John Venn
and the Friends of the Hereford Poor

John Venn
and the Friends of the Hereford Poor

by

Jean O'Donnell

Logaston Press

LOGASTON PRESS
Little Logaston Woonton Almeley
Herefordshire HR3 6QH
logastonpress.co.uk

First published by Logaston Press 2007
Copyright © Jean O'Donnell 2007

ISBN 978 1 904396 71 0

Set in Garamond and Times by Logaston Press
and printed in Great Britain by
Bell & Bain Ltd., Glasgow

Front Cover: John Venn by Edmund Wood Gill and presented to Venn by the artist 'as a token of his sincere gratitude and esteem' in 1879. This painting had hung in Venn's Hereford home, Beechwood, and in 1890 was offered to The Hereford Society for Aiding the Industrious by Venn's niece, Henrietta. It has hung in the Society's office ever since (Photo D. Foxton)

Contents

Acknowledgements

The main source of information are the archives of the Hereford Society for Aiding the Industrious. The main minute books from 1841–1926 and the early sub-committee minute books of the soup committee, the steam mill committee and the land committee have been valuable. The sub-committees were not recorded at a later date and only the main committee work is in bound volumes. The Deed Book and some correspondence was also consulted. I am grateful for the freedom given to me by the Society and Michael Cunningham to use the early records. Throughout the book I use 'the Society' to mean the Hereford Society for Aiding the Industrious.

I would also like to thank the University of Birmingham Library for the help of their Special Collections staff and the use of the John Venn's journal and notebooks. Thanks too for their use to the Church Missionary Society to whom they belong. Biographical information has come mainly from Dr. John Venn's book *The Annals of a Clerical Family* (1904).

Other material has come from the Hereford Record Office, such as the plans of Beechwood and Overbury Road, and the architect Bettington's preliminary drawings of Venn's Close.

Quotations from *Marianne Thornton*, E.M. Forster's portrait of his aunt, bring life to the description of her friends, the Venns. I am grateful to the Provost and Scholars of King's College, Cambridge and the Society of Authors as the Literary Representatives of the Estate of E.M. Forster who have allowed me to use them.

Dr. Derek Foxton has provided photographs from his collection for which I thank him.

My work has been enhanced by the guidance and editing of Andy Johnson after a long gestation; I am grateful to him for the careful delivery.

Preface

John Venn was one of the great Herefordians and his contribution to both the city and the county has been much overlooked. Jean O'Donnell's account of John Venn and the Hereford poor addresses these shortcomings and provides an insight into 19th-century life. John Venn's vision was an ability to see a way of combining industry and charity that was beneficial to all involved in his projects.

Much of St. Peter's parish became a small welfare state as the Portfields was built on and developed, while Bath Street owes its existence to the Hereford Society for Aiding the Industrious founded by John Venn to help the deserving poor.

That vision lives on today and the Society is still active and maintains its almshouses and grants from funds that were provided by the business acumen of its early managers and local philanthropists that were friends of the poor. This is a study from the early archives of the Society and the influence that John Venn had on it by a local historian who has spent some years researching her subject. She has also gained some knowledge from being a trustee of the Society. I urge you to read on and explore how it was done.

Mark Bricknell
Chairman
The Hereford Society for Aiding the Industrious
March 2007

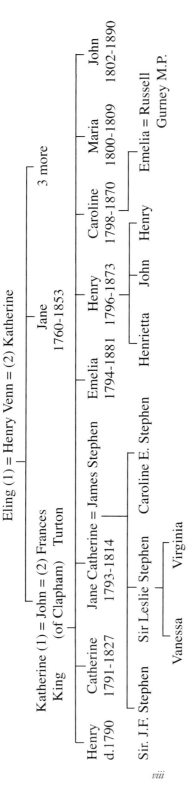

The Venn Family Tree

Eling (1) = Henry Venn = (2) Katherine

Katherine (1) = John = (2) Frances
King   (of Clapham)   Turton

Jane
1760-1853

Henry
d.1790

Catherine
1791-1827

Jane Catherine = James Stephen
1793-1814

Emelia
1794-1881

Henry
1796-1873

Caroline
1798-1870

Maria
1800-1809

John
1802-1890

3 more

Sir. J.F. Stephen

Sir Leslie Stephen

Caroline E. Stephen

Henrietta

John

Henry

Emelia = Russell
Gurney M.P.

Vanessa

Virginia

I THE MISSION

The conveyance known as The Fish Cart, on account of its dual purpose, swung into the yard at the rear of the City Arms in Northgate in the city of Hereford. A tall broad-shouldered man with a dark cloak around him, clasped at the throat with a brass chain, alighted and his baggage was unloaded beside him. This small cathedral city on the Welsh border was far from London and remote from the prosperous Middlesex village of Pinner from where the traveller had begun his journey some 30 hours previously. That traveller was the Rev. John Venn who had taken up the living at St. Peter's church in Hereford offered to him by Charles Simeon. He had bought it recently for the Simeon Trust, which he had set up to place Evangelical clergy when possible. A prominent evangelical preacher at Cambridge, he had studied with John's grandfather and was a family friend.

John Venn had not been destined to join the Church; his education had been tailored to a career with the East India Company. From Harrow school he went to Haileybury (the East India Company's own college) where he distinguished himself by winning, with other prizes, medals for Sanskrit and Hindustani. In later life he gave the gold medals to a Bible society to sell. This distinction won him a writership in the company's civil service. His father's friend, Zachary Macaulay, wrote of his success:

> The second son goes out to India in a few weeks with higher honours on his head, both literary and moral, than any young man has yet earned from the East India College.

In March 1820 all the members of John's family went to Slaters to have their 'picture taken' as John's sister Emelia wrote, so that John would have

1

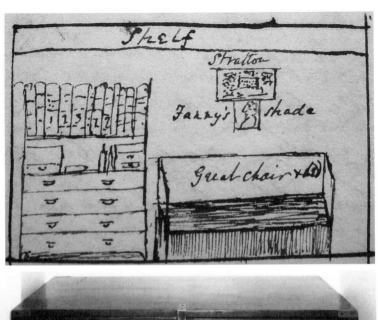

Figure 1 One of a series of drawings (University of Birmingham Special Collections) (top) that John Venn made of his cabin on the voyage on The Boyne, *this one showing a travelling chest (bottom) that was left in his will to Ann Turner and now resides in Canada with her descendants*

an album to take with him to India. On Wednesday 23 August 1820, aged 18, John embarked on board *The Boyne* and recorded in his journal:

> It is a fine free trading vessel of about 600 tons built in Bengal of teak wood and though having a motley crew of Indians, Negroes, Chinese and Turkish, making 64 men and yet well enough manned and managed, as in the case of most merchantmen returning to India, the Boyne has no cargo.

His account book reveals that he had £1,904 when he left for India, made up from his share of some property, a small legacy and gifts from friends and relatives. His journal recorded his powers of observation while at sea:

> The first 2 days of dead calm, but on the 3rd we met with the N.E. monsoon which will most likely take us up to the mouth of the river. Tuesday a young shark was caught. We saw it swimming about at the stern of the ship, a piece of pork on a hook was thrown in which in a few moments it came up to & seized; it was pulld on deck, it was about 6ft. long, very small indeed, yet so strong that it cd [could] nearly have broken a man's leg by the string by which it was held. There was a small sucker on it, that is a small fish that fastens upon sharks & whales & sucks their blood, being provided with an adhesive substance near its mouth. The shark was immediately caught at by the sailors to eat. Its jaw was perfect : it had three rows of teeth just like saws, which it can erect, or lie down at pleasure. This shark was 3 years old it appeared by its teeth, a fresh set coming each year till 7 or 8 years old.

His family received news of him in May, from a long letter that recounted his almost miraculous escape from shipwreck when *The Boyne* struck a sandbank.

The first year that John was in India he lodged with Mr. & Mrs. Thomason while he studied at the East India College for the writership examinations. Brilliant and hard-working he obtained medals in Sanskritt, Arabic, Bengali and Hindustani. He was then offered a good appointment in Calcutta. Just when he was about to take up his first post he was taken seriously ill with little hope of recovery. It was probably malaria as he had recurrent bouts of illness, and once he had sufficiently regained his strength he was then sent home on the six-month voyage to England to fully recuperate. He arrived back in July 1822 when Emelia, his sister, noted 'that it was a memorable day, for dear John has returned from India'. Characteristically, he recorded all his expenditure back on shore, noting that he went to have his hair cut for one shilling, his nails manicured for a further shilling and bought a toothbrush for yet another shilling. A leather waistcoat cost one shilling and sixpence. He also noted that he gave a poor woman sixpence; a typical act of generosity and carefully entered into his accounts.

When it became evident that his health would not stand the Indian climate he resigned from the East India Company and in the following year went to study at Queen's College, Cambridge, where his brother Henry was a Fellow. After a distinguished academic career as an undergraduate he was offered a Fellowship which he held until 1834 and was living in Hereford. It was at Cambridge that he came under the influence of Charles Simeon who was an Evangelical preacher at Trinity church and a friend of his father.

It was from his extended family that John Venn absorbed his compassion and visionary ideas. When his grandfather, Henry Venn, left his living in Huddersfield in 1771 his parishioners had given him a fine black cloak of Yorkshire woollen cloth; this was handed on like Elijah's, to the next prophet and it passed from Henry to John Venn's father and then to him. The symbolism of this mantle falling upon his shoulders evidently gave him his motivation for a life-long mission.

Henry Venn (1725–1797) was an eminent churchman who became an Evangelical after his marriage in 1750. He was a curate at Clapham from 1754, then vicar of Huddersfield until 1771. He was a friend of John Wesley and one of Lady

Figure 2 Queen's College, Cambridge, 1820

4

Huntingdon's chaplains. When he moved to Yelling it was near enough to Cambridge for him to inspire the young Charles Simeon. He retired to Clapham to live out his days with his son, John Snr., who was rector of Holy Trinity church.

Rev. John Venn Snr., born in 1759, had followed in Henry's early footsteps. He became part of a brotherhood of philanthropic and Christian men often called the Clapham Sect or, more scornfully by men such as Sidney Smith in the *Edinburgh Review*, 'The Saints'. William Wilberforce (1759-1833) is the best known member. He was returned to Parliament in 1780 and was a follower of William Pitt. He found his mission in the anti-slavery movement with ardent support from his Clapham friends, particularly Granville Sharp and Thomas Clarkson. In 1807 he ensured that the Slave Trade Bill was passed by 283 votes to 16 which prohibited British vessels from engaging in the Slave trade. Black slaves in the British Isles had already been freed by a court judgement in 1772. Many had been released into dire poverty and in 1786 it was suggested that land in Sierra Leone should be used for a new settlement. The first negroes were taken out in the following year. The climate was unsuitable and a series of diseases resulted in the deaths of many of the new settlers. In 1791 the Sierra Leone Company was set up with Clapham Sect members holding office and in effect running it. It was Zachary Macaulay's success as governor

Figure 3 Holy Trinity church, Clapham

that changed the Sierra Leone enterprise into a successful Crown colony. The 1807 Act stopped the slave trade up to a point, but it left the sugar plantations unaffected. It took the tireless efforts of the frail Wilberforce to get public opinion and Parliament to support a new Act in 1833 that gave slaves throughout the British Empire their freedom. To gain support for the Bill, the owners were compensated for their loss and Wilberforce declared to Thomas Babington Macaulay:

> Thank God that I have lived to witness the day in which England is willing to give £20 million for the abolishment of slavery.

Three days later he died.

Another dedicated abolitionist and evangelical, James Stephen, moved to Clapham to be near the Sect. He married, as his second wife, the widowed sister of Wilberforce. His grandson was Leslie Stephen; the first compiler and editor of the *National Dictionary of Biography* and father of Virginia Woolf and Vanessa Bell. James' son married

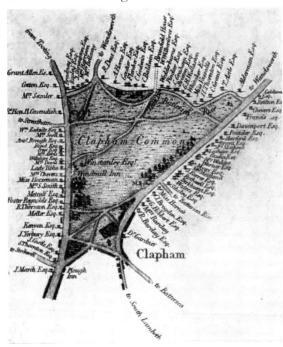

Figure 4 Clapham Common in 1800 showing the occupants of the adjoining properties (Lambeth Archives)

John Venn's sister, Jane Catherine (1793–1875). Other neighbours were Thomas Clarkson, Zachary Macaulay and John Thornton. It was wealthy banker, Thornton, who saw that John Venn Snr. was offered the living of Clapham in 1792. Of him Wilberforce wrote: 'Venn preached an excellent introductory sermon. I received the sacrament and had much serious reflection'. The houses of this close-knit community clustered round Clapham Common with Battersea Rise to the north where Wilberforce and the Thorntons lived.

6

The Venns began a programme of Bible study and district visiting. In 1802 they published a monthly review entitled *The Christian Observer* with Zachary Macaulay as editor. Other members of the Clapham sect established schools and Sunday schools in deprived areas of the countryside and poor parishes. In Clapham Rev. Venn saw that every child could learn to read. The British and Foreign Bible Society, formed in 1804, published and distributed bibles at home and abroad for the poor to read. Again it was the friends at Clapham who funded and formed the Society. Lord Teignmouth was President, Wilberforce was Vice-President and Thornton was treasurer. This missionary work was part of their daily lives and they helped to form other societies that sprang from Evangelism between 1799 and 1836. The Church Missionary Society, that now has a staff of 1,231 European missionaries working in Africa, India, Ceylon, China, Japan, Palestine and Iran, was founded in 1799 as the Society for Missions to Africa and the East. Then came the Religious Tract Society with Zachary Macaulay on the committee. Rev. John Venn Snr. was the first Chairman and John Thornton again was Treasurer. Closer to home the Rector set up the Clapham Poor Society where food, clothing, blankets and medicines were distributed to the needy by committees of local ladies. In 1800 Venn introduced smallpox vaccination to his parish.

This was the young John's inheritance and one he subsequently worked for with zeal.

Figure 5 John Venn at 18 (Venn Annals)

*Figure 6 Rev. John Venn Snr.
of Clapham (Venn Annals)*

The evangelical revival had brought with it a new doctrine of responsibility towards the underprivileged. Its first expression was the abolition of the slave trade for which Wilberforce and his friends worked so tirelessly. In England there was a move towards popular education and literacy so that all could read their Bible. Sunday schools catered for those at work including children, and gave the evangelicals a close interest in young children. They began to protest at the oppressive working life to which many of them were subjected in mines and factories, and at the ignorance and squalor of their home lives. From this raised awareness came the Factory Acts and industrial reform together with the provision of schools.

As well as the achievement of the abolition of slavery, the Clapham sect were anxious to take Christianity to India using the East India Company as the instrument. A Parliamentary Bill that Wilberforce introduced to give force to this aim was defeated., but nonetheless missions were taken there with increased zeal, allowing education to be extended and leading to reforms such as the abolition of the practice of suttee. Besides the freed Negro slave colony in Sierra Leone, a chaplain was provided for the new settlement of convicts in Botany Bay to care for their spiritual welfare.

Rev. John Venn Snr. remained in Clapham in the midst of his philanthropic friends until his death in 1813. His rectory was known for its sunny cheerfulness. His youngest son, John, was 11 years old when his father died and had spent all his formative years amongst these friends.

Figure 7 Clapham Old Rectory (Venn Annals)

The Thornton family children were to stay close to him with Marianne often visiting him in Hereford over the years. The links were confirmed when her brother, Watson, became vicar of Llanwarne and then a canon of Hereford cathedral.

John's mother had died when he was too young to remember her, just a year after he was born at the Clapham rectory in 1802. His father's sister, Jane, became his surrogate mother and moved in to look after the seven young children. She was greatly loved, but when their father married again she moved away and they missed her. However, on the death of their father she once again became mother to them when they moved to London. In her care on this occasion were Jane, Henry, Caroline, Emelia, and John. At that time they lived at Mabledon Place in Euston, and then moved to Harrow where John became a day boy at Harrow School. Emelia wrote in her journal that:

> John is to go to Harrow school & we are again to have a home of
> our own with our dearest aunt for our mother in a small house but
> a very cheerful one.

In 1814 they all moved into a larger house nearby at Harrow-on-the-Hill and, in October of the same year, a new piano arrived unexpectedly from Broadwards for Emelia. It was a present from aunt Jane. By this time, their sister, Jane, was being courted by James Stephen, the lawyer son of the older James. They were married just before Christmas in St. Mary's church on Harrow Hill.

On 1 June 1828 John was ordained Deacon by the Bishop of London in the Chapel Royal and, exactly a year later, he was ordained priest in the same place. The family had moved back to Mabledon Place so that John could live with them as he carried out his duties as curate of St. Mary le Strand, a very tough and exhausting parish. When ill-health returned from overwork he was offered the more congenial living of Pinner near Harrow by John Cunningham, a friend of the family. In March 1830 the family effects were moved from London to Pinner and they 'ate their first dinner in the house and drank tea in the spare bedroom'.

Emelia saw a vocation for herself and wrote in her diary,

> What an arrangement this will be if I am allowed to help him in the
> new parish & to devote myself to the only work in which my judge-
> ment tells me I can be happy, – the care of the poor.

For the rest of her life she stayed by his side to carry this out.

Aunt Jane remained in charge of the household and after the older children married or moved away she looked after John and Emelia until she died. Her great nephew, another John Venn, described his memory of her:

> Like other country-bred girls of the eighteenth-century, she was primed with recipes for everything which home resources could supply. As a boy, I remember her at Hereford, when she was verging towards ninety, still active in her domestic management, in which department, I suspect she rather distrusted the interference of her niece and nephew; and keenly interested in her garden about which the niece and nephew cared nothing. I have a distant vision of her with her keys in her hand, unlocking her store-cupboard, in which were ranged rows of pickles and other home-made stores.

John Venn never married; he had neither the inclination nor the necessity with his aunt and sister to care for him. Older than him, Emelia lived in his house from their time at Pinner until she died. When John arrived in Hereford with her he chose not to live in the old and crumbling rectory in St. Peter's Street, opposite his new church. Rev. Gipps, whom he was replacing, had lived in Castle Street amongst the more genteel members of society, but John Venn bought a small cottage with a large garden and wonderful views over the grassy fields towards the city and its cathedral tower. He could see his church, St. Peter's, and All Saint's with its crooked spire. Beyond was the dramatic edge of the Black Mountains, white in winter snow and with a black line above which a fiery sunset would often end the day. The house was in Parry's Lane, a turning by the toll gate, opposite Penngrove House and its gardens. A little further on was a thatched cottage where the painter David Cox lived. High on Aylestone Hill it was in a pretty rural area with stately villas scattered around in large gardens. The cottage was extended over the next 57 years until it became a large and convenient house called Beechwood.

In 1883 John Venn paid £200 for a parcel of former arable land lying in the Hill field, bounded by the new Overbury Road to the north and Beechwood to the south-east. (The name 'Overbury' is derived from the name of the manor of Overbury in Woolhope which was cathedral land and a prebend holding with Gorham. The farm still exists.) It was a new road in 1883 although it had been an ancient trackway to Walney Lane and

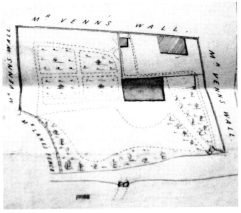

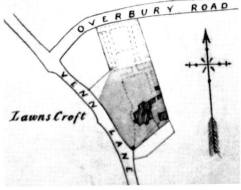

Figure 8 (top) Plan of the house and garden in 1840 (HRO)

Figure 9 (lower) Plan showing the extended area in 1891 (HRO)

the Lugg meadows. The house and land that he bought in 1840 included some in the Folly field which was a copyhold tenancy. This meant that he paid £60 to have name entered in the manor rolls although the field rent was one penny. The later acquisition gave him a larger garden and a frontage on to the new road for the Beechwood estate. When John Venn died in 1890 it was left to his nieces and nephews: Emelia Gurney, John Venn of Caius College and Sir James FitzJames Stephen. They sold it the following year to Benjamin Haigh Allen of The Priory, Clifford for £1,200. It was a marriage gift to his daughter who extended the house and opened a school. During the First World War Beechwood became a military hospital. It was sold several times after this and it was demolished finally to be replaced by sheltered housing for elderly people. Its former owner would have been pleased at this use for his land.

Born in 1784 and so a little older than her brother, Emelia Venn was a bright vivacious girl who loved travelling. With her well-connected friends from Clapham and elsewhere she had been in Europe at the end of the Napoleonic wars, when France was full of treasures stolen from the great museums and houses of Europe. She must have been very open and sociable for she once said that walking over the Aylestone Hill paths without meeting friends was ' like going through a Campo Santo' — one of the Italian cemeteries that she had seen on her travels. She was particularly fond of Italy. When she was 82 she claimed to visit friends at 40 different houses within reach and she was considered a lively and

Figure 10 Beechwood Venn's Lane (Derek Foxton Collection)

active old lady. In all John's schemes she was his supporter and often contributed financially.

She had no lack of children to spoil for their brother Henry's family were often there: John, Henry and Henrietta. They played cricket with their uncle and looked forward to their holidays away from Archway, in London, where their father had the living of Holloway. The youngest John Venn later wrote that he could remember travelling on the coach from Gloucester via Ross to Hereford. In July 1843 his father took them to Beechwood and left them there while he went to Switzerland and they became friendly with local children, including those of the Bulmers. Their Aunt Emelia was like a second mother to them, and she would go to London to select their governesses and their books so that they had the best. In adult life their nephew, John Venn, became an eminent mathematician and philosopher at Cambridge known by all children for his 'Venn's Diagrams'. He also translated his family diaries and journals from the shorthand in which they were written and added to his grandfather, Rev. John Venn's notes on his family history, publishing, in 1904, *Annals of a Clerical Family*. Both Emelia and John were taught shorthand by their father and used it for their personal papers.

2 LIFE IN HEREFORD

In 1833 when John arrived in Hereford the city was just emerging from the Middle Ages. A year before his arrival, a new local paper, the *Hereford Times,* had ben launched by Charles Anthony with a progressive and reforming attitude towards current political issues. The old city was ready for a social reformer who would tackle the problems of hunger, poverty and ignorance.

The Reform Act had been celebrated by jubilant Herefordians in 1832, in the anticipation that there would be a new way forward for the common man who was anxious to vote like his privileged fellows. After the passage of the Bill through Parliament they had gathered at an early hour in the evening and inspected the 'tasteful decorations' while the church bells rang and a procession of inhabitants paraded the streets preceded by a band and flags.

> On one of the flags was inscribed *Reform not Revolution.* By ten o'clock the City had presented a brilliant scene; the mansions of the rich and the humble dwellings of the poor exhibited a dazzling and continuous stream of splendid flames, occasionally diversified with soaring rockets and sparkling fireworks. Lit by gas from the new works were illuminated portraits of Earl Grey and Lord Brougham. The joy of the occasion was shown by the happiness that beamed in every face.

Earl Grey was a Whig prime minister whose aim was to abolish the rotten boroughs that were in the landlords' pockets, and to give representation to the growing industrial towns like Manchester and Birmingham. He was supported in the House of Lords by Lord Brougham, and by threatening to create new peers the Bill was passed. It had little effect in Hereford where there was a narrow male franchise restricted to householders with houses over a rental of £10 or owner occupied. In the following 1835 election the vote increased from 888 to 900; only 12 more. The city continued to return two members of parliament but the rotten borough of Weobley was abolished. Even with such a slight change the city saw itself moving into a new era.

Improvements had begun 50 years before when the old gates were removed to 'let in the fresh air' as it was said. More recently the old rows in the market place or High Town that had hung their projecting upper storeys over the narrow streets, with their rotting gutters and crumbling woodwork, were removed. They had once housed the butchery or shambles. Now only one fine house remained with its shop intact and the great door with the arms of the Butchers' Guild of London over its great nail-studded door. A notable architect, Robert Smirke, had been employed to build a new Shire Hall with money raised by a local rate, in a classical style of a Greek temple. This was used for the Assize Courts and to improve the social life with assemblies. Just a few years before, in 1819, it was reported that the spirit of improvement that 'whitewashed dingy antiquity' left filthy heaps of refuse 'as traps for the punishment of nightly passengers'.

In 1836 the area around St. Peter's church was improved. The removal of the two remaining houses of the Butcher's Row, east of the market place, made a spacious area from the Old House to the Guild Hall. The weighing machine stood by the new Shire Hall and St. Peter's cross

Figure 11 Butchers' Row, High Town. The Old House in the foreground has had the adjacent buildings of Butchers' Row removed but other rows fill the High Town up to the old Town Hall demolished in 1861 (Hereford Museum)

14

marked the end of the open market. From here Milk Lane (Offa Street) led across Packer's Lane in to St. John Street. In St. Owen's street, formerly Hungary Street, the large town houses added elegance to the area.

The new vicar, John Venn, found St. Peter's to be a fine old building with a large congregation. There were 1,800 seats of which 600 were free and without pew rent. It had pews with lofty sides and covered in green baize, galleries crowded under the arches, the clerk's desk, the high reading desk and the still higher pulpit standing in

Figure 12 Narrow Cabbage Lane in 1837 by David Cox. Located just off the market place the shops offered fish and vegetables

Figure 13 St. Peter's church in 1820 with Robert Smirke's Shire Hall to the right

15

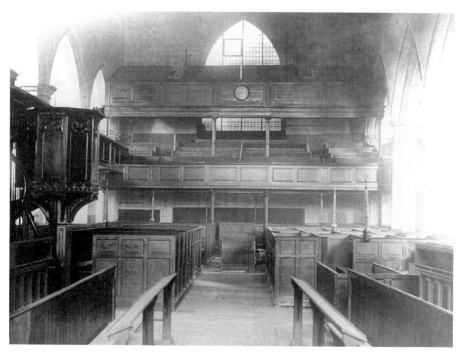

Figure 14 The interior of St. Peter's in 1884

the east end of the nave. There was a beautiful and large chancel. This was so long that it was supposed that someone reading from the east end could not be heard in the galleries and a glass screen was installed to cut it off. Communion was held in the chancel but readings were from the desk.

The previous vicar, Mr. Gipps, was very deaf and had installed, at a cost of £200, a paraboloidal sounding-board in which the preacher's head was concealed. The device sent a blast of sound down to the end of the church, but it sent back every whisper uttered by the congregation. He could not see them nor they him. It was quickly removed by John Venn who had a fine melodic voice. The spire, 160 feet high, was partially rebuilt in 1793 at the same time as other work was carried out, and further alterations were made by Charles Heather in 1836.

As has been mentioned, John Venn came from a background of writers and reformers who visited each other's houses, including his father's rectory in Clapham. His brother-in-law was Sir James Stephen, William Wilberforce and Henry Thornton were family friends and Zachary Macaulay's son, Thomas Babington, was a childhood friend. However, something in his make-up, perhaps resulting from his voyage to and time in India allowed him to work equally well with shoemakers and shopkeepers as with lawyers and politicians. He had a vision of a better society and believed in the victory of the good and perfect. He was a warm-hearted kindly man sometimes at odds with his narrow Calvinism.

Now, following his father's example he set about establishing a parish school for the young. He wasted no time in acquiring a site near his church, for in the year he arrived he bought a garden behind the Angler's Inn and then two houses next to it. The school was built on this garden land behind Union Street, John Venn laying the foundation stone on 19 July 1837 in front of more than 2,000 onlookers. The western range of the building had a pediment with the date over the central bay of the three. It opened as a parish school for girls and boys on 10 January 1839, teaching taking place in an open plan classroom, and included two houses for teachers. In about 1840 a separate classroom for infants was constructed closer to Union Street behind the Angler's Inn and this was equipped with moveable pews for divine service thanks to a grant of £80. John Venn's cashbook notes the payment in 1841 of £100 to Leonard Johnson for building St. Peter's Infant School and £80 for St. Owen's Infant School on the site of the destroyed St. Owen's church at the end of St. Owen Street. Leonard Johnson was a local builder and surveyor who had carried out the building of the workhouse and the new city gaol. In December this was followed by another sum of £37 5s. All the payments were entered in John Venn's personal cash-book and paid by cheque, but it is unclear whether he was subsidising all the building work or simply advancing the money.

Figure 15 The excavations before demolition of St. Peter's school in 2002 (Derek Foxton Collection)

At the commencement the schoolmaster was Robert Carpenter, who lived in the schoolhouse with his wife and six children. His wife found time to be the schoolmistress. Henry Yapp was schoolmaster in 1871; he had tried for the Headship of the Bluecoat school years before but was unsuccessful.

17

In later years the cottages at the front of the Gaol Street buildings were mortgaged to the Society for Aiding the Industrious that John Venn was to establish, and the gardens were used to enlarge the playground. A new Infants' school classroom was also constructed. There was a major rebuilding programme in 1904–5 when it was turned into an elementary school for girls to complement St. Owen's Boys' School. The Infants school closed in 1911 and it was replaced by St. James' Infant school. The girls' school was finally shut in 1983 and was demolished in 2002.

John Venn also took a close interest in the other parish schools as they were set up, particularly in the Scudamore school that had been funded by the Scudamore Charity. It had been proposed that a school was established on the British and Foreign system by the trustees of the charity. John Venn was strongly opposed to this on the grounds that it would 'excite party feelings', the British and Foreign system being that adopted by non-conformists, whilst the Church of England favoured the National School system. Instead he thought that the funds of the charity, which were intended to create employment and not schools, should be used to buy allotments and a farm for the labouring poor where 'spade husbandry' could be practised. He was a great advocate of this method of cultivation and saw it as more productive than ploughing. In the 1870s the tenants on the Portfields in the Society's model cottages and on the model garden were encouraged to grow their produce in this way. However, the local M.P., Edward Clive, was chairman of the Scudamore Charity and the rest of the trustees were men of influence, and so the school was duly opened in 1850 and is still in use.

St. Peter's Literary Institute was used for the Sunday school and the adult classes that were part of John Venn's vision of education for the working classes. It began in a room over the vestry but was soon located in Bye Street with lectures in the schoolroom. John had been greatly impressed by Professor Lee when at Cambridge. Lee had been a carpenter before an employer spotted his latent talent and sent him to be educated. His brilliant performance at Queen's indicated the potential of the underprivileged and uneducated working class and gave John a lifelong interest in encouraging their development. John taught and gave lectures in his institute. His colourful journey to India and life in London provided plenty of material to engage the minds of his young institute members. He made sure that there was a library and papers for them to read and encouraged their interest in the natural world of science.

It is hard to recapture the daily lives of the parishioners of St. Peter's as most of the detail is missing from minute books and other archives. Fortunately there is a lively account of the annual young men's tea party in a letter sent by Marianne Thornton when she was staying with the Venns at Beechwood in 1842. This was published by E.M. Forster in his biography of his aunt. She had been staying with her brother, Prebendary Watson Thornton.

> I will proceed to tell you about the young man's tea ... something kept me down in that room from eleven in the morning until near ten at night, not helping or being the smallest use, but amusing myself by seeing all the various witty devices, and hearing all the curious sayings of the Hereford people. It is etiquette for the Venns to have nothing to do with it until teatime, but I wanted to see all the proceedings, so Emelia went down with me and left me there while she went on into the town.

She went on to describe the scene, which must have been in the newly built schoolroom with the young men of the St. Peter's Literary Institute.

> The whole town of Hereford seems to have been wailing at the early frost which cut off the dahlias, that used to be their chief ornament; so as to make up they had sent not only mountain ash berries in haycocks, and branches of rosy apples, but forests of laurels and in every leaf a gold cross, a V, and a crown stuck on, and baskets of paper Dahlias with gold eyes and wire legs, and China roses in such abundance that I'm sure there can't be one left standing in the county ... pieces of rope had flowers tied on to them so as to make long festoons dangling at intervals all along the roof above the gallery, and very frightful it was to see the number of young men's legs dangling also among the beams, nailing them up. The youths were working like dragons, each having some pet idea of his own.

All the time Mr. Yapp, the parish clerk, was wandering around in his grey dressing gown. The gallery had green baize nailed to it so that bizarre pictures of idols, mummies, starfish and monsters could be added. There were two sailing ships, manned and rigged, whirling up in the air, then an enormous oil painting at one end with a bible. A text in gold letters was added. Beside the picture were two globes with two short military figures of plaster 'reading and praying'. As a contrast there was a pedestal covered with pink calico on which were various scientific curiosities used in the lectures: an electric machine, chemist's looking glasses (microscopes?), models of churches and a head with hair that stood on end when electrified. The two ladies found this particularly entertaining. There were models of classical buildings from Rome made of cork and stuffed animals; all part of the visual aids used in the lectures. The schoolmaster, Mr. Prout, had been labouring for months on a shipwreck of wood and pasteboard. Some contrivance made the sea move and the waves crashed until the vessel was wrecked. This all went on to the sound of a fiddle while a lifeboat went out to rescue the men. This was worked by one devoted youth who lay on his back and moved the machinery above him. When all was ready John Venn was to sit on a raised table with a dais with palms and paper dahlias above him.

After all this exciting preparation came the tea cooked and prepared by Mr. Yapp's family. They lit the gas at six o'clock, which illuminated it like daylight and the ladies went into a private classroom to have their tea and coffee. The youths were let in to the gallery to look down on all the abundance of 400 cups, saucers and spoons. When John Venn arrived, the lads rushed down and he sat on his platform while the show went on. Three to four hundred women and children crowded out the gallery to see the fun. 'John looked excessively happy and unconcerned too, and soon left his elevated place and walked about talking to one and another.' It became very uproarious when the shipwreck took place but John quietened them down by getting them all to sing *God Save the Queen*. Then there was a report on the past year's lectures and work followed by a talk full of funny stories by John, a bit of a sermon and prayers. John was 'all full of gaiety and goodness'.

Marianne Thornton adds that it was the sort of thing one could not see anywhere else. She commented that it was a cross between a mechanic's institute and a prayer meeting and gave John great influence over a class he would never meet socially in any other way. His sister told her that they were so fond of him that 'when he was absent a party of them met together to pray for his safety and welfare.'

The picture drawn by this account is that of a humourous and sympathetic pastor whose own enthusiasm for knowledge and science captured the imagination of his young parishioners. John Venn often lectured himself; in 1840 it was on The Wonders of Geology, then a fascinating new science. Some of the lectures were given by his childhood friend, Watson Thornton,

Marianne's brother, who was then Rector of Llanwarne and a prebendary of the cathedral., He was also chairman of the Poor Law Union and that must have made for some discussion and disagreement between him and John Venn on the plight of the poor and the treatment of poverty. He was a dim, fussy, joking youth according to his sister but he went to Trinity College, read for the Church and took holy orders. There is a portrait of him when he was 23 written by Marianne. She is over-awed at the thought of him standing where the venerated John Venn Snr. had preached.

> In hearing Watson read prayers for the first time in Clapham church on Christmas Day and he preached on Monday a quiet little sermon when there was no one but his sisters and cousins to hear him. There was something fearfully nervous in seeing him in *that* pulpit, but he was so composed himself, and though I say who should not say it, preached so well that I could not feel anxious to the end.

He had developed into a respectable preacher and 22 years later when she went to Cambridge with him for him to vote in the Parliamentary Election of 1847 she wrote that 'Watson was more amusing and ridiculous than I had seen him for years'. By then he was a canon of Hereford and married to Frances Webb. He died in 1855 when he was 53.

Figure 16 Watson Thornton preaching in Clapham Church, drawn by his sister, Lucy Thornton (Marianne Thornton)

At the St. Peter's Institute in Bye Street there was a library and reading room with newspapers. This provision continued until the Free Library opened in Broad Street in 1874 when the books were donated to it. Lectures were then held in the new Woolhope Room. The connection remained with more than books, for the Society that John Venn inspired donated £300 to furnish the museum with glass cases in 1892.

Dr. Henry Graves Bull, a leading member of the Society and the Woolhope Club, had been instrumental in the foundation and building of the Free Library in Broad Street together with Sir James Rankin who provided the funds. Unfortunately they did not cover all the costs and there was a debt to the City Council. A donation of £250 was made by the Society in January 1892 on the condition that the building could be enlarged by incorporating the two shops that had been created on either side of the entrance and the space used for the library. The front windows were changed to their original design and one room became a ladies' reading room.

Another of John Venn's early actions once in Hereford was to establish The Herefordshire Friendly Society in 1838 to provide a system of mutual support. The clerk was Thomas Day, later secretary of the Society. Connected with this was the Medical Club, the rules of which were printed in 1850. The bishop was the patron and it was well thought of by the local worthies. Meetings of the friendly society were held in Bye Street, probably at the Dispensary where the Society's office was to open three years later. Monthly premiums were paid to secure benefits at varying rates from 15 to 65 years of age. There was also provision for payments in the event of death. One curious rule was

Figure 17 Hereford Free Library in 1876

22

that no payment could be made to a mother during the month after child-birth. In 1947 the Herefordshire Friendly Society was still in existence with 73 members and an office in Offa Street.

John Venn published many pamphlets: one, in 1838, was his sermon against Sunday wakes which he had preached at Sellack. He described the wakes as 'the occasion of tumultuous and disorderly assemblings of both men and women, and of a debauchery, and a revolting profligacy, baffling all description.' These had commonly been held in the churchyards to celebrate the feast day of the church, but the drunkenness often led to brutal fighting in which some deaths occurred. He felt that he had to urge his fellow clergymen to stop these ancient festivities.

His early writing was passionate and full of fiery zeal. His condemnation of drunkenness and profanity stayed with him so that all through his life he preached total abstinence from drink. He urged that the working-man should not receive his wages on a Saturday night lest they be spent on liquor. He was also totally against work or entertainment on the Sabbath and in his later life he rebuked a working-man he met walking up Aylestone Hill on a Sunday who had been fishing in the river Lugg. He also condemned some of the social events connected with the Three Choirs Festival.

Included amongst other pamphlets of his that were published were: *An Earnest Plea for the Poor and the Rich; The Christian Ministry with special reference to the views of the Plymouth Brethren; The Office of Sponsors Briefly and Practically Considered* and *Church Membership*. The one that perhaps caused the greatest stir was that which detailed the debate he undertook with Canon Waterworth, provoked by the founding of Roman Catholic Belmont Abbey to which he was strenuously opposed. Roman Catholicism was an anathema to him and he challenged the priest to a public debate. The priest declined the invitation in favour of his brother, the Canon, and the debate took place in 1847 and was published under the title of *The Hereford Discussion*.

John Venn's Calvinism did not prevent him from believing in the inherent goodness in people, but he got into doctrinal difficulties with some of his congregation at St. Peter's who left the church and set up an alternative meeting at Mr. Humfrys' in Bridge Street, a prominent member of the church and a lawyer. This group subsequently built a new meeting room in Barton Road and they were known as the Brethren. They also met at a new chapel in Lugwardine and both meetings continue today.

It was in 1855 that John Venn, spurred on by Capt. Russell, had the idea of a missionary to work in the poorest parts of the city. George Chandler was duly appointed to the parish and financially aided by the Society. He commenced visiting the poor in their homes and held cottage and lodging house services when the opportunity arose. Later, a mission hall was built in Canal Street. In 1863 George Chandler's experience of the low morals he saw during his rounds led to the formation of the Female Rescue Society which helped young women in distress. For many years the Society gave grants to this cause and later, to The Haven home for delinquent girls when it was in St. Nicholas Street. When George Chandler died in 1901 he had been carrying out his work for 45 years. He had also helped with the Society's work and soon after the soup kitchen and dining room were opened in Crown Passage, he held a 'ragged school' in the evenings for poor children who worked during the day. The next missioner was Edgar Vigor who combined this role with that of probation officer for 23 years after giving up a post managing W.H. Smith's railway bookstall in London and then Hereford. He was followed by P.W. Brown who had previously been with the Church Army. The office of the missioner was in 22 Bath Street, on the corner of Kyrle Street, and near the Society offices.

This out-reach work in Hereford echoed the work undertaken by the Church Missionary Society. This is perhaps not surprising as the CMS had been founded in April 1799 in the first-floor room of the Castle and Falcon in Aldersgate Street in London by John Venn's father. Both John Venn Snr.'s sons, Henry and John, were intimately concerned with the CMS throughout their lives, Henry becoming unpaid secretary in 1840. When his health failed in 1846 he gave up his living in Highbury, travelling to the offices in Salisbury Square on most days. He was a leading member of the Evangelical party and stayed in post until the year prior to his death in

Figure 18 Henry Venn (Venn Annals)

1873. John always read the Annual Report to the large London meeting in the Exeter Hall every May. Their concern with the Church's missionary efforts overseas in the colonial settlements of India, West Africa and Australia came from the gargantuan efforts of the Clapham sect friends to establish practical help as well as Christianity.

Like his brother John, Henry was directly concerned with practical projects, to which end he made great efforts to find crops that would sustain the inhabitants of West Africa. Thus he sought advice from Kew Gardens on the cultivation of palm trees, cotton and tropical plants. In spite of this research the production of cotton in West Africa was a failure as the place was unsuitable in climate and soil. He also consulted cloth manufacturers about methods of spinning cotton and set up mills in Sierra Leone. Then he brought Africans to England to study methods of cultivation and production. His other great scheme was the introduction of a standard alphabet for all bible and prayer book printing in the many dialects of Africa and this was produced with the help of philologists in 1855. All this activity was ploughed into enterprises supported by the CMS. This practical application of Christianity was copied by John for his projects in Hereford carried out by the Society for Aiding the Industrious.

The brothers also shared a scientific view of the world that did not include literature or painting. Instead the wonder of the universe was to be found through a telescope or in the rocks beneath their feet. Henry was a serious man and lacked John's kindly humour but he had been on his own for some time after his wife died in 1840.

John Venn seldom left Hereford but he did travel round the country preaching for the CMS and always went to London for his annual delivery of Henry's report to the CMS at Exeter Hall. It was perhaps on one of these occasions that he used the opportunity to visit the Great Exhibition at the Crystal Palace in 1851, as recorded by Marianne Thornton in her journal. The party consisted of Marianne, the Venns and George Richmond, the society portrait painter. He was a friend of the Thorntons and painted their guardian, Sir Robert Inglis. His subjects also included Sir George Cornewall Lewis and Charlotte Bronte. She wrote: 'The Venns wanted to take everything back from the Exhibition to their parishioners at Hereford ... the hollow bricks, the dancing balls in the fountain that would amuse very old people more than a cat and be less trouble, and the jumping bed would be good for heavy young sleepers, and bonnets made of string would be wonderfully cool for Sierra Leone.' And they wanted to go back again; John

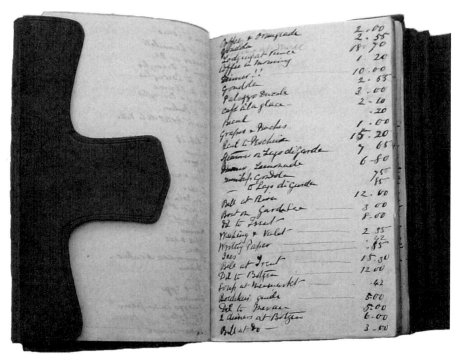

Figure 19 John Venn's travel journal of 1857 showing distances covered (top) and expenditure (lower) (Birmingham University Library Special Collections)

must have been intrigued by the technology and manufacturing on show. He would have been equally enthralled by the products and peoples of the overseas colonies of which he was so well informed from the missionary work organized by Henry.

One small notebook in red leather binding does record details of a holiday taken in Europe in 1857. John's companion was a Dr. Arthur Ransome (1834–1922), a distant relative of the well-known writer. The reason for their friendship is not known, indeed Ransome would have been a much younger man of 23. They crossed from Newhaven to Dieppe, then travelled by train to Paris, Strasburg and Zurich, Lake Como and Milan, then to Venice, back to Strasburg, on to Munich, Frankfurt, Cologne and Amsterdam, Antwerp, Ghent and Ostend. In all they travelled 1,313 miles by train. The railway really had opened up the Continent to the intrepid English traveller. John's notebook records that they also sailed 533 miles on steamboats, venturing up Lake Como to Riva, and on the canal from Cologne to Rotterdam. They used gondolas to view Venice. Items listed as expenditure include Baedeker guides, lemonade, orangeade, ice-cream, grapes and peaches. Exclamation marks against the cost of a dinner reveals that it was deemed rather an extravagant one.

Back in Hereford John Venn's interest in the welfare of young men who worked in the city was reflected by his work to form the Young Men's Christian Association. In January 1863 a meeting was held in St. Peter's schoolroom over which John Venn presided. The newly formed committee was allowed to use the room over the vestry in St. Peter's church for meetings with invited young men. In the same year the committee was re-organised to include the Congregational minister, Rev. Hill, as Vice-President. By September the association had affiliated to the headquarters in London. Two years later John Venn asked them to vacate the room as he was going to form a branch linked with St. Peter's. It is puzzling to know whether the schism was due to doctrinal disputes as had happened in the past or whether it was just some managerial difference. The original branch now found a room over some stables in Newmarket Street. The room there was opened nightly to members and their friends and a library was established. By the end of the year John was asked to amalgamate the two associations but he would not agree to this. The other branch continued under the guidance of Rev. G.H. Kirkwood for nearly 30 years. They moved to better premises in Widemarsh Street but by 1898 the lease on the current rooms was due to expire and by 1903 they were installed in Camden House and Hall which was bought by public subscription. The Hereford YMCA became the Divisional headquarters for Wales and the Border Counties in 1901 with an office in St. Peter's House. After John Venn's retirement only one branch continued; the one he started in 1863 and then abandoned.

One of John Venn's concerns was that the large area that was St. Owen's had been without a church since the end of the Civil War in the 17th century when the two parishes were amalgamated. A large and poor population had spread out on the fringes of the Portfields and near the barracks in Harold Street. Some of the worst slums were near the site of the former church of St. Owen and round the graveyard. (In 1914 Turk's Alley and other slum properties were cleared away and some 16 model dwellings were built.)

John Venn raised funds for a new church in St. Owen's by strenuous efforts. The site was in Bartonsham and was given by the Ecclesiastical Commissioners. In 1868 he was able to commission the diocesan architect and friend, Thomas Nicholson, to produce plans and build it. It cost £3,900 and it was designed in the Decorated style using sandstone from the Three Elms quarries with Bath stone dressings. The roofs were framed with pitch pine, boarded and felted and then covered with Whitland Abbey slates.

It was designed to seat 600 and all the seats were to be free — no pew rents here. There was a special reredos of encaustic tiles from Godwin's of Lugwardine. In 1872 an organ by Nicholson of Worcester was added.

On 23 December 1901 a fire destroyed the building except for the porch and vestry. It was as well it happened after John Venn's life had ended or it would have caused him considerable grief. It was rebuilt in 1903 by John Nicholson, son of its architect, who must have been anxious to restore his father's work.

3   THE POOR ARE ALWAYS WITH US

British society in the nineteenth century was poor by our standards. Most working class people experienced poverty at some time in their lives. The loss of work or illness could mean the family becoming destitute. However, poverty was regarded as an important element in society because feeling its pinch supposedly made the labouring poor work. Many early Victorians thought destitution and pauperism were the result of weakness of character and that the vagrants and beggars on the streets would infect the honest working poor.

Of the six parishes in the city, that of St. Peter's with St. Owen's (the latter had lost its church in the Civil War) had some of the poorest areas. The Poor Rates, which were levied in each parish, maintained a local workhouse and gave bread and money to families who were in dire straits from unemployment or illness. This system, managed by an Overseer, was known as outdoor relief because families were not taken to live inside the workhouse. The report of a Royal Commission in 1832 led to an Act of Parliament two years later that created what became known as the New Poor Law which combined parishes into Unions, abolished outdoor relief and produced a system of 'less eligibility'. Only those who were destitute and entered the workhouse could now receive help. In each Union of parishes the ratepayers elected a Board of Guardians to administer the workhouse as directed by Poor Law Commissioners. Conditions were harsh to stop idleness and improvidence and the standard of living was worse than that of the poorest labourer in work.

From the passing of the New Poor Law the rates dropped dramatically. In 1834/5 the sum of £49,257 was spent in Herefordshire. By 1838/9 the amount had declined to £41,100 in spite of a growing population. In April

1836 the 46 parishes in and around the city had combined into one Union and the first meeting of the Board of Guardians took place in May when 50 elected guardians and 14 J.Ps., also guardians, were present. The new Union Workhouse was built on two acres of land formerly belonging to St. Guthlac's Priory adjoining the County Prison designed by John Nash in 1798. The architect was Mr. Ploughden of Oxford, and Leonard Johnson of Hereford built it at the cost of £3,742. It had two wings where men and women lived separately; only children under 7 were allowed to be with their mothers. It opened in 1838, replacing the three smaller houses which had catered for the infirm and elderly, the destitute and orphans. In most years there had been only around 20 inmates, but the new workhouse could cater for 250. Several times the Board of Guardians asked for permission from the London Commissioners to grant outdoor relief rather than bring large families into the workhouse or split them up. This was always refused except in cases of sickness. Fear of the workhouse remained throughout the nineteenth century and some of the twentieth.

Opposition to the new law was widespread. It engendered terror in the poor who saw families divided on entry to the workhouse and children aged over 7 taken from their mothers. The aged were particularly vulnerable as they might be parted after years of marriage. Unmarried mothers and illegitimate children spent their lives inside unless they could work.

Figure 20 George Wythen Baxter, anti-Poor Law campaigner

There was political opposition too, and in Hereford a bookseller in St. Martin Street, George Wythen Baxter, collected evidence of the hardship it was producing and sent a petition to Parliament. His *Book of the Bastilles* contained many stories from the local and national newspapers that were both heart-rending and showed a flawed system at work.

Begging was an everyday occurrence and the *Hereford Journal* has many reports of 'Impositions upon the Benevolent'. Judgements were harsh, for whilst there was compassion for the 'deserving' poor there was very little for those who lied and cheated to get food. An example was the case of 16-year-old Charlotte Smith reported in the *Hereford Journal* on 2 December 1840. Her mother had been sentenced to 14 days' hard labour when she was found at home in the notorious slum of Friar Street, drunk and beating the girl. Charlotte was subsequently arrested 'for deception and begging' after the case was reported in the paper and brought before the mayor, Frederick Bodenham.

> On Saturday ... the case of the girl then proceeded, with Mr. Adams, Superintendent of police who stated that in consequence of a para-graph in the *Hereford Journal*, he directed her to be taken into custody. Mrs. Bulmer of Aylestone Hill deposed that as she was going home on Wednesday evening the prisoner accosted her, stating that her mother lived at Lugg Bridge, and expected to be confined shortly. The girl, who had a bundle, said that if she had the sum of 12 shil-lings she could have some baby linen, and stated that Mrs. Evans had given her 5 shillings. Mrs. Bulmer then gave her half a crown and at her request Mr. Charles Bulmer also presented her with 1 shilling and 6 pence. On inquiring of persons whose names the girl mentioned the witness found that they knew nothing of her, and the same evening having observed the paragraph in the paper, she sent it to Mr. Adams. Other evidence was produced, and the mayor, who observed that he had never heard of a more flagrant case of impo-sition, sentenced the girl to one month's imprisonment and hard labour. At the close of the inquiry, a man by the name of Powell, who afterwards described himself as a 'freeman of Monmouth and a Chartist', said he was the father-in-law of the girl, who, he observed, had done nothing wrong, and only told a lie to get a little bread. The mayor said he regretted very much that he could not punish him instead of the girl, for it was evident that he incited her to this act of deception.

He did, however, get two days in gaol for swearing at the police in High Town market place with 'unfounded imputations'.

Regulations in the workhouse were strictly enforced. Paupers were expected to rise when told and to keep themselves clean. They were not to make a noise when silence was ordered. Bad behaviour or language to the Union officers or to the other inmates was punished, and refusals to work or feigned sickness were serious offences. Punishments were rigid and laid down by the Poor Law Commissioners and then applied by the local Guardians. Mostly, it resulted in the withdrawal of food; particularly butter, cheese, tea, sugar or soup for up to 48 hours. Worse offences like bringing in alcohol or absconding resulted in appearance before a magistrate. Children were not punished by withdrawal of food but were more likely to have the cane.

Those between the ages of 5 and 9 were given 8ozs. bread, 4ozs. meat and 1oz. of cheese a day. From 1 to 5 years the bread was reduced by 1oz. and the meat by 1oz. Babies under 12 months received 6ozs. bread and an amount of milk. Some families were allowed outdoor relief because of temporary hardship such as sickness or unemployment but the children were frequently admitted during this period to relieve the families. Those on outdoor relief could not enjoy even this spartan diet. Food for adults consisted of three meals a day with bread, potatoes and rice as the staple foods with meat some days. Old people were allowed some tea, sugar and butter with the normal diet as a gesture to some humanity.

The daily routine for inmates proposed by the Poor Law Commissioners was as follows:

	Hour of Rising	Interval for Breakfast	Time for setting to Work	Interval for Dinner	Time for leaving off Work	Interval for Supper	Time for going to Bed
25 March to 29 September	6 o'clock	From 6.30 to 7	7 o'clock	From 12 to 1	6 o'clock	6 to 7	8
29 September to 25 March	7 o'clock	From 7.30 to 8	8 o'clock	From 12 to 1	6 o'clock	6 to 7	8

Half an hour after the workhouse bell was rung for rising, the Master or Matron performed a roll call in each section of the workhouse. The bell also announced meal breaks during which the rules required that 'silence, order and decorum shall be maintained', although from 1842 the word 'silence' was dropped.

Communal prayers were read before breakfast and after supper every day and Divine Service performed every Sunday, Good Friday and Christmas Day.

The Union medical officers were important for the treatment of paupers so that sickness or injury did not prevent them from working. Contagious diseases were also a problem and inmates were vaccinated against smallpox. The medical officers were also required to give sickness certificates and provide medicines to those paupers outside the workhouse. Contracts with three doctors were made in 1836 for one year but by 1842 there was an official appointment with a fixed salary. If the sick were admitted to the General Infirmary the bill was met by the Board of Guardians after their permission for the treatment had been obtained.

It was the policy of 'less eligibility' that made for hardship in the application of the New Poor Law and vulnerable people in the community came to dread the future that forced them to sell their meagre belongings and enter the 'bastille'. The failure of the system to help those who had fallen on hard times during agricultural depressions or poor harvests resulted in near-starvation for many families determined to stay together. The New Poor Law had been seen as a final solution to pauperism, an evil that endangered the moral fibre of the working-man; only by feeling the pinch of poverty could the labouring poor be motivated to work. The Old Poor Law that allowed wages to be subsidised was regarded as retrograde. Self-help and independence were virtues to

Figure 21 (top) Hereford workhouse in 2005
Figure 22 (lower) Map showing the layout of the Hereford Union workhouse

be encouraged and this was the view of society throughout the rest of the nineteenth century. Respectable artisans of the working classes shared this view; it was not confined to the wealthy.

Despite this broad agreement, opposition to the new system continued through the 1840s. There was a call from the Tories against the continuance of the Poor Law Commission and two petitions went from Hereford sent by George Wythen Baxter. One presented in 1838 had 1,707 signatures and was forwarded to John Feilden M.P. a formidable opponent of the new laws. He also presented others from Weston under Penyard and Linton in Herefordshire. When Baxter's *Book of the Bastilles* was published in 1841 it contained evidence of cruelty and neglect in the workhouses.

The Hereford Union had to respond to this. The local Tory M.P. for Herefordshire, Frankland Lewis, was one of the first three government Poor Law Commissioners in 1834 and in 1838 his son, the Whig George Cornewall Lewis, succeeded him in this post. In 1841 the Prime Minister, Lord John Russell, intended that the new Poor Laws should run for another ten years. Cornewall Lewis published a pamphlet with Nassau Senior, a lawyer with an interest in special and political issues who was also an adviser to the Whig party, explaining and defending the present administration of the laws. Many influential people were swayed by this but opposition from Tory M.P.s in the industrial areas of the North continued. In Herefordshire an Assistant Poor Law Commissioner from 1836 was Sir George Clive of Perrystone. Another friend of Cornewall Lewis was Edmund Head who was assistant Poor Law Commissioner for Breconshire and lived at Monnington Rectory with Gilbert Cornewall Lewis, George's brother. He eventually became Governor of New Brunswick in Canada. These intimate connections kept a tight network of control over the administration of the Poor Law.

The following petition was duly sent by the Chairman of the Hereford Guardians in response to the accusations published in George Wythen Baxter's book. Baxter had been very insulting about the Guardians of both Hereford and Ledbury.

To the House of Commons. 1841. Given to the officers
A Petition from Watson Joseph Thornton, Rector of Llanwarne and Chairman of the Hereford Poor Law Union on behalf of the Guardians and presented by Mr. E.B. Clive M.P.

'To the Honourable the Commons of England in Parliament assembled.
The Humble Petition of the Board of Guardians of the Hereford
Union.

Your petitioners have heard with much regret and surprise that
a statement has gone forth, that a rate on a tenement in the City
has been doubled — that infanticide and incendiarism have been
increased — and that unmarried mothers of children have declared
that they would rather die in a ditch than go in the Hereford
Workhouse. In reference to the first of these charges, your petitioners have to observe, that they have no control over the rating
of any particular parishes or tenements. It may happen that by the
revision of the rating on an individual house, such a rating may
have been increased, but as regards to the whole expenditure of the
Hereford Union, a saving of 26% has been effected by the management of your petitioners on the cost of the system before 1834.

Your petitioners have never heard of, and do not believe in, any
increase of infanticide or incendiarism within the Hereford Union
since that period. That the discipline essential to the moral improvement of unmarried mothers of children, and the religious habits
which your petitioners endeavour to establish in the workhouse,
may not at first be palatable to those whose lives have been passed
in dissolute habits, can by no means surprise your petitioners. They,
however, beg to assure your honourable House that they believe
fewer offences and greater comforts exist in Hereford workhouse
than in any other establishment of the kind, with which your petitioners are acquainted. Your petitioners have devoted their best
efforts towards rendering the workhouse available to the comforts,
welfare and moral improvement of the inmates, and a more frequent
and strict supervision of the house takes place on the part of the
guardians than in any other workhouse known to them. Your petitioners, since the building of the workhouse, not only give ample
opportunities to all respectable persons to visit the workhouse at
all reasonable hours, but a book is presented to all visitors for the
insertion of remarks, and your petitioners find the highest praise
given to the officers and arrangements of the house by almost every
visitor. Your petitioners beg leave further to state, that while discon-
tent and disturbance have prevailed in many parts of the kingdom,
more or less remote from the City of Hereford, no riotous assem-
blages, Chartist meetings, or other disorders, have taken place in
the district over which their duties extend, Your petitioners have

respectfully to assure your honourable House, that they are resolved to persevere with impartiality and firmness and without fear, favour or affection, in the arduous and unpopular task of relieving destitution, of detecting imposition, of discouraging profligacy, and of raising the moral character, and the physical condition of the lower orders. Through good report and evil report, your petitioners will continue to execute the duties entrusted to them, in the fullest confidence that the enlightened and reflecting portion of the community will not be swayed by vague accusations or unfounded statements. And your petitioners, as in duty bound will ever pray.

This defence was possibly generated by the combined attention of Lewis plus his local Commissioner, George Clive. It must have caused annoyance and some embarrassment that local opposition was taken up by politicians like John Feilden, a northern Tory M.P., and Richard Oastler, a factory reformer, who denounced the Poor Laws and their effects. Baxter had already published papers attacking the New Poor Law Amendment Act and had received support from influential Tories including Earl Stanhope. The accusation that the New Poor Law was not relieving hardship in Hereford was shown to be true by the destitution that arose from the year that the Union Workhouse opened in 1838.

In Hereford, the winters of 1838, '39 and '41 had been particularly harsh for the poor. In January 1838, the *Hereford Journal* reported that for 13 consecutive days there had been temperatures of just 5°F, 27 degrees below freezing. Resistance to entering the dreaded bastille was strong. The effects were obvious in St. Peter's and St. Owen's and a meeting was called in the vestry-room to consider what could be done. Committees were formed to collect subscriptions for making and distributing soup. The widow of the former vicar, Mrs. Gipps, had donated £5 and the names of donors were recorded weekly in *The Hereford Journal*, and soon soup was distributed four times a week. By February, 240 quarts had been delivered in St. Owen's parish where 941 people were fed. The population of the combined parishes in 1836 was 1,508, meaning that 62% were deemed to be in distress. This practical method of preventing the poor from starvation during the bitterest period of the winter continued until 1841.

However, the random application of relief according to available funds, and the charge that the poor had to pay inflated prices for coal because they could afford only small amounts at any one time, combined with another about adulterated food which appeared in the *Hereford Journal* in January

1841, prompted thoughts by John Venn to organise relief more effectively. He knew that work was still the answer for most families and so created some jobs for casual labour. The *Hereford Times* reported:

> In St. Owen's the admirable method of setting able-bodied persons to work and paying them for their labour, was adopted, and about 65 availed themselves of the opportunity.

However, all these schemes were random and temporary; none of them really helped to prevent families getting into a poverty trap. There was also unease among the middle classes about the disaffected workers of South Wales where Chartism and a call for political reform had produced agitation and riots resulting in the arrest of John Frost at Newport. A leader in the *Hereford Times* of 23 December 1840 commented that,

> It is neither for the happiness nor the prosperity of those who earn their bread by daily toil to be distracted by the conflicting political notions of the day. Such a state of society may, however, exist, that it is the bounden duty of all the well-disposed among the humbler ranks to associate together for the purpose of aiding in the endeavour to check the progress of destructive principles, and to extend the light of purer knowledge.

In 1839 there had been a rumour in Hereford that the Chartists had assembled on the hills and intended to make a descent upon the city. The report was without substance, but one of the causes was Mr. Well's circus that had advertised its troop of riders with posters stating 'That all shops be closed at six o'clock on Monday night' and at the bottom 'by order of the Management'. Some country men who read the bills without much attention took the announcement as one issued by the magistrates; they spread the rumour that the closure was due to an anticipated Chartist riot and ideas of plunder and massacre arose. Another circus bill announced that a humorous clown had as patrons Colonel Hope and General Expectation. The mere thought of such high-ranking officers in Hereford added to the idea of military operations. Another report said that the old mortar, Roaring Meg, then on Castle Green and which had been plugged up since the Civil War, was to be used against the Chartists. It was observed in the *Hereford Journal* that it would be more likely to injure those who fired it rather than those fired at.

Close proximity to the unrest in South Wales created this anxiety but it was realised that Chartism had been caused by social conditions. There was alarm amongst the Hereford middle classes and fear of revolution. Knowledge and reason went together it was thought. The idea of education for working-men was not a new one, indeed John Venn had already formed the St. Peter's Literary Institute.

There was also a move to establish an independent Mechanics' Institute in Church Street without the Anglican connections of the St. Peter's Institute. This was opposed by John Venn who claimed that his literary institute had 250 subscribers whose contributions helped to increase their library and if numbers fell it would not be so efficient. There was a meeting at the Guildhall where his views were read. The local M.P., E.B. Clive, moved a resolution to form a Mechanics' Institute saying that he thought only men with a particular religious bias would be admitted to Mr. Venn's institute. Although Rev. Barker corrected this idea and said that no one was excluded because of his denomination, the proposal had the support of the Dean and the opening of the rival institute was approved, the meeting concluding with a speech from Rev. Woodward who said:

> It was most gratifying that the higher classes did sympathise with the poorer, and if the day should come when the poor were universally set in opposition to the rich, a dissolution of the social fabric must take place, and the heaviest calamities to the nation would result. (cheers from the audience).

Other measures were needed to help the poor and avoid public unrest. In February 1841 distress was extreme from cold and unemployment and the workhouse was full. It was the year that saw Baxter's Petition to Parliament and Thornton's reply. John Venn was keen to provide a better method of helping the unfortunate and now called a meeting at the Guildhall in Widemarsh Street, to which men of influence were invited. At 12 noon, the mayor, F.L. Bodenham opened proceedings. By him sat the Bishop and the Dean. The mayor spoke about 'the way that indiscriminate and casual charity was ill-adapted to the purpose for which it was intended'.

When John Venn rose to his feet he told those present what pleasure it gave him to bring his proposals before so respectable and influential a meeting. It was subject of great importance to the industrious classes, and to the city generally. He then read his paper to them, outlining a prospectus of a proposed Society and its principles. He noted that:

> Every inhabitant of this City must have perceived and mourned over the sad state of our poor. There are many who entirely depend upon what they can get by importunate begging and a display of wretchedness; whilst numbers of a far more respectable character are suffering in patient silence the greatest distress. It is obvious that a great deal of charity is continually being given away, by bequests and by private individuals, and occasionally also, through public contributions but yet the sad state of the things described above is far from improving. The persons depending upon charity are becoming more numerous and more importunate; whilst the industrious, discouraged by their sufferings, and observing the success of clamorous appeals to the pity of the charitable, are in danger of losing their own spirit of independence. The rich themselves are also beginning very generally to feel that the whole system is radically bad, and to wish for a better to be introduced in its place.

The *Hereford Journal* reported that 'That there was considerable interest by the inhabitants at the lower end of the hall who expressed their concern and satisfaction.' The result was the formation of the Hereford Society for Aiding the Industrious.

Two of the guiding principles on which the Society was founded remained its underlying philosophy for many decades:

> That the truest charity is that which enables the workingman to maintain himself and his family in comfort and independence by his own prudence and industry.
> That the upper classes are bound by all considerations of benevolence, of morality, and above all, of religion, to try to place every working man in a situation which will enable him to do this.

By March the mayor reported that an office had been set up adjacent to the dispensary in 50 Bye Street, that proper agents had been engaged in order that the plans could be carried out and that the governing committee would meet regularly to agree the best methods of promoting success. The secretaries were Rev. John Venn and Mr. R.T. Barra. There was a paid assistant, Mr. Thomas Day, and an agent, Mr. Henry Yapp. Since 1835

Figure 23 The Hereford Dispensary and first offices of The Hereford Society for Aiding the Industrious

the poor had been used to attending the dispensary for here they received medical attention and medicine without payment. For over 40 years the Society was to operate from the adjoining premises.

Figure 24 In 1881 a new Dispensary was founded in Union Street by the efforts of Dr. Henry Graves Bull. The numbers of patients had increased to over 4,000 before the new building opened on the site of the old Bye Gate gaol. Families paid 3d. per week into the provident fund. The architects were James Davies and Lewis Powell

4 THE EARLY YEARS OF THE SOCIETY

At the end of the first year of its work the Society reported (on 15 March 1842) that they had formed several departments with their own sub-committees. One of these was concerned with the allotment of land.

They had obtained 28 acres of land and 21 of these had been let in small allotments of one eighth of an acre each. The rent was generally 15 shillings per piece but some were higher at 20 shillings. For this, the tenant had the land fenced, drained and manured and the tithes paid. The land, within a mile of the city, had been let at once to 172 tenants, and others were waiting. Another 7 acres at Clehonger had been taken by the Society, rather unwisely as it turned out, but had not yet been let. Other potential land had not been obtained as there was reluctance by farmers to part with land for cultivation by those who might buy their products. The main committee believed their enterprise had brought great benefit to the working-man and his family because it gave them an occupation when times were hard and enabled them to grow food. The Society appealed to landowners to let them rent more land so that 'the moral welfare of the working classes could be promoted' and the poor rates kept down.

There was also a feeling that spade cultivation in itself was good for people and it was recommended as part of the school curriculum. One of the great reformers that John Venn had come to know through the Clapham Sect was Lord Ashley, later 7th Earl of Shaftesbury. John met him frequently at the annual Church Missionary Society meetings in Exeter Hall where the earl took the chair. Born a year before John Venn they were contemporaries and shared their Evangelical ideals. The fight Ashley made for the white factory slaves that resulted in no children being employed under 9 years old and the shortening of their working hours, was just one small part of his social reforms. His strength of purpose was as strong as that of Wilberforce and in 1833 the Society for the Improvement of Factory Children was formed. This was the year that John Venn came to Hereford. A majority of the clergy were in favour of limiting working hours for children and saw it as an opportunity to give them some education and save their ignorant souls. It was known as *eternity* work.

Shaftesbury's fight in Parliament for the ten-hours bill followed, and as a result factory hands found they no longer had to labour into the night and that they finished earlier on a Saturday. This also meant that men and women saw more of their children and family life improved. He also fought for the prohibition of employment of women and children in the coal mines, and for a ban on chimney boys. He took homeless children from the streets and gave them a training ship for seafaring: the *Arethusa*. He campaigned for the repeal of the corn laws, against American slavery and many other noble causes. Shaftesbury's energy and compassion was for the working classes.

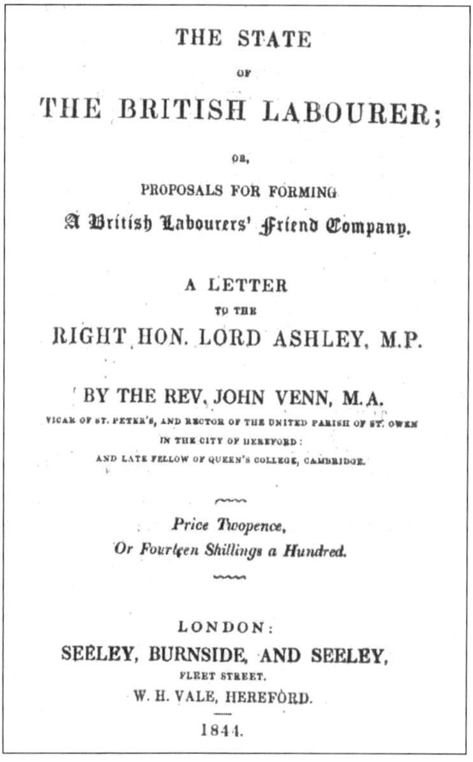

THE STATE

OF

THE BRITISH LABOURER;

OR,

PROPOSALS FOR FORMING

A British Labourers' Friend Company.

A LETTER

TO THE

RIGHT HON. LORD ASHLEY, M.P.

BY THE REV. JOHN VENN, M.A.

VICAR OF ST. PETER'S, AND RECTOR OF THE UNITED PARISH OF ST. OWEN
IN THE CITY OF HEREFORD:
AND LATE FELLOW OF QUEEN'S COLLEGE, CAMBRIDGE.

Price Twopence,
Or Fourteen Shillings a Hundred.

LONDON:

SEELEY, BURNSIDE, AND SEELEY,

FLEET STREET.

W. H. VALE, HEREFORD.

1844.

Figure 25 Title page from
The State of the British Labourer

It is perhaps no surprise, therefore, that a pamphlet John Venn wrote in 1844 entitled *The State of the British Labourer* in which he made proposals for forming a British labourers' friendly company that would facilitate the letting of small allotments of land to help the agricultural poor, was addressed to the Earl of Shaftesbury. 'The condition of our agricultural poor is deplorably bad' he wrote. 'The rate of wages in Herefordshire is about seven shillings a week, with a liberal allowance of beer or cider. But many cannot obtain work.' Shaftesbury was at that time piloting a Bill though Parliament to facilitate the use of small allotments and for the regulation of loan societies. Both of these provisions were to become part of the strategy of Venn's Society for Aiding the Industrious in Hereford.

At its meeting on 16 March 1844, the allotment sub-committee under its chairman R. Hereford and with John Venn present, made several decisions. One of the principles they stated was that after the initial fencing, draining and manuring the tenants should continue their own manuring. It was decided to print a leaflet on 'Hints' which would be given to each tenant. Prize money was to be donated by some of the committee and local worthies and small cash prizes for first, second and third in a variety of categories were to be given. More typically, 'the land committee [or allotment sub-committee] met on Tuesday, June 25th, at ten o'clock in the Bye Street office and then went to inspect the allotments and adjudge the prizes.' At this time land was rented out in Friars Lane, Whitecross, Barton no.1 and Barton no.2 (two separate fields), Hunderton, Bartonsham and Litley. In July it was reported that some tenants were not cultivating their holdings properly, and it was resolved to warn them that their tenancy would be terminated if they did not meet the requirements. At the next sub-committee meeting it was agreed that Richard Jones at Litley was to be told to quit. The following year another Jones was found guilty of theft and asked to leave.

In 1845 Edward Poole, a landed gentleman of Homend at Stretton Grandison and owner of Barr's Court, a small estate, offered the Society 31 acres at Barr's Court and associated farm buildings. The rent was £3 per acre, which was cheap as the usual rate was £5. In January of the following year the secretary was requested 'to take all necessary measures for setting out a piece of land at Barr's Court adjoining the canal, in allotments.' Fencing was good oak pale hurdles, and 'quick' hedging was also used. For the farm, seed was purchased: lucerne, mangle wurzel and 2 acres of potatoes plus 5cwt. of guano from Peru for manuring the crops, with another 48 tons of manure for the wheat crop. Mr. Llanwarne was asked to act as farm manager. But by June the reason for taking on the farm had gone. The intention had been to provide work for unemployed labourers but instead there was a shortage of workers for the farm, and it was thought desirable to give it up as soon as possible. In August 1847 Mr. Llanwarne was asked to dispose of the wheat crop and the hay-rick, and the land that was to be retained for allotments was now divided up into pieces of one eighth of an acre by Mr. Fosbrooke, the surveyor. The remaining allotment holders had entered the awards and the first prize at

Figure 26 Middle Basin Hereford and Gloucester Canal. The rural aspect of the city land through which the canal was cut is illustrated by the presence of a rick for either bark or hay on the left. The Hereford and Gloucester canal reached Hereford in May 1845 after a protracted delay in the stretch from Ledbury due to lack of funds. When the railway line and Barr's Court station was opened in 1854 the use of the canal declined. The Poole family continued to let land to the Society and the last piece consisting of 8.14 acres in Plough Lane, Canon Moor was transferred to the City Council as late as 1972. It is now a trading estate

Barr's Court was awarded to Thomas Lloyd and £1 2s. 6d. was donated by Edward Poole for the purpose.

When the canal was excavated near the estate some of the top soil was left in heaps of which two piles were offered to the Society. Some of it was requested by James Jay, a member of the committee, who undertook to replace it with stable manure.

By the seventh annual meeting in 1848 the Society was letting out 52 acres of land to 352 tenants. Money prizes were awarded as usual: 10s. for first, 7s. 6d. for second and 5s. for third. These were handsome awards. The committee recorded that they had heard that the system of allotments was being widely and rapidly extended throughout the kingdom; and that they had been informed that in many places the experiment of increasing the size of the allotments, in some cases to a considerable extent, had been tried with great success. They agreed that early consideration would be given to doing the same if land could be obtained, but this does not seem to have happened. (In 1887 the Allotments Act required the local authority, then the sanitary authority, to acquire land and provide allotments for the labouring population at a reasonable rent. Only then did allotments become widely available.)

Slight complaints were received by the Society from the tenants over the years, mainly concerning the state of the fencing. Just before the First World War, in 1913, there was a serious complaint about the new householders of the Hereford Co-operative Housing Estate known as the Garden City. This new development in Barr's Court Road was next to the allotments and the fences round the new homes were inadequate. Complaints about trespass on the allotments were made and the matter was referred to the Chief Constable.

At the same time Hereford Council decided to widen Coningsby and Monkmoor Streets so that allotment holders there were given notice to move out. The same thing happened in Friar Street, but the council officers had pegged out the new road over the allotments before the tenants were given notice to quit. They were, naturally, very angry. The secretary of the Society at the time, Mr. William Garrold Lloyd, wrote to the *Hereford Times* and the *Hereford Journal* about it so that all the tenants knew what was happening, but he added that it was a pity the allotments 'inspired by the late Revd. John Venn that have existed for nearly 70 years ... now have to be discontinued'.

Many of the early allotments in Hereford were created by the Society. In 1941, a hundred years after the formation of the Society, Mr. Marchant, the then chairman, pointed out that there were still 140 allotments in use and well cultivated. The last allotments to be sold were at Plough Lane in Whitecross, behind the Plough Inn, and now an industrial estate, together with 8 acres at Canonmoor that were sold for building land. Competitions were held for tenants and certificates awarded as late as 1961.

One other of the Society's initial schemes was a loan department. Between £1 and £10 could be borrowed by anyone bringing a proper recommendation and one good security (probably an individual who would cover any loss). Ten pence in the pound was deducted for interest before the loan was received and a compulsory loan-book cost 3d. After three weeks the money had to be repaid in instalments of 8d. per £1. In the first eight months of the scheme 131 sums had been lent amounting to £538. The loans were financed by sums of money lent by patrons who received 3% interest. In 1848, 630 loans totalling £2,472 were made. Today loans continue to be made for helping education and small businesses.

There was also a provident bank that took deposits in the Society's office every day. These small sums could be withdrawn at any time, upon a fortnight's notice in summer and a week's notice in winter. During the first year 3,057 sums had been deposited amounting to £159 4s. 2d. This fund was an encouragement to save and to pay rents when they were due. The Savings Bank in Packer's Lane (East Street) did not deal in such small sums so this provided a safe way of keeping money for a rainy day.

The Society did not make its own direct payments to 'distressed persons', but did undertake to administer such payments on behalf of donors having

Figure 27 James Jay J.P. at the office (HRO). He was a remarkable figure as he stood 6 feet 4 inches in height and was as thin as a lamppost. A solicitor and known as Lanky Jim, he was mayor of Hereford twice, in 1847–8 and 1862–3 and worked hard for social improvement. He had a strong personality and was outspoken in public affairs. This sketch dates from the late 1840s when he was mayor at the time the steam corn mill opened in 1848. In 1844 he served on the allotment sub-committee and in 1847 he was on the new mill sub-committee

undertaken their own investigations into the need. There were 60 such potential beneficiaries in the first year, but 40 had been sent away as 'utterly undeserving' with £24 4s. 5d. granted in relief to the others. The main committee considered that this method of charity by application to the Society had checked the amount of begging and benefited 'the industrious and deserving'.

Another early concern of the Society was the cost of coal. Until the railways brought cheap coal from South Wales in 1854, the price prevailing in Hereford was high in winter months. The Society therefore hired a large yard at a rent of £8 a year that was capable of holding 500 tons. Then, by borrowing the capital, 395 tons were bought at summer prices and resold by delivery to the door in the winter at the cost of 11d. a hundredweight. This was a reduction of 5d. on previous winter prices and over 4,727 separate deliveries were made in the winter of 1841/2. The slight loss of £25 to the Society was deemed worthwhile, and may also have brought down the general price of coal in Hereford. The poor were urged to pay a deposit in the summer and before 1 November so that they could receive the benefit of a further penny reduction and save themselves from 'a state of miserable anxiety'.

The number of tons of coal sold in the severe and protracted winter of 1846 rose to 1,047, more than double that of the previous year. Much of it was sold at 6d. per hundredweight.

All this charity had been efficiently managed to the extent that the office and coalyard had been set up leaving a small balance of £8 in hand. In former years £400 had been expended on indiscriminate relief, but now it was expected that far more could be done for an annual expenditure of £120.

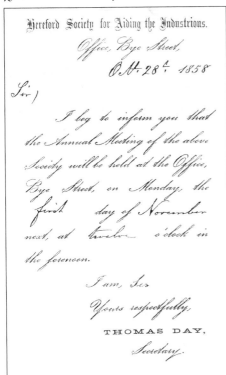

Figure 28 Notice of Annual Meeting, 1858, sent to the Society members by the secretary, Thomas Day

Employment was a major concern of the Society and it had been hoped that by keeping a book of vacancies in the office and registering those looking for work the Society could carry out the role of a labour exchange, but few employers made use of the scheme. The Society did issue a plea for wages to paid on Fridays or Saturday mornings rather than on Saturday evenings when pay would often be dissipated in buying alcohol.

5   THE SOUP KITCHEN

Production of winter soup had remained one of Venn's primary concerns and became an important activity of the Society. By 1847 the disastrous failure of the potato crop in England as well as Ireland co-incided with a series of bad harvests and low employment. It had become the Hungry Forties. John Venn told that year's annual meeting that 'the committee bore testimony to the patience and resignation with which the working classes had borne their severe privations and sufferings'. The Society's soup had kept whole families from starvation during 1844, and in 1846, 33,239 quarts of 'good, wholesome and nutritious soup' were made.

In 1847 it was decided to step up soup production, and in January a special appeal was made in the *Hereford Times* for funds and ingredients. It was intended to produce 100 gallons a day at 1d. a quart. More furnaces had to be installed in the shed behind the office to cope with this heavy demand. Contributions in kind were requested, especially peas, rice or vegetables. Rice was used in place of the scarce potato. As the winter freeze continued — the *Hereford Times* reported that 'in the month of January just ended the temperature was 9.25 deg. lower than the corresponding month in 1846' — it was realised that the increased soup sales were running at a loss of £10 a week at the same time that hundreds had to be turned away each day as demand exceeded supply. In addition crowds of applicants beset the Society offices in Bye Street seeking cheaper coal.

The work of the soup committee of the Society had begun on 12 December 1844 and it met every week under the guidance of its chairman, Dr. Edward Morris. Eight gentlemen served on it, including Charles Brunsdon who later became President of the Society. They resolved to buy a full-sized Papin's Digester (an early type of pressure cooker) and

Messrs. Yapp and Knill offered to acquire other necessities such as scales, a block and cleaver. Butchers were asked to give tenders for the supply of meat and advertisements were placed in the local papers asking for help. Distribution was by ticket and 500 were printed on stiff card and entitled the bearer to a quart of soup at a penny a ticket. Mr. Knill offered to receive the money and tickets. He and Mr. Yapp were asked to find the best recipe so that they could start production as soon as possible. By the next meeting most things had been purchased and Mr. Yapp reported that he had bought six stones of beef at 4s. a stone, two cows' heads at 2s. 9d. each and two bags of peas at 6s. 3d. per bushel from Mr. Hooper of Woolhope. Two bushels of peas and a bag of turnips had been donated. Mr. Knill was asked to superintend the making of the soup to a given recipe and sell it three times a week on Tuesday, Thursday and Saturday from 11 o'clock in the morning. Mrs. Phillipps was employed to make the soup at 2s. 6d. per day, this high rate of pay reflecting the hard labour it involved.

The recipe below, dated 28 February 1845, is recorded in the Soup Committee Minute Book and was handed on through the years:

Receipts for making 80 gallons of soup

80 lbs. of gravy beef	10lbs. parsnips
1 head	12lbs. leeks
1 skin	4 good heads of celery
3 pecks of good peas	6oz. black pepper
1½ pecks of good flour	6oz. mustard
5 good turnips	3oz. ginger
4lbs. onions	½oz. chillies
10lbs. carrots	salt to your taste

Bundle of sweet herbs such as thyme, winter savory-mint, notted marjoram, a portion of each boiled in a muslin bag.

The hard labour and time involved in making such large amounts of soup was daunting, as recorded in the minute book of the soup sub-committee:

Commence previous day about 3 o'clock. Put the peas to soak in a tub till morning. Clean the vegetables and cut up in small diamonds. Fill the furnace with the proper quantities of cold water (say about

60 gals. for 80 gals. of soup). Cut the meat into small pieces, thoroughly crack and break the bones, then put meat and bones with pepper, salt, chillies, vegetables & sweet herbs (in muslin bag), on to boil for 3 or 4 hours or till every bit of meat leaves the bones. It is then left for the night, the fire being made up and covered with ashes so as to keep the soup simmering till 1 or 2 o'clock.

Next morning (about 5) make up the fire, skim the refuse off the peas & adding some fat skimmings from the meat to the peas boil the peas in about 20 gals. of water till quite soft which they will be in two hours if they are good peas. At the same time (5 o'clock) put the rice into the large furnace. In the time the peas are boiled have all the bones taken out of the bottom of the furnace, then add the peas and liquor, boil all together till 9 or 10 o'clock. The flour should then be mixed smoothly with cold water & added gradually to the mass, being careful that the soup boils briskly & is kept stirred while thickening is added. Afterwards smother up the fire with ashes to prevent burning and keep stirring till served at 11 o'clock am.

When the bones are taken out, it is usual to place them in a 4 gallon digester with water & the sweet herbs, and in due time four gallons more of excellent soup will be ready to add to the next making.

The comment is added that the greatest care and cleanliness are required.

The container used for the extra cooking was the Papin's Digester which consisted of an iron cylinder with a wooden handle on either side, seated on a circular base of the same diameter. The base served as a little furnace and had a door at the front where the fuel was burned. Over the perforated part of the furnace a second cylinder of strong metal was placed and hermetically sealed by a circular lid which was screwed down by another lid on top and strong iron catches. This allowed the temperature to rise beyond boiling point reaching high pressure inside. This was particularly useful for softening bones and faster cooking.

Soup was made most years between 1 November and 1 March. In January 1847 soup was made daily (except for Sundays) and 3,608 gallons were sold in ten deliveries to the other city parishes at a loss of £5 3s. Two weeks later Mr. Knill reported that the demand could not be met because of the small size of the furnaces. Two larger furnaces were ordered, to be built by Leonard Johnson.

In the following years normal production was resumed. In 1851 the bishop offered the use of St. Peter's church house for the soup kitchen and it was fitted out with furnaces, but fine weather delayed the start of operations until the New Year. Dr. Henry Graves Bull, who had arrived five years earlier in the city, was appointed to the committee in the following year and took an active role in the work of the Society, serving on the soup committee for ten years.

Only two years after the kitchen had moved to St. Peter's church house the Society received a letter from the diocesan architect, Mr. Nicholson, requesting that the furnaces be removed and they were reinstalled in the premises behind the Bye Street offices. Leonard Johnson was asked to erect a temporary shed near the Soup House to shelter those waiting and Mrs. Phillipps resumed her labours on 20 December. She continued to make the soup until 1856 under Mr. Gollins' supervision and each year a temporary shed was built. By 1872 John Venn, having retired, began to play a more active part in affairs and he was in the Chair on 27 June when Mr. Nicholson, now architect to the Society, presented a plan for a new dining room to the members. This was to be erected in the space between the soup kitchen and the unused cottage behind the offices in Bye Street, since renamed Commercial Street.

The soup kitchen was constructed behind the premises that the Day family had sold to the Society in 1871. The dining-room had its entrance in Union Passage, formerly Crown Passage, and is still recognisable by the two doors, one that allowed ticket holders to enter and the other to leave.

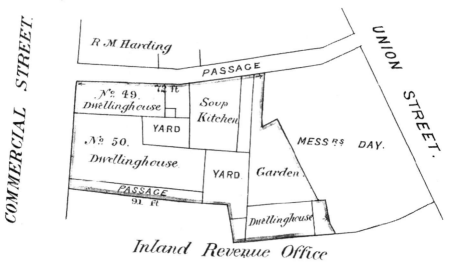

*Figure 29 Plan of the buildings adjacent to Union Passage c.1871
showing the location of the Soup Kitchen*

Designed by Thomas Nicholson, it has an open hall with large tie beams and a version of a queen post roof that took its inspiration from a medieval dining hall. The skylights provided ventilation. Mr. Nicholson's bill for his work was £42 5s. 8d. The kitchen cost £300 and was built by Welsh and sons, but the fine dining room was built by Beavan for £221 12s. Between the wars it was given a polished sprung floor and was used as a dancing school. The kitchen and earlier soup house was rediscovered in the 1990s after it had been hidden by more recent buildings. It has a large oven in one corner that was used by a bakery. The outside walls are clearly visible although now enclosed, and a door and passage linked it to the dining-room. Again it was open to the roof and provided an airy room. Today it lies behind a shop in Commercial Street.

Slight changes began to creep in. Australian beef and lamb were now used; mostly boiled or tinned. The cook was now Mrs. Burrowes, who was allowed a female assistant. From 1875 until 1882 there is a gap in the minute book as the soup sub-committee was dormant. This was due to the

The new premises at the rear of the house in Bye/Commercial Street consisted of a dining room and kitchen. There was a built-in oven in the kitchen that is still there. Figure 30 (left) shows the dining hall end of the premises, whilst Figure 31 (right) shows the entrance off Union Passage

opening of refreshment rooms in the dining room behind the office that sold soup all the year and was managed by the main committee. There was a request for the display of religious tracts and temperance publications in the room but the committee asserted bravely that the Society was founded on non-sectarian principles and it should adhere to them. The Society did decide, however, to pay for two daily newspapers and two copies of *Cottagers and Artisans*, a popular monthly periodical, as well as texts and pictures for the walls. By August 1877 it was resolved to let the house in Bye/Commercial Street which contained the refreshment rooms at a rent of £40 per annum. Unable to find a tenant, the Parker family who had been managing the refreshment rooms were given notice and the ladies' committee was asked to run them.

In the event they were let to an independent team of women who were given a subsidy of £30 to make soup for the poor as part of their general activities. This was sold at 2d. a quart. They were also 'to endeavour to promote the welfare of the working classes in whatever way they think best.' They were given permission to take in lodgers or to start a school of cookery on their premises but they were required to use a name that would disassociate them from the Society. They were advised to serve cocoa, coffee, tea and American drinks every day. By the following April the managers of the refreshment rooms had resigned and the ladies' committee wished to discontinue the business. In the event they changed their minds and kept going until August 1882 when their account was overdrawn by £49. As it was felt that the poor did not frequent the refreshment rooms often enough, it was resolved to close them. Instead, the soup kitchen was to be resumed in the winter months in the same manner as it had been managed in the past.

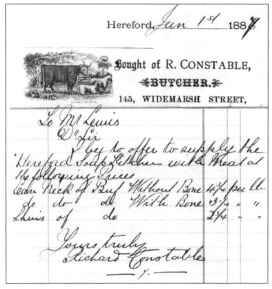

Figure 32 A tender for supplying the ingredients from which to make the soup

Thus, as from the winter of 1882, soup was made once more every day except

Sunday under the guidance of George With who was an indispensable servant of the Society (see pp.96-97). A realisation that the soup cost 1½d. to 2d. per quart to make caused the Society to raise the price for non-subscribers to 1½d. a ticket. In the following years production was transferred to the new purpose-built premises next to the new office in Bath Street when detailed records cease or are lost.

The ingredients for soup at this time still include mustard, pepper and chillies to give it a hot flavour.

Once the soup kitchen had moved to the corner of De Lacy Street in 1885, next door to the new office premises, the old regime was resumed. Tickets were issued and soup collected by entering one door and leaving by the other. There was also a dining room where it could be eaten. Directly the winter temperature dropped, soup making was resumed and continued until demand declined with warmer days.

Later minute books recorded the use of the soup kitchen after the First World War. On 13 March 1922 the soup kitchen was closed at the end of the winter. It had served 5,426 gallons of soup at a loss of £202 17s. 1d. In 1923 it was opened on 27 November and sales were resumed. The day after Christmas it was reopened for poor school-children. It was then kept open on Mondays. In 1924, 4,141 gallons were sold with a loss to the Society of £93 19s. while the boiler in the soup kitchen was worn out. The soup kitchen was used through the Depression and some Herefordians can still remember the queues that waited outside the doors on

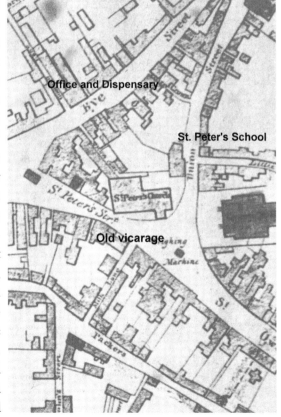

Figure 33 Map of 1841 of St. Peter's marked with places associated with John Venn

the corner of De Lacy Street. One of the few benefits of the Second World War was that school meals and British Restaurants provided cheap food and the soup kitchen was no longer needed.

6   THE MILL

Once the protectionist Corn Laws were repealed in 1846 the working classes looked forward to cheaper bread. The laws had increased the cost of imported grain by imposing a tariff. The factory owners of the northern industrial towns were opposed to these restrictions as they were

Figure 34 Signing a petition against the Corn Laws

in turn forced to pay higher wages to their workers, who could otherwise not afford bread. The opposition to the Corn Laws was led by two Members of Parliament: Richard Cobden and John Bright. The Tory land-owners were led by the Prime Minister, Sir Robert Peel, but he changed his views when the distress caused by the potato famine in Ireland and the agitation of the northern workers against the protectionist Laws finally convinced him that they had to go.

Even if the grain was cheaper (some was gleaned from the fields after the harvest), the cost of milling it could still be excessive.

Figure 35 Gleaning the aftermath

The idea came to John Venn that the Society should build its own mill where the industrious poor could have their grain milled or where they could buy flour at low prices. This was an inspired vision that was to produce an extra dividend in the form of income and employment for the Society for years to come. After he had put forward his ideas, a special sub-committee, chaired by the then mayor, H. Bullock, was established to work out a scheme. Members of the committee were Rev. Venn, Messrs. Vale, Jay, Smyth, Webb, Lanwarne, Johns, Brunsdon, Braithwaite, Newton, Lee, James and Dr. H.G. Bull. In August, at a special meeting of the Society, with the Bishop in the chair, the plan outlined was greeted with enthusiasm even though £3,000 was required to finance the scheme.

It was agreed to purchase a piece of land just outside Byster's Gate, at Brookside, for £200 from Mr. Charles Spozzi of Castle Street. At this time the city ditch, which ran in front of the land, was still full of water from the Eigne Brook. On the other side was the medieval city wall, which rose to a considerable height by the site of the old City Gaol, now replaced by a new prison in Gaol Street. The path beside it had been known as the Sally Walk from the willow trees that grew beside it and was a favourite place for a Sunday afternoon stroll. Near to the new Commercial Square, with the prestigious Kerry Arms Hotel, it was an area ripe for development.

In August an appeal for loans was published in the two local papers. The proposal was to build a modern and efficient steam mill at a cost of

£3,000, capital which had to be raised. Offers of help with the purchase of machinery and the erection of the buildings on favourable terms were made, but the sum was to be raised from subscriptions and loans. The *Hereford Times* applauded the idea:

> Other places were building steam mills for the benefit of share-holders but Hereford would be almost exclusively the only town in which there is a mill of this kind established on a principle of pure benevolence.

By the end of the month the scheme had been given the go ahead and the land purchase made. Messrs. H.O. and A. Robinson of Millwall, London had been involved with building other mills and offered their services to undertake the plans and specifications at no charge and to install the engine and machinery at cost price. Leonard Johnson offered to build the mill on the same terms.

By 5 August a draft agreement for the engine and machinery had been drawn up by Messrs. Robinson and laid before the committee. At this meeting it was resolved that a brick chimney should be substituted for the iron one in the plans and alterations were made in the contract. Bricks for the building were offered by Mr. Newton for 44s. per thousand which was accepted, and by 28 August an agreement for supplying the mill was signed with Messrs. Robinson. Cast-iron pillars were to be used to strengthen the floors and supplied by Robinsons. Leonard Johnson put forward plans and specifications for approval with some changes. One of these was an alteration to the roof, which would save £18.

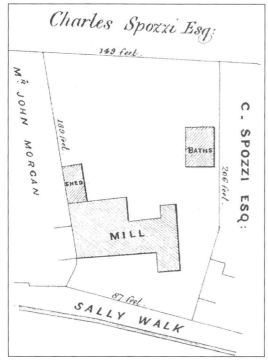

Figure 36 Plan showing the mill in Sally Walk

By October building work was progressing well and it was resolved to give £3 to the workmen as a gratuity for drink according to their efforts, with the distribution left to the foreman. Drink was then a normal way to reward labourers. Thoughts turned to the running of the mill and Robinsons were asked to engage an engine driver at a salary of not more than 18s. a week who would take up his duties when required. In November, Leonard Johnson was due to install the boiler with the agreement of the contractors, and the Society's secretary was asked to find lodgings for the men who were to install the machinery. It was now time to look for a miller and enquiries were made of a Mr. James. When he was interviewed he offered his services for 21s. a week. William Vigor was also seen and offered the same terms. The following January the choice was left to Messrs. Robinson, as consultants, but both applicants failed to gain their approval. Mr. Knowles was finally engaged for a year with the stipulation that he could be sacked instantly for misconduct and that all his time as miller and stone dresser, between 6am. until 6pm., should in the service of the Society. He was offered 30s. a week and £3 for his travelling expenses from Gloucester for the interview. At the same time John Stewart was engaged as stoker for the boiler at a wage of 21s. a week.

In February 1848 the contractors were asked to procure a bolter, to sieve the bran out of the meal, for the mill. The well underneath was to be sunk four or five feet deeper than had been planned and fenced off for safety. A Mr. Jennings was paid 12s. for a grindstone.

In the meantime cash was required to meet the bills and attempts were made to raise £2,000 by issuing shares at £25 each at 4% interest. Some offers were made for mortgages on the mill but all fell through and erstwhile investors were reluctant to part with their cash. John Venn and his sister Emelia put up some funds at 4% interest and offered to raise the rest. This offer was gratefully accepted in January 1848.

On 6 March Leonard Johnson was requested to finish the work at the mill by the end of the week so that it could begin production, as the machinery had now been installed. Two weeks later Robinsons were asked to let their workman, Oswald, make an addition to the hoisting jack and to fit a mercurial gauge and dial plates for the engine to measure the temperature. Leonard Johnson was requested to partition off the machinery as quickly as possible under the direction of the miller, and to board the top of the engine room. Completion of the project was delayed by the lack of the elevators, which had not yet been installed by Robinsons. Considerable dissatisfaction was expressed about this, and in March they were told to forward the elevators in compliance with their contract.

By the end of the month Robinsons had replied to the effect that their expenses so far incurred amounted to £1,062 4s. 9d. and they requested an assurance that payment would be made as they believed that they had fulfilled their contract. This evidently did not please the committee who felt otherwise, and that several things remained to be done to make the mill and machinery work efficiently. The inconvenience caused by the delay in the installation of the elevators was also noted and the Secretary was asked to send a copy of the committee resolutions to Messrs. Robinson, indicating that they would seek to enforce the terms of the contract.

On 5 April Mr. A. Robinson came before the committee and stated that the present bushes needed replacing with more efficient ones, that the jack tackle needed adjusting for lowering, and that the elevators would be erected immediately. On hearing this news the committee agreed that the contract had now been fulfilled and Mr. Robinson was thanked for attending the meeting and explaining the situation. On the following Friday Mr. Robinson tried out the power of the engine and its efficiency in front of several members. It performed by driving all three pairs of stones and the dressing machine with ease. Each pair of stones had ground 61½ bushels within the hour and all had worked admirably. The whole committee expressed their appreciation of Robinsons' work 'with the exception of the elevators'.

The mill started work, according to the mill's Stock Book, on 7 June 1848 with a delivery of wheat amounting to 104,950lbs. at a cost of £525. 0s. 1d. By 18 September 1848, just three months later, the pay roll included the secretary and two clerks, Knowles the miller, James the engine driver, Higgins,

Figure 37 James Jay was mayor and on the committee in 1848

61

Owen the stoker (who had temporarily replaced Stewart), Phillips and Dallow. There was some casual labour mostly for hauling coal. A surplus had been made of £34 15s. 2d.

From the MILL STOCK BOOK 1847–52
EXPENSES

oil	£3	12s.	
twine & tow		10s.	5d.
coals	£119	15s.	6d.
hauling coal	£2	2s.	1d.
poor, road & church rates	£1	10s.	
income tax	£0	7s.	3½
carriage of flour	£5	6s.	1d
stamps	£1	2s.	2½d.
interest paid	£33	3s.	2d.
sacks	£14	5s.	0d
utensils	£2	0s.	8d.
sundries		13s.	0d

Balance	Sales	Expenses/Wages
1848/49 £221 4s. 8d.	£1150 4s. 9d.	£929 0s. 1d
1849/50 £204 16s. 7½d	£1371 7s. 0d.	£945 5s. 8½d.
1850/51 £684 17s. 11½d	£1708 0s. 7d.	£1,023.2s. 7½d

It was decided by the committee that one-tenth of the profit from the mill should be divided between the workers, a sum that in 1855 amounted to £191 10s., the whole profit having risen to £1,914 14. 10d. The largest amount went to the manager, Thomas Day, who received £120. His assistant, William Lewis, had £40, while Bruton, Dallow, Owen, and Owen jnr. all received lesser sums. Equivalent allocations continued for some years until the amounts were deemed too large.

In the meantime the miller, John Knowles, had been dismissed in February 1849 with two weeks' wages. As a result new regulations had been drawn up for the operation of the mill and the services of the employees. The hours were long — 5am. until 9pm. — but now there were to be two millers covering these hours, working ten hours each. The new regulations included:

That grists be received & ground every day, one pair of the wheat stones & the barley stones being kept for that purpose, and the second pair of wheat stones for manufacturing flour for stock but the two pair to be employed for the latter purpose until 9 o'clock.

All grists when dressed shall be weighed off as soon as possible & shall be required be remarked and removed to the first floor of the store room until called for.

The working classes if in attendance at the mill always to have the preference in their grists being attended to.

Further regulations are given in Appendix 2, and provide an indication of what was expected of the workers and their requirement to attend to the needs of the poor at all times.

In July 1849 it was decided that larger stones should replace the small ones then in use, a task that Mr. Newman was asked to undertake. His estimate was £11 9s. 10½d., but he agreed to take the old stones in exchange. Mr. Newman was summoned again in September because the gear for driving the larger pair of stones was not effective, and was asked to remedy the problem, work for which he would be paid. An estimate was also received and agreed from Messrs. Haden for the machinery necessary to drive the stones.

In September 1850 the secretary reported that a spare runner stone was necessary to facilitate the milling work and a Welsh runner was agreed. During the following month damage to the machinery occurred and John Higgins was suspended until there had been an inquiry. The damage is not detailed in the minutes, but he was reprimanded and fined a sovereign towards the expenses. In October the state of the engine was again causing consternation and Mr. David Glasgow of Birmingham was requested to come and examine the whole of the machinery. At this time a clock was purchased and also a gutta percha speaking tube, a very modern means of communication between workers that had two cones connected by a flexible air pipe. Attention to the fact that it was about to be used was made by blowing a whistle.

On 8 November 1850 David Glasgow duly arrived and made his inspection, subsequently pointing out the defects of the engine to the committee. He was requested to make a new cylinder two inches wider in diameter than the present one, also a new piston, a new force pump barrel and valves. Intriguingly, he was also asked to furnish a plan for heating water by using the waste steam from the boiler for baths and wash-houses to be undertaken in the future. In addition he was to provide a plan for a new boiler to work either with or separate from the present boiler. The upright shaft to the engine room needed removal and he was asked for an estimate that was to include:

> a frame, bed, a pair of mill stones of the same size as the others in the situation of the present upright shaft, to remove a smutting machine into a loft and gearing for the same, in order to lengthen the main shaft at the N.W. end, to drive the elevators and treat the same if found necessary and expedient.

It is clear that a major overhaul was necessary, only two years after the mill had opened. Glasgow's estimate of £95 was accepted, whilst Leonard Johnson was required to do some building work.

John Owen, the engine driver, proved an innovative mechanic and was presented with £2 at Christmas for inventing a contrivance for burning the smoke of the boiler and reducing the level of pollution. There was an emphasis on the effects on the local environment as the substitution of the brick chimney for an iron one, so more pleasing to the eye, indicates. This is surprising in view of the vast amounts of smoke then overhanging every industrial town.

In February 1851 concern was expressed about the encrustation arising from the impurity of the water and the state of the engine. It was decided to alter the pipes so that the force pump could work in cold water. There were other adjustments. The smutting machine was moved and the dressing machine was altered to drive at the tail instead of the head. The meal-dressing bin was also enlarged. In September, John Owen was given a gratuity of £6 for the alterations he had made in the pipes and heating box of the engine and also for planning and erecting pipes for procuring warm water for the baths. His son worked the engine while he did the necessary work. By December the committee resolved to erect an additional boiler house and rooms, work that Leonard Johnson was requested to undertake. They also approved a second cylinder to the engine supplied by Messrs. Haden. A new dressing machine was also needed. By June of the following year Messrs. Haden were asked to install a new fly shaft for the engine.

In 1864 a large extension to the mill was made. Charles Brunsdon, who was a lawyer and member of the committee, and William Evans had to negotiate the contract for the work with William Bowers, builder, whose tender was eventually agreed for £860. The surveyor, Thomas Davies, supervised the work and made the drawings.

The specifications give some insight into the original materials used in 1847 as the new ones were to be as similar as possible. All the bricks had to be made by William Godwin by machine at Lugwardine brick works. Earlier bricks did not come from here but were to match the existing. Fifty-eight columns were ordered, to be the same as the existing ones. Other local materials included stone from the Three Elms quarries used to support the iron columns. The same stone was used for lintels and plinths round the door frames. York paving was used for the floor and sleeper walls. The slates on the roof were carefully removed for use again when it was raised and the new part had to match with best Bangor Countess slates each fixed with two copper nails. Fifty-two iron rods were used to bolt and fasten the existing beams into the extension. Two sets of open stairs were inserted to reach the upper floors. On top of the roof a shutter was put in a dormer to give access to the lead gutter. The new windows had to match the existing ones and Newcastle Crown glass was used. Inside the new

Figure 38 Plan of the mill extension of 1864 showing the side elevation

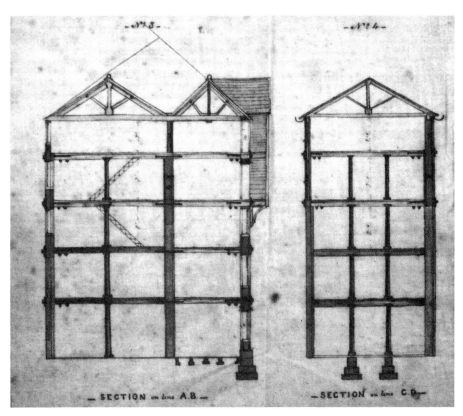

Figure 39 Mill extension cross-section of 1864, showing iron columns on piers, two stairs, and the timber walls for the hoist

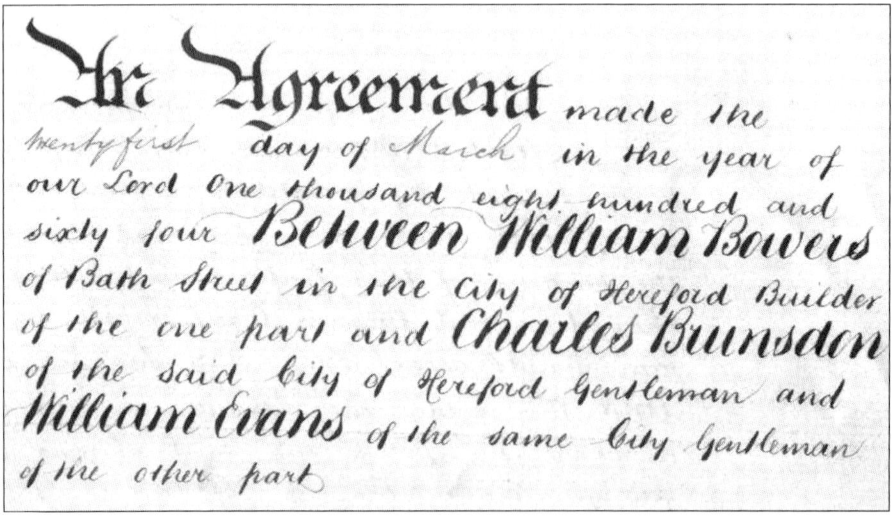

This Agreement made the twenty first day of March in the year of our Lord One thousand eight hundred and sixty four Between William Bowers of Bath Street in the City of Hereford Builder of the one part and Charles Brunsdon of the said City of Hereford Gentleman and William Evans of the same City Gentleman of the other part

Figure 40 Agreement for work on the extension of 1864

walls were 'lime whited' and every part, new and old, that needed it was given four coats of plain paint.

The main driving force behind the mill throughout this period was Thomas Day. From the day that the Society was founded in 1841, Thomas Day was manager of its offices until his death on 28 December 1869. He was a shoemaker by trade with premises in Broad Street which he ran with his brothers, Edwin and Henry. They all lived in Bye Street in a house behind the Society's offices that fronted on to Union Street. He was one of John Venn's most trusted Sunday school teachers and also preached at Wellington every Sunday. He showed such aptitude for the work that he was made manager of the corn mill as well as assistant secretary to the Society. In 1856 he was also clerk to the Herefordshire Friendly Society. He had to learn about flour milling, but by 1863 he was listed as a miller in city directories when living at 119 St. Owen Street. In 1865 Thomas Day was presented with a bonus:

> That the sum of One Hundred Guineas be presented to Mr. Day in testimony of the grateful appreciation by the committee of his services and of his constant endeavour to promote the best interests of the Society.

His assistant, William Lewis, was given 35 guineas, Thomas Bruton 10 guineas and Fred Hollings received 7 guineas. The enterprise was paying dividends for all their hard work in overseeing extensions at the mill and increased production. The following year the two clerks were given a rise to £70 a year, and in 1869 Thomas Day was again rewarded.

> The clear profits of the corn mill from the time of its establishment about twenty years ago now amounted to above £17,400 whilst its bad debts during that time have only amounted to under £400. And as much success is so much owing, under God's blessing, to the great judgment and unwearied energy of Mr. Day, this Committee feel it to be their duty to increase his salary from £350 to £425 a year and they have the greatest pleasure in doing so.

Every day of the week he would visit the mill between 11 and 12 o'clock at night to see all was secure. The well gates had to be locked and the mill was lit outside with oil lamps. This hard-working zeal probably contributed to his early death, as the committee sadly observed. When Thomas

Day died on 20 February 1871 the Society called a special meeting to record their 'unfeigned sorrow' at his demise and to 'express in the highest possible terms their estimation of his abilities as a man of business and of his character as a Christian'. His widow was given £300, which was the difference between his annual salary and what he had earned, and the committee asked to put up a tombstone recording their grateful appreciation of his services and character.

His son, Thomas Day jnr. was offered a position as clerk in the hope that he would assist in the mill business, whilst William Lewis, who had been his chief assistant, was promoted to assistant secretary at a salary of £300 a year. In addition an agent was appointed to gain orders in South Wales, thus giving the new manager time to attend to the mill affairs. The loss of such a main stalwart meant that a radical re-organisation took place with the clerks managing different departments.

Following Day's death, the Society also agreed to purchase the premises owned by the Day family — Edwin, Ann Whybrow Day, and Henry Day

— which consisted of two houses occupied by the Society offices and the cottage built at the rear at 49-50 Bye Street. The properties were valued by Thomas Davies at £1,140 for the houses and £140 for the cottage. The family offered to leave the money on loan at 5% until the Society paid it off. It had been bought in 1855 in equal shares by the brothers evidently to provide a nearby base for Thomas Day, and perhaps to furnish some capital for the Society. In his will Thomas left his share to his sons and also his 'messuage and heridi-taments situate in the village of Welyington'.

The financial success of the mill must have surprised the members of the Society. On Thomas Day's death the profits

Figure 41 Thomas Day,
Secretary and Mill Manager

of the mill for the past 22 years were recorded as £20,124. These had paid off the mortgage, expanded the mill and enabled the charitable work to flourish. It had already financed the washing baths heated by the surplus steam from the mill and which contributed to the health and cleanliness of the poor (see next chapter).

For 22 years from 1852 there is a gap in the Mill Minute Book, presumably because the mill was being run smoothly and capably. The mill sub-committee evidently did not meet from 1852 and the Stock Book ceases in 1852/3. In 1870 the main committee heard that no.2 boiler had been repaired by Messrs. H. Smith and Co. and that a contract had been signed with the Gas Company to lay gas on to the mill. The sub-committee was only resumed when alterations were necessary in 1874.

In 1874 the new sub-committee oversaw plans for a new boiler house and settings for the boilers that had been drawn up by Thomas Nicholson, who had played a large part in Society enterprises of the 1870s. A tender for the work for £573 4s. was accepted from William Bowers. The old engines and boilers were to be replaced and sold off or sent to auction. Plans for the foundation of the new engine and donkey pump and for two pairs of stones which were to be moved to the old engine house had been prepared by a Mr. Umpherson and Thomas Nicholson. Mr. Bowers was asked to undertake this building work for £222.

In May 1883 the Society's assistant secretary, Mr. Lewis, laid before the sub-committee letters from Mr. McDougall, the engineer of the Manchester Steam Boiler Association, and from Mr. Umpherson, the maker of the steam engine at the mill, about the corrosion of the face of the flange of the valve chest of the high pressure cylinder. It was recommended that an entirely new cylinder with Ingles and Spencer's Gorliss valve be erected. Messrs. Nayler & Co. had first been called in to look at the corrosion and give advice and they had prepared plans for the new cylinder, which had been approved by Mr. McDougall, and they quoted the sum of £153 to complete the work. The secretary reported that it was first necessary to tighten the engine crank brasses laterally as they had worn from the thrust of the engine stroke and that there was no possibility of closing them. All the work was carried out.

A new era began with the death of William Lewis in 1900 after 56 years of service to the Society; over 30 as manager and secretary. His successor was William Garrold Lloyd. He was far removed from the humble shoe-maker and preacher, Thomas Day, the first manager. Lloyd was born in

1857 at Whitchurch, near Ross on Wye. He was educated at Worcester, Liverpool and a college at Weston super Mare. His work for the Society started in 1878 as a traveller in flour for the mill and he worked his way up to assistant secretary. He made a good marriage in 1883 to Emily, daughter of James Moore of Monkhide Court, Yarkhill. The expansion of the mill and the business of the Society required managerial aptitude and business sense in which he was proficient. He became a director of Hampton Park Brick and Tile Works in his spare time and was on the committee of the Working Boys' Home. From 1918 he also served as a J.P. His home was at Oaklands, a grand villa in Bodenham Road.

By 1910, Garrold Lloyd was reporting a demand for soft white flour made wholly from English wheats. As the woolly nature of English wheat required more dressing surface than the ordinary mixture of two-thirds hard foreign wheat, this meant that a new centrifugal dressing machine was required to do the work efficiently. He was duly authorised to purchase a second-hand machine for not more than £25. However, the business was not doing well, the travellers' expenses were reduced and a Mr. Matthews was given notice.

There then began to be problems with transport. The usual method of moving the flour to the station was by horse and wagon but there were accidents. In June 1910 one of the cart horses ran away while transporting a load of flour to Barr's Court Station, causing damage to a lamp-post and to a bicycle belonging to Mr. Bennett, a butcher in Commercial Road. He settled for 30s. but it cost £3 to repair the lamp-post. The Secretary commented that, 'Very little damage was done to the horse or wagon', but it may have been the old black horse that was shot later in the year by the vet. In 1912 it was decided to purchase a steam wagon at the cost of £496. The business that was promoted by the travellers was important and it was decided that to be effective a motor-car was necessary. At the start of 1911 it was resolved to buy a standard Austin two-seater for Mr. Baskerville, the commercial traveller. The agreed second-hand price was £125. It only did 25m.p.h., which was too slow for its first owner who had acquired a Rolls Royce! By October of the same year another car was bought from Mr. James Fryer of the Green Dragon Garage. Perhaps this was faster as it was a new four-cylinder Swift, with lamps and fittings that cost £140 in cash when the Austin was traded in. After the First World War a motor wagon was bought from Shrewsbury for £1,265 and the use of steam suddenly seemed archaic.

By 1913 the mill was losing money: a financial statement in February of that year showed a loss of £239 9s. 1d. in the past four months. The Secretary explained that it was the result of the disastrous wet weather during the previous August and September which meant that little English wheat had been purchased and foreign wheat had largely been used. Garrold Lloyd then presented a report on the necessity to install new machinery in the mill and a special meeting was called. The effect of reconstruction, new machinery and electric power was considered with regard both to the business of the mill and upon the

Figure 42 Mill cottages adjacent to the mill itself and fronting Bath Street which have recently been replaced by the Magistrates' Court

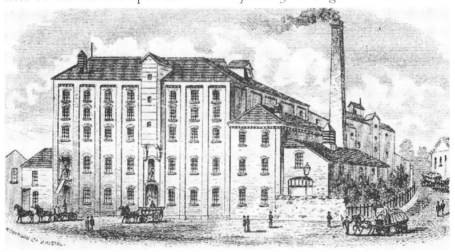

Figure 43 The steam mill at the beginning of twentieth century. The horses and wagons are coming from the yard past the baths (see next chapter), to load at the front

operation of the adjacent baths. It seemed that running costs would be reduced and the quality of the flour would be improved which, in turn, would lead to increased sales. Whilst considerable capital would be needed to modernise the mill, it should once again become a paying concern. The committee decided to go ahead and agreed to close the mill and baths so that the work could proceed.

Estimates were requested from Messrs. Thomas Robinson & Co. of Rochdale, Messrs. Samuelson & Co. of Banbury and Messrs. Breddon & Fowler of Stockport for the installation of the machinery An estimate was agreed with another firm for electric motors: The British Thompson Houston Co. of Rugby, and three of different horse power were ordered at a cost of £555 14s. 4d. These were connected to the City Council's cable. The work was not before time as there was a loss for the year of £893 8s. A loan of £5,000 was obtained from the bank to finance the work once a full review of the Society's assets had been undertaken. However, the final cost exceeded this at £6,023 7s.

By January 1914 the new machinery in the mill was working well and the output was improving daily. However, at about the same time, the demand for flour fell by nearly 25%. According to the Secretary, this was due to the mild weather, a good supply of vegetables and potatoes, together with good wages.

On 4 August 1914 a special meeting was called to discuss the impending war. The mill manager was present to give an account of the flour and wheat in stock, the wheat already bought for delivery and sales engagements. It was resolved to continue business as usual but staff were told they could join the army if they wished. It was agreed that all sales had to be for cash except for those who had an account with the mill, and that English wheat should be bought for stock with finance from the bank.

By the time of the next meeting four men had enlisted and a fifth was waiting for a regiment. They were: F.M. Rudge, a junior clerk; H. Preece, a self-raising flour packer; G. King, a loader; A. Cale, a warehouseman and Mr. Baskerville, a traveller. A junior clerk, 17 years old, was engaged to fill the gap. The loss of staff to the forces caused a change in recruitment policy when the first woman was interviewed for the position of clerk. Duly appointed, Gertrude Preece was to be paid 10s. a week after a month's trial. She was found suitable and her wages rose to 12s. and then to 15s. after three months. The ledger clerk, Claude Workman enquired whether the Society would assist him if he joined the Royal Flying Corps, for he helped keep a home for his mother and sister. The committee generously offered to keep his job open until the end of the war and give him £50 a year until then. The young clerk who took his place, H. Chandler, was appointed at £60 a year rising by annual increments of £10. However, he was called up the following year and another woman, Miss N.B. Morris, was taken on who was paid 12s. a week for six months and then 15s. In 1917 Mr. Baskerville was given £80 a year to help him. He had joined the Royal Garrison Artillery. The South Wales Traveller, Mr. W. Arnett, was robbed of £5 worth of silver on his way home from Cardiff while in a train carriage. — lawless days resulted from lack of manpower and police — and he was given £5 by the Society so that he should not be out of pocket after his many years of service. Despite the drop in demand for flour early in the year, the annual balance sheet for 1914 showed a profit on the mill operation of over £1,000 — a great improvement — and of £467 6s. 9d. on the Society's whole business.

Figure 44 William Garrold Lloyd J.P. in the garden behind the mill. He served the Society for 58 years from 1878 to 1936

Profits at the mill continued to rise with the demand for flour. In the four months up to 30 April 1915 the accounts showed a profit of £2,085 2s. 10d., although there was some concern that the value of the large stocks of wheat had fallen due to the market price. This was not stored at the mill itself in case of incendiary bombs but at the Society's warehouse in the Portfields.

The Society was indignant when it received a bill for Excess Profits Tax. The

Secretary wrote and pointed out that they had made a considerable capital investment in new machinery as that installed in 1884 was completely worn out. They never speculated in corn or wheat as their purchases were balanced daily where possible and the profits arose from the new machinery. It was agreed they did not pay income tax and they were given a balance of over £2,600 for wear and tear on the current year's profits.

In the meantime costs of railway transport, wages, electric power and sacks were all increasing. The Secretary was also instructed to insure the buildings, stock and machinery against attack by enemy aircraft. The huge increase in the price of Manitoba wheat that had risen by 47s. to 77s. a quarter was a cause for concern. It seemed unwise to have too much in stock in case the price fell and so it was decided to sell some on the open market and then have an option on it for future stocks. Nevertheless, final profits for the year were up again, to £2,880, after writing off depreciation and bad debts.

By May 1917 the government had taken control of the flour mill. The Secretary had been ordered to take stock on the 12th and the books were balanced up. To comply with the regulations ordered by the Ministry of Food, alterations and additions to the machinery were made. Profits increased to £6,488 and Mr. Garrold Lloyd's salary was raised to £500 a year with his annual bonus a generous £300.

After the war things slowly returned to normality. In 1919 the Society received £2,000 for the use of the mill from the Flour Mills Control Committee and control over production was resumed in 1920. There was an improvement in the machinery in order that whiter flour could be produced.

In 1919 the mill workers' wages were increased as a result of Trades Union agreement with the government. This was by 7s. 6d. to the same wage as the foreman, George Leach, who now also required a rise to £4 10s. The hours of work were also agreed. Shiftmen worked 44 hours a week, day workers 47 hours, carters and lorrymen 48 hours. This reduction meant three or four more men were required to work the mill. This is the first mention of Union activity.

Employment of women was no longer favoured by the Society when the Secretary reported that it would be advisable to have a young man in the office rather than one of the girls and that a former employee, Geoffrey Chandler was unemployed. He expected to be paid £200 a year, which the committee thought too much and he accepted a job as ledger clerk for £180. (It might be that Geoffrey was the brother of the H. Chandler who had been called up at the start of the First World War, or that they are one and the same person, the minute book confusing initials.) Miss Morris remained as the only woman employee. In 1923 she resigned to get married after six years with the Society. They wished her every success and voted five guineas for a wedding present. She was replaced by a young man at 15s. a week.

In 1922, Tom Owen, one-time mill engine driver and stoker, was reported as seriously ill after 52 years of service. He had requested and been given a lighter job in 1911 when he was 59 as rheumatism was making the stoking difficult. He was granted a pension of £2 8s. a week, but soon after he retired he died and his widow was granted 10s. a week for a pension.

In 1923 Charles Swales, the mill foreman, injured his hand in the rollers of the machinery and had a finger amputated. In 1936 he became manager of the mill and was given the lease of 11 Kyrle Street with its large house and garden for £25 a year. He worked at the mill until it was sold in 1948 and then joined Hereford Flour Mills Ltd. as a company director. He was still in his house when Kyrle Street was renumbered in 1951.

Figure 45 The flour mill in 1932 (Derek Foxton Collection)

75

The mill buildings closed in 1957 after being empty for some years and were then sold to *Berrows Journal* of Worcester who had acquired the *Hereford Times* which was printed there until the building was resold.

7   THE BATHS

The decade of the 1850s saw many changes and a new vision of the outside world. In Hereford the advent of the railways from 1853 and the consequent improvement in transport brought about new employment opportunities and fresh markets for produce. It was possible to visit London in a day and to go on seaside holidays. The Great Exhibition at the Crystal Palace in 1851 was widely reported on and visited by the working class as well as the wealthy. It introduced products from overseas as well as promoting innovation and design from Great Britain and enjoyed six million visitors.

Far from the metropolis, improvement became urgent in Hereford when it was discovered that the growing population, 11,156 in 1851, had a disproportionately high death rate for this and previous years. Major contributions to this rate were waterborne diseases and tuberculosis.

From its foundation, living conditions in Hereford had slowly declined in common with other ancient towns in Britain. An increasing population and uncoordinated urban growth produced unhealthy conditions. Manufacturing had been confined to flannel, hats and gloves, with some boat building along the banks of the river Wye once the river was used for transport in the late eighteenth century. An iron foundry was constructed in Friar Street in 1838, but transport costs of the raw materials and the finished products before the advent of the railway proved too great; 20 years later it was used as a brewery. Two smaller foundries producing goods used locally managed to survive. With the arrival of the railways steam coal began to arrive from South Wales and there was hope of increased prosperity. Before this the bad roads and the almost total reliance on agriculture had combined to keep Hereford a poor place.

Some physical improvements were made when the Paving and Lighting Act of 1774 was adopted and overhanging buildings were removed, streets widened and cleansed and footpaths maintained. The medieval city gates were demolished and 'no obstacle offered to the free sweep of the winds' nor to the traffic. What the City Commissioners failed to do was to fill in the ditch that continued to carry its filthy waters round the town as an open sewer and then spit them out into the Wye at Greyfriars and Castle Mill. The mill ponds lay with great stagnant pools around the north and east of the city, any damming up of the waters causing floods on Widemarsh and the surrounding area.

In 1848 the Public Health Act was introduced by Lord John Russell's government. One of its provisions was to establish a Central Board of Health that could, where the Act was not adopted locally, intervene and hold an inquiry into a high death rate. This is what happened in Hereford where the death rate was 27 per thousand, nearly as bad as northern industrial towns. When the subsequent inquiry was opened by Thomas Webster Rammell on 5 January 1853 local resentment was expressed against government interference. A local commissioner of Paving and Lighting was also afraid that the citizens 'might be put to a frightful expense'.

It became clear that the appalling sanitary conditions were mainly due to the poor drainage and lack of proper public water supplies. Two-thirds of the houses had common privies with cess pools or 'bog holes' as they

*Figure 46 Rent Day in the Cellar (*Punch, *1850)*

78

were locally called, many of them in cellars. These had to be emptied but this was expensive and was often delayed until they were overflowing. The cess pools were constructed of bricks without the use of mortar, meaning that foul water could percolate through into the gravel in which the wells were sunk. It was not just the poor who were affected — the mayor, Charles Anthony, had the oldest water-closet in the city that was supplied with water from a force-pump in the cellar, but even this refinement drained into a cess pool in the garden. A new one had to be created every few years and he had already had three. 'What is to be the end of it?' he asked, 'are the back premises in every street to be converted into cess-pools?'

In the poorer areas of housing the privy accommodation was very limited. In St. Owen Street there were 10 to 12 cottages to two privies. Pipe Lane (Gwynne Street) had eight houses to one privy, but the worst place was Friar Street which had 20 to 30 dwellings to one privy. The implications for the spread of disease is obvious and it is surprising there were not more epidemics.

When the eminent physician and member of the Society, Dr. Henry Graves Bull gave evidence he ended with the words, 'I do not think the sanitary conditions of this city can be rendered such as it ought to be until each house is properly supplied with water'. Samples were taken from the well in High Town, opposite the Sun Tavern, from Dr. Bull's

Figure 47 Dr. Henry Graves Bull came to Hereford in 1841, just at the time the Society was formed. He gave support to its work for the rest of his life, helping with the dispensary in 1842 and with the Herefordshire Friendly Society. He joined the staff of the General Infirmary in 1864. He had many interests, particularly in natural science. He was an author of the Herefordshire Pomona, *a prominent member of the Woolhope Naturalists' Field Club and chairman of the committee that established the Free Library in Broad Street in 1874. He died in 1885 (Woolhope Club Library)*

own well in Harley House, St. Ethelbert's well, the Town Clerk, Richard Johnson's in St. Owen Street, the river and the Moor spring that fed the Widemarsh and Yazor brooks. None was found fit for drinking.

There was evidence of blocked sewers, overflowing graveyards, live-stock filth in the streets, and candle factories in Bewell Street that stank and produced maggots for fishermen. All this vile neglect was exposed and the final report by the inspector recommended that change should be imposed unless the city undertook it of its own accord at once. Without delay and under threat they employed the surveyor, Thomas Curley, to design the necessary improvements. Once the plans were drawn up an Act of Parliament was necessary to implement them. The Hereford Improvement Act of 1854 duly provided new waterworks, more efficient drainage, a new cattle market and a public cemetery. The expense was paid for by rates and market tolls. The new waterworks were finished by October 1856, the total cost being £12,000. By 1880, with the construction of the water tower on Broomy Hill, every house could be supplied with water. The new sewage works still emptied the effluent into the river, but it drained the cellars and the waters of the town brook flushed it. By the 1870s new methods of sewage treatment were adopted and land was bought near the river for this purpose.

*Figure 48 Domestic Sanitary Regulations for the Middle Classes (*Punch, 1850)

Keeping clean for the poor was a constant battle. Cheap housing provided little in the way of domestic comfort and over-crowding and unsanitary conditions led to disease. Even middle-class houses had limited access to water and sanitation. In the poorer areas of Hereford like Friar Street and St. Owen's, there was only one lavatory for many households and a public pump. In wet weather drains overflowed and the city ditch became an open sewer. Personal hygiene was limited, for with no adequate water supply, washing was very difficult and the poor made do with the river or other open pools of water. There were public areas by the river for clothes laundering, romantically portrayed in paintings. There were subscription baths for gentlemen in the clubhouse on Castle Green but they were limited to affluent Herefordians. In 1844, as part of a move for moral improvement, a National Commission for Baths and Washhouses was set up to encourage the building of public baths.

In April 1851, Thomas Nicholson was asked by the Society's baths committee to draw up a plan for eight washing baths at a cost not exceeding £450. Public meetings followed which gave approval for the project, the details of which were then fine tuned.

It was agreed that the cubicles for the more affluent were to have carpets, bells for assistance and be provided with fine towels. The rest had cocoa-nut matting and no towels. As all the men would have worn hats or caps, hat pegs were needed. Other amendments made by the Society's committee to the draft plans included:

- That the partition between the several baths be raised one foot higher.
- That latch keys be substituted for the locks on the bathrooms and closets.
- That the baths be numbered.
- That bells and carpets be provided for the first class baths.
- That the 2nd and 3rd class be provided with cocoa-nut matting.
- That two scrapers, door mats and umbrella stands be provided.
- That three hat pegs be provided for all the baths.
- That curtains be provided for the shower baths.
- That the seats be partially boarded up.
- That looking glasses be provided of three sizes.
- That two dozen of fine towels be provided for 1st class.
- That thermometers be procured for the use of the baths.

The annual subscription was fixed at £1 10s. for the 'first class' user and £1 for the 'second class'. Presumably the 'third class' user paid an admission charge on each visit.

Figure 49 Entrance into the washing baths (Derek Foxton Collection)

The brick building was situated behind the mill on the land bought from Charles Spozzi. The excess steam from the mill boilers was used to heat the water and warm the rooms. There were also overhead showers.

At the beginning of March 1852 the committee ordered that the ground in front of the bathhouse be cleaned, laid out and planted, with an iron fence to separate the road to the baths from the mill. The cement around the baths was to be painted.

Sarah Prosser was engaged for three months as an attendant on Wednesdays and Saturdays from 2 o'clock to 5 o'clock at 3s. a week for the medicated baths that contained added sulphur (saline baths cost 1s. 6d.), and at 6d. for first class baths and 3d. for second class at other times. The stoker at the mill, John Owen, was to help at the baths and for the sum of £15 he and his son were to attend at the baths from 6 until 8 in the morning and from 5 until 6 in the evening and also when medicated baths were required. They were also to assist on Saturday evenings until the baths closed and at other times when required. It was their job to maintain the machinery of the baths in good repair, and to clean the boilers at least once a fortnight. The baths were open during the summer from 6am. until 9pm. and on Saturdays until 10pm. The hours of separate bathing for females was between 10am. until 1pm.

For publicity it was decided to put cards and pamphlets in the inns and public institutions of Hereford and neighbourhood, and medical men and all subscribers were to be supplied with a copy of the prospectus, while 500 handbills were to be distributed to the working classes.

The annual operating loss to the Society amounted to £60 and by May 1858 renovations were already needed: a sulphur box was replaced and a leakage in the drains stopped, whilst new carpets were laid in the first class baths. Two dozen new towels were ordered. Then prices were reduced and the rights that accompanied the first and second class annual season tickets were extended. Children of the local parish schools were allowed to use the baths on Tuesdays and Thursdays at a halfpenny a time.

In 1870 John Venn persuaded the Society to build a swimming pool adjacent to the washing baths. Again Thomas Nicholson was asked to design it. It had a capacity of almost 40,000 gallons, the water being pumped from the mill well by steam power. Exhaust steam also heated the pool's water. The bath was 51ft. 9ins. long by 23ft. 6ins. wide and 4ft. 10ins. deep. Lined with plain white tiles, the pool was one of the earliest public baths in the country.

On 11 October 1871 Dr. Bull was in the Chair of the sub-committee when interviews took place for the post of swimming attendant. Possible candidates had all been investigated with regard to their character and qualifications. Hugh McDowell was selected and offered 18 shillings a week to start on 1 November. It was thought desirable that he be provided with a distinctive uniform. The committee was also anxious that he should live close to the baths and so he was offered a cottage nearby. As part of his duties included the washing of towels, drawers and bathing dresses it was

Figure 50 The baths in Venn Road. The washing baths is at the front while the swimming bath, now the Masonic Hall, is at the rear

decided to purchase 'a washing, wringing and mangling machine'. Furniture for the changing cubicles had yet to be installed and the instructions and regulations to be displayed in conspicuous places. Finally, a large board had to be erected with the words 'To the Swimming Bath' at the corner of Bath Street and Commercial Road. The baths opened on time on 13 November and were in use for 55 years.

Soon after the swimming pool opened it was decided that the hard water from the well should be replaced by soft water from the town reservoir on Broomy Hill. To achieve this many alterations in the supply pipes were needed. It was found that some of the old pipes were defective and these were replaced. At the same time repairs were made to the engine and boiler at the mill. There were complaints by the public in the *Hereford Times* about the closure of the washing baths and the inconvenience caused during this process, and on 5 December 1871 a member of the committee wrote in reply:

> that they wished to promote the cleanliness, health, and enjoyment of each class of bathers, and if, in the outset and under exceptional circumstances, a little inconvenience may have been occasioned to some, I believe the public will be considerate enough to make allowances for this.

In 1904, 16,213 people used the swimming baths and generated £280 in receipts; the following year the number dropped slightly to 15,845 although receipts rose gently to £287; in 1908 numbers had increased to 18,107 (accounted for by the regular swimming classes from 1906 attended by the newly opened elementary school of St. Owen's), and in 1909 to 18,664, but receipts remained largely static. At this time the charge for a swimming lesson for adults was 1s. while for children it was 9d. The sessions lasted half an hour and 'no person was to enter the Bath without drawers'.

A letter from the Headmistress of the High School for girls, Miss Krabbé, reveals class attitudes at this time for she wrote to the Society stating that: 'Some of the parents of her scholars objected to the mixed bathing of their daughters with the children of the elementary schools. This received a cool reception for in reply the committee instructed the Secretary to send Miss Krabbé a list of the hours set apart for ladies' bathing and to tell her that the committee were unable to reserve the swimming bath for any one school. In 1911 a request from young lady shop assistants found more favour and a Thursday evening was set aside for ladies for two hours.

It was around this time that it was recorded that:

> The swimming bath is emptied daily in the busy months and is well washed out. The temperature being kept as nearly as possible to 74 degrees. This is warmer than the river or City water except in very hot weather. In the winter the swimming bath is covered with a floor for the use of a gymnasium club, badminton or dancing or any other purpose for the recreation of the citizens at low charges.

A report to the committee was made on the swimming baths on 11 July 1910, when the had been open for nearly 40 years. At this time the baths were in operation from 6am. until 9pm. on each day of the week from 15 March until 31 October The swimming baths closed during the winter months but the washing baths remained open on Wednesdays, Thursdays, Fridays and Saturdays at the same times with separate sessions for the sexes. Women, however, were given fewer hours at 27 while men had 62.

In 1913 the baths had to be closed while the mill next door was converted to electricity. The Society, anxious about depriving the public of the baths, made an informal approach to the City Council to see whether they would purchase of the baths and any adjoining land to use for the benefit of the city. The answer was not satisfactory as the transfer would have amounted to a gift so this was refused and the baths temporarily closed in October. Discussions took place with the City Surveyor, John Parker, as to the best means to heat the water, and it was agreed that the only practical solution was to reuse the old boiler from the mill, the City Council subsidising the cost by £100 for the year. However the boiler was found to take one ton of coal a day to heat the baths, a much greater quantity than had been anticipated.

By 1914 the baths had made a loss of £207 1s. and the City Council was requested to raise their subsidy to £150 (a sum that they had originally offered) as the Society could not afford the loss to continue. In the negotiations that took place between the end of 1914 and early 1915 various courses of action were proposed, including that the council either leased the baths and the adjoining two houses in Kyrle Street, or even acquired them for £2,000. In the end the council agreed to increase their annual subsidy, whilst the Society was to seek advice on providing heating at a lower cost.

The First World War in fact proved a boon to both baths for they became in great demand. Early on the First Home Battalion of the Herefordshire Regiment was granted permission to use them on four days of the week for a payment of £5, a fee that did not include 'soap, towels or costumes'. Another unit that was recruiting at the Drill Hall also asked to have the facilities for the men. This was agreed at a charge for a bath of 3d. per man including soap and towel. A request to reduce this was sent from Western Command, Chester and it was agreed to charge 2d. 'in order to assist His Majesty's forces'. The attendant at the baths received a rise in his wages and the female attendant, Mrs. Stephens, was given two guineas towards extra expenses incurred by the soldiers of the Third Battalion Herefordshire Regiment. This was possibly for extra bath cleaning and towel washing after training sessions. The girls from the Munitions Factory at Rotherwas also made good use of the baths.

In the winter the pool was covered with a floor as usual and the room was used for gymnastics and dances.

In 1915, 23,396 people used the baths and the Society felt they had to keep them going with the continued subsidy from the City Council.

In the meantime financial pressure mounted from another quarter when purchasers of the Society's debenture bonds requested an increase in the interest rate to 4½% in line with Government War Bonds. For many years since it was formed such loans had financed the Society in its work.

In 1919 the Secretary reported that the gas lighting was not sufficient in the winter and it was resolved to convert it to electricity. The necessity of urgent repairs to both baths was a problem and it seemed that it would be throwing money down the drain as the Society wished to close them. As a result of discussions with the City Council, the latter offered another £25 a year if the Society kept them open until 1921. Even so the Society only carried out basic repairs and decoration and in January 1921 a letter was sent to the council pointing out the condition of the baths as 'dirty, and in a deplorable condition'. This time the Society asked the council to take them over on a repairing lease for 99 years at a nominal rent, but the council countered with an offer to do all the repairs and pay £250 a year if the Society would agree to keep the baths open. This they did.

In February 1926 the Society once again announced that they wished to close the baths stating that space was needed for the mill and the boiler

Figure 51 Cartoon from the
Hereford Observer

house was to go as the boilers themselves had become dangerous. These now only provided the heating for the baths.

The subsequent proposal by the council that they should build a new swimming baths in Edgar Street was met with a storm of opposition and open criticism of the Society for closing the baths, as the citizens of Hereford had come to consider they belonged to them. The arguments blew up into a war of words between the *Hereford Times* and the *Hereford Observer*. There were headlines such as 'Do the Citizens own the Baths?', and 'A Challenge to the Industrious Aid Society'.

So many questions were asked that the Society was forced to publish its rules or Memorandum of Association. It was then suggested that the Society's profits were not being used in accordance with these. The Society kept a discrete silence on their affairs which only led to more speculation. As a result they were asked to publish the balance sheets since 1914. Mr. Humphrys, a well-known local solicitor who had acted for the Society when it had become incorporated in 1884, added to the furore when he wrote that he was not satisfied with the conduct of its business. There were furious debates in the council chamber in the Town Hall in which Cllr. Hiles-Smith said he was firmly opposed to the provision of new baths, mentioning that local people could not pay the present rates and that 500 had been summoned for non-payment as it was. He added that 'The Poor Rate had gone up by 3d. in the pound to relieve the poor devils who could not get a mouthful, and yet they were suggesting spending £20,000 on new baths.' He also felt that the Edgar Street site proposed for the new baths was an outlandish place to build them — it had been selected for a new rubbish destructor but one of the conditions attached to its financial support was that the excess heat produced should somehow be used. In spite of much criticism, Cllr. George Britten, the deputy mayor and member of the Society's committee put their case to the council and renewed the offer made in 1921 of a repairing lease and a peppercorn rent for the baths. The Society, however, was unanimous that they would not continue to operate them on a long term basis but would, however, run them on a limited basis if the council installed new boilers. The council now had to decide whether they would erect new baths for £14,000, or put in new boilers at the old baths costing £2,000 to enable the Society to keep them going for a limited period. As it was likely that the loan from the Ministry of Health for the waste destructor would be withdrawn if the waste heat could not be utilised, adding to further pressure to raise the rates in any event, the decision was made on 1 May 1926 to build a new baths.

The two old bath buildings were then given to the council who sold them the following year for £1,000 to Masonic Halls Ltd. Two years later they bought 1 and 2 Kyrle Street for £925. This complex is still used as the Masonic Lodge, where the white-tiled swimming bath, where so many Hereford schoolchildren learned to swim for over 50 years, remains under the present floor.

8 THE PORTFIELDS

Once the mill had proved successful and was making a yearly profit, the mortgage from the Venns was repaid. The Foundation Deed for the property is dated 7 March 1853 and noted a mortgage to Miss Venn of £4,000 dated from the previous year. In this they agreed to transfer the property of the mill, bath-house and baths to the Society who were to adhere to the objects of the Society. Over future years as the Society needed capital to develop new projects, the mill was remortgaged to the Venns until the loan could be paid off.

The first purchase in 1856 was the land and two cottages next to the mill and baths:

> All that piece of meadow or pasture land whereon corn mills and baths have lately been erected situate near the Town Brook in the Parish of Saint Peter in the City of Hereford. Two thousand six hundred and forty-one square yards adjoining to and having land late of John Morgan but now Leonard Johnson on the west side.

The land had been let out as allotments and had been manured and fenced by the Society for some years. In 1864 meadow land called Portfields, by the road or way called the Sally Walk, leading from Bye Street to St. Owen Street on the south and lands of Charles Spozzi, was purchased from Rev. Morgan who had already been leasing it to the Society. After Canon Morgan's death the Barn field was acquired for £1,050. Evidently it had been a farm for it contained Beasthouse Fold and shed, plus cottages and outbuildings on the boundary.

In 1866 Charles Spozzi's will allowed the acquisition for £3,000 of his land adjacent to the mill premises which included cottages at Portfields

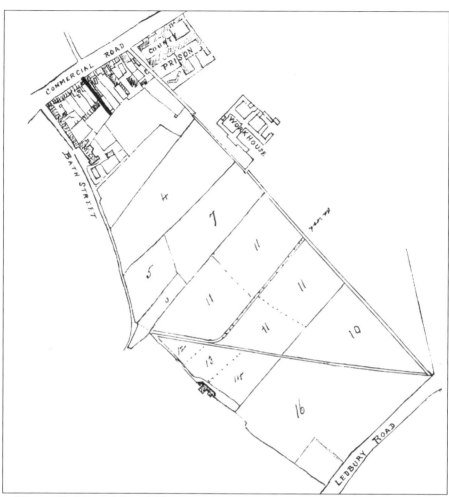

Figure 52 Map of Portfields c.1855, before Venn Road (later Kyrle Street) was made, the numbers being those shown on the tithe map. Only the washing baths are shown and the land of the Portfields was divided into allotments. The present foot-path to Ledbury Road is an ancient route that originally led to Scutt Mill. As well as Venn Road, the Society also created St. Guthlac Street; the vicarage for St. Peter's was built at 1 Ledbury Road in 1871; land was sold in 1874 for the Working Boys' Home (now Herefordshire Council Offices) and subsequently more land was sold on which to build St. Owen's Elementary school in Symond's Street. In Bath Street, Wye Terrace and the other frontages were developed and sold by the Society and eventually the rest of the land was sold to the council for working-class housing round Central Avenue. Almshouses were built in 1938 on the experimental garden and part of the farm. The pig cots were used during the Second World War and disappeared with the remaining farm buildings during the street widening of 1967

90

or Byster's Gate. There was also a garden of three acres lying behind the Zion Chapel, now the Baptist Church, bounded by the allotments and the road to the workhouse which was bought in 1866 and became the Kyrle Street estate. In 1869, after the death of Canon Morgan, the Barnfield was acquired. This was an area of 8 acres and cost £1,050 plus a payment to the bishop of Hereford in lieu of tithes of £1,156. A further 8 acres known as the Old Pledge was purchased from Dr. Morris in 1872. It was at once remortgaged to Mrs. Morris and to Miss Venn to secure the £1,800 plus the £830 needed for its purchase.

All this capital was loaned at 4½% interest, and allowed the whole of the Portfields to be acquired by the Society and be developed for the benefit of the people of St. Peter's and St. Owen's. The Society was the first institution in the city to act as a benevolent entrepreneur, and the income from the mill now secured the capital to develop innovative ideas. These came, as always, from John Venn. As soon as he had retired in 1870 he put forward a series of new plans, which had been fermenting in his active mind. The land in the Portfields, to the south of the mill, had been acquired in the 1860s and let out as allotments. Now it could be used for new initiatives:

> The honorary Secretary having expressed his conviction that the position of the Society would now justify the committee in extending their operations for the benefit of the working classes suggested:
> That a swimming pool should be constructed [see last chapter].
> That ten cottages should be built on the Society's land with every convenience utilizing waste and refuse matter of the house, plus an establishment for Moule's Patent Earth Closets, plus 1 acre.
> Two trained nurses to be employed visiting the sick poor.

These inspirational schemes probably astounded his committee for John Venn added that he would undertake to borrow whatever money might be required on his own personal security at 4½%. At once Dr. Bull proposed that the swimming bath be built and Mr. Evans the cottages, while Mr. Turner urged the medical members to make all necessary arrangements for the nurses. Once more his vision had inspired their enthusiasm. At 68 John Venn still had this extraordinary gift of creative imagination and compassion that he used for the welfare of his parishioners.

The last proposition was an extension of the aids for the sick scheme that the committee had been operating for the last five years. Items for helping the sick poor were purchased, including water and air pillows for invalids, and iron bedsteads and blankets for onward sale in weekly instalments. A sub-committee managed the scheme. A District Nurse was engaged in December 1870 and by September of the following year she had made 1,168 home visits and had 64 patients on her books. Her duties included the management of illness, providing extra linen and blankets, invalid chairs and giving nourishment when it was needed. Her account for 1871 was a modest £9 6s. that included medicine. In August 1872 the Society was informed that a nurse training institution had been set up by a charitable lady and that she had undertaken to nurse the sick poor 'gratuitously'. The committee therefore decided to dispense with the services of their nurse at the end of the year and expressed their entire satisfaction with the way she had performed her duties. By 1876 three Champion washing machines were acquired to rent out to those that needed them. Apart from scrubbing boards there were few alternatives for doing the laundry except elbow grease, but by the 1860s roller wringers and a variety of mechanical washing machines had been invented.

Figure 53 The Model Lodging House, showing food on the table, a cloth, carpet, books and piped water to the kitchen sink (Punch, 1850)

The housing conditions of working people had concerned John Venn since he arrived in Hereford. The poor of St. Owen's parish in particular lived in some appalling cottages close to the old graveyard of the church and at a lower level. There were frequent outbreaks of diseases like typhoid. In 1849 Venn had attended a City Council meeting and explained his ideas about the improvement of 'cottage residences'. He produced drawings of model cottages and asked to purchase four acres of land at Widemarsh, but nothing came of the proposal.

Twenty-one years later he still held his views that working people prospered with good housing and Venn proposed that the Society erect ten model cottages, each with a sixth of an acre of land with a piggery and henfold, together with some fruit trees. He suggested that a model garden should accompany the scheme so that the tenants could learn the best methods of gardening and manuring. To that end a shop and laboratory would manufacture and sell manure and dry earth for closets made with Mr. George With's patent formula which he was already selling for the Society's allotments.

Ten years earlier, in the 1860s, there had been a great debate about the disposal of human waste. Some wealthy houses already had water closets but waste still emptied into cesspits and the excess water found its way into wells and ultimately into water courses with all the consequences for public health. Henry Moule, vicar of Fordington, in Dorset, was born a year before John Venn, in 1801. He became convinced that water closets polluted the environment and he wrote that 'the cess pool and the vault are simply a natural abomination'. He had converted his own family to using buckets after his own cess pool became a smelly nuisance. When he noticed that all the family waste vanished when he buried it in a ditch he realised that earth was a very effective way of disposal. He built a shed and mixed the contents of the buckets with dry earth. This way he found he could recycle the contents and add them to his garden and so produce better crops. In 1860 he produced a particular commode with a bucket under the seat and a hopper behind it containing dry earth. When the handle was pulled the required amount of dry earth was released into the bucket to cover the contents. He took out a patent in 1860 and followed it with others. Thus was the Moule Patent Closet Company founded and manufactured earth closets, including expensive models in mahogany. The closet was often positioned in a shed or privy that provided shelter from the elements. He wrote several pamphlets and papers and managed to convince a great many people including *The Lancet* that his was the correct method for an improvement in comfort and health. It duly became the favoured method for use in school lavatories.

John Venn was an enthusiastic supporter of his fellow clergyman's ideas and it seems that he corresponded with him because Rev. Moule wrote to the Society advocating that they purchase chalk to use in his process. It was then resolved that Moule's paper should be printed and circulated throughout the county and that a specimen earth closet be ordered from Messrs. White and Co. to be kept at the office of the Society for public inspection. George With, who became Secretary of the Society was, amongst other skills, a chemist, and refined the method with his own chemical recipe and it was sold on the Society's premises. Over time earth closets were found unsatisfactory and were replaced by water closets. Nevertheless earth closets were still used in rural schools until mains drainage replaced them in the 1960s.

The houses were laid out along the new Venn Road and the builder was Mr. Pritchard who gave the most competitive quotation of £2,300 with £334 13s. for the piggeries and henfolds. The architect was Thomas

Figure 54 2 Kyrle Street. This was George With's laboratory where he produced his earth closet mix and worked on experimental manures. In 1876 Hereford Corporation laid on gas and a lamp at the corner of Venn Road for the sum of £16 14s. 1d.

Nicholson who had just completed the swimming baths and who was an enthusiastic supporter of all the Society building schemes.

The tenants were to be required to collect the waste and refuse matter of their houses for turning into manure, whilst the slops were collected in an irrigation system for use on the gardens. The manure was not to be sold and tenants had to agree to show people round the model enterprise. Unsurprisingly the tenants were to be carefully chosen:

> Care being taken to obtain honest and sober and industrious tenants. These tenants are to be selected principally from the class of mechanics and labourers, and those that know something of, or have a taste for gardening to be preferred, and such as have children.

It was noted that:

> Any industrious man of ordinary intelligence, who is placed in favourable circumstances, can live with God's blessing, in comparative comfort and find for himself and his wife and children, healthy and interesting and profitable employment for all their leisure hours at almost all seasons of the year, and at the same time pay a remunerative rent to his landlord. It is hoped therefore, that the tenants will constantly bear in mind the immense importance of the success of this undertaking to the welfare of the working classes throughout the kingdom; and of the great obligation which rests upon them to do their best and make it succeed.

Figure 55 The outbuilding at one of the houses in Kyrle Street housing the original earth closet with its ventillation pipe

It was the first model garden estate in Hereford and preceded the Garden City

95

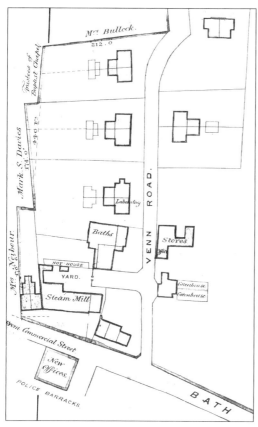

houses in Barr's Court Road by 30 years. Generous prizes were offered for upkeep, produce and for the best-written accounts of the methods of cultivation. The rents each week were reasonable: four-bedroomed houses at £1 8s., three-bedroomed at £1 4s. and two-bedroomed at £1. The experimental nature of the scheme with all the extras such as the trees, piggeries and henfolds meant that the rents did not reflect the investment made by the Society. On the other hand it was hoped to demonstrate that where land could be acquired cheaply, model cottages could be constructed.

In 1882 the tenants comprised a publisher's clerk, the Society's analytical chemist (George With), an ironmonger's assistant, one of the builders

Figure 56 Plan of Venn Road showing mill, baths, laboratory and greenhouses

that built the cottages, the clerk to the Society (a Mrs. Lucy), a brewery manager, a cattle dealer, a railway police inspector and a dentist's assistant. Clearly they were not the poor, but the aspiring working class who would abide by the regulations and fulfil the expectations of the Society. Two of them were employees of the Society, whilst number 11 was the house attached to the experimental garden and where, at the opening of the enterprise, the Head Gardener lived. He had to look after the experimental gardens and hot houses, the shop and the dry earth establishment. In 1872 Thomas Tranter was appointed to this position, who had previously been the gardener at Athelstan Hall on Aylestone Hill, living in the stableblock next to the Hall.

George With, who worked part-time as the chemist for the society and who was headmaster of the Bluecoat school, was appointed in May 1876 as a paid Secretary to the Society at a salary of £150 per annum with one of the model cottages opposite the gardens, rent and tax free, to be used as offices and laboratories. George With had made his name making optical lenses and was a prominent and honorary member of the Woolhope Club where he enjoyed showing members biological slides through his microscopes. He had been appointed headmaster in November 1851, supported in his application by the Dean of Hereford. The rival candidate was Henry Yapp, the son of the St. Peter's parish clerk, who was promoted by John Venn. There was no ill-feeling over this for George With was the 'most clubbable' of men. He was always a forward-looking and innovative teacher and when he asked to leave after 25 years, his committee placed on record their regret and thanks for the efficient and able manner in which he had conducted the school. He was a moral and intellectual force and introduced science to his pupils. John Venn, however, persuaded him to give up his full time teaching post and take on his role in the Society at the same salary.

His personality was described as 'sweet and winning'. He fostered many scientific projects and had a single-minded devotion to his ideals. A memorial in the cathedral records his devotion to yet another activity — the choir of which he was member for 30 years.

Once appointed Secretary to the Society he became firm friends with John Venn who valued his intellectual

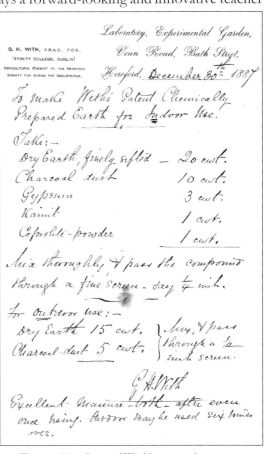

Figure 57 George With's recipe for manure which he patented in 1879 (No. 1168). It was recorded as an invention of 'Improvements in Treating and Preparing Earth for use in Commodes and Earth Closets'

gifts and dedication. He soon became his right-hand man and for many years read the lesson in church. His duties were to superintend the garden, farm, model cottages and the Society's allotments plus the new refreshment rooms in Commercial Street behind the office.

There were difficulties with the operation of the experimental gardens, however, and by the following year, November 1877, much of the land was released as allotments and only 2½ acres were kept for experimenting with new manures. It was also decided to let the Head Gardener's cottage and hothouses at a fair rent.

When Thomas Tranter moved to Venn Road to become head gardener he had a wife, Harriet, and three children. He faced a difficult future becoming self-employed and paying rent for his house. However, he took on the house and garden as a business, running a stall in the Butter Market selling vegetables whilst the Society ordered celery, onions, parsnips, carrots and swedes from him for their winter soup. However the business appears not to have prospered, for a year later he owed the Society £114 and was threatened with legal proceedings. He had made losses on his onion crop and suffered disease in the potatoes. Nevertheless, he managed to pay off all but £10 of the debt the following year, but continued to be dogged by bad luck: hard frosts, leaks of manure into his hothouse and disease. In 1882 his rent was reduced by £3 because there was no hot water to his pipes in the greenhouse behind the mill. As his debts mounted once again a new lease was reached in 1885 when his holding was reduced so that the mill garden containing the steam-heated greenhouses and the loft over the piggeries behind, were no longer his to use. In June the greenhouse behind the mill was moved to a new position behind his house to help him and new hot water pipes were laid on, but by the next month he was ten months in arrears.

Figure 58 The Head Gardener's house, no. 11 (now 4) Kyrle Street

Figure 59 (top) The farm buildings
Figure 60 (lower) The farm bailiff's house in Bath Street, all since demolished
(Derek Foxton Collection)

In spite of support from William Lewis, the mill manager and Secretary, he was finally evicted in 1887 when his goods were confiscated. He went to live at number 2 Whitecross Road where he continued his business as florist and market gardener in the Butter Market.

Subsequently other tenants tried to keep the garden productive but it was finally taken over by Kings Acre Nurseries. In 1916 they wrote to request a new boiler for the greenhouses as it leaked and was worn out. One was supplied for £12.

In 1872, as soon as the cottages were completed, Venn proposed an ideal model farm. There were to be stalls for 32 cows, two ranges of hen houses and piggeries to help the working classes to have a wholesome diet containing milk, eggs and bacon. There would be a house for the bailiff, a bakery and store rooms. American beehives were to be purchased. He also planned to employ boys after school hours so that they could afford to stay on longer and complete their education, whilst also feeding them a nutritious diet from the farm. Mr. Chandler, the first City Missioner, was employed to teach skills to local poor boys in the evenings and at weekends, and was given a rent-free house as recompense.

The farm proved a disaster: the cows were never bought and the first delivery of hens all died. The piggeries were used at various times for alternative uses. The profits from the mill soon began to be absorbed by the over ambitious plans. In 1876 the loss was £1,316 and in the next year the pigs and most of the poultry had to be sold off. It was decided to return the land to allotments that became known as Portfield Gardens., whilst the model warehouse, cellar and storerooms were let out to Pulling and Co., a local gin distillery, as a store. In 1899 a new water closet was put in for allotment tenants and repairs were made to the buildings. The warehouse next to no.11 finally disappeared when Kears motors took it over and built round it as Vaughan Street was created in the 1920s.

The name of Venn Road was changed in 1890 to Kyrle Street and Parry's Lane, where John Venn had his home, Beechwood, was renamed Venn Lane after John's death in the same year.

9   MANY CHANGES

In 1881 Venn's sister, Emelia, died quite suddenly. He wrote immediately to their close friends, the Money-Kyrles at Homme House, Much Marcle.

Feb.26/81

My Dear Friends,

I have sad but yet joyful news to tell you. My beloved sister last night left this world of sin & sorrow & entered into the joy of her Lord.

On Sunday last we were having our little service together in my study at 12 o'clock when she suddenly became pale & sick & with great difficulty we got her up to her room. It soon passed away, when she had a slight return on Monday & Tuesday but on Thursday morn. she was so much better that my niece, Mrs. Russell Gurney (who was staying with us happily) determined to return home. Suddenly, however, a rather severe attack came on: & she stayed. The next day however (yesterday) she felt so well that I thought all cause for anxiety was removed. But at 4 o'clock it returned with fearful violence: & after nearly five hours of suffering so sad to witness, she fell asleep in the Lord, & was at rest.

Her mind was perfectly clear at the time & she joined every now & then in repeating potions of texts or hymns & amongst others the Te Deum, with great energy.

For nearly eighty years we have lived together excepting the two years when I was in India — was there ever a brighter mind combined with such depth of feeling than hers.

But I would not have her back, I delight to think her warfare is ended & I shall soon join her in the presence of the Saviour we love.

I have many letters to write so farewell. May God stir us all up to live wholly for Eternity.
Truly
Ever yr most loyal servant,
J. Venn

There were glowing tributes to Miss Venn in the *Hereford Times*. As the daughter of Rev. John Venn of Clapham and one of the founders of the Church Missionary Society her life-long interest in the movement received much comment. Her brother Henry was honorary secretary and her own nursery governess was the first to go out as a missionary under the auspices of the society 'which the Venn family have done so much to foster'. She was highly regarded for her piety and for her 'sweetness of disposition'. Her kindness to the poor and her general affection for them paints an appealing portrait of an energetic and compassionate woman who lived until she was 86 years of age. Her funeral was almost a public event and was conducted by the vicar of St. Peter's, Rev. G. Bennet. Her niece, Emelia, and nephews, James and Leslie Stephen, were present as mourners. From the church there was a long procession to St. Peter's burial ground where she joined her aunt Jane in a family grave. A poor woman who stood at the graveside is quoted as saying, 'Well, she always had a smile ready for everyone!'

The following letter to William Lewis, the Society Secretary and manager, written in John's own strong hand only a few weeks after his sister's death, reveals the nature of the man:

Aylestone Hill,

March 25/81

My Dear William,
I borrowed £700 of Henry Powell (Mrs. Russell's Servant) at 4½ per cent. & £100 of James Moses Powell at the same rate of interest.
I did this of course for their benefit.

But now I should like to pay them off: & I will thank you therefore to transfer £800 out of my current account with the Soc. to them.

If quite convenient to you, would you pay £300 to my account at the Natl. Provincial bank?

I hope soon to go down into the Town; and then I shall see you & your dear wife & little ones.

I trust you are quite recovered now.

God bless you & yours: & enable us all to live in the full enjoyment of the glorious hope.

Yrs. most truly,

J. Venn

By 1885 much had changed. The Society had sold off its houses and office in Commercial Street and built a more convenient arrangement opposite the mill in Bath Street. This was built on the corner of the 'new' street, or De Lacy Street as it was named. This road contained terraced houses for the policemen (who then also doubled as firemen) stationed at the building round the corner. 1885 was also the year that Dr. Graves Bull died, meaning that the Society lost one of its key promoters and supporters, and John Venn one of his close friends.

The new Society building was designed by Willet and Wakling as offices and a soup kitchen at an estimated cost of £550 to £590. In the event the tender accepted for the building work from a Mr. Pritchard was some £100 higher, at £659. The premises included a kitchen and dining-room for the supply of soup. While the foundations were dug out Mr. Pritchard's men found the old city ditch with its sloping sides and a buried willow tree from the Sally Walk. By June 1885 the new buildings were ready and a brass plate was ordered to be put on the gate.

The new offices were to coincide with a reorganization of the business. In the past the Society had tended to raise funds either by seeking donations or by mortgaging its properties to the Venns on short term arrangements, using the profits from the mill to pay the interest and to eventually reacquire the assets. But John Venn was now 82 years old and other arrangements needed to be considered. In addition, recent losses incurred on some of the enterprises of the last ten years had raised the spectre that if action was not taken swiftly enough in future, spiralling debts would lead to the outright sale of property. It was impossible to borrow money without better security than that which currently rested on a personal memorandum signed by members of the committee. There was to be a new society, albeit with the same name, The Hereford Society for Aiding the Industrious, with similar objects. It was to be incorporated as an association limited by guarantee and was to apply for a licence to the Board of Trade under section 23 of the Companies Act of 1867. As so constituted the Society would be able to borrow and give a proper legal

Figure 61 The new Society offices and soup kitchen, Bath Street
(Derek Foxton Collection)

security under seal with the property of the Society as security. At the same time the committee was reorganised with a President, the first of whom was Charles Brunsdon. John Venn's signature is one of the ten committee members who agreed to these actions, and it is difficult to know whether he signed with a light heart, seeing how his early plans had matured, or with sadness at the need for the changes.

On 5 August 1885 at an extraordinary meeting the old Society was dissolved and the new incorporated Society was founded. From the start the policy of the new Society was far more stringent and when the finance committee got to work it recommended the closure of the model garden which was to be let out along with the farm premises. The loss on closing the model garden had amounted to £183, a considerable sum. George With was retired with John Venn's help over his pension, and under his supervision he was to carry on making manure at no.1 Venn Road while John Venn undertook to make up any deficit up to £250 a year for another two years. The value of the manure department to be taken on by John Venn was £81 14s. 10d., whilst the fittings in the laboratory were bought by George With for £2. The arrangement for the removal of the soil from the closets at the mill, baths and model cottages was to continue as before with George With being paid £20 a year for the labour and the medicated earth he supplied.

Figure 62 Elevation of the new offices and soup kitchen to De Lacy Street

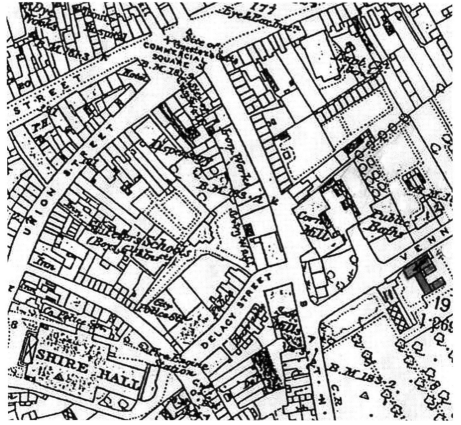

Figure 63 Map of the northern end of Bath Street showing many places associated with the activities of The Hereford Society for Aiding the Industrious. The new offices faced the mill on the corner of De Lacy Street

Rationalisation meant that bad tenants like Thomas Tranter were evicted and others were reminded that their rent had to paid. The provident branch or savings bank was discontinued on the grounds that Penny Banks were now provided in most places and there was also a Post Office Savings Bank. Many of the small benevolent schemes like aids for the sick were also abandoned. Land in Bath Street was staked out ready to be sold for building and a new fence was put up taking part of the land of the model garden rented by Thomas Tranter. The Society was keen to relet the house and land at no.11. By the following year the old premises in Commercial Street were sold at last to Mr. A.G.E. Boulton for £2,000.

At the end of 1887 George With applied for permission to occupy the cottage used as a laboratory until June of the following year in return for his services looking after the other cottages and allotments. It was clearly pointed out that this did not allow him use of the garden opposite on the other side of the road at no.11. In January he gave notice as expected that he would be leaving in June.

The house that Thomas Tranter had vacated was painted and papered and repairs were undertaken to the house and greenhouses at the cost of £18 17s. 6d., work carried out by William Pritchard. A new Gem stove was installed in the back kitchen at a cost of 35s. The premises were then let for £40 per annum to a Mr. Rogers.

John Venn was still playing an active role in various projects and in the committee work. He still preached and there is an account of him in a letter that appeared in the *Hereford Times* in October 1938. This relates that on the morning of 30 September 1884, when it was a warm day, the 'eminent divine' attended St. Nicholas church and, wearing a long flowing surplice, took his seat in one of the cross pews at the north-east end of the church. At the appointed time, and not changing into a black preaching gown as was at the time his practice, he slowly ascended the tall pulpit, being closely followed by the then rector, the Rev. Samuel Holmes, till he was safely installed. Then to a rather small congregation, in his usual impressive style he discoursed on the text 'now we see as through a glass darkly'.

In 1890 there was a change in the Society's financial practice. It had been customary from the early days of the mill to devote a fixed proportion of the profits as a bonus to the commercial servants of the Society every year. This was now discontinued and any future bonus for individuals depended on the committee's decision. This action was taken after John Venn's death and there is no doubt that he would have opposed it.

John Venn died on 12 May 1890 at the age of 88 years, for 55 of which he had carried his evangelism to the people of Hereford. He had declined any advancement in the Church and had devoted himself to the welfare of his parishioners.

His health had been wonderfully good up until a month before his death, indeed many of his friends thought he would live into his nineties. John Venn had a weak heart, but his robust constitution and careful diet had long kept it from being a problem. In time his heart began to fail and John took to his bed. After a week he lost his natural cheerfulness and his power to converse with friends gradually failed him. By the Sunday it became obvious that his end was near; prayers were said at church services but during the early hours of the following day he died with his niece, Emelia Gurney, at his side.

The funeral took place on the following Friday at St. Peter's church. The coffin was conveyed on a hearse with glass sides and covered with flowers. The chief mourners were Emelia, his niece, Rev. Dr. John Venn, his nephew, Rev. Henry Venn, another nephew and his wife. Mrs. Money Kyrle and Miss Kate James joined them as close friends. They were followed by mourning coaches containing the doctor, Thomas Turner, and John's solicitor of many years, Mr. W.J. Humphrys plus the household servants. At the church were the Bishop of Hereford, the dean and ministers of every denomination, together with a large congregation. The procession was met by the curate, Rev. Hugh Williams, Bishop Maredon (a former curate of John Venn), Rev. H.P. Prosser (the rural dean), and Rev. G.H. Kirkwood. The *Hereford Times* reported the funeral on 17 May:

> The order of the procession was:- Industrial Aid Society, Herefordshire Friendly Society, citizens, choir, clergy, doctor and solicitor, bearers, hearse, mourners and undertakers. The route to the burial ground was through St. Peter Street and Commercial Street. Most of the shop windows in the city were darkened with shutters, and many blinds were drawn down through the funeral and St. Peter's church bell was tolled. Bath Street flour mills and other premises conducted by the Society for Aiding the Industrious were closed for the day.
>
> It will be remembered that the old burial ground was renovated and a handsome stone arch entrance was erected facing Commercial Road as a memorial to the late Miss Venn. Her brother's funeral is the only one that has come to this grave-yard since then, and the

first that has passed under the arch entrance, which it may be added, bears near the keystone the appropriate words: Spea, Pax. Mr. Venn's grave is the same, which had previously received the body of his late sister over whose remains was placed a stone covering. The sides of the grave were steined, and the upper part was clothed with laurel.

The Venns were the last burials, for the graveyard was then closed and the ground has been neglected over time. It was noted early in the next century:

> The burial ground alas! is in a state of disorder, affording evidence of heedless indifference and unseemly disrespect to the immortal dead, enough to sear the eye and grieve the heart. What a striking contrast to the Municipal Cemetery and the many county church-yards whose grounds are beautifully and reverently kept.

This tribute was placed in the minute book of the Society that he created:

Figure 64 Buried in St. Peter's burial ground are Rev. John Venn, Emelia Venn and their Aunt, Jane Venn

108

The committee unanimously desire to place on record their deep sense of loss sustained by the Society by his death. He was its sole founder and for this purpose incurred personally very heavy pecuniary responsibilities. For many years he took the warmest interest in all its operations which the committee feel have conferred and will in the future bestow great benefit on the industrious classes of the City, whose spiritual and temporal interests Mr. Venn always had most earnestly at heart.

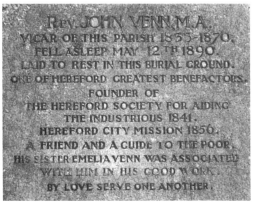

Figure 65 The memorial arch into St. Peter's graveyard designed by E.H. Lingen Barker and carved by Thomas King in 1881, restored in 1970. It had been erected by Emelia Gurney, John Venn's niece, in memory of John's sister, Emelia, but today the arch is often erroneously thought to have been erected after John's death as a memorial to him

Figure 66 The arch now carries a tablet with an epitaph inscription of appreciation to both John Venn and his sister, Emelia

A fund was started to provide a Venn Ward at the General Hospital for 'Incurables' which operated until the advent of the National Health Service in 1948. It was also resolved by the Society that a piece of land should be kept for some kind of memorial, a proposal which manifested itself in Venn's Close memorial homes (see below).

Following his death the name of Venn Road was altered in 1891 to Kyrle Street after Captain Money Kyrle, a loyal committee member for many years. Instead, the road on Aylestone Hill where John Venn had lived at Beechwood was renamed as Venn Lane in place of Parry's Lane.

Complaints were soon made about the state of Kyrle Street due to bad drainage, and the question of widening it and putting in sewers was referred to the appropriate sub-committee, who in turn referred it to the City Surveyor, Mr. Parker, for specifications and an estimate. This included replacing the fencing after widening and for substituting water closets or lavatories for the old earth closets in the cottages and baths, so beloved of John Venn and George With, and connecting them to new sewers to be laid down by the council. The tenants were asked to give up some of their front gardens to allow for the work, but as they were to be given notice if they refused; none did.

Refusal to grant permission for an additional bedroom to Mr. Rogers in no.11 meant that he gave up his tenancy in 1893 and it was let to a Mr. J. Bowen, but he was soon in arrears and was given notice to quit six months later. The next tenant stayed less than two years. An experimental gardener named Cross then applied to take on the house and garden in 1898 for a longer lease of up to 21 years provided the Society would make some alterations including an additional bedroom. He also offered to pay 5% of the cost. This must have been accepted as at the end of 1900 the Society

Figure 67 The Working Boys' Home and Meadows Hall

paid £17 for a new boiler to heat the greenhouses. The warehouse and shed next door were let in 1903 to The Kings Acre Nursery Company for £30 per annum.

When the City Gaol was built by Leonard Johnson a house for the prison governor was built behind it. This mid-19th-century building had a classical front with a porch. When De Lacy Street was constructed in the 1880s the house became the home of the Chief Constable. It was apparently part of the Society estate for rent was paid to them. The last Chief Constable to live there was Mr. Freeman Newton, O.B.E., who moved in to this large establishment near the police station in 1927. The street and the house were demolished when the present police station was erected.

Further down Bath Street land had already been sold in 1876 from the Portfields to the trustees of the Working Boys' Home who wished to build a new house for their orphans. The first house opened in Workhouse Lane and was supported by charitable donations. The boys were described as 'ill-clad, dirty, and apparently totally uncared for by those to whom they belonged'. Within two years the numbers increased so that a new home was necessary, and the Society sold them a ¾-acre plot from the land facing Bath Street for £335. Their aims were in accordance with the Society's and John Venn was patron. It provided shelter, training and work

Figure 68 Land was sold facing Bath Street and the garden at no.11 Kyrle Street was reduced and an iron fence was erected. Wye Terrace was then built by William Bowers who also had his yard there for many years

for homeless boys. The building cost £2,000, with a further £500 for furniture and fittings, and was designed by George Haddon. It was opened on 1 February 1877, with Mr. & Mrs. Cuffe as its first master and mistress. The boys sold bundles of firewood round the city and ran messages, but the home was always struggling to raise enough money to expand. Later it added a training school, the Meadows Hall and rented more land from the Society for cultivation.

Between St. Owen Street and Ledbury Road, on land that the Society owned near St. Peter's vicarage in Ledbury Road, were two areas of gravel. The Boys' home leased them for a while and no doubt the boys were employed digging out the gravel and sand. Later, the City Council leased the pits. They were a considerable asset until they were built over.

10 THE RECENT HISTORY
OF THE SOCIETY

On the northern perimeter of the Portfields beyond Kyrle Street and on
Commercial Road lay the Hope Pole Inn. This came up for auction in
1896 on the death of its owner, Mark Davies of Hunderton. The Society
felt that its acquisition would allow the creation of a useful approach to its
Bath Street estate from Commercial Road, and decided on purchase at the
subsequent auction.

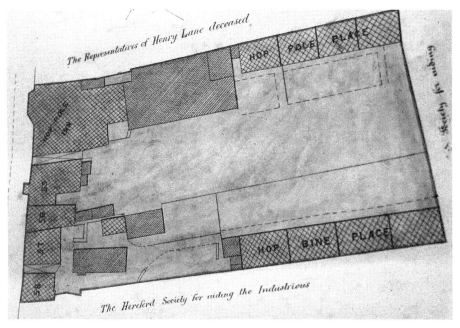

Figure 69 Plan of Hop Pole Inn and courtyard cottages

It was offered for sale in two lots: the first lot comprised the Hop Pole Inn with Mr. Joseph Jupp as landlord, along with four shops at 55-58 Commercial Road, Hop Pole Place where there were four cottages, and Hop-Bine place with another four cottages. They were typical of the small courtyard developments that lay behind frontages on to the main roads. The second lot was a further four cottages in Monkmoor Street. The whole was purchased for £4,000 with a part mortgage from the Bulmer brothers.

Once Mr. Jupp's tenancy ended in 1898, the Hop Pole was let to Messrs. Arnold Perrett and Co. for one year. It contained a bar, bar parlour, tap and smoke room as well as a market room and a dining room. At the rear was a new stable block for 30 horses.

A sketch plan was drawn up in 1900 for a road 30 feet wide through the property to Kyrle Street. It was shown going through two arches, but doubts were expressed about getting permission for this entry. The Society then decided to sell the property, but after it had been offered to Arnold Perrett who declined it as it was in such a bad state of repair, it was resolved to pull down the existing buildings, including the four cottages called Hop Pole Place, but keeping provision for the new road. By 1903 the plan for the road as prepared by the City Surveyor had been approved by the council, and tenders went out for rebuilding the Hop Pole. One for £1,495 was accepted from a Mr. Davies, and in 1904 it was ready to let at a rent

Figure 70 Hop Pole elevation by W.E. Britten

of £150 per annum. In the event it was let to the Hereford Public House Trust Ltd. for £120 p.a. plus half the tenant's profit. It was continually in need of repair and suffered from dry rot soon after its construction.

A valuation in 1897 gives an idea of the assets then held by the Society, although the new office and soup kitchen are not shown separately but included in the Bath Street estate. The Hop Pole estate is shown to have been a considerable investment and it proved to be a constant problem. Indeed, the *raison d'être* for its acquisition, the access road to Kyrle Street, was never built, although there is still a passageway leading into Kyrle Street, which formerly led to the Portfields. The Gaol Street mortgage shown on the valuation was on the cottages in front of St. Peter's school. Income from allotments was low but the two estates in Bath Street were a valuable asset. A surprising amount was owing to the mill.

1897   Valuation of property

	£	s	d
Mill and baths building	14,238	2	4½
Hop Pole Estate	4,133	18	4
Commercial Road estate	614	15	6
Portfields estate	8,881	10	0½
Bath Street estate	4,289	7	6
Canon Moor	26	10	1½
Barr's Court	10	18	8
James Howell mortgage on 23 Broad St. L'minster	300	00	0
Gaol Street mortgage	450	00	0
Gaol Street mortgage Interest Account	6	9	0
Invalid- value of stock	20	14	3
Loan accounts owing	213	13	8
Friars Lane allotments arrears	2	16	9
Barr's Court	16	15	3
White Cross	12	6	0
Barton	2	18	0
Portfields	21	14	9
Canon Moor	8	11	0
Bath Street revenue	37	1	7
Capital and Counties Bank Deposit account	1,500	00	0
Mill debtors	7,957	12	2
Mill value of stock in hand	3,065	13	1
TOTAL	46,084	13	0½

The land next to the Hop Pole, with four shops, was subsequently sold to Greenlands Ltd. where they built a furniture repository that stands today as a handsome red brick warehouse with a Dutch gable and terracotta dressings, recently redeveloped as apartments. Interestingly, in 1916 the builder who worked for the Society, William Bowers, bought nos. 3, 4, 5, 6, 9 & 10 Kyrle Street for £1,550 and sold on nos.3, 4, 5 & 6 to Greenlands so that they had access to the rear of their premises — a reverse of the process which the Society had intended! The joint ownership of 5 & 6 with the Commercial Road property continued until recently.

*Figure 71 Hop Pole and Greenlands Depository built 1903
by Walter William Robinson, as they look in 2007*

The Society still owned the Hop Pole in 1919, but the Herefordshire Public House Trust Company had been wound up in 1917 and the lease was taken over by the Peoples' Refreshment House Association Limited. In 1930 it was finally sold to the Public House Trust Refreshment Association for £4,556 13s. 4d.

Over the years more of the Portfields landholding was sold. In 1902 a new elementary school was required and land was sold on which to build St. Owen's School, which opened in 1905 in the present Symonds Street, named after the then Chairman of the Education Committee. In 1907 the council was looking for a site for a new Grammar school and the area of the gravel pits near Ledbury Road was considered but rejected because the Society wanted too much for this valuable piece of land. Instead, the new boys' school was built in Widemarsh Street.

The earliest council housing in Hereford had been built under powers contained in the Housing of the Working Classes Act of 1885. Further Acts enabled Hereford Council to buy land at Barr's Court where they put in the infrastructure and leased it to Co-operative Housing Ltd. Architects Groome and Bettington then constructed 85 cottages that housed over 400 people, the first residents moving in during 1909. This new estate became known as the garden city because of its landscaping and layout. Other small schemes followed at Green Street, St. Owen's

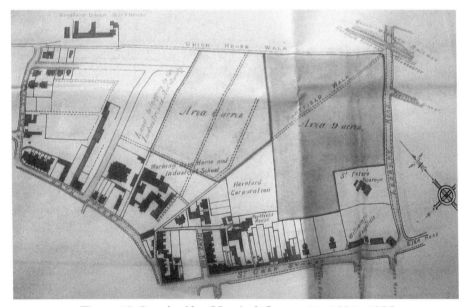

Figure 72 Land sold to Hereford Corporation 1921–1925

117

Gate, Cannonmoor Street, Edgar Street and Greenland Road; most of them the result of slum clearance.

After the end of the First World War the Society refused an offer for their Portfields land of £300 an acre. Instead they offered 15 acres for £5,000 'with the object of benefiting the working classes in the future as they had done in the past,' pointing out that the Society had already spent

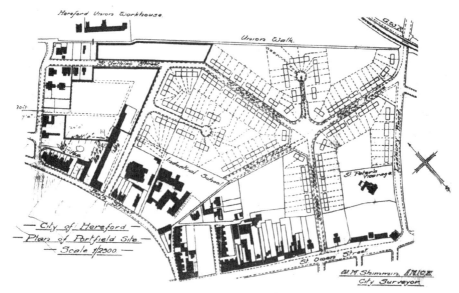

Figure 73 Central Avenue development

Figure 74 Central Avenue

118

Figure 75 The old model garden storage buildings are incorporated into this motor workshop on the corner of Vaughan Street

£905 on developing roads and sewers. In the end a price of £4,750 was reached through arbitration. In 1921 work began and gas pipes from St. Guthlac Street were connected to the Portfield housing site. A new road was joined to St. Guthlac's across Society land and 57 yards was donated to the council. In 1922, 34 more houses were built on the Portfields and the Society parted with more adjacent land and gave a grant of £250 towards the development. Sadly, notice was given to the Portfield Allotment holders that they would have to vacate their holdings from February 1925 so that the development could be completed, but some of the model farm land was kept for allotments until 1937. The Society was asked to make a new road on their land in 1925 and the main sewer was connected. St. Guthlac Street had already been developed at the Kyrle Street end by the Society but the rest was included in the council development. Vaughan Street was laid out by taking land next to the stores that had been part of the model garden. The stores are now a motor workshop.

The sale of 1 & 2 Kyrle Street in 1929 to the Masonic Lodge had added to the accumulated funds of the Society and by 1936 nothing had been done to use them or provide an adequate memorial to the Venns as had been promised at the beginning of the century. This became a problem when a national weekly, *John Bull,* published an article on old charities in May 1936 and selected the Society for special attention. The headline was

'£50,000 Mystery Charity'. It began: 'One of the most strongly entrenched and commercially successful of old charities and one which has lost much of its original character exists in the cathedral city of Hereford,' and went on to suggest that it was conducted in so secret manner so that local people were unaware of its operation. It also pointed out that the whole of its profits must be devoted to its declared objects under the conditions of its licence from the Board of Trade, yet the circulation of its annual accounts to members had ceased in 1923. *John Bull* accused the Society of not operating the soup kitchen, distributing cheap flour to the poor or of making grants of blankets or medical aids to the sick. It hoped the members knew what the Society did with the funds, for no annual report was published and so the local community was in complete ignorance about the Society. To this indictment was added the comment that no one knew how much money was voted to the members of the committee. It admitted that there was no obligation to disclose the finances of the Society but urged the members to dispel the air of secrecy and let the public know of their good work. The long-serving Secretary and manager, William Garrold Lloyd, had died on 1 January 1936 so was spared the publicity and enquiries.

The new secretary was Mr. E.G. Morgan who had to present a new image of the Society. Changes were soon made in the method of keeping its accounts: the charitable side of the enterprise was separated from the mill and rent was paid over to that account. In addition Charles Swales was promoted to the position of mill manager and remained so until the mill was sold in 1948.

The furore prompted action by the committee so that in 1937 a decision was taken to build almshouses in Bath Street on land where the farm and garden stood, and as a Venn memorial. The architect was Edward Bettington and Messrs. Howard and sons built the ten cottages and maisonettes together with a caretaker's house around a garden and fish pond in what became called Venn's Close. It was enclosed by a wall and entered via a gated archway.

The houses were intended for elderly widows and spinsters and were opened in 1938. The small estate was described at the time:

> The lay-out of the Close is L-shaped in plan with a fine stone archway, opening up onto Bath Street, forming the main entrance. The buildings, in five groups, including eight suites of flats, are erected round a beautiful quadrangle with a lily pond in the centre. The houses are built in hand-made bricks of warm texture, with hand-made roofing

tiles, and with the artistic boundary walls and gateway, they make a delightful addition to the architecture of the City.

Each house or flat, contains a large living room, a bedroom, a scullery with tiled dado and modern conveniences. Gas is laid on to cookers and boilers, and electric light is installed throughout. Every care has been taken in the colour schemes to make the homes as artistic as possible, and in the blocks containing flats, sound and fireproof floors have been provided.

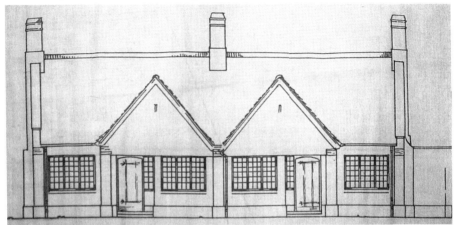

Figure 75 Bettington's design of 1937 for Venn's Close

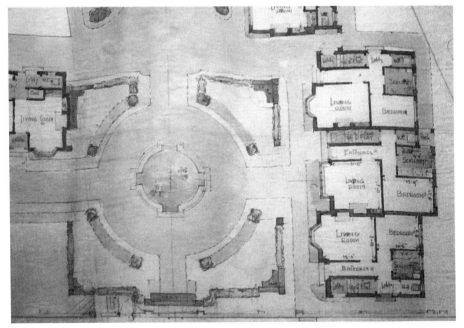

Figure 76 Bettington's design for a pond and flower beds as a central feature

121

Figure 77 Venn's Close in 2004

Once the mill premises were sold in 1948 there was a large capital sum with which to construct some more almshouses. In 1952 land was purchased in Friar Street for £425. By May 1953 plans were submitted by

Figure 79 Venn Memorial Homes, Friar Street, for single women and widows

a Mr. Robinson for the new almshouses intended again for spinsters and widows. In December 1953, a tender for £18,748 19s. 11d. was accepted from builders W. Powell and Son. Open space in front of the buildings was to be maintained by Hereford Council. The John Venn Homes were opened on 24 November 1955.

The Society's offices were still on the corner of Bath Street and De Lacy Street, but these were compulsorily purchased for £10,400 in 1967 as part of the land acquisition for the new inner relief road, and the subsequent new police station.

The Society's remaining funds were then all converted to stocks and shares to provide a portfolio that would produce an income to maintain the almshouses and generate a surplus to use for grants to worthy causes and deserving claimants. The office was moved to 38 Widemarsh Street, but an increase in rent in 1997 made the Society decide to construct a small office in Venn's Close which was opened in June 1998. As in the past, the officers and committee members meet monthly to discuss applications and to make grants. The welfare of the tenants of Venn's Close and the Venn Homes is also of concern. The Society is under close scrutiny by the Charity Commissioners and audited accounts have to be sent to them annually and to the members. Although the charity's work is not well

Figure 80 The Secretary, R. Michael Cunningham and the Hon. Chairman Mark Bricknell in the office at Venn's Close in 2006

known today there is a display in St. Peter's church which outlines the work of John Venn and the history of the Society.

Today's community has been transformed by state welfare and abject poverty no longer exists but there are still those who are deprived of education and opportunity need a helping hand to become industrious and to have their ambitions fulfilled.

APPENDIX I

Leonard Johnson & Thomas Nicholson

Leonard Johnson, 1789–1862

Leonard Johnson became an important contributor to the modernisation of 19th-century Hereford. He first made his name as the builder of the two wings added to the General Infirmary in 1834. Then came the Union Workhouse in Kennel Lane. This conformed to plans drawn by Ploughdon of Oxford; as also used in other towns. After some work to the College of the Vicars Choral, he then built a new front to the Bluecoat school. Soon after, in 1838, came St. Peter's parish school in Union Street for Rev. John Venn. When Bye Gate prison was removed in 1841–2 Johnson rebuilt it in Grope Lane, later Gaol Street. Although it is mainly of brick like his other buildings, he designed a façade of rusticated stone. The accommodation was in separate cells with exercise yards, and space and facilities for weaving and making mats and rugs from coconut fibre. It also served as the Police Station.

With the removal of the ancient City Gaol the Hereford Improvement Commissioners planned the area to be known as Commercial Square; so renamed in 1855 when the ditch was in-filled. Johnson took down the picturesque Packers' Inn and replaced it with the Kerry Arms in 1846. This hotel stood on the site of the Bye Gate into the city and so was given height and importance with an embattled parapet to emphasise its former history. Today it still gives the appearance of a fortified entrance into the medieval city as it stands facing all comers from the north-east.

In the following year, 1847, he was given the commission by the Society to design and build the new steam corn mill (see p.59). The same year he bought some land on the corner of the present Bath Street on which he built himself a house *c.*1850, with a garden behind. It later became a Servants' Home and Registry, noted in 1890 in Jakeman & Carver's Directory at 12 Commercial Road. This gave employment and lodging to female servants. He went on to rebuild the Deancry (now part of the Cathedral School) in the Cathedral Close in stone in a plain symmetrical style. In 1850 he became the first City Surveyor and as such gave evidence on the state of the sewers and drains to the Public Health Inquiry that led to the Improvement Act of 1854.

His brother, Richard Johnson, was the Hereford Town Clerk; a role he played with distinction. His daughters gave their three houses in St. Owen Street for a site for a new town hall that was completed in 1904. Leonard died in 1862 and was buried in St. Peter's graveyard. Johnson's Hospital by the Workhouse were almshouses named in his memory in 1862.

Thomas Nicholson, 1823–95

Thomas Nicholson is best known as a designer of churches and schools, but he also undertook several important commissions for the Society. He was born at Everton, Liverpool, in 1823 but moved to Portsmouth with his parents as his father was a naval captain. Thomas Nicholson trained as an architect and set up in practice in Hereford in 1845 when he was 22 years old. His home and office was in the old vicarage in St. Peter's Street near to the parish church where John Venn was the incumbent. He had four children by his first wife, Eliza, who died in 1864 aged 38. He re-married soon after and, according to the 1871 census, lived in he house with his wife, Emily, together with his elderly mother, Elizabeth, and a nursemaid, as at 47 Thomas had become a father again. Another daughter was born two years later. There was also a cook and a housemaid.

Figure 81 Thomas Nicholson's house and office, 6 St. Peter's Street, the former vicarage (English Heritage)

In 1868 he undertook the design and construction of the new St. James' church for John Venn. In 1871 he was appointed Hereford Diocesan Surveyor of Ecclesiastical Dilapidations and then Diocesan architect. In that year he built St. Peter's Infant school for John Venn's successor, Rev. G.B. Bennett, and also a new vicarage for St. Peter's in Ledbury Road funded in part by John Venn. It was a substantial red brick house with decorative diapering of blue brick and with sash windows. The south arcade of St. Peter's was completely rebuilt by him between 1880–85, at the same time that much of the rest of the structure was restored.

His work for the Society had begun in 1851 when he was requested to draw up plans for a building housing eight baths at a cost not exceeding £450 and heated by the excess steam from the mill. Five days later the plans were ready and by January of 1852 the baths themselves. Naturally it was to Nicholson that the Society turned when John Venn suggested a swimming baths in 1870 using the steam and water again available from the mill and his plans were adopted on 28 November.

It became desirable to build a dining room and kitchen for the distribution of the Society's soup and in 1871 Nicholson designed both to be built behind the office premises in Bye Street, since renamed Commercial Street.

His next challenge provided by John Venn was to plan a street of model cottages and an experimental garden next to the baths in what became Venn Road. Soon after he designed the farm buildings and bailiff's house for the unsuccessful model farm on the Portfields. Much of this work was financed by borrowed capital from the Day family who put up £1,500, Miss Withers £200, Miss Bishop £1,100, Miss Braithwaite £200 and Mr. & Mrs. McAlister £1,750. These were not inconsiderable sums and they show a commitment to the Society and its work.

Thomas Nicholson seems to have done little work for the Society after this, probably being fully committed to his work as Diocesan architect.

His eldest son, John Anthony Thompson Nicholson was also an architect and carried on the practice after his father's death. It was his firm that rebuilt St. James' church after the disastrous fire that destroyed it in 1901. John became ARIBA in 1882 when he was 26 years old, his sponsor being Frederick Kempson, a Herefordian friend of his father and Diocesan architect for Llandaff.

APPENDIX 2

Regulations for the Mill Workforce

• The deduction in weight to be allowed for waste in grinding & grists shall be as small as possible but shall not exceed one pound and a half per imperial bushel.

• All wheat etc delivered at the mill for grinding shall be entered by the miller in a book for that purpose, who shall give a receipt for the same & no grist shall be returned by either miller without the receipt being stamped at the office.

• The foreman shall make an entry of the quantity & weight of all wheat purchased for the society on its delivery at the mill and give the certificate provided for that purpose acknowledging its receipt.

• The foreman shall during the week he commences at 5 attend to the stones and dress flour until 9, afterwards he shall attend to the first floor. He shall receive all wheat making the necessary entries. He shall deliver out the grist also all flour, gurgeons, bran etc for the office; and to other persons producing a ticket but no flour, gurgeons etc shall be delivered (except for the office) without the usual ticket. He shall dress & keep the stones in good working order; he shall oil the bearings & gear on the first floor and keep the whole of the first floors in a clean and orderly manner. He shall during his week commencing at 9 after the miller has left in the evening attend to the stones until time of leaving work and on Saturdays and at other times when needful he shall assist with the grists.

• When a third miller employed and found necessary to work all night the foreman to commence at 7 in the morning and leave at 7 in the evening attending to dressing stones and the other work as distributed before & the second & third miller to work 12 hours alternately.

• The second miller shall during his week in the morning dress flour & during the day attend to the spouts & gristing, making the proper entries and also when necessary assist in dressing the stones & such other work as may be wanting.

• The miller who commences at 9 shall weigh off (if not done before) all flour etc dressed and send it up to the store room.

• The assistant to the miller shall attend to the hoisting tackle, elevator, smutting & dressing bins, the oiling of the bearings & the greasing of the gear on the upper floor. He shall keep in order the grists sent up for grinding & dressing, shall keep the bins supplied with wheat for grinding, he shall previous to his leaving work at 6 o'clock fill the bins with a sufficient quantity of wheat to grind until the next morning, he shall be careful to attend to the instructions of the foreman & miller in all things.

• That the assistant to the miller shall give immediate attention to all applications for sacks for wheat, shall register all sacks delivered out & shall take care of farmers' sacks & keep the upper floor in a clean orderly manner.

• That the machinery be oiled every morning at 9 o'clock and the driving gear be greased every Tuesday & Friday at the same time. The bearings & gear on mill floor by the stoker, - the upper floor by the assistant & the middle floor by the foreman who shall see that each person keep their several departments in a clean & orderly manner.

• No part of the machinery shall be suffered to run in gear when not wanting but shall be immediately put out of gear when finished using.

• The stoker is expected to get up steam at the appointed time and start and stop at all times the miller may require & shall give any assistance in moving & hoisting sacks that he may be able to do without neglecting the necessary attention to the boiler etc. He shall properly attend to the oiling of the engine & keep his department in a clean & orderly manner & shall not leave the premises during the time the engine may be at work. He shall also every night lock up the well & gates & put the keys in their proper place.

• Every one engaged in the mill is expected to be punctual in commencing work at the appointed hour, all extra time will be paid for at the rate of wages & all time lost from irregularity will be deducted.

• The stoker shall register in a book provided for that purpose the exact time each morning at which the mill is started & the time made by each person engaged during the day.

• No articles necessary for the use of the mill or engine shall be obtained without an order from the office.

• No person engaged at the mill will be allowed to smoke in or about the premises.

• That a book be kept accessible to all for the entry of any wants or matters necessary to be attended to belonging to the machinery of the mill etc & also of any complaints of neglect, disorder, or inattention in any person engaged in the mill.

• An immediate & courteous attention is expected to be given to every person coming on business to the mill by all engaged therein.

• Although the duties of each person has been set forth as near as possible, it is expected that those engaged at the mill will cheerfully render such assistance to each other as circumstances may require.

• Every implement in the mill shall be kept in its proper place & only employed for its proper use & the various work done at its proper time.

Bibliography

Fenn, R.W.D. *The Life and Times of Sir George Cornewall Lewis, Bart*,
    Logaston Press, 2005
Forster, E.M. *Marianne Thornton*, Edward Arnold, 1956
Hennell, Michael M. *John Venn and the Clapham Sect*, Lutterworth Press,
    1958
Howse, Ernest Marshall *Saints in Politics*, George Allen and Unwin, 1953
Venn, John *Annals of a Clerical Family*, Macmillan & Co., 1904

Index

McDowell, Hugh 87
Mechanics' Institutes 38
Medical Club 22
missionary church in Hereford 23-24
Moore, Emily 70
Morgan, E.G. 120
   Rev. 89, 91
Morris, Dr. Edward 49, 91
   Miss N.B., clerk 73, 75
Moule, Rev. Henry 93-94
Moule's Patent Earth Closets 93-94

National Commission for Baths and
      Washhouses 81
National School 18
Nayler & Co. 69
Newman, Mr. 63
Newton, Mr. 58
Nicholson, John 28, 127
   Thomas 25, 52, 69, 81, 94-95, 126-
     127

Oastler, Richard 36
Old House 14
Overbury 10-11
Owen, stoker 62
   Jnr. 62
   John 64, 87
   Tom 75

Parker family 54
   John, City Surveyor 85, 110
Parry's Lane 10, 110
Phillipps, Mrs. 50, 52
Phillips, Mr. 62
Pinner 9-10
Ploughden, Mr. 30
Poole, Edward 43, 44
Poor Law 29, 33-34
   'less eligibility' system of 29, 33
   outdoor relief 29
   (*see also* Workhouse)
Poor Rate 43, 44
Portfields (*see under* Society for Aiding
   the Industrious)

Powell, Henry 102
   James Moses 102
   Lewis 40
Powell, freeman of Monmouth 31
Preece, H. 72
Pritchard, Mr. 94
   William 106
privies 79
Prosser, Sarah 82
Prout, Mr. 20

Queen's College, Cambridge 4

Rammell, Thomas 78
Rankin Sir James, M.P.
Ransome, Dr. Arthur 27
Religious Tract Society 7
Richmond, George 25
Robinson, Messrs. H.O. & A. 59, 60, 61
Rogers, Mr. 106, 110
Rudge, Mr. F.M. 72
Russell, Capt. 23

St. Guthlac Street 90. 119
St. Mary le Strand 9
St. Owen's church 28
   parish 28
   Elementary school 90, 117
   Infant School, Hungary Street 17
St. Peter's burial ground 107-109
   church 15-16
   church house 51-52
   Infant school 17-18
   Literary Institute 18, 22
   vicarage 10, 90, 126, 127
'Saints, The' 5
sanitary conditions 76-80, 93-94, 95
Scudamore Charity 18
   school 18
Scutt Mill 90
Senior, Nassau 34
sewers 78-80
Shaftesbury, Lord 41, 42
Sharp, Greville 5
Shire Hall 14, 15

Submarines at War
1939-1945

First Published by Blandford Books in 1982 as
"The Underwater War 1939-1945"

Republished in 2004 by
Periscope Publishing Ltd.
33 Barwis Terrace
Penzance
Cornwall TR18 2AW
www.periscopepublishing.com

A CIP record for this book is available from the
British Library

ISBN No 1-904381-22-7

To The Girls They Left Behir

Contents

ERRATUM: The caption to the illustration on page 77 should read
British U-Class. The entry in the Index for British S-Class should
read British U-Class.

Acknowledgements

I have so many people to thank for help of one kind or another that the following list is bound to be incomplete; I sincerely apologise if any of the invaluable photographs, advice and fragments of first-hand information given, sometimes without a formal record, are omitted. Where, exceptionally, more than one print of the same photograph has been provided I have acknowledged what I believe to be the original source.

First and foremost I am truly grateful to my wife Eve for expert, patient assistance and constant encouragement throughout the lengthy preparation of this book.

For research, I am, above all, deeply indebted to Gus Britton whose broad knowledge of submarines, especially those of World War II, is exceptional and probably unequalled. My gratitude also goes to the remainder of the staff and helpers in the Royal Navy Submarine Museum—particularly Micky Budd, Lindsay Pirie, John Lambert, Mrs J R Corcoran, and, for technical diagrams, David Hill.

Amongst numerous books used as a basis for research, the works of Clay Blair Jnr, Dr J Rohwer and J P M Showell have been notably valuable; and I am grateful to Ruari McLean for permission to quote from his experiences, awaiting publication, with the Free French Navy and to Jon Wenzel for the use of excerpts from a unique study of the Japanese submarine force.

For photographs, documents and advice my thanks go to: the Trustees of the Royal Navy Submarine Museum; Cdr F C van Oosten (Director of Naval History, MOD Netherlands); ECP Armées France; The Imperial War Museum; National Maritime Museum; Lt Cdr Mike Wilson (Naval Historical Branch); the Staff of Flag Officer Submarines; the Staff of the Portsmouth RN Museum; RAF Historical Branch; Novosti Press Agency; Bundesarchiv Koblenz; K W Grutzemacher; C R Haberlein (Naval Historical Center, Washington); Pacific Submarine Museum Pearl Harbor; USN Submarine Museum New London; Cdr A B Catlin; Captain W L Siple; Vice Admiral Tatsuo Tsukudo; Cdr Z Orita; Vice Admiral Longonesi-Cattani; Cdr Borys Karnicki; Vice Admiral Sir Arthur Hezlet; Captain R W Blacklock; Mrs P R Compton-Hall; Captain M L C Crawford; Lt Cdr Mathew Todd; Cdr J Devlin; Captain Guy Griffiths RM; Lt Cdr George Honour; Captain M Hatcher MN; Arthur Robinson; Captain J S Stevens; Vice Admiral Sir Ian McGeogh; Col H G Hasler; Cdr E A Woodward; Captain A D Piper; Captain W A Stewart; Lt Cdr M Hayes; Captain J P Belmont USAF; Rear Admiral D A White; R Kerr; Mrs V Stephen; Lt Cdr P J Walker; the late Jan Honeywill; Leonce Peillard; Captain Claud Huan; Captain W A Stewart; Count Nicholas Sollohub; Lt Cdr A J D Burdett; G Taylor; Alexander Fullerton; Lt B Charles; Cdr J Whitton; Lt J R Menzies; Mrs E Barton; Cdr P C Chapman; Cdr R B Lakin; Captain H F Bone; Captain G E Hunt; Captain J O Coote; Captain J E Moore; John Batchelor; Lt Cdr P M Staveley; the following British submariners: G Selby; L Stannard; S Glazebrook; H G Wood; L W Benson; F Cocks; E Brandwood; S Biggs; A Mallett; C Anscomb; G Aveling; G Kimbell; R A D Green; J McCurrach; R R McCurrach; A Philp; G Svenson; R Hernaman, N Drury; R C Fry; F Miles; W Higgins; J Brighton; G Buckett; F Boston; G Curnall; G Clough; L C Hooton; J Richards; T Kirkpatrick; S Law; G A Luck; A H Miles; R Radwell; L Davis; Maurice Perratt; the following wartime U-boat commanders, officers and men: Cdr A Schnee; Captain H Wessels; Captain W Dommes; Captain P Cremer; Lt W Seiler; Captain W Schulz; Lt H Geider; Lt F Sack; Lt R Conrad; Cdr S Koitschka; Lt K Kamper; F Waruschka; J Eckert; H Schmidt; F Peters; K Franzen; A Wickbolt; Dr W Pohl; K Boch; Max Schadhauser; E Schmeckenbecher; H Stark; K Conen; K H Esser; K Bernt; F Kaspras; J Ahme; H Kotter; T Glasmacher; W Menzel; G Hogel; A Walczak; C Lewitz; F Stoldt; W Solling.

Title page
HMS *Taku*, true to her motto 'Won by Valour', was one of the few early T-class to survive the war. She saw active service from Benghazi to the Barents Sea, sinking and damaging 68,000 tons of enemy shipping. Of the five different commanding officers who scored successes in her, Lt Cdr Arthur Pitt was the top scorer with 36,340 tons to his credit. In April 1944, whilst trying to penetrate the mine fields guarding the Skagerrak, *Taku* was badly damaged by a mine and subsequently withdrawn from service. With two angled midship tubes, a T-boat had a bow salvo of ten torpedoes. The single tube later added aft, however, gave a very poor chance of hitting the sort of targets which the British expected, so the midship tubes were later reversed: this arrangement still left a powerful bow salvo of eight fish and increased the stern salvo to a useful three. However, only six tubes were internal: torpedoes in external tubes could not be worked on at sea and were apt to be less reliable so that 'mixed' salvoes did not always achieve the exact spread and spacing intended.

Contents page
Type VIIC U-boat adding to the numbers surrendered after the cessation of hostilities in May 1945. The crew of *U-826* are waiting resignedly under British guard to receive the new arrival alongside.

6

1 Fact and Fiction

There are now about 1,000 submarines in the navies of the world. At any one time about 250 are hidden, submerged and supposedly ready for action. Why they are there and what they may be capable of doing are questions most easily answered by looking back a little.

The history of the underwater war of 1939–1945 is particularly relevant because it was the last time that submarines were in action. Submarines have not fired a shot in anger since that time, when they had an unparalleled effect on the outcome of the war. The immensely powerful submarine forces of today, which have replaced the omnipotent surface battle-fleets of the past, only have simulated battle-experience to work with and develop from; and that, in the past, has proved notoriously unreliable. So many false conclusions were drawn in the pre-war years from unrealistic trials and exercises at sea, erroneous calculations on shore and misrepresentation in high places that it is worth a close look at what submarines were able to achieve, and not achieve, when it came to real action: and that may throw a little more light on the murky underwater threat today.

The difficulty lies in sifting true experience from false or over-written accounts: and these abound. One way of finding out what actually happened is to take a look from below, through the eyes of wartime submariners themselves. However, some caution is necessary. For one thing, when submariners got together it was (and still is) their habit to take opposite sides, automatically, in any given discussion; and for another, they were apt to use rose-tinted periscopes when staking their claims to success. But their view gives an intimate insight into the nature of underwater war—which was not what it seemed on the surface—and may suggest which side to back when histories conflict. That is the purpose of this book.

In the days when a tot of rum was issued daily to ratings in the Royal Navy, there was a pleasant custom of giving 'sippers' to a messmate—a taste rather than the whole tot. A few chapters about the submarines in action can do no more than offer 'sippers' to the reader; but many here are taken from bottles that have not been too often uncorked—at least not publicly.

A model of Bushnell's *Turtle* constructed from the best available data. The accounts of its attack in 1776 on HMS *Eagle* lying at anchor in New York Harbour, are more legendary than factual. Supposing an attack did take place, the operator would soon have been immersed in exhaled carbon dioxide and would not (in British submariners' terms) have known whether it was Christmas Eve or the Marble Arch. The auger at the top is attached to the back-pack delayed-action explosive charge by a lanyard.

The Irish-American inventor John Philip Holland who designed submarines in America, originally to destroy the hated British fleet on behalf of his fellow Fenians. However, business acumen allowed his most successful design to be sold to the Royal Navy which launched the first British (Holland) boat on 2 October 1901 at Vickers, Sons and Maxim, Barrow-in-Furness. The original New

Before getting immersed in the second underwater war it is useful to take a brief glance at what led up to it, if only to see how hard it is to sort out fact from fiction. Submarine history is said to go back for more than two thousand years; but it is bedevilled by misunderstanding and exaggeration to the point where a submariner today with, of course, the benefit of modern technological and physiological knowledge, has to discount much of what was written until at least the latter part of the twentieth century. The Dutch physician, Drebble (1572–1634), for example, has often been hailed as the 'Father of Submarine Navigation';[1] but it is impossible to believe that his boat, in which King James I of England (a nervous monarch at the best of times) was rowed down the River Thames, was capable of submerging fully, still less of being controlled beneath the surface. Like most early so-called submarines, it was no more than a tightly covered, airless rowing boat which could be weighted down to an awash and partially concealed condition.

Even quite well documented inventions like David Bushnell's *Turtle* must be taken with a large pinch of sea-salt. Sergeant Ezra Lee's immortalised attempt, on 6 September 1776, to attack the British flagship *Eagle* which was lying off Staten Island in New York harbour is not at all likely to have taken understandably made the best of a good story; but there is no reference to any kind of attack above or below water in HMS *Eagle*'s journals covering the years 1776 and 1777.[2] In particular, the (much later) assertion that Admiral Lord Howe was so alarmed that he lifted his close blockade and sailed away to safer waters simply is not true; he stayed where he was and evinced no signs of alarm whatever! There is undoubtedly a solid foundation of fact behind the legend; but all that can confidently be said is that George Washington's remark (made 11 years after the event) praising Bushnell's device as an 'effort of genius'[3] was fair with regard to its concept irrespective of dubious practicalities. Covert attacks of this kind would have been ideally suited to a weak maritime power threatened by a powerful enemy fleet. The *Turtle* and *Eagle* affair was the first attempt to mount what might now be called a submarine deterrent. As such it fully deserves its place in history.

Several more underwater attacks involving mines (then usually, and confusingly, called torpedoes) and semi-submersibles, in which Robert Fulton and other unnamed American citizens were involved, were said to have been launched during the war of 1812–1815. These well publicised efforts, all of which were abortive, drew violent cries of indignation from Great Britain. While an American paper felt able to report that 'the much ridiculed torpedo is obtaining a high reputation,'[4] the British press variously described the American use of underwater weapons as unhuman, barbarous, infamous, knavish and ignoble. HMS *Ramillies*, with Nelson's Captain Hardy in command, was cited specifically as a target for these infernal engines of war; but the log of HMS *Ramillies*[5] makes no mention of them. Nor can any reliable contemporary record be found to substantiate a statement that Hardy filled up his ship with American prisoners-of-war as a counter-deterrent to torpedoes, although crews were, in the normal way, taken off prizes and either put to work or confined on board.

America reacted vigorously to British criticism and retorted that the English themselves had paid Fulton to experiment with similar weapons and were being hypocritical. So they were: but the cause of all this invective was largely a figment of a well-fanned public imagination. It is tempting to think that fear of a supposedly powerful new weapon was the underlying motive for these exchanges in the press; but that would be overrating the threat as it appeared to commanders at sea. Fear of submarines would indeed grow and it was to be carefully fostered by interested parties; but it did not become a meaningful factor in international politics until some seventy-five years later when submersibles at last became a demonstrable threat. Before that, underwater warfare was based more on words than action. The principal and continuing lesson to be learned from that era was not to trust the newspapers in regard to submarines!

It was with the greatest reluctance that the principal navies of the world at last allowed themselves to be dragged below the waves which Britannia had ruled, with a few lapses here and there, for centuries. Even the most sail-bound Admirals and the most prejudiced politicians could not fail to perceive that if the submarine was a success it meant the end of surface fleets as they knew them. Nearly one hundred years earlier the noble, much respected Admiral Earl St Vincent had said of Pitt, the then Prime Minister, that he 'was the greatest fool that ever existed to encourage a mode of warfare which those who commanded the seas did not want, and which, if successful, would deprive them of it.' This weighty, much quoted but profound observation was made to Robert Fulton in 1805: it summarised policy towards submarines for a very long time to come. In similar vein in France, Admiral de Crés, at the Ministry of Marine, curled his lip at Fulton's *Bateau-Poisson* (*circa* 1800): 'Your invention is good for Algerians and pirates but learn that

The shape of things to come. HM submarine *No 1* at Vickers in 1901; it was to be nearly 60 years before this almost ideal shape again took to sea – driven not by gasoline but by nuclear power.

9

France has not yet given up the seas.'

By 1900, with the ugly, stunted, fishy creature actually at sea and showing its warlike capabilities nothing too bad could be found to say about it in Europe. In England the epithets were particularly violent. It was an 'underhand form of attack', thundered Admiral Wilson, VC, Controller of the Navy, 'treat all submarines as pirates in wartime . . . and hang all the crews.' The Admiralty, at his back, remarked with smug satisfaction: 'we know all about submarines; they are the weapons of the weaker power; they are very poor fighting machines and can be of no possible use to the Mistress of the Seas.'

Of course, all this was sheer wishful thinking. Every navy with a large surface fleet profoundly hoped that submarines would magically disappear and never be seen or heard of again. But it was not to be. Savage epithets were thereafter increasingly hurled at submariners and their craft as they progressed, rather jerkily, towards the twentieth century. When allied with Mr Robert Whitehead's Device of the Devil, the free-running torpedo, the potent combination provoked more furious arguments. European politicians and Admirals spoke of 'stooping from our lofty ideals' (France) and this 'damned un-English weapon' (Great Britain) when submarines started to become an unavoidable fact of life at sea. But they were not speaking from a moral standpoint (al-

though that was what they wanted people to think); they were plainly afraid that, if submarines could do what submariners claimed, underwater craft would wreak havoc upon the splendid imperialist fleets which had won empires and dominated the oceans for so long. Their fears were to be fully justified.

Outside Europe, there were snide inter-service comments about the capabilities and usefulness of submarines when they were introduced into the United States Navy; but there was little criticism politically in America except, as usual, on grounds of cost and priorities. A leading armour manufacturer summed up a dominant misgiving when he said: 'We will oppose submarines. For if they succeed, Congress won't appropriate for so many ships.' The foremost figure in underwater design, John Philip Holland, experienced years of frustration in America and wrote bitterly, in 1887, that he was 'totally sick and disgusted' with the lethargy of the Navy Department. But he won through in the end. The only notable public shaft directed at his ultimately successful *Holland VI* came in July 1899 from Miss Clara Barton, the first President of the American Red Cross: after a brief dip in the little craft on a cold, rainy day off Sag Harbour, the first woman to go down in a submarine sharply reprimanded the bespectacled, school-masterish Irish-American for inventing a 'dreadful weapon of

HM Submarine *No 1* to the Irish-American J P Holland's design, but with the invaluable addition of a periscope designed by Captain R Bacon (the first Inspecting Captain of Submarines) for this 'damned un-English weapon' as the Controller of the Navy called it when an order was placed for the first five boats on 8 October 1900.

war'. Holland, unabashed, replied prophetically that submarines 'would serve as a powerful deterrent to international conflict.'[6]

In Europe, after Holland had more or less proven the efficiency of his submersible, a curious attitude of ambivalence started to prevail. It required a good deal of weasel-wording amongst politicians. Mr Arnold-Forster's speech in the House of Commons on 18 March 1901 was typical: 'I will not say much about submarine vessels,' he explained (sensibly, because he knew nothing about them), 'but I will say that I am glad that the Admiralty . . . took the view that it was wise not to be found unprepared in regard to this matter. We have a great amount of information about these boats, but we do not attach an exaggerated importance to it. But we believe that an ounce of practice is worth a ton of theory . . . we are comforted by the judgement of the United States and Germany, which is hostile to these inventions (*sic*), which I confess I desire shall never prosper.'

During the years leading up to World War I, submarines were sometimes strongly favoured, sometimes actively opposed and sometimes blindly ignored. The fact is that only a scattering of enthusiasts in the various navies had more than a vague idea of how they worked and few, with the notable exception of the Royal Navy's Jackie Fisher and his stalking horse Admiral Sir Percy Scott, cared to raise their voices.[7]

The United States Navy did not try to maintain its early strong position and, whilst Britain eventually caught up with the submarine idea and became vigorously occupied in developing a war-worthy vessel, France, which had displayed such marked enthusiasm for the submarine initially, relaxed her efforts and allowed the British to reduce her lead rapidly and, by 1912, to overtake her. By 1914 the French submarine fleet was numerically smaller, and technically little further advanced than her 1905 flotillas: many of the boats were obsolescent and some were still steam-driven.

What was to become the most effective submarine force in the world started inauspiciously in Germany. Although Krupp-Germania at Kiel had already built three submarines for Russia, it was not until 1905 that they received the order to build *U-1*. The first U-boat owed its design to the Spanish engineer d'Equivilley who in turn was much indebted to French experience. During the 1914–1918 war, when submarines first demonstrated their enormous power, opinion amongst the Allies crystallised (through skilful press-handling) into doctrine to the effect that German U-boat men were cowardly and bad but Allied submariners were heroic and good. The dogma was to be proclaimed again in 1939. Outside submarine circles, and even inside a

top Right
Part of the British underwater Fleet (three Hollands and one A-class) *circa* **1905.**

Centre Right
The large wardroom in the Royal Navy's M-class (*circa* 1918) **was a great deal more comfortable and spacious than in the boats of World War II.**

Bottom Right
UB-*119* in World War I did not look, with its clean functional lines, very different to many boats in the navies of World War II.

few of them, this extraordinary distinction, spawned almost entirely by propaganda—admittedly an essential weapon of war—still persists quite widely among the former Allies. The two underwater wars were not fought by chivalrous, knightly battles. All war is murderous: that is its nature; and submariners were particularly skilled at dealing destruction and with it, necessarily, death. The Germans, as losers in both wars, saw their (very few) U-boat contraventions of the seaman's code proclaimed and punished whilst the Allies, as winners, were not arraigned. But any belief that there was some kind of clear-cut division between U-boat men and Allied submariners in their conduct is arguably untenable and invidious.

Submarines between the wars tended, for political reasons, to be kept hidden in the background. Consequently, with the exception of the German U-boat arm so purposefully revitalised from 1935 by (then) Captain Karl Doenitz, the tactical and strategic influence of submarines was neglected. In England the Submarine Service regarded itself as a private navy and was treated as such by the other specialist branches. This led to the Submarine Service not being properly integrated into the Royal Navy and to widespread ignorance amongst the other specialists regarding the potentialities—and the weaknesses—of the submarine arm.[8] The situation was much the same in other navies outside Nazi Germany.

It is necessary to glimpse something of this lengthy history, littered with lack of logic, ignorance, dual-thinking, hesitancy and wrong reporting in order to understand why, as the various nations entered World War II,

Top Right
USS *R-27* prior to launch in September 1918.

Centre Right
HMS *E22* at Harwich 1916. This was one of the Royal Navy's first experiments with carrying aircraft on submarines, and one of the first aircraft carriers on any kind. The aircraft are Sopwith Babies and they were intended for shooting down Zeppelins well away from the British coastline.

Bottom Right
Sail and steam. HM Submarine *K3*, one of the notorious 1917 steam-driven submarines intended for Fleet work with speeds up to 26½ knots on the surface. Nearly one half of the class was lost by accident, mainly because they were ordered to work with the surface fleet. The dangers of doing so have been forgotten.

so many submarines were poorly prepared for the coming battle. Perhaps submariners themselves, serving in the most silent of services, were principally to blame for not advertising their wares well enough. That is not something they can be accused of today: but whether the current advertisements can be wholly trusted is debatable; history suggests, as will be seen, that they may not be entirely accurate if put to the test of war.

Top Right
Bow view of HMS *M2*. She originally mounted a 12-inch gun but this was later removed to make room for a watertight hangar for a Parnell Peto seaplane. *M2* was lost with all hands on 26 January 1932, probably due to over-enthusiasm in attempting a rapid surface when the hangar door and access hatch were opened simultaneously. The Japanese took careful note of the design for their own World War II submarine aircraft carriers.

Bottom Right
The 12-inch gun, taken from a nineteenth century *Colossus*-class battleship and mounted in three M-boats (1917–18), was a far from stupid idea in view of torpedo unreliability at that time and much, much later! Although the gun had to be reloaded on the surface because the housing was not watertight, the submarine had only to broach to fire a round. Although never proved in action, each 850 lb shell would have done enormous damage both to ships and shore installations, the shells were a great deal cheaper than the cruise missiles developed in modern times from the same concept!

2 The Order of Battle

The indecision which dogged submarine development between the wars resulted in most boats that sailed to fight World War II being little different, basically, to those which had fought the first underwater war a quarter of a century earlier. They tended to be larger, longer-legged and a little more comfortable but there had been no giant strides forward. Propulsion was virtually unchanged and maximum speeds submerged were still around 8 knots.

Under the terms of the Versailles Peace Treaty of 1919 Germany was not only denied a U-boat arm but also prevented from maintaining an ability to design and construct a future underwater fleet. The latter prohibition was cleverly circumnavigated by German designers and constructors who had kept in close touch with each other after the Armistice. In 1930 they set to work on one submarine for Turkey and five for Finland.

The Turkish *Gur* was laid down in Spain in 1932 and furnished with machinery made principally in Holland. She was, in fact, the prototype for two Type IA, 862-ton U-boats built in 1936. These were not very successful, principally because they were over-engined; they were relegated to training duties at the outbreak of war. The Finnish submarines were much more interesting. *Jane's Fighting Ships* naively noted that the last of these, the 250-ton *Vessiko* was built as a 'private speculation'[1] by the German firm A/B Crighton-Vulcan at Turku on the south-western point of Finland. She was actually the model for the Type IIA U-boat. She was used, without ostentation, as a training vehicle from 1931 to 1936 for future German U-boat crews. Great care was taken to conceal the true purpose of *Submarine 707*, as she was known throughout the Baltic, and a rumour was put about that she was destined for Esthonia which she certainly was not. A German officer, Commander Barttenburg, and an Engineer Assistant were appointed to the Finnish Naval Staff and in the Spring of 1931 a German crew arrived in the special service ship *Grille* to take *707* through her trials.

With the exception of four engine-room ratings, the entire complement consisted of young German officers. Each springtime thereafter the *Grille* arrived with a fresh team for *707* and in this way a score of potential U-

The four submarines of the R-class all operated in the Mediterranean and although younger than the O-class were too large for service in that theatre of war. Three were lost due to enemy action and the fourth, *Rover*, acting as a floating power station to the damaged cruiser *York* in Suda Bay, Crete, was bombed and left unfit for further operational service. *Rainbow*, seen here in 1932, was sunk on her second patrol in a gun duel with an Italian submarine.

Right
Five classes of British submarines in commission in 1939 lying alongside at Fort Blockhouse with Portsmouth Harbour in the background. Two O-class and one U-class are in the far trot.

Below
Of six of this minelaying class only *Rorqual* survived, *Seal* being captured by the Germans and the other four, *Porpoise, Grampus, Cachalot* and *Narwhal* all being lost through enemy action. *Porpoise* and *Rorqual* were the most successful of the group, *Rorqual* spending three years of service in the Mediterranean.

boat officers each year received six months training in sophisticated attack methods at the expense of the Finns and without any complaint from the outside world.

Meanwhile, another very promising German design was being thoroughly tested by the supposedly Finnish *Vetehinen*-class. This 490-ton ocean-going boat was to become, with very little modification, the German Type VIIA.

The 1935 Anglo-German Naval Agreement cleared the way for open expansion of the U-boat arm. It was signed on 20 June and, during the preceding conference, Admiral Schuster admitted that 12 250-ton boats had already been laid down and 12 more would be added during the year. German tonnage was restricted to 35 per cent of British equivalents in all classes except for U-boats which could be built up to 45 per cent. The latter percentage meant that Germany could legitimately build U-boats totalling 24,000 tons. The Royal Navy at that time had 59 submarines in commission of which 20 were in the 1350 to 1805-ton bracket with one, HMS *X-1*, of 2425-tons. The remainder were between 410 and 760 tons and that was approximately the size the Germans were aiming for. The Admiralty may have reckoned on Germany only building 45 per cent of the British total in numbers rather than in tonnage which would have resulted in only 26 U-boats: it is hard to understand otherwise why the British, without consulting the Dominions or France, still less America, signed the agreement so readily.

Lessons of history less than twenty years old were forgotten; but absolute (and misplaced) confidence in the new Asdic underwater detection device apparently made the agreement seem perfectly acceptable. As it turned out, internal arguments within the German Navy were a much more effective restraint on the building programme than any treaty.

In July 1935, immediately after the signing of the Agreement, a certain Captain Karl Doenitz was suddenly ordered by his Commander-in-Chief, Admiral Raeder, to take over the submarine arm. Doenitz had had an undistinguished submarine career in World War I but was noted for exceptional leadership and organisational ability in the peacetime surface navy. He was not, at first, overmuch pleased by the idea of becoming the U-boat chief but Raeder was an accurate judge of character. It was to prove probably the most perceptive appointment made in the Armed Services of any nation before or during World War II.

Doenitz immediately applied himself to the task with a single-minded sense of purpose that was to endure unbroken for ten years and twenty days until finally, as head of the German Government, he authorised the signing of the instrument of surrender on 8 May 1945. But despite the unassailable logic he advanced for a fleet of 300 U-boats, only 46 boats were ready for action—a fortuitously large proportion of the 56 in commission—when at 1330 on 3 September 1939 the Naval High Command signalled: 'Commence hostilities against Britain forthwith.' Only 22 boats were suitable for service in the Atlantic. The rest, small 250-ton 'canoes', were for coastal work and could not contribute to Doenitz' unswerving aim to destroy trans-Atlantic shipping. Although larger long-range boats, in the proportion of one to three, were also needed the bulk of the U-boat fleet should, he reasoned, consist of small, quick-diving submarines with a low silhouette and a high speed on the surface where they would primarily operate. A slightly enlarged Type VII met these requirements admirably: the result was the Type VIIC and the first of the class were ready early in 1939. They displaced 769 tons on the surface and had an endurance of 8,850 miles at 10 knots with a maximum speed of rather more than 17 knots. With no periscope standards and a conning tower only 5.2 metres above the waterline, they were hard to see from an average ship beyond a few miles even in daylight; by night, end-on, they were practically invisible. They could dive in less than half a minute and could go down to 100 metres without strain and to just over 200 metres if hard-pressed. Their speed submerged was 7.6 knots for two hours, 4 knots for 80 hours or 2 knots for 130 hours. Depth and endurance at high speed were twice as good as in submarines elsewhere. Type VIIC U-boats were the principal weapons with which Doenitz, soon promoted to Admiral, set out to wage war on commerce.

In September 1939 Britain had 58 submarines but there were only 21 boats in home waters and five of these were more than ten years old. A further 11 boats were building but British submarine strength, in terms of availability where it was most needed, was less than that of Germany. Most pre-war exercises involved boats performing in the role of a loyal opposition: but commanding officers, especially on the China Station, had seized every opportunity of practising submerged attacks so that, at the outbreak of World War II, the majority were highly skilled professionals. It took time to call the eastern veterans back but when they returned they quickly made their mark.

The strategy and tactics adopted in the Royal Navy by Rear Admiral Submarines were diametrically opposed to those of his German counterpart. Doubtless he would have liked more boats (and he had more than enough trained officers); but numbers meant less than they did to Doenitz. RA(S) had no intention of embarking on surface pack-tactics like Doenitz who intended to direct groups of U-boats on to convoys; fast warships were the principal targets for the Royal Navy and the British War Plan disposed submarines along lines in individual patrol areas where, far from chasing targets, they waited for the enemy to come to them. Thus, in the Royal Navy of 1939 submarines were, in the Admiralty mind, little more than mobile mines.

Britain's world-wide commitments made Depot Ships necessary as well as bases and in 1939 four large, well-fitted ships were in commission. They were vital to British submarine strategy and the enemy, who had no such dependence, knew it. A depot ship had sufficient mess-decks, workshops, stores, torpedoes and provisions (including up to 4,800 dozen bottles of beer) to care for about 12 submarines. Unfortunately, whenever 'Mum' sailed sedately out of harbour she became a prize target. Her great length and slow speed made her easy to hit as the British found to their cost when HMS *Medway*, 580 feet long and making only 14 knots on her double-acting Doxford diesels, was sunk in the Eastern Mediteranean by *U-372* in June 1942.

Unfortunately, the most important British base, the island of Malta, was not fortified against predictable attacks from the air. It would have been a simple matter to build submarine shelters beneath the fortress as submariners had asked in 1936: the cost would have been about £300,000 (about the cost of one submarine); but the proposal was turned down by the Cabinet in July 1937. As the naval historian Captain Roskill remarked it 'was one of (Britain's) most expensive negligences'.

It was the quality of the officers and ratings in all services which decided the effectiveness of the submarines themselves. In Nazi Germany men were drafted to U-boats more or less irrespective of their own inclinations provided that they were medically fit.[2] But in the Royal Navy submariners were almost entirely volunteers. Out of 3,383 men mobilised in 1939 only 108 were pressed, although the ratio was to increase indicatively upwards as the war developed. Submarine pay and hard-lying money undoubtedly helped recruiting, nearly doubling the wage packet of many submariners. No upper limit was fixed for ratings but it was agreed that a captain should ideally be between twenty-five and thirty years old: he was arbitrarily (and sometimes wrongly) reckoned to be over-age at thirty-four, whilst the few who rocketed to command in their very early twenties were thought (unfairly in most cases) to lack judgement.

A handful of boats from other navies whose countries were threatened with German occupation flocked to join the British submarine service soon after the outbreak of war. They included the Polish minelayer *Orzel*, a brand new Dutch-built boat, and *Wilk* which had been constructed by the French firm of Augustin Normand in 1930. Both escaped from the Baltic. *Orzel*, interned by Esthonia in Tallin harbour, slipped her guards on 18 September 1939. Stripped of all navigational equipment, she eventually found her way to Rosyth in October using a home-made chart and arrived safely, after some unlooked for adventures and a gallant but fruitless patrol in the Baltic. From there the Poles made their way to Dundee where Allied non-British submarines were to gather for wartime patrols on a proper footing. The Norwegian *B-1* made an even more heroic effort to join the group. On 10 April 1940, the day after Norway was invaded, *B-1* cast off in a heavy snowstorm and bottomed in Narvik Fjord. She lay there for five days, surfacing briefly for orders that never came, but it was impossible to recharge batteries or replenish the air with so many German air and surface units above. On the fifth day the exhausted

Top Right
The Asdic set in HMS *Oswald* at the beginning of the war. This rudimentary set (not significantly improved for many years) was sufficient to tell when it was safe to come to periscope depth from deep, to transmit and receive signals by SST (Morse) and to count revolutions but if used to gain attack data luck played a major part.

Centre Right
The control room of a British U-class submarine at 60 feet. These outstanding boats were originally designed for A/S training but were quickly brought into operational use at the beginning of the war when their potential was realised.

Bottom Right
USS *Narwhal* showing clearly how large this submarine was. Eight re-load torpedoes were carried externally under the forward and after gun decks.

Captain at the periscope of an old US Navy submarine, probably a training boat, with no conning tower attack centre.

crew anchored their boat, trimmed it right down so that only the top of the conning tower was showing and went ashore to rest; but by daylight they could see that the conning tower was dangerously conspicuous so the First Lieutenant rowed out and climbed on board, opened one of the main vents, raced up the conning tower, shutting the hatch behind him, and left *B-1*, deserted, to settle on the bottom. The crew retreated on horse-drawn sleighs to Harstad. A month later they received secret orders to return and raise their boat. *B-1* was duly brought to the surface and, with rapid makeshift repairs, was able to head out to sea on 18 June. She arrived safely in the United Kingdom but, sadly, was found to be in too bad a state to be used for anything more than anti-submarine training which, nonetheless, was very valuable to the war effort. Most of her crew transferred to one of the three British U and V-class submarines made over to the Royal Norwegian Navy.

Most of the Dutch boats also avoided capture. Of their 27 commissioned submarines, 15 were in the East Indies but, between 12 and 16 May 1940, the 12 operational boats in Dutch home ports, together with two more which were not quite complete, safely reached the British submarine base at Fort Blockhouse, Gosport. Three were fitted with schnorchels, the first operational boats in the world to be so equipped, but the Royal Navy shortsightedly saw no need to adopt the device: it would have

proved invaluable in the Mediterranean. The Dutch also provided a merchant flagship, the *Columbia* which was converted to a depot ship at Dundee and for a year from August 1941 she mothered Allied submarines there.

By comparison with Germany and Great Britain, France and Italy had extraordinarily large submarine arms. Between the wars both governments had engaged in extensive building programmes, with France leading until 1930 when Italy started to overhaul her. It is not easy to perceive clearly the aims of either country and, in any case, they probably changed over the years; but the large submarines which France constructed, including the giant *Surcouf*, were more suited to the widely proclaimed (but seldom demonstrated) traditional French strategy of a *Guerre de Course* than to defensive warfare. France was consequently suspected of having failed to ratify the Washington Treaty of 1922 with regard to commerce-raiding by submarines. For long France, rather than Germany, had been England's traditional enemy and history probably coloured French naval planning. But the real reason for the large French submarine building programme was that submarines were the cheapest possible way of exercising sea power; and any nation that had a sufficient number was bound to receive due attention at the conference tables of the world. In September 1939 France had 77 boats in commission of which 38 were ocean-going, 32 coastal, six mine-laying and one, *Surcouf*, a cruiser. After the collapse of France, seven French submarines operated with the Free French naval forces which were based on Britain and four boats were taken over by the Germans. But the French boats were not all up to 1939 warfare standards; the *Narval's* machinery, for

instance, 'had to be heard to be believed'.[3]

When Italy entered the war in June 1940 no less than 84 submarines were operational: the remainder of the 150 boats commissioned were in refit or undergoing trials. They were markedly inferior to all German U-boats: comfort played too large a part in their design. They were, in the main, good-looking vessels, capable of showing the Italian flag with pride; but their huge conning towers made them easily visible on the surface and they were slow to dive, clumsy when submerged and poorly equipped. It was hard to avoid the impression that the Fascist submarine service was intended more for show than action. There was scant evidence of realistic pre-war exercises; and the very special teamwork demanded of an aggressive submarine crew was lacking in the Latin temperament although individuals were brave enough: the outstanding successes of Italian human-torpedo volunteers and swimmers were emphatically to prove that.

When Italian submarines arrived at Bordeaux to join forces with the German fleet in 1940 the first order from Doenitz was to 'cut short their towers to make them less visible'. That was unfortunate because some of the boat's cooking arrangements were built into the superstructure. However, the point was quickly taken care of. 'When they came', grinned a German U-boat commander, 'the Italian boats had *four* galleys—one for Officers, one for Chief Petty Officers, one for Petty Officers and one for the rest. Then, quite quickly,' the smile thinned, 'German advice prevailed. *One* galley was enough.' Italian submariners operating under German orders were not, perhaps, entirely happy!

Russian statistics were, as always, imprecise. But when the Soviet Union entered the war in 1941 there were probably well over 200 submarines in commission. The Russians had by far the largest submarine fleet in the world and it was entirely intended for defence. A fair proportion of the boats were newly built; but their designs were outdated and their weapon systems were antique. Due to Stalin's pre-war purges, only a quarter of the Soviet submarine officers had served for more than two years; and all submariners were governed by a system of centralised and very strict control which severely hampered their fighting ability. Successful submarine operations everywhere demanded freedom of action for commanding officers but that was denied by political commissars who watched every movement that a captain made. It was extremely unwise in the Soviet navy, even in peacetime, to admit that an operation had been a failure; so lessons were neither looked for nor learned. Technical and tactical

Depot ship HMS *Medway* with her flock

development suffered accordingly; and the potential of the vast Soviet underwater fleet was never to be realised.

Japan acquired her first submarines towards the end of the Russo-Japanese war in 1905. Thereafter, for many years, Japanese designs were based upon proven foreign types, especially the British L-class. Great emphasis was placed upon sea-going qualities in the rough waters around Japan but no particular purpose was evident in their submarines. Even when the first large trans-Pacific boats were built there were no concrete plans for their employment although the provision of aircraft in some implied reconnaissance for the surface fleet. However, the Imperial Navy eventually came to the conclusion that in the event of war with the United States (which by 1935 was regarded as inevitable) the Phillipines, Borneo and Indonesia should be invaded immediately; after that the Submarine Fleet would assume a defensive role aimed at the attrition of American naval vessels when the enemy fleet steamed northward, bent on retribution but in an exhausted condition. It was a strategy of the sort that is more likely to have been concocted in Staff Colleges than at sea; and it was to be proved wholly unrealistic.

At the London Naval Conference of 1930 the Japanese delegates fought for a larger submarine arm than the other major powers. The size and number of capital ships and aircraft carriers were limited by the conference but the building of submarines was thereby unintentionally stimulated.[4] In the

This chart, sketched from a souvenir of HMS *Maidstone*, shows how far-ranging and important a depot ship's support operations were in war.

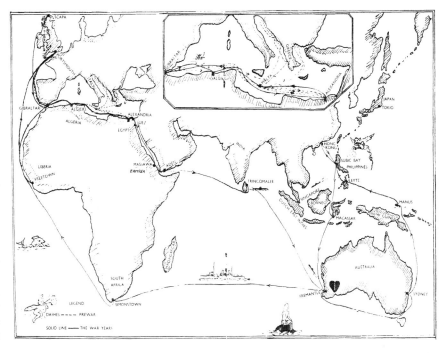

Top Left
Depot ship preparing for war operations.

Top Right
The torpedo body flat in HMS *Medway*. Of the additional 90 torpedoes being carried as deck cargo when *Medway* was sunk in 1942, 47 floated free and were saved.

Bottom Left
The bakery aboard a depot ship.

Bottom Right
Baths and laundry were the most popular reasons for a depot ship's existence!

end, Japan had to accept submarine parity with the United States and Britain, but in 1934 midget submarines began to be built under the direction of Captain Kishimoto Kaneji to swell the numbers. These prototype two-man, 49-ton craft, which carried two torpedoes, were credited with the exceptionally high underwater speed of 19 knots; if that was true they must have been difficult to handle. Special mountings to carry the midgets were fitted to a number of large submarines and they could be manned through a trunking without surfacing. There was no shortage of volunteers and, on the face of it, they were potent units; but in war they were to fail dismally. Meanwhile, irrespective of treaty limitations, plans were made for increasing the number of large boats as well.

On 8 December 1941, the Imperial Navy had 65 operational boats with a further 29 under construction. Of these, 48 were rated 'first class' and it was upon them that Admiral Yamamoto relied for carrying through a new plan for submarine employment. Instead of awaiting the arrival of a hopefully exhausted US fleet in Japanese controlled waters, Yamamoto now planned on a decisive fleet action, centred around his aircraft carriers, at the earliest possible moment. Submarines would not lie in wait for targets well clear of the surface action but would be closely tied to the fleet in the big battle itself. The decision was to have far reaching results during both the Pearl Harbour and Midway operations where Japanese submarines were robbed of their two greatest assets—surprise and freedom to manouevre.

In the United States submarines, as a strategic force, were not highly regarded before the war. A defensive strategy engendered the belief, copied in Japan, that the role of submarines was to sink warships advancing towards the unending coastline. This, in turn, generated peacetime exercises that were to be of little use in creating experience for the coming war and safety became the first consideration when exercising against high-speed naval targets. The danger of being rammed in peacetime could not be ignored when public opinion was sensitive and when, within the Navy itself, internecine conflicts were constantly at work. Exercises had not only to be safe; they had to be successful (on paper) in the light of the creed current in the USN that only excellence merited promotion. Consequently, when America was at last forced to go to war with 112 submarines, 64 of them elderly, their commanding officers were overcautious and the admirals were overconfident.

The submarines themselves were made up of widely assorted classes ranging from 520-tons upwards; but the tendency was to go for bigger boats with much greater comfort, larger crews, heavier weapon-loads and longer range, higher surface-speed capabilities than European boats. Sophisticated equipment, including radar and advanced fire-control systems, was given high priority but underwater performance and diving times were no better than elsewhere.

Between 1936 and 1941, building stabilised around Fleet submarines of the P and new (1937) S and T classes. All were rather more than 300 feet long and displaced from 2,000 to 2,370 tons with speeds around 20 knots on the surface. Complements ranged from 55 in the P-boats to 85 in the T-class and the crews were to become even bigger as the war went on. Two medium-sized boats were built, *Mackerel* and *Marlin*, but submarines smaller than the standard fleet-type found no favour in the fleet. The P-class and its successors had all-electric drive with four diesel-generators. Besides more important engineering advantages, diesel-electric propulsion did not drain the battery like direct-drive diesels (which could not, generally or reliably, be run astern) when manoeuvring in harbour. Hours of re-charging were thereby saved after entering harbour which reduced harbour watchkeeping, improved maintenance and enabled captains to be generous in allowing junior officers to gain valuable experience in ship-handling.

The comparative roominess of the large fleet boats, however, had an inbuilt disadvantage. It was much more difficult for a captain to maintain intimate contact with all that was happening throughout the submarine. He depended, sometimes far too much, on instrumentation (which was by no means always reliable) and, although no bad thing in the long term, he had to delegate a good deal of responsibility, especially to his 'Exec' who, much more than in other navies, was a true second-in-command. A submarine captain in the USN needed an exceptionally strong personality and roving habits, like Lcdr Dudley Morton in *Wahoo*, to imbue the whole crew with his own fighting spirit. Unfortunately, in 1941 personality and spirit were too often lacking and a sizeable proportion of USN peacetime captains were to fail the tests of war.

US Navy O-boat used for training. The practise of leaving hatches open and unwatched underway, even in harbour, was extremely unwise and it is strange to see it here in a training boat.

3 Mechanics

Control and trimming submerged was similar in all submarines and was not the black art that submariners made it out to be. It was very difficult to trim accurately enough to achieve exact neutral buoyancy (a 'stop trim') although all boats were designed so that, when fully manned, stored and fuelled, they would displace, when dived, their own weight in salt water of a specific density (the neutrally buoyant condition). In practice, a boat's bodily weight changed continually at sea as fuel, stores and weapons were used and as sea-water density altered. Density was significant and in some areas unpredictable but sharp changes could be helpful: HMS *Parthian*, for instance, was able to sit, stopped, on a layer for two-and-a-half hours while being hunted in the Mediterranean. Hull compressibility was also an important factor: instead of flooding in water to go deep it was necessary to pump out considerable quantities—typically 75 gallons for every 100 feet—to prevent a boat becoming negatively buoyant as it went deeper, compressed and so displaced less.

There were a number of compensating and trimming tanks in each submarine but only three were generally used when dived—the forward and after trimming tanks and a tank amidships. These allowed bodily weight and the trim angle (or pitch) to be adjusted. German U-boats used reduced high-pressure air to blow water from forward to aft and *vice-versa*. It was a quiet and simple method of balancing a boat; with the trim tanks at each end split in two, a pressure could be maintained in one tank of each pair and a cock had only to be opened on the appropriate line to send water from one set of tanks to the other. This method did, however, lead to minor air leaks and the occasional need for total tank-venting which could build up an undesirable air pressure inside the boat. Submarines in other navies used a small pump for the same purpose. Bodily weight was adjusted by an amidships tank, flooding into it direct from the sea by external pressure or pumping water out through a powerful main ballast pump which could also be used to discharge water from

any other tank or compartment. Separate bilge-pumps took care of the oily bilges which would have contaminated the main trimming lines and led to traces of oil floating to the surface in action.

Compensating and trimming tanks were mainly contained within the pressure hull. Fuel tanks were compensated, as fuel was used, by sea water admitted to the tanks themselves; the difference in specific gravities between oil and water resulted in a boat becoming heavier and this, too, had to be compensated by pumping water out.

The trim was calculated by simple arithmetic before leaving harbour and roughly checked by reading the draught marks at full buoyancy. If possible, a trim dive was carried out as soon as the 20-fathom line was crossed and, when dived thereafter, the trim was adjusted continually by trial and error. When diving it was only necessary to open

HNMS *O–14*: **engine room platform.**

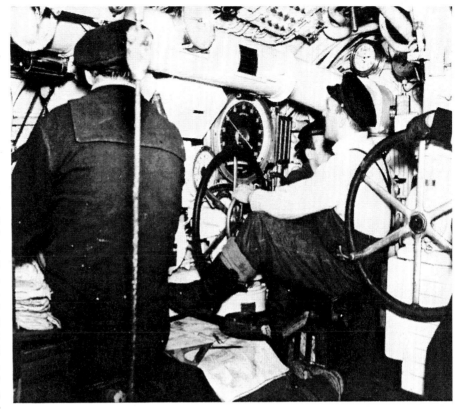

the main vents which allowed the supporting air in the main ballast tanks, mostly outside the pressure hull, to escape. Surface buoyancy, which differed greatly between classes, was thus destroyed and the boat, then in theory neutrally buoyant, was able to dive at an angle regulated by the forward and after hydroplanes whose effect naturally depended upon speed through the water. A special tank forward, 'Q' or 'Negative', was used to speed up the rate of diving and changing depth; it had a capacity of several tons, gave temporary bow-down negative buoyancy when flooded and was blown just before reaching the desired depth. It was then vented inboard, markedly increasing air pressure in the boat. Submarines were able to submerge fully from high speed on the surface in times varying, in most classes, from 27 seconds to 1 minute depending on the size of the boat and its course in relation to the sea and swell. Some of the larger types took considerably longer to dive, particularly the minelayers with external mine rails and, principally for this reason, large boats were dangerous to operate in restricted, heavily guarded inshore waters. If heading into a heavy sea, diving could be held up interminably and it was best to run on the surface with the sea abeam if possible. It was also much easier to keep periscope depth with a beam sea. Conversely, a steep sea or swell from ahead or astern could cause a submarine to broach from periscope

Top Right
Control Room of Dutch submarine *O-14* **(Lt Cdr G Quint). The British depth gauge shows the boat is at periscope depth (which was then measured from the surface waterline rather than from the keel as it is now). Dutch submarines fought with great distinction in the Mediterranean and Far East.**

Centre Right
HMS *Graph* **(ex** *U-570***) and HMS** *Simoom* **in 1943. The British S-boats were broadly comparable to the Type VIIC U-boats but were markedly inferior in diving depth and endurance at high speed submerged.**

Bottom Right
The upper conning tower hatch of HMS *Taku*. **The stirrup and clip fastenings were peculiar to British boats and made the hatch much easier to control when surfacing with a high pressure inside the boat, than to wheel-and-spider arrangement usual in other navies.**

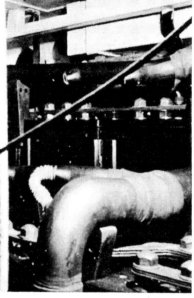

depth. There was also a danger of pooping on the surface with a following sea so that revolutions had to be increased or decreased to avoid making the same speed as the sea itself. Fortunately for submariners, it did not seem that these factors were understood by anti-submarine aircraft when assessing a submarine's course while attacking with bombs or depth-charges.

When changing depth normally a submarine's bow was simply pointed up or down by the hydroplanes which were also able to keep a boat level at the ordered depth at speeds down to about one and a half knots provided that the trim was not more than half-a-ton or so in error. If the trim was bad more speed had to be used; this drained the batteries needlessly so that good trimming was very important to a submarine's safety in more ways than one. The trimming officer was, naturally, a target for criticism by the whole crew, and especially the captain if the periscope dipped during an attack. One U-boat pricked the Chief Engineer's sensibilities more gently than most by putting on a recording of the well-known German song 'All right, we'll do it alright, we'll get the thing done yet' when he was endeavouring to catch a trim. Others, particularly in British boats, criticised the trim more crudely or asked sarcastically if somebody had forgotten to blow Q.

Men passing through the control room could change the fore-and-aft trim significantly and it was often a rule to ask permission before going either way. Sending men forward or aft at the rush was, in fact, an effective and rapid way of correcting a steep angle and many boats were saved in this way from plunging to the bottom under attack or when the trimming officer had simply got his sums wrong. Six men weighed the same as 100 gallons and could move much more

Top Left
Typical British motor room and switchboard: looking from aft in HMS *Pandora* **with the engine-room beyond.**

Centre Left
One of the main battery compartments in HMS *Oswald* **showing some of the ventilation arrangements vital for cooling the cells and dispensing potentially explosive hydrogen.**

Bottom Left
Control room of HMS *Upright.* **The hanging lights were supposedly shock-proof but seldom survived depth-charging.**

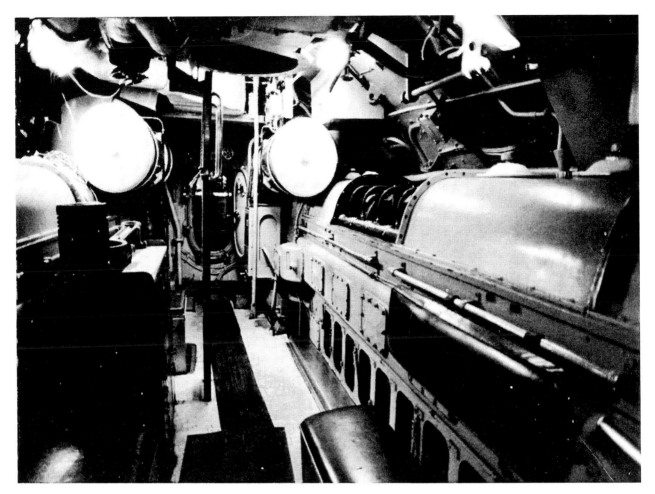

Top
The after engine room in a US fleet submarine showing clearly how much easier it was to keep clean than the equivalent in other navies.

Bottom Right
The engine room of HMS *Unruffled* **with its reliable Paxman Ricardo engines. In rough weather on the surface with the engines roaring and the boat pitching and rolling submarine life could be very grim.**

quickly than an equivalent amount of water passing along the trim line.

Diving depth depended, of course, on the strength of the pressure hull and this was a factor not only of its thickness but also on its circularity with the least number of hatch openings to spoil the line. German U-boat hulls, particularly the Type VIIC, were exceptionally strong and these boats could go twice as deep as most of their equivalents in other navies. This was due to their having well-shaped hulls between $\frac{3}{4}$-inch and $\frac{7}{8}$-inch thick instead of just over $\frac{1}{2}$-inch as in most British boats. That, in turn, was made possible by omitting certain features common to British submarines, which submariners would surely have given up if the advantages had been realised. Incredibly, it was insistence on a reliable magnetic compass in a certain position, to supplement the

Top Left and Right
Watertight doors (shown here in a US fleet boat) were not strong enough to resist pressure at any great depth and, in any case, the flooding of one compartment, in practically every class of submarine in all navies, prevented a submarine from diving safely by sheer weight of water. However, doors like this were sufficient to isolate compartments for escape from relatively shallow depths and were very useful to prevent the spread of fire or gas in the event of damage. Inter-compartment ventilation trunking and voice pipes could be shut off by valves which had the same resistence as the doors.

The hydroplane controls in USS *Cero*. The deep depth gauge above was shared by both operators. The lower of the two inclinometers registered up to 30 degrees but the deliberate use of steep angles was avoided because of equipment breaking loose, possible battery spillage and the fact that the bow (or stern) might be dangerously deep while the control room depth gauges still showed an acceptable depth.

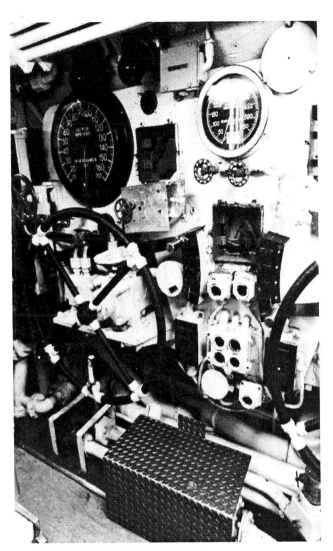

The diving controls and 'Christmas tree' in USS *Torsk*. Rows of red or green lights signified the state of major hull openings, vents and valves.

US submarines measured depth from the keel (see depth gauges) while British and most other Allied boats used the surface water line as a reference; this difference gave rise to a number of misunderstandings.

sufficiently serviceable gyro, that was much to blame for restricting the diving depth of British boats. The magnetic compass was positioned, outside the hull, vertically above the helmsman and British designers would not accept steel within seven feet of it although the Germans were content with three feet and accepted a moderate performance thereby. The conning and gun towers and their surrounding areas in British boats had therefore to be built of bronze which was extremely heavy and prevented thicker steel being used for the main hull. There were, of course, other factors. U-boats did not have so many internal watertight bulkheads (which did not contribute much to a submarine's safety in war) and they did not have special escape hatches (which, anyway, in war were

often locked externally in British boats to prevent them jumping when depth-charged). Germany also accepted a lower reserve of surface buoyancy. In other words, in the Royal Navy, unnecessary and unwarlike features which supposedly contributed to safety in peacetime actually militated against effective avoiding action and survival in war. In this and other structural and engineering matters there was reason to think that seamen, constructors and engineers in the Royal Navy found it difficult to communicate with each other; or else the Admiralty failed to set its sights on the right targets and priorities for fighting efficiency. In the latter respect the German Type VIIC had only four torpedo tubes forward and they could be included in a circular cross-section of the

hull; the six tubes demanded by the British, whether tactically justifiable or not, required an oval bow and hence weakened the structure.

The understanding between operators and technical experts was undoubtedly better in the US Navy where officers were all trained in engineering. However, the USN still did not achieve such effective, practical designs as the Germans who were ruthless in eliminating all but strictly *wartime* capabilities. The Germans were also prepared to sacrifice long-life economy for immediate operational benefits. Their batteries, for instance, had a short and thus expensive life; but they had an exceptionally high capacity which, although making them rather slow to charge and apt to overheat, endowed the Type VIIC with

virtually double the submerged performance of comparable Allied submarines.

There were two very different kinds of diesel-propulsion. The US Navy favoured diesel-electric drive with diesel-generators connected to the battery which in turn drove mechanically independent main motors. The system allowed any number or combination of the four diesel engines in fleet boats to be run at one time and made running maintenance at sea much easier with plenty of power always in hand; the advantages in harbour have already been noted. Moreover all-electric propulsion enabled engines to be built for steady, optimum high-speed running unrelated to propellor-shaft revolutions. American main motors, too, were designed to run at quite high speeds which were electrically efficient; but they carried the penalty of noisy reduction-gearing between them and the propellors. The Royal Navy only adopted a diesel-electric system in the U and V classes although these too could be clutched for direct drive if required. Most other submarines everywhere, including German U-boats, had direct drive. This meant that a common shaft ran from the engine to the propellor through the motor (which doubled as a generator) with or

HNMS *O-19* using her schnorchel on trials. When the German and, much later, other navies adopted the device the exhaust was discharged below water. As late as April 1944 the US director of Naval Intelligence wrote that 'although this device might be used in dangerous areas, the likelihood that it will take in water in almost any sea is felt to make its use impractical'.

The most usual type of schnorchel fitted in German U-boats.

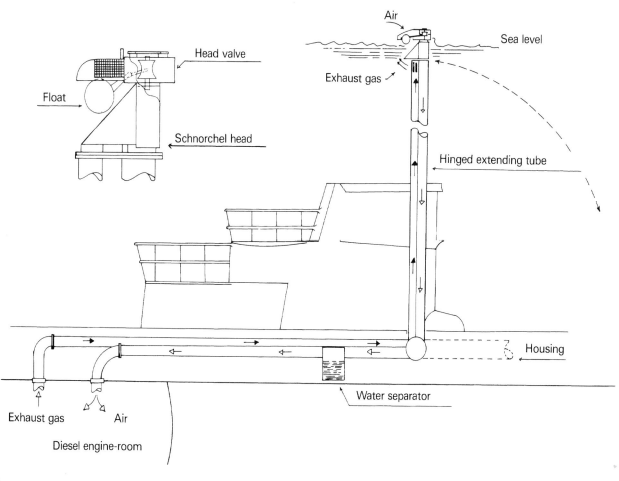

without the tail shaft connected by a clutch for a running or a standing charge. The principal disadvantages were that the engines had to be clutched in or out when surfacing and diving; and that engine-speeds had to be directly regulated to the required propellor rpm which implied mechanical inefficiency and imposed limitations on the type of diesel engines installed.

There was a simple way of improving efficiency and hence economising on fuel with direct drive; it was almost always used by U-boats but was not appreciated, apparently, by other submariners even when an extended range was badly needed. This was to propel on the surface on one screw at a moderate speed around nine knots with a running charge on one side and a standing charge on the other. This gave the Type VIIC, helped by twin rudders, a surface

endurance 10 per cent greater than at the same speed on both shafts. Pre-war engineering trials by the Royal Navy, conclusively demonstrating this not very difficult concept, were largely disregarded for no known reason by submarine operational staffs.

On balance the German Type VIIC was thought by many submariners to be the best design anywhere for its purpose: when eventually equipped with a schnorchel it was outstanding. Even critics who said it was cheap and nasty (an unwittingly flattering description) had to admit that going to sea in HMS *Graph* (ex *U-570*) was an exhilarating experience which, frankly, was more than most submariners could say about their own boats in World War II. The underlying reason for the Type VIIC's comparative excellence was not, however, due to any particular German technological ability; it

Top Left and Right
Parts of pre-fabricated Type XXI U-boats lying on the quayside at Hamburg after Germany's surrender.

Centre Left and Right
Type XXI U-boat stern sections photographed while under construction at Hamburg in January 1945. German U-boat construction was always rapid and reliable but the methods which were designed for the new electro-boats were exceptionally advanced.

was simply that this class of submarine was built as a carefully planned 'package deal': it was a complete *weapon system* intended for war and war alone.

29

4 Life Below

Submariners created an artificial world in which they lived for weeks and even months on end. There were few complaints that amounted to anything more than the traditional grumbling enjoyed by seamen everywhere, and even that was overridden by unmistakeable pride. Men not only learned to adapt physically; they also, to a greater or lesser degree, reshaped their personalities. It was only the few that were unable to make these changes within themselves who were genuinely unhappy. Submariners were always packed together, frequently exhausted and quite often terrified; but provided they believed they were doing a worthwhile job—as a team—they were content. Habitability, or lack of it, was not a factor that greatly influenced morale; and there was no evidence to suggest that, given equal operational success, the crew of a relatively comfortable American fleet submarine was any happier or more determined than the 'Sea Lords' crowded together amidst the squalor of a German U-boat on a long-range tropical patrol.

Morale depended on success; and success depended, ultimately, upon the captain—far more than the weapons and material under his command. Men were willing to risk their lives with an aggressive, capable captain although they certainly did not think in such straight-forward terms. Danger was not foremost in their thoughts and it was rare, even at the worst period in the British Mediterranean campaign or when the Atlantic tide turned against the U-boats, for anyone to consider that his own boat might not return; or at least that is what most wartime submariners, looking back, say now. It did not matter if the captain was no gentleman (whatever that might have been); or if he drank too much in harbour; of if he brought the wrong girl to a party; or even if he was harsh and overbearing: if he hit the target and brought the boat back intact, his personal qualities were overlooked. But if he was weak or hesitant the discomforts of life below broke surface and the foundations of a unique and demanding form of discipline crumbled.

It was often the case that adversity, which included appallingly bad living conditions and moments of extreme danger, welded a crew so tightly together that, as Theodore Roscoe, the renowned US Naval historian, says of USS *Puffer*'s ordeal on 9 October 1943, 'men who subsequently made several successful patrols on *Puffer* were still outsiders—not members of the gang. They had not been through *the* depth-charging.'

Every submarine acquired, one way or another, its own personality but the welding together of a crew still left ample margin for individual eccentricities that varied even more widely than the conditions, internal and external, under which these remarkable men served.

German U-boats were not designed for comfort; they were built for action. Doenitz ensured that his men had the best of everything available but his boats were entirely practical. Everything was subordinated to fighting ability. One boat of a class was mechanically the twin of another which greatly simplified training and maintenance. They were not built for a long life; but that was not because of disregard for life itself. The boats, like their crews, were intended only for war; and no war would last for twenty years—which was the designed life of Allied submarines.

A Type VIIC U-boat sailing for a long patrol carried the bulk of its provisions stacked along the passageways to form a false deck. Clothing was wedged behind piping and into every corner. There were two heads but one of these was also packed with stores and in no sense could the one remaining be called a convenience, let alone a comfort station. The stench of oil fuel and human bodies pervaded everything and in heavy weather seasickness contributed its own foul odour. Fortunately, a submariner's sense of smell had a knack of deserting him—at least until the conning tower hatch was opened. It would have been pointless, at sea, to insist on uniforms but the German cold-weather leather gear and oilskins were superior, for their purpose, to anything issued in other navies including the USN. After the fall of France, when huge quantities of Allied materials were captured by the advancing German armies, British battledress proved particularly popular in U-boats[1] but the 'Sea Lords' wore what they liked and only the captain was distinguished by the white cap which he donned on formal occasions.

In the bitter Atlantic winter it was impossible to find any clothing that would entirely keep out the cold and wet, especially when a boat was racing at top speed through high seas with the low bridge structure on which Doenitz insisted. The bridge was continually swamped and there was a real danger of being washed off despite safety harnesses: U-706 lost two men overboard on her first patrol. It needed drive, spirit and outstanding leadership to claw ahead of a convoy in the teeth of an Atlantic gale. Cooking, for long periods, was out of the question and it was then that the long, spicy sausages, hanging incongruously from the deckhead amongst the torpedo tubes, were most appreciated.

Kk Wolfgang Lueth told of life below when speaking on the 'Problems of Leadership in a Submarine' to a convention of Naval Officers at Weimar on 17 December 1943. He was talking primarily of his experiences in command of U-181.

'It is my job as a submarine commander to sink ships. To do this I need a co-operative crew so that everything clicks . . . life aboard is monotonous for long periods. For many long weeks one must be able to bear failures, and when depth charges are added life becomes a war of nerves . . . life aboard a submarine is unnatural and unhealthy . . . there is no constant change between day and night for the lights have to burn all the time . . . the captain must attempt to compensate for these disadvantages as far as possible . . . there is no regular time for sleeping, since most of the fighting is done at night. Continuous responsibility rests with the captain for weeks and he must be alert at all times.'

Most of Lueth's Petty Officers were married and 'the rest were honestly engaged'. He considered that an advantage: 'though I know that a woman can break a man's fighting spirit, I also know that she can give him strength, and I have often observed that married men return from their leave particularly well rested for a new mission.' That was very true and British submariners, more than any, benefited from wives who threw all security to the winds and came to be near them whenever they could guess their port of

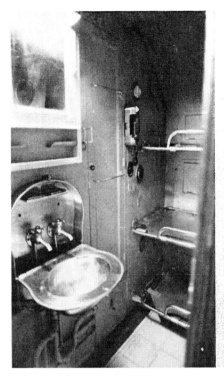

return. Indeed, submariners everywhere, in or out of wedlock, drew strength from the girls they left behind—and they were all too often left behind for ever. Those widows, wives and sweethearts deserve to be remembered.

Lueth had his own ideas about punishment. If china was broken the mess attendant had to eat out of a can for three days. Minor misdemeanours resulted in a man being deprived of smoking or, if he was a scat fan (a popular card game) he was forbidden to play for three days. One man who took more than his fair share of the rations was given 'the silent treatment' for two weeks. After that

period the case was closed.

Lueth stressed the need for a precise routine being adhered to. It was a matter of honour for the watch to be relieved on time. In submarines everywhere, in fact, unpunctual reliefs caused more quarrelling than any other human failing. Waiting an extra three minutes on a sea-swept bridge bordered the bounds of tolerance and reason.

Alcohol was not normally allowed in a U-boat but the crew could 'take a swig from the bottle now and then on special occasions, as when a steamer is sunk, if it is someone's birthday or if somebody gets soaked while working on the upper deck.' During an attack a 'Victory bottle' was uncorked in anticipation and the Victory March was prepared for playing as the seconds passed. If, after two minutes, there was no explosion the waiting was ended with a crew-chorus of 'Schiet!', unmistakable in any language.

During supper in *U-181* there was an evening concert of records. Sundays started with the popular German tune 'Yes, this is my Sunday song, to stay in bed at least till ten'; and if anybody had any clean clothes left he changed into them. The evening concert ended with the *Abendlied* sung by the Regensburg Domstatzen choir. Before sailing every man brought on board enough illustrated magazines to make up a general pool which distributed six new ones each Sunday. (Some American boats adopted the same practice; if anyone cheated by looking at the comic strip ahead of time he was treated 'silently' like Lueth's offenders.)

The head, noted Lueth, was sometimes a problem when there were inexperienced hands aboard who did not know how to work it. A notice was installed to 'make it short' and there was a notebook which every visitor had to sign. If the head was not clean, the last man who signed it had to make it so. The little verses in the book gradually became so numerous that they could 'fill half an evening of entertainment'.

There were occasionally cases of venereal disease—by no means limited to German submarines—which might be cured by drastic treatment on board; but in *U-181* shore leave was stopped without warning three days before sailing so that men would not 'make a last quick visit to a whore house'. This precaution was probably neglected by another captain who, on return to harbour 'would form up his men and, placing himself at their head, march them to the local brothel'[2] Lueth forbade nude pictures because 'if you were hungry you should not paint bread on the wall'. Allied submariners might have thought he was worrying too much about sex and submariners; sex reared its head in submarines everywhere but conditions at sea were not suitable for serious salaciousness! In harbour, of course, things were different .... Venereal disease was always a problem for submariners living in close quarters and symptoms seldom appeared until after a boat had sailed. Prophylactics were issued free but if, as British submariners maintained, they were made from disused, heavy duty bicycle tyres, they may have been discarded with unfortunate results. The German High Command viewed the increasing number of cases in French ports with alarm. By 1942 it was regarded as cowardice before the enemy to become infected and the victim rendered

himself liable to hard labour for up to ten years. The logic behind this harsh rule lay in the ease with which those who did not wish to sail in a U-boat could contract the disease; but there was little evidence that the excuse was deliberately sought.

U-boat officers were not allowed to listen to American or British jazz. Whether they liked it or not had nothing to do with the matter; 'they simply must not like it, just as a German man must not like a Jewess. ...' Lueth was a devoted Nazi and felt that his men's 'national socialist spirit with revolutionary ardour' gave them an important advantage over the Anglo-Americans; but, that apart, his brand of leadership would have been admirable in any navy.

Not all U-boat captains were like Lueth. One captain of *U-606* rewarded a trivial offence, such as the purloining of a packet of cigarettes, with a term in prison or on the Russian Front. This captain, weak and inefficient, was accompanied by a tyrannical First Lieutenant and morale was poor. Shortly before Christmas 1942, *U-606* limped into Brest with major defects resulting from a disorganised dive when threatened by a destroyer. On New Year's Eve the petty officers went politely to wish their captain a happy new year. They found that a party was in progress and on opening the wardroom door saw a vast array of bottles, some extremely dishevelled officers and a number of partly or entirely naked women. After a few moments of shocked amazement, one of the petty officers spat out a 'short but vulgar word' and slammed the door. The captain, however, had had the forethought to invite the Flotilla Commander to the party and the affair was eventually hushed up.

The crew of *U-606* were not entirely confident when they put to sea for what was to prove their last cruise on 3 January. The First Lieutenant's nerve gave way during a counter-attack when *U-606* broke surface after a dangerously deep dive to well beyond 200 metres while avoiding a Polish destroyer: he lost control of himself and ran through the boat, trying to get out through the after hatch. Later, after a bizarre series of incidents on the surface under gunfire from the Polish destroyer *Burza* and the American *Campbell*, most of the crew abandoned ship but the First Lieutenant, Engineer Officer and a handful of ratings stayed below until the firing died away; then they came on deck and kept the cold out with a meal of sausages and champagne laced with rum. Just before they were taken off by the Allied ships, a Petty Officer seized the opportunity to pay off old scores. He went up to the First Lieutenant, saying 'I have waited a long time to do

this', and hit him hard across the face. He then jumped overboard. One of the other survivors was heard to cry 'What sins have I committed in my life that I should be sent to such a boat.' The story of *U-606*[3] was extraordinary and, happily for Doenitz, exceptional.

Much was made by the Allies from 1943 onwards about a supposed decline in U-boat morale. It was wishful thinking. U-boat men, with very few exceptions, continued to live their life below with the same cheerful acceptance of its hardships until the bitter end.

British commanding officers did not air their dedication as openly as Lueth. There were some flamboyant characters amongst them and the best recognised that, like it or not, they were in show business of a kind; but, whether hamming it up or not, a calm confident act (for, often, it was no more than an act) was essential. Usually they advertised their beliefs and successes in rather jerky understatements. It was not customary to extol Winston Churchill or to sing 'Land of Hope and Glory'. In fact, patriotic music and lectures were not considered necessary to enliven the crew in a British submarine which was a little—a very little—more comfortable than a German U-boat except for the tiny British U-class which bore the brunt of the underwater war in the Mediterranean. A good picture of one of these small submarines was painted by Signalman Gus Britton in a letter home from HMS *Uproar* in the Mediterranean in 1943:

'We have lockers about the size of coffins and also two smaller ones and a small table in the fore-ends. Hanging from the "ceiling" there are about fifteen hammocks so if you want to move around you have to do so in a crouched position. In one corner there is a wash-basin and to use it you have to squeeze behind the tail of a torpedo and put a hand either side of the coxswain's hammock. Potatoes and cabbages are piled in one corner and, as it is as damp as Eastney beach, after six days there is a horrible smell of rotting vegetables and refuse is only ditched at night; and on top of that there is the smell of unwashed bodies. .... At the moment we are doing about eighteen hours dived every day so you can guess it is pretty thick at night. Before I go any further don't think that I am complaining because I really love submarines and this sort of life and I wouldn't swop it for anything.

'What a blessed relief when, at night, comes the order "diving stations" and about ten minutes later the order "blow one and six". The boat shudders as the air goes into the ballast tanks and then up she goes! I am at the bottom of the ladder in the darkened control room and sing out the depth which I can see on the submarine's gauge—25 feet—20—15—10—5; and then the Captain opens the hatch and up rushes all the foul air just like a London fog[4] and if I don't hang on I would go up

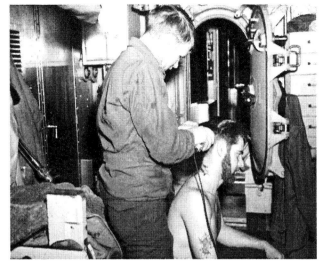

Life below in USS *Stickleback*. (*Stickleback* was lost when she was rammed and sunk by USS *Silversteen* off Honolulu on 29 May 1958. The entire crew of 82 was saved.)

with it as well. Beautiful, marvellous air . . . we are provided with some top-notch waterproof gear[5] but the water always seems to find a weak spot to trickle into. Up on the swaying bridge, with a pair of binoculars which you try to keep dry to have a look round between deluges of water, soaked and frozen and saying to yourself "why the **** did I join!" Then, when you are relieved, you clamber down the ladder, discard all the wet gear and go into the fore-ends, have a cup of cocoa, turn in and, as you fall asleep, you think "well its not such a bad life after all."'

During the critical years from January 1940 to November 1942, the British Submarine Service had the good fortune to be commanded by Admiral Max Horton who had had a most distinguished record in submarines during World War I. His intimate understanding of life below conferred a significant advantage over senior commanders in other navies. Max Horton was a well-matched opponent for Karl Doenitz and was ultimately to beat his U-boats when he left submarines and headed the anti-sub-

marine war as Commander-in-Chief Western Approaches from November 1942 onwards. But Horton's ruthless insistence on efficiency did not make him popular. In September 1941 he summarised his ruthlessly high standards in an address to all officers and men in harbour at Malta:

'. . . it is not a kindness to overlook slackness or mistakes. It is really great cruelty to do so—cruelty to wives and relatives of the man you let off and his shipmates and to yourself. There is no margin for mistakes in submarines: you are either alive or dead.'

Like Doenitz, Horton did his best to ensure that his submariners had the best of everything despite wartime difficulties. Admiralty Fleet Order 3072/42, at his insistence, made it clear that no food-rationing for submarines was to be enforced. This worried the Paymasters. The Superintendent of the Malta Victualling Yard observed worriedly that 'the only consideration is presumably that of cost' and a Paymaster

Lieutenant noted with alarm that the General Mess Allowance was 'exceeded by some four pence per man per day': it was cheap at the price if the Captain of the First Submarine Flotilla was correct in minuting that 'at a conservative estimate these men (his submariners) eat at least eight pounds daily.'

However, submarine menus were scarcely appetising. The coxswain, who was responsible for messing in British boats, had little or no training in catering (although he was carefully instructed in how to distinguish horseflesh from other meat) and was mainly worried about keeping his books straight. A qualified cook was not always carried; and even if he was, his task was not easy. Night was often turned into day on patrol so that cooking could be done while on the surface; but the heat in the galley at night was still fierce and sweat was freely mixed with other ingredients which included oil fuel and cockroaches. The bread embarked on sailing soon grew stale and after ten days even the most parsimonious coxswain was forced to admit that cutting off successive layers of green mould on the outside of each loaf left too little edible crumb to make the job worthwhile. The solitary chef then added baking to his repertoire and the delicious aroma which resulted almost overcame, for a brief half-hour, the hideous smells that normally pervaded the whole boat. With fresh water strictly rationed and seldom available for washing, except in a communal, greasy bucket, the chef, after a session of

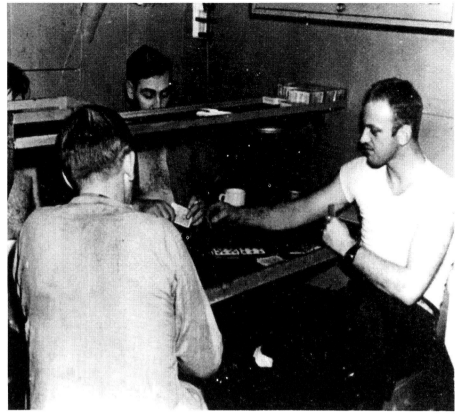

Off watch in USS *Parche*

A cake like this one, in an American submarine, was very seldom found in British boats where the ultimate delicacies were Cheese Oosh (a flat, leaden form of soufflé), HITS (Herrings in Tomato Sauce) and Baked Beans ('Windy Beans', known as *Haricots Musicales* in French submarines).

kneading dough or mixing rissoles, was apt to be the only man on board with clean hands—but that was only *after* his mixing operations were complete. . . .

Favoured British items were HITS (herrings in tomato sauce), Palethorpe's precooked sausages (snorkers), Baby's Heads (tinned steak-and-kidney puddings) and Train Smash which was a plateful of tinned Harris' bacon, each slice neatly separated by greaseproof paper, canned tomatoes and scrambled dried eggs (35,840 breakfast portions to a ton of egg powder, much more easily transported to a remote submarine base than 3,000 dozen eggs). When eaten for breakfast in red lighting, guts-and-blood Train Smash was devoid of all colour. For an evening meal, Cheese Oosh—properly speaking 'Hoosh' (an Eskimo word), derived from the Canadian Navy—was the ultimate in high living. This dish, made from a recipe mercifully known only to a few, was a deliberately flat and solid soufflé; it was roughly equivalent in density to the chocolate 'Brownies' which thudded heavily onto mess tables in the US Navy around the middle of a favourable forenoon.

Rum was issued at the rate of one-eighth of a pint per day per man but this did not include officers who never drank at sea (although they made up for it in harbour). It was a constant problem to know when to issue spirits: a tot of 120 proof rum could have an interesting effect on a man already tired, short of oxygen and over-supplied with carbon-dioxide during a long dive. Junior ratings were supposed to have their tot mixed with two parts water to prevent it being kept; but rum was usually issued neat on the questionable grounds of it then being less soporific. Ratings sufficiently removed from the control room sometimes saved up their rum rations in a 'blitz bottle' for consolation during a depth-charge hammering. Since every man, during a submarine's commission, drank seven and three quarter gallons of rum, its transport and storage presented a sizeable security problem. Rum containers suffered an uncommon amount of 'breakage' in transit, and, on board, a generous amount of 'spillage' was allowed for by the Admiralty.

British food was adequate if not imaginative although stewed prunes and kippers for breakfast on the first day out in a list of meals prepared by one Supply Officer was inventive enough; that must have stifled criticism from the start! The principle difficulty lay in getting rid of the waste. Gash of all kinds was pushed into reeking buckets and bags and ditched, as a carefully planned evolution, on surfacing. Over-flowing containers were hauled up the swaying conning tower in

Top Left
The forward mess in HMS *Tempest.*

Top Right
The forward torpedo compartment of *U-552*, **the famous Red Devil boat which, under the command of Erich Topp, was the third highest scorer of the war, sinking nearly 200,000-tons of Allied shipping. Turning-in fully dressed was usual in boats everywhere because the crew were liable to be called to diving or action stations at any moment and every second counted.**

Bottom Left
The crew of HMS *Graph* **(ex** *U-570*) **were hand picked, older and more experienced than usual. The mess-traps in this photograph were decidedly British!**

Bottom Right
The game of uckers, as played in submarines, was not at all the same as the polite and gentle game of ludo played ashore!

near darkness on the end of a rope and the contents, weighted to make sure they sank quickly, were jettisoned over the side as quickly as possible so as to reduce the period of vulnerability during which the boat might lose valuable seconds in diving. Inevitably, disgusting garbage was spilt as buckets caught on the ladder rungs; it was a messy operation but gave the crew a cathartic feeling of relief when it was over.

The heads were a continual hazard and in some boats they were open to view adjacent to living spaces. Blowing the contents out to sea when submerged required the permission of the officer-of-the-watch because of tell-tale bubbles; and no less than eleven distinct operations were required. A mistake resulted in an unpleasant occurrence known as 'getting your own back'. One German boat, *U-1206*, was actually lost as a result of the captain himself (Kptlt Schlitt) making an error in the drill which resulted in a flood of seawater penetrating the battery compartment below and generating chlorine gas: *U-1206* was depth-charged by an aircraft when it broke surface to ventilate and the boat had to be

abandoned.

Life below was similar for most Allied submariners; but the French, particularly, enjoyed something approaching real cuisine despite having to use, for the most part, basic British provisions. Good wine, of course, helped. Perhaps it was for fear of spoiling the palate that smoking was forbidden at all times in French boats. British Liaison Officers, Signalmen and Telegraphists were embarked in Allied boats not to assist in their operations, let alone give advice, but to ensure the security of British signal procedures and ensure that orders and signals in English were properly understood. Sub-Lieutenant Ruari McLean in FF Submarine *Rubis* reported that '*Rubis* is a French submarine, not a Free French one . . . patriotism and loyalty is not to de Gaulle (who, however, they admire) but to France and is as strong as an Englishman's to England . . . if they are captured by Germans they may not be shot but if they are captured by Vichy Frenchmen they certainly will be shot . . . they are fighting Germany for France not for Britain. . . .'

Life below in *Rubis* circulated around vigorous arguments and excellent food. The French were constantly critical of all English habits and the Liaison Officer came under fire at every meal for eating from the back of his fork and for drinking soup from the side of a spoon. Spirited discussions included the possibility that the King of England was a Jew and that the papacy was invalid for a number of imaginative reasons. (No serious submarine conversation anywhere was impeded by unnecessary facts or inhibitions). On one memorable occasion there was a detailed debate on how best to furnish a bedside table for a honeymoon. McLean, who was well liked anyway, was accepted into the company with more interest than had, until then, been evident when he produced a parcel sent from his (maiden) aunt from New York: unwrapped, it proved to be a selection of six celebrated erotic novels. Rousselot, the Captain, claimed he could smell perfume on them.

The chef in *Rubis* was a genius called Gaston and he had interests ashore outside his galley. He had liquid, pathetic eyes that went down particularly well with the women of Dundee and he was currently sleeping with both a mother and her daughter. Gaston produced his greatest culinary masterpiece in August 1941 when *Rubis*, badly damaged and unable to dive, had crossed the German minefields in the North Sea and was at last under escort by the Royal Navy and RAF. The whole crew came onto the casing because a battery fire made it impossible to remain below; the upper deck galley fire was lit, and Gaston went to work. The officers very properly took their meals abaft the conning tower and the crew were relegated to the casing forward. Dinner started with soup, accompanied by port or sherry, and was followed by cold ham, cucumber and salad on silver dishes, anchovies, spring onions, hard-boiled eggs, hot French tinned peas and new potatoes. Fruit salad and dried apricots washed down with two bottles of white burgundy were offered as a sweet; and the picnic concluded with coffee and cognac as the sun went down. It was an excellent example of how the French were able to put war in its proper perspective.

It is difficult, even now, to form an accurate picture of life below in Soviet submarines. British submariners operating from Polyarnoe found that the base was dismal and certain essentials were lacking. Commander G P S Davies RN begged Admiral Horton on 13 November 1941 for 'a supply of bumph (service brown) to be sent to us as opportunity offers. It is unknown in this country and Admiralty Fleet Orders are liable to give one piles'.

There were frequent air attacks on the base at Polyarnoe and the Russian Commander-in-Chief worked in one of a number of shelters tunnelled into the solid granite rock. Life was hard. It was forbidden to sell liquor to naval officers and ratings on the base but the edict seems to have been avoided because Captain Third Rank Zhukov managed to come by plenty of the hard stuff somehow and was relieved from the command of *K-21* for his addiction to the bottle ashore. Red wine was sometimes issued to submariners but the normal ration of alcohol was 100 grams (3.5 ounces) of vodka at noon each day. Food in Russian boats was dull, even by British standards, according to a Royal Navy stoker who was victualled for six months in a Soviet submarine; but he was probably missing the huge family-economy size bottles of tomato ketchup and brown sauce that decorated all British mess tables. Herring figured largely on the menu in Soviet boats but the celebration meal prepared on 5 December 1941, Constitution Day, by the cook of submarine *D-3* was special and devoid of fish. The cook, according to the Division Commander, 'went out of his way to turn the ration of groats and canned beef into a dinner worthy of the occasion', while somebody else prepared the traditional borsch.

Electric radiators—30 in the large K-class—were installed for keeping crews warm in winter at sea and steam pipes were led from shore in harbour. These measures did nothing to dispel the chill emanating from commissars who wore uniform similar to other officers but had vermilion between the stripes and no oak leaves on the cap. A commissar was responsible for welfare, food, pay, routine, punishment, requests, advancements, leave and, above all, the political instruction of the ship's company. He also kept a fatherly eye on the political leanings of the officers and countersigned orders but not (it was thought) actual operation orders. Captain, later Rear Admiral I Kolyshkin (a submarine Division Commander during the war) made several rather endearingly naive references to commissars in his memoirs, amongst them one who 'gloomily frowning, with brows angrily drawn together, looked as if he were always discontented . . . in reality he was the kindest of men . . .' This commissar (Gusarov) apparently stayed on the bridge 'almost the whole night long'. In this respect he outdid the captain and 'nobody knew when he slept. In the daytime he could be seen . . . presiding over a short meeting of agitators, having a talk with the editorial board of the wall-newspaper or simply talking to the men in his taciturn but extremely sincere manner.'

The icy cold Soviet winters and the long-lit summer days were far from ideal for submarine operations of any kind. Twelve days on patrol, with a total of seventeen days out, were all a crew could be expected to undertake with reasonable efficiency. Conditions in Russian submarines were probably far worse than those of their Allies but, to Russian sailors, they were so much better than those endured by the civilian population that they may have seemed idyllic. A particular pleasure for Russian crews was to come ashore and watch films like Snow White or Robin Hood (both with Socialist overtones) provided by the British Staff and approved by the Communist Party.

American sailors had the best of everything and would never have tolerated sub-standard conditions although there was a tendency, especially amongst the officers, to adopt a frontiersman attitude to life below to emphasise its ruggedness. Stubble-darkened jowls were, in fact, quite unnecessary: Kleinschmidt electrically operated distillers produced about 700 gallons of water each day and American submariners, unlike those in other navies, were not short of water for washing; many boats carried a commercial washing machine and it was possible to wear clean clothes throughout a long patrol. Efficient Freon air-conditioning plants were also fitted and the British Assistant Naval Attache in Washington remarked that there was a 'noticeable absence of smells from cooking, smoking or other gases' and that 'the well-known submarine fug is never pesent as long as the plant is kept running'. Smoking was usually controlled but the air conditioning was said (wrongly) to prevent the atmosphere from becoming foul if the crew were only allowed to smoke for twenty minutes in every hour when dived. Air-conditioning had the obvious advantage of keeping the boat cool but, much more importantly, the dehumidifying effect reduced the number of electrical defects suffered in other navies due to damp. This last invaluable advantage was not, however, noted by British visitors—or, at any rate, the submariners amongst them did not think it worth reporting—while American submariners took sound engineering practices for granted and did not trouble to point them out.

After a week at sea, the BNA reported that vitamin pills were issued to the crew every day and 'a noticeable improvement in health has resulted and, in particular, they appear to help in relieving constipation.' That was doubtful: it was the sophisticated heads which helped in relieving this common submarine problem; in the modern boats, instead of

Fore-ends of typical U-boat on war patrol. Despite the comparatively luxurious food and happy smiles, life in a U-boat was all too often grim and short. Well over 700 boats were lost on operations and 784 were lost in all; some 30,000 men went with them to the bottom out of 39,000 serving in U-boats during the war.

the bridge must be *completely* full. Only one (coloured) steward was able on every occasion to meet his requirements: the rest invariably spilled the contents during the long and difficult journey up the conning tower ladders. At the end of the commission the executive officer at last persuaded the steward to reveal his secret. The hugh ebony face split into a grin. 'Well, ah guess ah can tell you now,' he beamed, 'ah always takes a good mouthful at the bottom of the tower and spits it right back where it belongs when ah gets to the top—sah!' Discipline and morale had been properly preserved to the last by a simple expedient which any submariner would have thought entirely sensible—a good example of sound submarine common-sense!

Lieutenant Commander G C Koziolkowski — better known as 'George' to everyone in the British Submarine Service. This gallant and popular Polish Officer, who succeeded the famous Borys Karnicki, commanded *Sokol* during her second commission patrolling from Malta 1943–44. Polish Officers and sailors quite often wore something like a hair-net but this habit was most emphatically not indicative of an effeminate nature as their fine war record shows — ashore as well as at sea!

being blown direct to sea whenever used, the heads drained down to a large sewage tank in the forward torpedo room which could be discharged when operationally convenient. It did not always work: in *Hawkbill* sea pressure leaked into the tank and eventually lifted the relief valve with potentially castastrophic results which were only avoided by the valour of Ensign Rex Murphy who waded into a 'miasmic fog' and held the valve shut for one interminable hour until the boat could surface.

In American boats attention was paid to details which other navies did not bother about but which cost little in terms either of space or money. Waterproof bunk covers, for example, enabled men coming down from the bridge or going off watch in dirty clothes to take a rest without soiling the bedding. Decor, too, was given due attention. Sometimes it was startling. At the height of the Pacific war Mare Island Navy Yard despatched the following message requesting the authority to paint the interior compartments of USS *Trigger*: '. . . Torpedo Rooms light pea green, Wardroom light green, Control Room and Maneuvring Room sky

blue, Engine Room dark sky blue, Crew's Mess Light blue X University of California scientists recommend for morale and phycological reasons X'. Everybody wanted to help US submariners; but it was sheer size—four times the space for only twice the number of men—that made habitability in American submarines so superior by comparison with others.

Most of the US Pacific submarines carried a pharmacists mate and valued him highly. Corpsman 'Doc' Lipes in USS *Seadragon* removed a troublesome appendix after a two-and-a-half hour operation 'with the help of God and a long-handled spoon'. It was one of three operations of that kind before the doctors ashore stopped what they unkindly called an 'undesirable medical practice'. One crew, though, faced a far worse prospect than any surgeon's knife when their captain, determined to cure any submariner's most usual complaint, marched into the control-room from the engine-room blowing soapy bubbles from a 12-inch grease-gun converted into an enema syringe.

The formal language of wartime patrol reports and the sometimes biting endorsements from above (occasionally abetted by disloyalty from below) gave the impression that American submariners took life too seriously. They certainly worried about the effects that their patrol reports would have; but, inside the boats themselves, a rich, basic and sometimes black humour prevailed. It was typified by the tale of a captain whose idiosyncracy was to demand, with threats, that every cup of coffee delivered to him on

5 Finding the Way

With a potential draught, in effect, of 50 fathoms or more, submarines needed even more careful and precise navigation than surface vessels. They had to operate inshore and close to minefields; they had to keep to narrow safety lanes on passage to avoid attack by friendly forces and stay within strictly delineated patrol areas on arrival so as not to risk mutual interference; and they had to be in the right place at the right time to intercept enemy units.

Unfortunately, submarines were not well equipped to meet these requirements. They did not carry specialised navigating officers like their sisters on the surface and there was neither room nor protection for chartwork on the bridge. When on the surface, bearings from landmarks and sextant readings had to be sung down the voice pipe to the plot in the control room below where they might or might not be heard and written down correctly. The enemy was not so considerate as to tell the world, in war, about changes made to buoys, navigational marks and beacons; and leading lights and lighthouses were usually extinguished except for brief periods when required by his own forces. Radar, from a navigational point of view, was still in its infancy: bearings were inaccurate and ranges from a submarine radar aerial so low down were not dependable; they did not show the nearest point of land but only those peaks which were above the radar horizon, hills or mountains well inland. Gyro compasses were temperamental and easily upset by violent angles, interruptions in electrical supplies and depth-charges. Gyro precession, significant in Northern latitudes following a rapid alteration of course, was not—could not—be allowed for; and navigators, wherever they were, did not, as a rule, appreciate the importance of frequently checking a gyro against the sun.

Even in an ideal position, where shore marks were clearly visible, a three-bearing fix, from which all three lines should have passed through a point, often resulted in a sizeable 'cocked hat' due both to gyro error and to the physical difficulty of taking a bearing on the bridge with the sea or spray washing over. Standby magnetic compasses were unreliable and difficult to steer by

because the repeaters swung lazily. The compass itself was encased in a brass housing outside the hull, to obviate as far as possible the submarine's own magnetic effect, and the compass rose was reflected down to the control room by a series of mirrors. The reflection became indistinct or clouded if moisture entered the projector tube, as it often did, and however much care was taken to adjust compass deviation by swinging the boat before sailing on patrol, deviation soon became an unknown factor as the submarine's inherent magnetism changed, unpredictably, due to the buffeting of the sea.

Speed, and hence distance run, was, in theory, obtainable from log readings but these were notoriously inaccurate. The Chernikeef type log, which slid downwards through the hull, depended upon a small propellor which quickly became decalibrated or choked by weed; and the Pitometer type, fitted in the same way, depended upon the measurement of water flow through an open tube device which was also easily blocked. Even when operating perfectly neither kind of log was trustworthy at all submarine speeds and was only reasonably dependable over a narrow range of, say, five knots at medium speed: either side of this bracket, and particularly at the very low speeds between one and three knots which a submarine used for long periods dived on patrol, the readings could be wildly misleading.

Nonetheless, inexperienced commanding officers and navigators had a touching faith in the navigational sensors at their disposal which sometimes included an automatic plotting table purporting to show the submarine's position at any moment by a beam of light projected upwards onto a plotting sheet; this instrument had its own deficiencies as well as a facility for compounding compass and log errors. No wonder that submarines so frequently found themselves far removed from their dead-reckoning and estimated positions when their true positions eventually became apparent after a long while, sometimes days on end, without a fix. It is only surprising that submarines did not more often find themselves in serious navigational difficulties, equipped as they were with less than trust-

worthy instruments and manned by navigational teams who, in many cases, had a lack of training and expertise that would not have been tolerated in an average merchant vessel. The boats which had an officer from the Merchant Navy or Coastguard—RNR or the equivalent—did not always realise how lucky they were!

Navigators, like trimming officers, were fair game for the rest of the Wardroom. A favourite ploy (invented quite independently, it seems, in the USN and Royal Navy) was to prime the officer-of-the-watch, in mid-ocean, to call down some imaginary bearing of land. The best results were observed if the navigator was enjoying a quiet nap from which he could be shaken to plot the 'fix'. His panic-stricken reactions never failed to draw applause from an appreciative audience. It might be said that submariners, as a race, were easily entertained.

Away from land every opportunity for taking sun, moon, planet and star sights had to be snatched. Sight-taking with a sextant was treated as an evolution; if surfacing primarily for that purpose it was combined when possible with ditching gash—which made matters no easier for the navigator competing in the conning tower and on the crowded bridge with a hustling gash party, the lookouts and the sea itself. The smallest drop of water on the sextant mirror made sight-taking impossible and the instrument had to be wrapped tenderly in a towel when not actually bringing the observed body down onto the lurching, irregular horizon which, with so low a height-of-eye, made the task doubly difficult. The 'exec' was primarily responsible for navigation in American boats (assisted by excellent quartermasters) but German commanders relied upon the equivalent of a specially trained warrant officer to take sights. Most British captains thought sight-taking far too important to entrust to Vasco (the navigator) and did the sextant work themselves; but they were quite happy to delegate the long and boring working-out of the sights when they were taken! It could easily take an hour to plod through the spherical trigonometry (which actually amounted to no more than straightforward arithmetic) before arriving at a solution which almost invariably produced a large cocked hat; this led to thinly veiled hints from Vasco to the effect that the captain was incapable of reading sextant angles, and to more direct accusations from the captain that the navigator was incapable of simple addition and subtraction. Some boats carried rapid reduction tables derived from air navigation manuals which greatly shortened the time required to produce a fix: but the Royal Navy and most other services clung doggedly to Inman's Nautical Tables with their long columns of five-figure logarithms.

It was naturally a temptation to surface at noon for a meridian sun-sight which gave an immediate latitude and a handy gyro-check without lengthy calculations; but the word quickly spread through both German and British submarine services that boats were being caught napping in this way by aircraft who were apt to appear, as an unwelcome interruption, coming out of the sun whose angle the sextant was measuring. It was reluctantly conceded by both sides, quite early in the war, that it was a great deal safer to surface at dawn or dusk for star-sights than to take the easy way out at mid-day. Some submariners brought bubble sextants into use; these, by providing an artificial horizon, obviated the need for taking star-sights at dusk or dawn which were the only times when stars and the true horizon could be seen together. Others were, sensibly, reluctant to use this device which required a stable platform and was intended for less precise aircraft fixes; it was apt to give misleading results on the unsteady bridge of a submarine in heavy weather.

Some USN submariners claimed that they pioneered a way of taking star-sights by night against a dark horizon by using telescopes converted from binoculars cut in half. Apart from involving a lot of explaining to the

Top Right
Navigation on the bridge of a submarine markedly lacked the refinements of that on a surface ship as can be seen from the hand-held chart here on USS *Cero.*

Bottom Right
Lt J P King RNR correcting charts in the wardroom of HMS *Unison.* **While en route from Bizerta to Malta and, for safety, included in a convoy,** *Unison* **was fired on by a 'friendly' ship: Lt King was killed and the captain, Lt Daniell, and two lookouts were wounded. The books in the rack here include, ironically, a recognition manual as well as the old nursery favourite,** *Black Beauty.*

Top Left
The triangular navigational D/F aerial on the after casing of HMS *Unshaken*. **It was a doubtful asset, apt to give misleading results and not often used in war.**

Top Right
Wheel, compass and navigational D/F aerial on the bridge of HNMS *O-16*.

Bottom Left
'Faithful Freddy', the standby magnetic compass, normally stowed below, being 'swung' in HMS *Stonehenge*.

Supply Department, the home-made device must have led to alarmingly inaccurate fixes. It was another of several instances, more noticeable in the USN than elsewhere (although no navies were entirely innocent), of instrument readings being taken at face value and accepted without enough justification.

With all these uncertainties, very careful dead-reckoning was an essential part of submarine navigation and this required particularly careful hand-plotting using precise speeds determined against specific shaft revolutions when running over the measured mile on trials. Due allowance had (or should) subsequently have been made for speeds being lessened by increasing fouling of the hull. The dead-reckoning (DR) position was then converted to an estimated position (EP) by applying tidal streams and currents predicted by tidal atlases which seldom, however, gave accurate figures (during the war) for currents below the surface: keeping track of the EP, hour by hour, was a painstaking process but was well worth the trouble.

After a prolonged action, when speeds and courses had frequently been altered, it was particularly difficult to reckon the boat's final position from the scribbled log kept in the control room. Submariners who trusted automatic devices, or who believed unquestioningly in hasty unsupported fixes without checking the EP by hand-plotting were soon lost. Keeping the EP up-to-date, though, was sometimes very hard. For instance *U-763* (Kptlt Ernst Cordes) was discovered by destroyers off Selsey Bill on 6 July 1944 and forced, blind, to evade their attentions, which included 550 depth-charges, for 30 hours. During this hectic period accurate dead-reckoning, let alone proper allowance for tidal streams and currents, was impossible. When *U-763* finally drew clear the echo-sounder showed depths incompatible with the supposed position some 20 miles north of Cherbourg and navigational D/F bearings made no sense. Cordes concluded that he was probably between the Channel Islands and he steered north towards what he hoped was deeper water because he had already grounded several times. Early in the morning of 8 July he ran aground again. When at last he cautiously came to periscope depth he was faced inescapably with visual proof that he was actually in Spithead, the most famous of all British anchorages! Probably because there was so much shipping and activity in the area, his presence was not suspected and he was able to work his way safely back to Brest. No submarine had adequate navigational facilities to keep track of its movements in circumstances like those in which *U-763* found herself and singularly little attention, in any navy, was given during the war to improving them.

Echo-sounding, to compare with the depths shown on the chart, was a help but E/S transmissions were close to the frequencies to which hydrophones and Asdics were tuned; they could be detected unmistakeably at long range. It was possible to limit these transmissions by making a 'snap sounding' but the reading given was not then necessarily correct; a shoal of fish below the submarine or even a patch of cold water could give a false depth which might not be recognised as such by one or two transmissions alone.

Medium-frequency direction-finding (D/F) aerials, for use with commercial shore-based M/F D/F beacons, were fitted in many boats but the line of bearings gave only a vague indication of position due to bearing inaccuracies. The most potentially useful radio aid evolved from a German long-range navigational system with a curious history. In February 1943 British radio monitors detected some strange signals being radiated on a frequency of 316 K/cs from a vast aerial array at Quimper near Brest. They soon discovered that these transmissions were beamed to give bearings of hitherto unknown accuracy out to one thousand miles for German ships, U-boats and aircraft in the Atlantic. No special aerial was needed in a submarine and the radio operator simply had to count a series of dots and dashes which gave the boat's bearing from Quimper when referred to a special chart. Further stations were discovered at Petten in Holland, Stav-anger in Norway and then at Lugo in neutral Spain. The British government's first thought was to send a strong protest to Spain but, upon reflection and at the suggestion of Dr R V Jones, Head of the Scientific Intelligence Department at the Air Ministry, it was decided to keep quiet and make use of these transmissions for Allied aircraft. Since the Germans called the system 'Sonne' (Sun) and the Allies were going to find their position 'with sun' the Spanish words *con* and *sol* were put together to make the name CONSOL for Allied use. CONSOL cut air navigation errors down from the customary 30 miles (and sometimes more) over the Atlantic to a mere five, which was the same degree of accuracy as U-boats were now enjoying in their major operating areas against the convoys. Unfortunately, Allied submariners seldom operated in areas where cross-bearings, and hence fixes, could be obtained. LORAN, a more sophisticated radio aid was more useful but was fitted very late in boats outside the USN. Meanwhile, Sonne became invaluable to German submariners and aircrews when, rarely, aircraft were made available to co-operate effectively with U-boats; however, it came too late, like so much German technology, to influence the battle to any real extent. When the Allies came to know about it, it is questionable whether they made the correct decision to let it continue for their own benefit, rather than jam the frequencies or by some means stop the transmissions which were giving Doenitz so much help.

Submarine navigation was, then, generally more of an art than a science although it was a good deal more scientific in some boats than in others! Submariners who admitted to themselves that neither navigational facilities nor training were very good were able to allow for the errors which were bound to occur; and, despite the difficulties, the most successful captains, perhaps more by a submariner's instinct than by calculation, had a knack of turning up at the right place at the right time. It was the navigationally overconfident captains who ran into trouble.

6 Communications

It was seldom possible for a submarine, especially a German or an American boat, to operate effectively without communicating with its shore operating authority. Communications were not welcomed by submariners who preferred to be fully independent; but with a submarine's small radius of search, commanding officers had to be directed towards certain targets or ordered to shift patrol to likely areas; and this involved a good deal of signal traffic.

Broadly speaking, signals were sent *to* submarines but submarines were only exceptionally expected to send messages to shore. The most important exceptions were enemy reports (to which anything else of immediate interest, such as a weather report, was added); and these were collated at base (*e.g.* BdU) and broadcast to other units. Any radio transmission from a submarine at sea (necessarily H/F as a rule) risked interception by monitoring stations which were able to measure the bearing of the transmission by direction-finding—D/F—but not the range. Two widely spaced stations could report cross-bearings which, if plotted on a chart, intercepted at the approximate position of the boat transmitting. However, that position was far less precise than submariners had feared before the war: bearing inaccuracies (according to intelligence reports to BdU) resulted in average errors of 60–80 miles at a range of 300 miles from the intercept stations and often amounted to much more. The least error reported was 30 miles and the largest 325 miles—the latter at 600 miles from the D/F aerials. However, when H/F D/F (Huff-Duff) came to be fitted in Allied escort vessels towards the end of 1941[1] the same technique could be used tactically at sea, with much greater accuracy at closer ranges, to pinpoint U-boats passing the reports on convoys which were so essential to Doenitz for homing wolf-packs in to the kill. The use of radio by submarines was always a calculated risk but commanding officers who kept quiet for the sake of safety were not apt to be forgiven.

Submarines could normally only listen to HF traffic on the surface although some boats were equipped with raisable masts which could be used at periscope depth for both transmitting and receiving. Traffic was therefore usually passed from shore on Very Low Frequencies (VLF), typically around 16 kilocycles (16 Khz), whose ground-waves followed the curvature of the earth and enabled submarines to listen at periscope depth virtually worldwide. The wavelengths for such low frequencies required proportionally long transmitting aerials ashore as well as very powerful transmitters. VLF transmitting stations were fundamental to both Axis and Allied submarine operations and it is difficult to understand why greater efforts were not made to render them inactive either by bombing or sabotage. A concerted effort to destroy them, or even put them out of action temporarily, would have had a profound effect and they would have been difficult to replace quickly since the ideal length of VLF aerials was reckoned in kilometres. The reason why shore radio installations were not attacked was probably that the enemy codes on all sides were, at one stage or another, broken, and the information gained was decided to be so valuable that highly secret monitoring stations had no wish to halt the flow of intelligence. If this was so, it was arguably a wrong decision and it must have arisen from the security restrictions which enabled code-breakers to deal in very high places without necessarily going through normal military channels.

Since it was extremely undesirable for submarines to acknowledge the receipt of VLF messages, which they would have to do by using HF frequencies vulnerable to D/F, they were broadcast and repeated at regular, predetermined times throughout the day to ensure reception. Rugby VLF transmitter, for instance, broadcast routines every four hours and repeated messages at least three times; it was therefore mandatory for submarines to read at least every third routine but they also kept constant watch, when possible, for priority signals which were broadcast at any time. Each signal was numbered and the numbers preceded each routine so that a boat knew if it was missing any of a series. This was important not only to ensure that all relevant messages were received but also to avoid the need to steer an optimum course, towards or away from the transmitter, for long periods at

periscope depth when this was not necessary and might well interfere with operations. W/T routines had a considerable effect upon the conduct of a submerged patrol: the optimum course might drain the battery if it was adverse for maintaining depth in relation to the sea; and if a submarine inadvertently went a few feet deep, even for seconds, vital encoded groups were missed and these could not afterwards be filled in by guesswork.

The commanding officer took a personal interest in radio procedures and no transmission could be made without his authority, confirmed by the officer-of-the-watch on the bridge who ensured that nobody was touching the aerial. Aerials attached to the bridge were a particular hazard, especially for anyone relieving himself over the side (in the absence of a 'pig's ear' funnel inside the bridge); practically any liquid was an excellent conductor of high-voltage electricity!

Radio operators were carefully chosen and felt their responsibilities keenly. They kept long hours on watch and their job required intense concentration, especially in U-boats listening to merchant ship chatter in a foreign language on the 600 metre wave-bands. In many boats radio-men doubled as hydrophone, asdic and radar operators until specially trained ratings became available. They worked hard but at least they did not have to endure the rigours of bridge watch-keeping. Like all submariners the men at the morse-keys were staunch individualists and several had a dangerous weakness: they could not resist adding their personal signature to the signals which they sent. This was easy enough to do by fractionally deviating from the standard length of dots and dashes at the end of a signal; these made the operator (and hence the boat) just as easily recognisable to an enemy interceptor as to a friend at the legitimate receiving station. It was a practise that proved hard to stamp out and resulted in a good many Allied boats being finger-printed by German monitoring stations.

All except the most urgent enemy reports were encoded. The beginning of each message specified the classification and by whom it should therefore be decoded. The task usually fell to an officer and very highly classified messages were dealt with only by the captain himself. Before the advent of decryption machines this was a process which could take half-an-hour or more: the groups of figures had to be subtracted from rows of other figures in secret signal publications and then referred to 'dictionaries' to find the words they represented. Signal books were a constant source of anxiety for the unfortunate communications officers. They had to be mustered page-by-page and courts-martial resulting from the loss, or more often mislaying, of a single sheet were common.

The security of codes was obviously paramount but the ability to break them was an even more closely guarded secret. When the German Enigma encryption machine was introduced, Doenitz believed its messages were unbreakable, presumably on the advice of the B-service whose own success in breaking Allied signal traffic told Doenitz most of what he wanted to know about convoy sailings. No form of encryption guaranteed total security although certain one-time-only systems came close to it. However, code-breaking could take an unacceptably long time unless computers like the British Colossus were used. The British knew of the Enigma system as early as July 1939 when a Polish crypto-analyst gave the Admiralty two machines. These, by themselves, were not enough to crack the codes but a windfall occurred on 9 May 1941 when *U-110* (Kptlt Julius Lemp) was heavily damaged by depth-charge attacks following an attack on convoy *OB318*. Lemp blew his disabled boat to the surface and the nearest escort, HMS *Bulldog*, at first turned to ram but then decided to see what could be recovered from *U-110* before finishing her off. The U-boat's crew were taken off and sent below decks, where they could not see what was happening, while a boarding party, painfully conscious of the probability of demolition charges exploding, clambered down the conning tower and into the tiny

Top Right
Radio shack in a US fleet submarine.

Centre Right
HMS *Osiris* **showing her aerials and the mast primarily used for HF communications. Masts of this type were hydraulically raised but were clumsy and gradually phased out.**

Bottom Right
HMS *Seadog* **showing aircraft recognition flares on the after periscope standard. These were considered very necessary in the event of 'friendly' aircraft appearing even when the submarine (as seen here) was being closely escorted through Allied-controlled waters.**

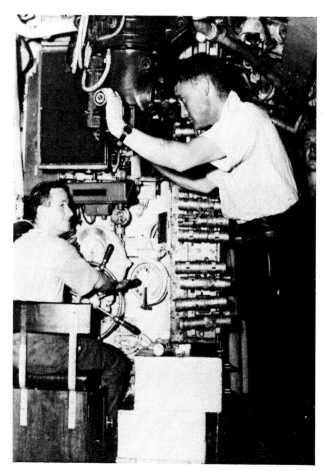

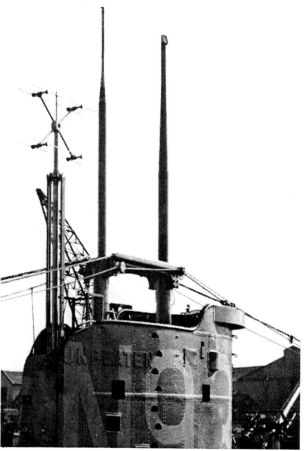

Opposite Top Left
Radio operator in *U-73* **(Type VIIC). This rating, as in all navies, had to be a cut above the average and in U-boats was expected to gather intelligence from Allied merchant ship 'chatter'.**

Opposite Top Right
Recognition signal flares in the control room of a British U-class submarine. These were mounted on the bridge and fired by a lanyard if a threatening aircraft was thought to be friendly: a submarine often dived, nonetheless, to be on the safe side!

Opposite Bottom Left
HMS *Unbeaten* **was fitted with aircraft radar and IFF (Interrogation Friend or Foe) in September 1942 but it did not save her from being sunk by an RAF aircraft at 0220 on 11 November well within a bombing restriction area. Airguard radar could by no means be trusted to give certain warning of an approaching aircraft.**

Opposite Bottom Right
VHF aerial arrangement on HMS *Scythian* **between the periscopes.**

Below
HNMS *O-19* **surfacing. Like most Allied boats the VLF reception aerial was strung from forward to aft along the length of the jumping wire (port side in this case).**

radio office opposite the captain's cabin. It is still not know why Lemp's crew were unable to carry out the standard orders for destroying secret equipment and papers; but the search party were able to bring back the Enigma machine with a signal already set up for sending together with associated code books. The settings were valid only until the end of June but the information gained was enough to enable the Allies (including some outside a hitherto tightly-knit group of code-breakers) to decrypt a proportion of the signals passed in Hydro code. The staff at BdU did not realise that the system had been compromised and continued to use it. The men of the powerful code-breaking organisation in America were, incidentally, far from pleased; they already had enough material to solve their puzzles and were afraid that the incident would jeopardise future work. It would, anyway, be wrong to think that the *U-110* haul contributed in any major way to the defeat of the U-boats in the Atlantic; breaking down the messages still took a long time and scarcely affected the tactical situation at sea.

The success which American crypto-analysts enjoyed in reading Japanese classified radio traffic was much more significant; it was on the basis of Ultra despatches from the code-breakers (the word itself was given the highest classification) that the direction of US submarines over the vast Pacific largely depended. Whether such dependence was altogether a good thing is debatable; it certainly seems to have distracted submarine operators from the advisability of planning a sound objective strategy. Admiral Fife's description of moving his submarines here and there like 'playing checkers' (in response to Ultra reports) can hardly have been welcomed by submariners.

Despite rigorous security, the American press deduced, from a fairly minor breach in the Navy Department, that the enemy 'mail' was being read and the Chicago Tribune published a story to the effect that the United States knew about Japanese intentions before the Battle of Midway. This caused alarm and despondency amongst the code-breakers and resulted in an intensive witch-hunt, probably emanating from the White House itself; but the Japanese missed the significance and the USN continued to be well briefed about forthcoming operations.

HF, VHF and, exceptionally, LF frequencies were used by American submarines in co-ordinated operations which were closely controlled by a senior commander from one of the boats in a three or four-submarine pack unlike the shore directed German wolf-pack operations. Their susceptibility to D/F was recognised but Japanese intercept capabilities did not constitute much of a threat. The real danger lay in using TBS (Talk Between Ships) VHF sets like telephones; there was a

Signal grenades from the 2¼-inch recognition pistol can be seen at the bottom of this picture of the control room in HMS *Safari* (Lt R B Lakin in October 1943). Flashing and pyrotechnic recognition signals were changed frequently, usually every four hours, and this seems to have presented a problem to the crews of Allied A/S aircraft, especially those of the British Coastal Command.

strong temptation to talk all the time instead of getting on with the job!

The only absolutely secure methods of communication (with automatic discipline built-in) were by directional lamp and semaphore but these were, of course, limited to a few miles. British boats were particularly proud of their signalling (which was frequently misused to send highly personal messages of an inflammatory nature to 'chummy ships') and the qualified signalman in a British boat was seldom left to rest in peace. At any moment on the surface a shout for the 'Signalman on the bridge' brought him racing out of his bunk, often inadequately clad, to grab the Aldis lamp en route from its stowage in the tower and answer a distant flashing light that might be friend or foe. The shout was also the cue for everyone else to flatten themselves against the bulkhead: speed in answering a challenge was vital and the signalman wasted no time on apologies if he knocked somebody flying as he leaped for the ladder to the bridge. Signalmen tended to be well-built—perhaps because one of their jobs was to hold on to the captain's legs in the tower when opening the hatch on surfacing with a pressure in the boat!

Neither normal communications nor code-breaking were glamorous occupations but the radio-warfare experts wielded enormous power at the highest level. However, if communicators in their various ways supplied submariners with the seeds of success they did not themselves reap much reward. They deserved more thanks and recognition than they actually received.

Semaphore used to be a quick, reliable and, above all, secure means of sending signals but is no longer taught in most navies.

7 Underwater Weapons

'The only use of the *Holland*', said Admiral O'Neil USN in 1900, 'is to discharge torpedoes, and no weapon is more erratic.' There were plenty of submariners to agree with him forty years later.

Torpedo propulsion was generally based upon the Fiume heater system first introduced in 1909 to supersede compressed air alone. It used fuel oil, which was sprayed into a combustion chamber with compressed air at reduced pressure and ignited; water could also be injected to control the operating temperature and generate steam. The combination of hot gases drove a piston engine. The German Mark G7A, the USN Mark 14, the British Mark VIII and the Japanese Types 89/95 were all variants of this basic engine in a 21-inch (530 mm) diameter body.

Payloads were generally six to eight hundred pounds of high explosive (the best was Torpex) and their elegantly simple thermal propulsion system drove them at about 45 knots to their targets out to about 5,000 yards—provided that they were correctly aimed, kept on course by their gyro mechanisms and maintained at the set depth by a hydrostatic mechanism which Whitehead, who first demonstrated the 'Device of the Devil' in 1867, had called 'The Secret'. Unfortunately, submariners did not understand the secret very well: war was to show all too clearly what peace-time practices had failed to reveal: torpedoes by no means always ran at the desired depth. No navy was wholly exempt from erratic depth-keeping; misses due to torpedoes running too deep were common during the first two or three years of war.

Depth-keeping difficulties were accentuated by the widespread adoption of magnetic exploders. These worked on the principle of a ship's magnetic field abruptly altering the effect of the earth's constant field when a torpedo ran under its target. A warhead had far more effect detonating below the keel than when striking a ship's side; a single torpedo could break the back of a merchant vessel from below and severely damage the strongest warship. The magnetic exploder would, therefore, economise in weapon expenditure; and that was a matter of the utmost importance if numerous targets

were expected in areas far distant from bases where further supplies of torpedoes could be embarked. By the middle of 1942 Doenitz was becoming impatient for a reliable magnetic pistol, pointing out that between January and June it had taken 816 torpedo direct hits to sink 404 ships (which was not, in fact, at all bad); but his demands were never met. The British wanted magnetic pistols for a different reason; their principle targets were battleships and cruisers which were difficult to sink with contact heads however many fish struck home.

For a long time a combination of torpedoes running deep and the unreliability of influence pistols denied submariners on all sides the success that they deserved. The underlying reason for these compounding faults was undoubtedly the lack of adequate trials. This was particularly marked in Germany and the United States and both navies found themselves bedevilled by similar problems. It was, of course, costly to carry out test firings; but economies in peace were to prove exceedingly expensive in war. There were other factors, too, which militated against exhaustive proving trials; these included scientific self-assurance backed by commercial interests, secrecy (although this was poorly preserved) and, for Doenitz, political and practical restraints on conducting exercises in the Atlantic where his underwater war was to be fought.

The other trouble in Germany was that the Torpedo Experimental Establishment, in charge of torpedo development, built a torpedo, tested it and then itself decided whether or not it was fit for operational use. Doenitz rightly believed that the whole process 'should never be left in the hands of one single authority'.[1] The situation was somewhat similar in other countries, especially in the United States where the Gun Club (the Bureau of Ordnance) with its Newport Torpedo Station was self-accounting. Much important torpedo research before the war was conducted by Ralph Christie who, later, as a Captain and then an Admiral in the South Pacific war, found himself obliged to defend the torpedoes against outspoken complaints by his commanding officers. Lcdr 'Red' Ramage in

Trout told Christie 'if I get 25% reliable performance on your torpedoes I'll be lucky . . .' and Lcdr 'Moke' Millican in *Thresher* complained that during an attack on a Japanese submarine his weapons had 'merely clinked 'em with a clunk'. Christie was not prepared for any 'wrangling in print' and said flatly that the torpedoes 'were fine'. Millican was ordered back to the States for rest and new construction.[2] The Gun Club kept close ranks and its members' insistence that torpedoes ran true was backed by a fair number of successes.

It was difficult to account satisfactorily for widely varying performances everywhere: patrol analyses depended almost entirely on the narratives of commanding officers who were understandably subjective and, anyway, found it impossible to maintain a detailed log of fast-moving events. Only the man at the periscope really knew what was happening and he was not going to make himself look a fool. Every submariner realised that there must have been human as well as material faults. On occasions, in all navies, stop valves were not opened; top stops were not checked down; safety devices were not removed; air vessel pressures were wrong; and even propellor clamps were left on. But it was equally clear that the weapons themselves were far from dependable. As Doenitz said about torpedoes in his diary for January 1940, 'we were thus back to where we were in 1914–18 . . . confidence was in every way very much shaken.'

In the U-boat arm, very important strategic opportunities were lost due to faulty torpedo performance, first exemplified by the attacks that failed against HMS *Ark Royal* on 14 September 1939 and HMS *Nelson* on 30 November 1939 (although a mine laid by *U-31* five weeks earlier seriously damaged *Nelson* in December). The captain of *U-56* (Oblt Gunther Zhan) was so depressed after delivering his attack on *Nelson* through a screen of 12 escorting destroyers and hearing, as he thought, three torpedoes hit but fail to explode that Doenitz 'felt compelled to withdraw him for the time being from active operations and employ him as an instructor at home.' In point of fact, nobody in *Nelson* heard torpedoes strike and Zahn's account

47

Top
A torpedo being partially hauled back from the
tube for checking in the Netherlands submarine
O-14.

Bottom Left
Japanese Type 95 21-inch torpedo tubes. The
Automatic Inboard Venting arrangements were in
fact *semi*-automatic but worked well. This six-tube
bank was typical of most classes except for the
I-400 class which had eight bow tubes for'ard split
into two sets of four tubes located in separate
compartments one above the other. The firing
gear, using low pressure air, was largely modelled
on British systems. The bow caps, however, were
worked by an air motor driving a worm and
quadrant instead of by a hydraulic ram. As in
practically all submarines everywhere following
the disaster in HMS *Thetis* in 1939, positive
interlocks prevented a bow cap and rear door
being opened at the same time.

Centre Left
The TI (Petty Officer in charge of the torpedo
department) of HMS *Taku* checks the tubes.
Extreme, painstaking care and constant
maintenance in very difficult surroundings was
essential if the tubes and torpedoes were to
function correctly. The personal supervision
exercised by the TI was directly reflected by the
success of attacks or otherwise; in *Taku*, it was not
in doubt with 30 torpedo hits on 15 important
targets out of 84 torpedoes fired and spread to
cover possible errors.

Centre Right
After torpedo room in a US fleet submarine. The
amount of water let in to compensate for the
difference between the weight of a torpedo and a
tube full of water after firing was not
automatically compensated as in British boats: an
inlet valve was manually opened for a given time
according to depth.

A very successful British commanding officer, Lt P C Chapman looks at the excellent tube arrangements in a Type XXI after the end of the war.

was probably not correct; neither for that matter, was the German belief that Winston Churchill was on board at the time. In the case of *Ark Royal* the two torpedoes fired by *U-39* (Kptlt Glattes) both missed astern and exploded in the wake: Glattes had under-estimated *Ark Royal*'s speed by four knots and Doenitz was therefore wrong to put all the blame on the torpedo failures for alerting the escort who subsequently sank *U-39*, the first German submarine casualty of the war.[3]

However, Doenitz was right in believing that the torpedoes fired by *U-27* (Kptlt J Franz) on 19 September 1939 exploded prematurely when fired at what was thought to be a 6000-ton cruiser (actually a *Tribal*-class destroyer); but it was not prematures that brought about the destruction of *U-27* which followed. The U-boat had been seen on the surface before diving for her attack and HMS *Fortune* had already initiated an A/S action before sighting two upheavals on the bearing.[4] Notwithstanding tactical errors by commanding officers Doenitz reported to the Naval High Command[5] early in 1942 that 40.9 per cent of misses had been caused by mechanical failures and that there was evidence of negligence in the preparation of torpedoes before issue in the Torpedo Department in the Naval Dockyard at Kiel and in the firing trials held by the Torpedo Experimental Establishment.

Four officers and officials were court-martialled and the Naval High Command was assured that the reasons for the court-martial had now been overcome: 'that this is so is proven by the successes since achieved against the enemy'.[6]

One interesting and subtle reason for torpedoes running deep was found during the German enquiries and it may well have

been a contributory, undiscovered cause elsewhere. During a prolonged dive, air pressure built up in a boat due to unavoidable small leaks from the HP air lines. The balance chamber of a torpedo was not designed to resist an insidious increase in ambient pressure over a long period; when the fish was fired the hydrostatic valve was thereby already biased and Whitehead's Secret was un-balanced, taking the torpedo deeper than set. It was a classic example of what could happen when equipment was not tested under realistic operation conditions.

The statement earlier in the war by the captain of *U-35* (Kptlt Ewerth), after his boat was sunk and he was captured on 28 November 1939, to the effect that he was highly satisfied with German torpedoes (which gave the Allies cause for concern) can only have arisen from his wishing to impress the British interrogating team.[7] Other captains were not so happy. In *U-47* Gunther Prien, of Scapa Flow fame, complained that he 'could hardly be expected to fight with a dummy rifle'. He spoke for submariners in most navies: the thought that the extreme risks which they continually ran could prove nugatory was not conducive to good morale. But, nonetheless, attacks on all sides continued to be pressed home.

The Royal Navy suffered comparatively little from poor torpedo performance. This was probably due to the large number of torpedo firings carried out before the war on the China station. Submariners contended that such failures as there were could be excused by bad 'prepping' in Depot Ships before the fish were taken on board. For example, unsuccessful salvoes from HMS *Traveller* (Lieutenant M B St John) during a Mediterranean patrol in July and August

1942 'may in part be explained by the disorganised base (Haifa) from which the submarine had started.'[8]

British non-contact CCR pistols, which had been produced 15 years before the war but were brought late into service, were as defective as they were elsewhere and 're-sulted in many otherwise successful attacks being nullified, chiefly by premature firing':[9] they were seldom used after the initial disappointments although the mills of God ground slowly and it was not until the end of 1944 that Flag Officer Submarines formally ordered them to be discontinued.

The Japanese, who had many torpedo setbacks due to poor engineering standards before the war and who were long unable to produce air vessels to withstand the high pressures required for acceptable ranges, improved their technology to such an extent that, by 1940, their weapons were remarkably reliable. Oxygen enriched air was used in some models to avoid tracks, improve engine performance and (because of the smaller air flask) increase the weight of warhead to as much as 880 lbs. Contrary to popular belief amongst the Allies, the Japanese did not equip their submarines with the very long-range 24-inch torpedoes found in their cruisers and destroyers: quite apart from constructional difficulties in the submarines themselves, it is difficult to see how anyone thought a 20,000 metre, straight-running submarine weapon could be exploited ex-cept, perhaps, when attacking dense

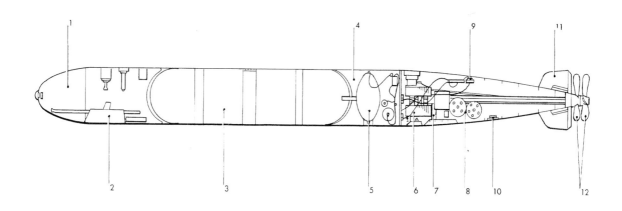

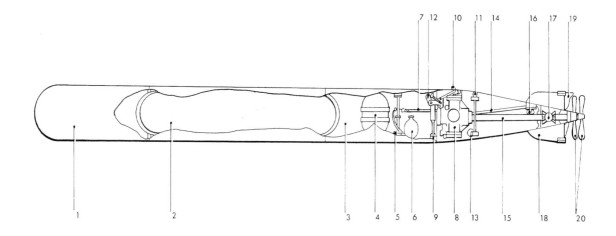

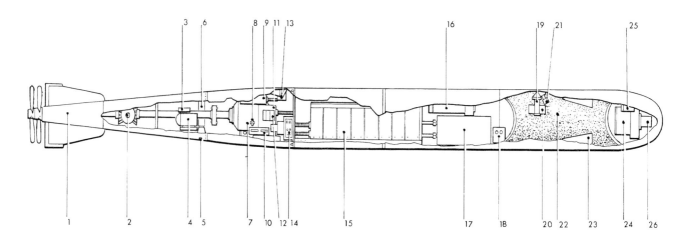

American Mark XIV Topedo (*Top*)
1: Warhead 2: Exloder Mechanism 3: Air flask 4: Water compartment 5: Fuel flask 6: Engine 7: Depth mechanism 8: Gyro 9: Starting gear 10: Cable connector 11: Tail Assembly 12: Propeller

British Mark VIII Torpedo (*centre*)
1: Warhead 2: Air bottle 3: Balance chamber 4: Fuel bottle 5: Depth gear 6: Main oil bottle 7: Gab rod 8: Engine 9: Main reducer 10: Air lever 11: Gyro angling 12: Generator 13: Air blast gyro 14: Diving rod 15: Main propeller shaft 16: Safety valve 17: Tail gearing 18: Stabilizing fin 19: Rudder 20: Propellers

German Type V Acoustic Torpedo (*Bottom*)
1: Tail unit 2: Contra-rotating gear 3: Discriminator box 4: Gyroscope 5: Depth control gear 6: Touching lever switch 7: Motor 8: Converter for pistol supply 9: G switch 10: Pistol distributor box 11: Generator for homing gear supply 12: Charging plug 13: Starting level 14: Main switch (motor) 15: 36 cell battery 16: Pistol amplifier 17: Compressed air reserve 18: Fusing delay 19: Contact (inertia) pistol 20: Coil operating pistol 21: Solenoid locking pistol propeller 22: Warhead 23: Pick-up coils 24: Acoustic amplifier 25: Thermal relay 26: Acoustic receiver

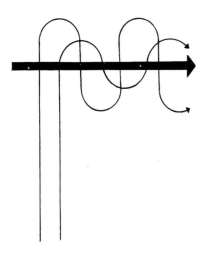

German pattern-running torpedoes (FAT).

convoys—and that was not what the Japanese intended. The 24-inch Type 93 Long Lance torpedo was, however, the basis of certain suicide submersibles. Most midget submarines carried 18-inch Type 97 torpedoes with a range of 3,000 metres at 40 knots. The Type 97 was equipped with serrated net-cutters, in the form of a four-armed starfish, on the nose: the device was adopted by the Germans for their own midgets but its efficacy was very doubtful.

Electric torpedoes, which were trackless, had obvious advantages although they were necessarily slower at, typically, 30 knots (against 45 knots) out to 5,400 yards (reduced to 28 knots and 3,300 yards if the battery was not electrically pre-heated). Except in the German Navy, where they had been well proven before the war, submarines were slow to adopt them. U-boats almost always fired electric torpedoes but maintenance and temperature requirements prevented their use in external tubes. Electric torpedoes had the disadvantage of needing to be checked every four or five days: in U-boats one torpedo was hauled back each day so that three were always ready in the tubes.

By far the most significant battery-driven torpedo was the German T5 Zaunkoenig (Wren) or Gnat (German Naval Acoustic Torpedo) which was in service by 1943. The T5 had directional transducers in the nose which gave signals to turn the rudders and steer the weapon towards a noise source, predominantly the wide-band frequencies produced by a target's propellors. It was designed, primarily, for retaliation from deep against A/S vessels who were forced either to stream decoys, noise-making 'foxers', astern (which seriously impeded their own Asdic performance) or keep outside the range

bracket—about 8 to 18 knots—in which a T5 could both hear and home on its target. Another emerging requirement in the U-boat arm in the face of strengthening A/S opposition was met by pattern-running 'Curly' FAT (Feder Apparat Torpedo—Spring Apparatus Torpedo) and LUT (Lageunabhangigertorpedo—torpedo independent of target's inclination) torpedoes to improve the chances of hitting with a browning shot at a convoy or a loose shot from deep against a single ship; but they increased hit probabilities less than Doenitz was informed. The weapons were, anyway, only available in penny numbers at the time when they were most needed although they were sufficiently plentiful by the end of 1944 to allocate five Gnats and three or four 'Curlies' to many boats.

Despite engineering and mathematical hopes for something better, torpedos everywhere were most effective if two or more were fired in a range bracket from 600 to 2,000 yards and set to run at an appropriate depth to hit but not so shallow as to be affected by the sea state. It was fish with these modest settings that achieved most successes.

Quite heavy gun armament was fitted to most submarines. It broke up streamlining, making the boats noisier and slightly slower than they should have been; but, for some unaccountable reason, disappearing guns, which had been invented as far back as 1908, were not introduced. Gunfire was particularly useful for shore bombardment and against small shallow-draught targets. Unlike torpedoes, there were plenty more shots in the locker if the first salvoes missed. Two or three hundred rounds of ammunition could be carried and a dozen rounds were enough to settle the fate of most small ships.

The USN opted for the heaviest guns that could be fitted. USS Nautilus had two 6-inch monsters although smaller 4-inch weapons were more usual in most boats. Type VII U-boats had 88 mm and Types IX and X boats had 103 mm weapons, all forward of the conning tower. A 4-inch (100 mm) was found to be the ideal calibre; its ammunition was not too heavy to hand up the tower for quick firing and 35 lb HEDA shells did far more damage than 3-inch and 12-pounder shells. For example, a wooden junk was sunk by two rounds from HMS Thrasher's 4-inch gun but it took 46 3-inch rounds from HMS Statesman to destroy a similar target. Two British boats, Shalimar and Seadog, innovated a gunnery wolf-pack patrol in the Far East in July and August 1945. They communicated by VHF voice and used time-of-flight stop-watches to distinguish fall-of-

shot for spotting. The results of this experimental operation were impressive with a dozen small vessels sunk; but, between them, they expended 1,075 rounds of 3-inch HEDA which the Captain S/M, Second Submarine Flotilla considered too high. By contrast HMS Thrasher and HMS Spur, using 35 lb 4-inch ammunition, averaged only 21.3 and 12.5 rounds respectively per vessel sunk in individual gun actions against equivalent targets.[10]

The rate of fire was, incidentally, far less than the 10 or 12 rounds per minute expected. British analysis showed that it varied, in fully worked up boats, from 2.2 rpm to 7.4 rpm. The hitting rate varied from 11 to 53.8 per cent with around 30 per cent at 6 rpm in reasonable weather conditions.

· Gunnery had, of course, one great disadvantage. It was summed up well in the German Naval High Command's Handbuch fur U-bootskommandandten issued in 1942 to all U-boats:

'The U-boat as an armament carrier is fundamentally a contradiction in itself. It is not constructed for gunnery action on account of its limited stability, its low and unsteady gun and observation platforms which are directly exposed to the sea's motion. Strictly speaking the U-boat is inferior to every surface warship in an artillery battle. For the U-boat, as opposed to its surface opponent, is rendered completely vulnerable in every artillery duel as one hole in the pressure hull can prevent the U-boat from being able to dive and thus easily leads to the loss of the boat.'[11]

Most boats had light, portable anti-aircraft machine guns which could be brought up to the bridge and fitted on stanchions when needed on the surface. Submarines regarded these as last-ditch weapons; but they were handy for shooting up floating mines, terrifying the occupants of small boats and, sometimes, for relieving the captain's feelings. They were virtually useless against aircraft although a few were hit by lucky bursts and some may have been put off their aim when coming in to attack.

However, on 31 May 1943, a week after giving the order for U-boats to withdraw from the Battle of the Atlantic, Doenitz discussed with Hitler ways in which the trend (a euphemism for defeat) might be reversed. One proposal, promptly put into effect, was to equip U-boats with four-barrelled 20 mm AA cannons for protection against the clumsy Liberators and Sunderlands which were making the passage through the Bay of Biscay so hazardous. Most U-boats already had 20 mm or 35 mm AA guns on a platform abaft the conning tower but now, especially when transitting in a group, the Flak vierling

Bow-loading a torpedo into a Soviet M-class
submarine in the Baltic Sea.

Loading a torpedo into HMS *Unbroken* at Malta.
Embarking a full load was not the simple
operation it appeared; it could easily occupy an
entire day and a conscientious TI would then
spend a great deal of time checking and further
'prepping' the fish prepared by the Depot Ship or
Base. The USN eventually adopted a policy of
recording the men concerned with preparing
torpedoes all along the line; this had a most
salutary effect on torpedo performance.

Top
HNMS *O-21* **loading a torpedo. Like all Dutch
submarine operations, torpedo loading was
accomplished with the minimum of fuss and
maximum efficiency. Although there seems to be
little supervision at this stage of the operation,
one can be confident that all was well!**

Bottom Right
**For several excellent reasons Wrens were a
welcome addition to the ship's company of a
submarine base. Here they are helping to load
torpedoes on board the ex-American HMS** *P-556*
**at the Alma Mater of British submarines, Fort
Blockhouse, Gosport in 1943.**

53

with armour to protect the bridge and gun-platforms, offered a formidable amount of fire-power. Special 'plane traps', *U-211*, *U-256*, *U-271*, *U-441*, *U-621* and *U-973* had, as well as the quadruple mounting, a 37 mm and two 20 mm guns. All this was not enough. It deterred maritime patrol aircraft to some extent but light US aircraft operating from carriers in relays were hard to hit and, attacking continually from different directions, swamped the defences. Bloody battles ensued and U-boat personnel losses were severe.

The lessons learned about gunnery boiled down to one: it was not worth the candle unless it was the only possible method of defence or unless the target was incapable of fighting back. As surface sailors had said about submariners in general a couple of generations earlier, submarine gunnery was 'no occupation for a gentleman'.

Submarines were ideal vehicles for mine-laying. Unlike surface minelayers they laid their fields unseen, and were far more accurate

Top
Crew exercising with their deck gun at the New London, Connecticut submarine base on 4 November 1943.

Bottom
The Oerlikon gun in HMS *Splendid* used mainly for holding up small vessels. As an anti-aircraft weapon it had little value in submarines but could be off-putting to an inexperienced pilot.

than aircraft. The disadvantage was that minelaying operations usually involved a long passage to and from the area concerned and detracted from torpedo operations. The United States Navy had only one purpose-built minelayer, the 3,000 ton *Argonaut (V4)* built in 1925; but in 1942 she was hastily converted to a troop-carrier capable of transporting the 120 marines which she took successfully to Makin Island. When Mark X-1 mines, suitable for discharging through standard torpedo tubes, became available, fleet submarines were dispatched to plant fields at the eastern entrance to the Inland Sea, in the Gulfs of Siam and Tonkin and off Cape Padaran. There was not much enthusiasm amongst the American submariners for minelaying but it was admitted that if all torpedoes were unlikely to be expended during a patrol a submarine could advantageously carry a mixed load.

The German Type XA and XB boats were specifically designed as minelayers with mines stored in vertical shafts in the saddle tanks (like the French *Rubis*—see Chapter 11) and in the after section of the hull; a few Type IXs were also modified with eight vertical mineshafts in place of torpedo reloads. Up to 66 mines could be carried in a Type X. The Russians probably had a similar system but at least one boat had a roller conveyor system under the casing and the L-class had two stern launchers. Those Japanese boats which retained 21-inch tubes mainly used German tube-laid mines which were magnetic.

German U-boats laid 327 mines off the eastern American coastline resulting in 11 ships being sunk or damaged. However, seven ports also had to be closed for a total of 40 days and this was a significant figure, equivalent in effort to a great deal of tonnage being sunk. No U-boats were lost on these operations. Unfortunately, some deterrent minefields laid by the United States Navy, to keep U-boats clear of anchorages where convoys assembled, resulted in several Allied ships being lost or damaged.

The Royal Navy had six *Porpoise*-class purpose-built minelayers, each carrying 60 standard Mark VIII moored mines; but only HMS *Rorqual* survived the war. They had a power chain-conveyor system installed at the stern below the mine rails which were laid along the pressure hull and enclosed by a high casing; the periscopes were moved over to starboard to give a clear run. Mines were usually dropped from 116 to 120 feet apart which, at 2.5 knots, meant a manageable dropping interval of 30 seconds. When submarine mines were built to fit 21-inch torpedo tubes the requirement for special

minelayers lapsed. It seems extraordinary that torpedo armament should willingly have been thereby sacrificed when it had been proved entirely practicable to instal minechutes for 14 mines in the ballast tanks of E-class submarines during World War 1; disregard of this simple, inexpensive type of stowage was probably due to the British insistence on preserving a huge reserve of surface buoyancy, far more than the Germans deemed necessary.

A total of 658 mines were laid by Allied, mainly US, submarines in the Pacific where the minelaying effort came to be concentrated. This resulted in 27 Japanese ships being sunk or damaged beyond repair and another 27 damaged but repairable. Therefore, for each dozen mines laid, one was successful. No submarines in the Pacific were lost while minelaying.

Mines were a very formidable submarine weapon and could be laid as a deterrent to shipping as well as for purely offensive purposes. They were particularly well suited to the Soviet navy where political control did not affect operations as it did with such serious results during torpedo attacks. However, torpedoes, in western navies, excited the public imagination much more than mines which tended, in consequence, to be undervalued and poorly provided for in submarines.

Embarking 3-inch fixed ammunition in HMS *Untiring*. **The ammunition was struck below in the magazine and passed up manually through the conning tower and down through a bridge port. U-class submarines had no gun tower hatch.**

8 Attack

An attack did not start only when mastheads appeared over the horizon. The foundations were laid very much earlier and the whole crew, not just the attack team, were involved. War histories forgot to record the enormous amount of preparation needed in harbour before sailing on patrol: huge quantities of stores, exactly accounted for, had to be carried on board and stowed; engineers had to sweat over recalcitrant cylinder heads; seamen had to guide a dozen or more 21-foot, ton-and-a-half torpedoes down through a narrow, circular loading hatch and then attend to their mechanisms with a watchmaker's precision in cramped, cavernous surroundings where garage mechanics would have refused to work on the clumsiest agricultural machinery. Nor could historians have known how it felt to give up the last few precious hours ashore to study charts and operational orders, align the tubes and periscopes, dessicate binoculars, work out the trim, muster secret signal publications page by tedious page and carry out a thousand-and-one essential checks on every piece of equipment on board.

Only selfless teamwork made it possible for a captain to bring his boat into a position where the torpedoes could do their work.

Ultimate success was due as much to the stokers aft as to the torpedo-men forward and the 'oilies' deserved a lot more credit than they got for successful operations. Good management was needed to direct the many diverse skills in action but it was wrong to call the captain a One Man Band.[1]

Nevertheless, the captain was the only man to know everything that was going on in action, and he personally controlled an attack to a much greater degree than in surface ships. The art was to use the members of the attack team as extensions of his own senses and that required—for all concerned—training, training and more training.

Training for submarine command should therefore have been exceptionally thorough, but it was not always so. Wartime pressures shortened the time available and the USN believed anyway that prospective commanding officers learned the trade best on patrol although some (by no means all) went for a few weeks to an Attack Teacher ashore. In retrospect the USN policy seems to have been wrong; American captains were not as well grounded in tactics and periscope useage as their opposite numbers in the Royal Navy who underwent exhaustive (and exhausting) periscope schooling during a mandatory

'Perisher' course. Apart from not learning the drill properly it was very difficult for an officer to discover his personal failings—tendencies to under-range and inclinate wrongly for example—without a Perisher or something like it. Dutch, Polish, Greek and Norwegian officers joined British commanding officers' qualifying courses when they could be spared and coped admirably with the English language; at the height of an attack fundamental expressions proved to be remarkably similar in any language!

It was what Churchill called a commanding officer's 'ice-cold brain in danger' that mattered and (though not admitted in such dramatic words) that was what a Perisher aimed for.

Each officer made twenty-five or thirty dummy attacks in the Attack Teacher followed by as many as possible in a specially assigned submarine at sea. Each attack was analysed in detail and ruthlessly criticised by Teacher, a senior and experienced commanding officer. Torpedo running errors were taken into account by drawing discs from a bag. A black disc signified that the torpedo did not run at all; and although Teacher sometimes unbent sufficiently to sympathise if the dummy fish were un-co-operative, it was a salutary reminder of torpedo imperfections and underlined the importance of firing adequate and carefully calculated salvoes, spread (with appropriate spacing to avoid 'gapitis') so as to allow not only for course and speed errors but also for torpedo anomalies. U-boats, mainly attacking at point-blank range, seldom had to worry much about target estimations or consider spreading: one or two torpedoes usually sufficed. American captains tended to select salvoes and spreads rather arbitrarily and without due consideration of hit probabilities. The latter were a good deal lower than might be expected and it was advisable to close the range if possible so that the target's length absorbed miscalculations in aim-off. The Russians did not understand spreading and spacing techniques at all. They generally followed the philosophy of one of the Tsarist captains in 1916 who invariably fired all his fish as quickly as possible on slightly diverging courses: 'We just go puff, and some torpedoes must hit.'[2] He was being very optimistic.

Control room of HMS *L-23* at diving stations during 1939. The three L-boats serving in World War II were completed shortly after World War I but were occasionally used operationally as well as for training after 1939. The man on the left is a 'sparker' manning the hydrophones.

After attacking a convoy off Zante in September 1941 and sinking one ship, *Rorqual* was rammed by another ship and lost both periscopes.

A Perisher started in the Attack Teacher with a nice, simple, straight–course, slow-speed target model moving on wires and wheels over a glassy sea against a blue horizon. An artificially focused periscope in a revolving cubicle represented a submarine control room and a Perisher's attack team was made up of his fellow trainees (who were not over-anxious to see their captain score hits). Zigzags, weaves, higher speeds and escorts were gradually introduced while Teacher laid bare each Perisher's soul with tigerish licks of his rasping tongue. British torpedoes could not be continually angled before firing so it was necessary to point the submarine's bows (or stern if stern tubes were being used) ahead of the target and wait for the DA (Director Angle) to come on. Rapid mental arithmetic and nice timing were needed if the submarine was to achieve an ideal firing range of about 1200 yards on the target's beam and still catch the DA. This required bursts of high speed deep and blind on the best closing track for the target's last known course; and meanwhile the target might change course radically.

Coming up from deep to periscope depth at the wrong time risked ramming. If Teacher had to take over and order the submarine deep again, the unfortunate Perisher knew that his chances of passing the course were slim. The one-minute rule was strictly observed: that meant going deep when

an oncoming ship was one minute away at its maximum speed which, for a destroyer, implied a range of one thousand yards. A decision had to be taken when the ranging height in feet—funnel, mast or bridge—equalled the number of minutes of arc subtended at the periscope which meant the range was 1150 yards. Submariners reckoned rules were meant to be broken but this one was worth remembering even in action.

Some officers had a natural periscope eye. Others never succeeded in acquiring it. The worst got 'lost in the box' and were not able to keep a mental track of where targets and escorts were; they were quickly and mercifully weeded out. Attack instruments in British and most European Allied boats were rudimentary but sufficient.[3] A hand plot was the most reliable indication of target speed—the most important parameter—which could be checked by a propellor revolution count or the position of the second bow wave or, often enough, an educated guess! Course was estimated visually from the angle-on-the-bow. It was easy enough to inclinate when the target presented a fine aspect but much more difficult in the closing stages of the attack when it was nearly beam on: a last minute zig was hard to detect. There was a marked

The control room of HMS *Rorqual* with plotting table on the right.

A relatively minor penalty of not going deep quickly enough for a destroyer: a bent periscope following a dummy attack by a destroyer with all too realistic results—collision.

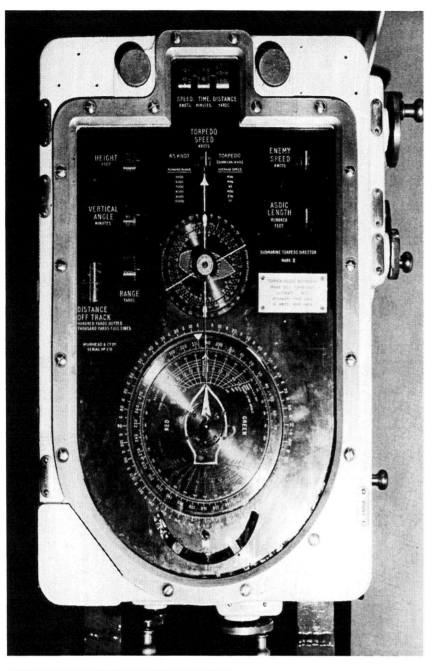

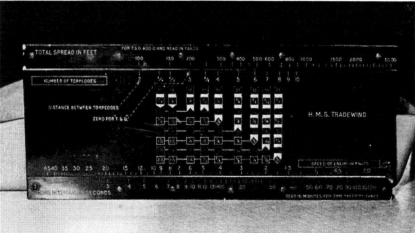

tendency for inexperienced officers to over-estimate angle-on-the-bow and hence mislead the plot into giving too slow a speed which resulted, of course, in the DA being too small and the torpedoes missing astern.

British periscopes incorporated a gunnery-type range-finder by which one image could be balanced on another to measure the angle subtended against a known height. The angle was then easily converted into distance. American periscopes, however, only had a graticule lens graduated in minutes of arc; a stadimeter slide-rule was used for translating a comparatively rough angular reading into yards. If (as happened in all navies) a target was thought to be larger than it really was, gross over-ranging as well as over-estimation of target length was bound to result, seriously degrading the fire-control solution. Sonar bearings were another significant source of error in the USN. They were inherently inaccurate (sometimes wildly so) but were trusted implicitly. Mathematical problems aside, blind sonar attacks simply did not work in action.

American fire-control was outstanding in one respect. The angle-solver for calculating DA was broadly similar to the basic Is-Was or slightly more sophisticated Fruit Machine in British boats; but there was also a TDC (Torpedo Data Computer) which continuously generated a firing angle and applied it electrically to the gyros of torpedoes waiting in the tubes. When the fish were fired they automatically turned to the calculated hitting track with an appropriate angular spacing between them. This meant that the boat itself did not have to turn on to a firing track and there was thus no danger of altering course too late and missing the DA. That was the theory and it greatly simplified tactics; but it did not always work out like that. The system sometimes lagged and torpedoes did not always accept large angles—at least, that is what certain post-war trials suggested. It would have been better to restrict angles to near zero or a set 45 degrees or 90 degrees (as the Germans preferred, sometimes, with a

Top Left
The British fruit machine which superseded the 'Iswas'. Although supplied from the gyro this machine did not track continuously and had to be completely reset at each observation.

Bottom Left
The invaluable Greek slide-rule used in British and certain other Allied navies to calculate linear spread and spacing and named for the officer in the Royal Hellenic Navy who markedly improved it, Lt Cdr E P Tsoukalas.

similar system); for otherwise the successive stages of continuously supplying angle-orders to the torpedoes aggregated mechanical, electrical and human errors; and inaccurate ranging accentuated the problem of parallax. It was also possible that some torpedoes fired at short intervals with a narrow spacing collided, causing explosions wrongly taken for hits. Counter-mining by adjacent fish would have resulted in another reason for unjustified celebrations. These possibilities are suggested because they could well account for a number of so-called torpedo malfunctions and at least some of the numerous wrongful claims by American submariners which were illuminated by post-war analysis.

However, whatever its inaccuracies, continuous angling offered a chance of shooting at threatening destroyers which the other Allies were seldom able to do. Down-the-throat shots were sometimes successful at ranges around 1,000 yards and the Submarine Operations Research Group credited US submarines with 104 hits out of 452 torpedoes fired at close range on track angles of less than 20 degrees. This, presumably due to fire-control discrepancies, was less than the mathematical 30–50 per cent probability of one hit on a destroyer with a tight spread of four torpedoes at 1,000 yards. It was a valuable technique; but if, as was said of at least one captain, he deliberately exposed his periscope to entice destroyers into turning towards, he was a very rash submariner indeed. Four torpedoes fired on a *broad* track (given that course and speed estimations were correct within 20 degrees and two knots) had a 70–90 per cent chance of one hit at the same range on the same target so it was a good deal safer to stick to standard tactics.

Boats in other Allied navies had to fire straight-ahead or straight-astern hosepipe salvoes which achieved the effect of spread and spacing by the target's own movement across the single line of torpedo tracks. This method had obvious disadvantages but it ran the least risk of errors arising between the periscope and the torpedoes. British and Allied 'hosepipes' scored 1363 hits out of 3220 attacks (42.3 per cent) and 1040 ships were sunk out of 5121 torpedoes fired (20.3 per cent). In the USN 1314 sinkings were achieved by angled fire with 14,748 torpedoes (8.9 per cent).

The proportion of German hits to torpedoes fired was very much higher because most attacks were made on the surface from only a few hundred metres against slow, steady targets. To achieve results, the instructions given to U-boat captains did not err on the side of caution as the following

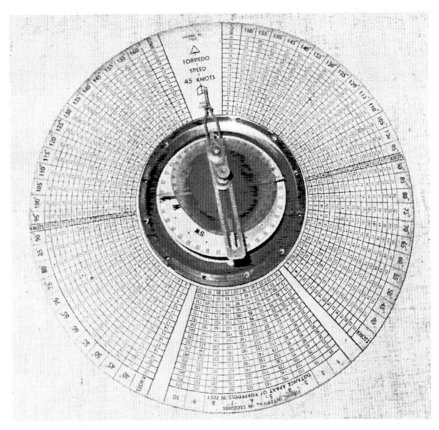

A British Iswas and DA disc. This rudimentary calculator was perfectly adequate for determining aim-off but did not give the captain a continuous picture of what was happening.

extracts from the Commanding Officers' Handbook shows:

'. . . dive only when an immediate hazardous fight is expected on account of an enemy escort's close proximity . . . serious miscalculations may occur by night, therefore *go in as close as possible* . . . even if the U-boat is sighted while making its attack it should still be impossible for the enemy to avoid the torpedo [but] even at night minimum range is 300 metres . . . do not fire prematurely from an over acute angle, an inexperienced torpedo gunner [presumably referring to the First Lieutenant who worked the bridge torpedo director sight during the usual surface attacks] is inclined to take the angle for more obtuse than it really is. Therefore, keep your nerve and do not fire too soon . . . distance is easily underestimated . . . one is *always* further away than one thinks, particularly at night. [Doenitz was assuming that small targets would not be mistaken for large ones.] Stick it out and go nearer . . .'

Successful attacks were duly rewarded in all navies. It was impossible to be entirely fair but tonnage sunk was generally the dominating factor in the German and United States submarine services. Doenitz checked claims as carefully as possible and there was relatively little exaggeration by U-boat captains despite Allied propaganda to the contrary; but use of the T5 acoustic-homing torpedo, available from 1 August 1943, gave rise to false claims of Allied escorts sunk due to the fact that these weapons were invariably fired amidst 'confused noises in a skirmish which could only be appreciated by one who has experienced it'.[4] These claims, in one convoy battle in September 1943, amounted to 12 destroyers 'definitely sunk' and three 'probably sunk' by Gnats. Analysis shows that only two sinkings, HMCS *St Croix* and HMS *Polyanthus*, were achieved by *U-305* and *U-666* during that particular skirmish.

American claims were considerably in excess of actuality throughout; this led to some embarrassment when the JANAC analysts had done their counting which showed a spectacular drop in several scores, the greatest disparity being Cdr Roy M Davenport's credits while commanding *Haddock* and *Trepang*. These were reduced from 151,900 to 29,662 tons with eight ships instead of 17 being sunk. There was a natural temptation to exaggerate successes; and in the stress of action or while avoiding counter-attack deep it was easy to think wishfully when explosions of all sorts were clearly heard. Some guidelines for medals were formulated with regard to tonnage but were not strictly adhered to. A US Navy Cross, for instance, was to be awarded for sinking at

Top Left
US fleet submarine conning tower looking forward towards the wheel and showing the access hatch from the control room below.

Top Right
The conning tower attack center in a typical US fleet submarine looking aft.

Bottom Left
Some of the attack instruments in the conning tower of USS *Torsk.* **Submariners might argue that far too much reliance was placed on instrumentation in the USN and its dangers are implied by the lettering on the dial at the right— 'correct solution'. When dials matched and the solution 'tracked' convincingly, commanding officers had a marked tendency to believe that the settings were correct forgetting sometimes that, as with all computers, it was the original inputs that governed the quality of the solution.**

Centre Right
Part of the control room of a US fleet submarine showing the plotting tables.

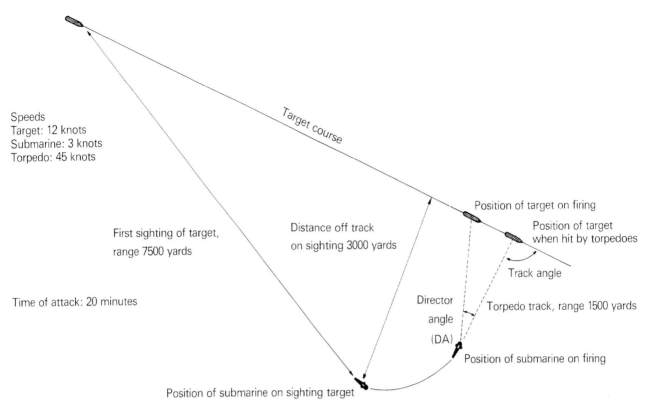

Speeds
Target: 12 knots
Submarine: 3 knots
Torpedo: 45 knots

Target course

First sighting of target,
range 7500 yards

Distance off track
on sighting 3000 yards

Position of target on firing

Position of target
when hit by torpedoes

Track angle

Time of attack: 20 minutes

Director
angle
(DA)

Torpedo track, range 1500 yards

Position of submarine on firing

Position of submarine on sighting target

Simple attack with straight running torpedoes

Typical spread and spacing of a four-
torpedo salvo. This was achieved either
by the target's movement across the
single track of a hosepipe salvo or by
angular spacing.

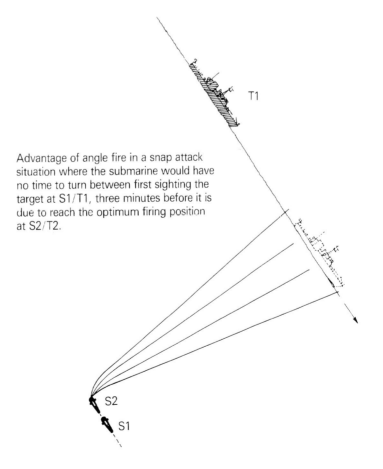

Advantage of angle fire in a snap attack
situation where the submarine would have
no time to turn between first sighting the
target at S1/T1, three minutes before it is
due to reach the optimum firing position
at S2/T2.

T1

S2

S1

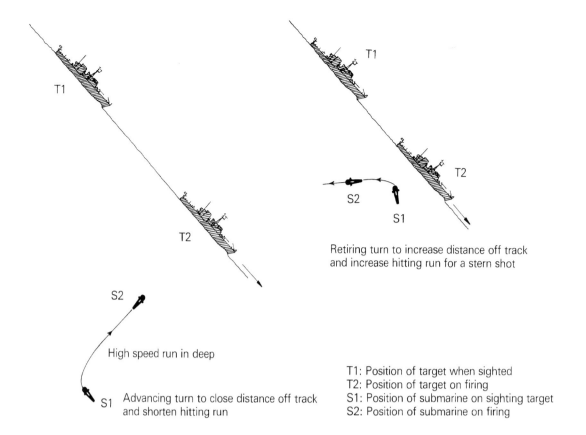

Retiring turn to increase distance off track
and increase hitting run for a stern shot

High speed run in deep

Advancing turn to close distance off track
and shorten hitting run

T1: Position of target when sighted
T2: Position of target on firing
S1: Position of submarine on sighting target
S2: Position of submarine on firing

least three merchant vessels totalling 15,000 tons, a cruiser or above, two destroyers or submarines, or one of each: but individual actions were quite rightly judged according to circumstances. In general, U-boat captains were awarded the Knight's Cross for 100,000 tons and the Oak Leaves for 200,000 tons. Only one U-boat captain seems to have hoodwinked the High Command; and he was awarded the highest decoration of all, the Knight's Cross with Oak Leaves, Swords and Diamonds for what later came to be known as unjustified claims. This was Fk Albrecht Brandi (*U-617*) whose surviving colleagues say he gave a grossly exaggerated account of his exploits in the Mediterranean which included the sinking of HMS *Welshman*, a fast minelayer wrongly taken for a large cruiser. In the main, though, submariners of one navy did not grudge the medals of another when they compared notes after the war; friends or foes, they knew that they deserved them. The highest decorations were everywhere awarded sparingly but in Germany the modest Iron Cross was liberally handed out to reward ordinary U-boat 'soldiers' and it gave them a great deal of pleasure.

Russian medals were difficult to equate with those of the other Allies. They looked splendid but they did not, apparently, confer the same privileges as in the Tsarist days when Lt R W Blacklock RN was awarded the Order of St Vladimir 4th Class with Swords for services rendered during World War I. St Vladimir entitled the wearer, amongst other

honours, to visit any state school for girls, taste the food and remark on the quality!

Submarines returning from patrol displayed their results in different ways. A U-boat strung tonnage-pennants from its periscopes and American submarines flew a series of small rising-sun flags for men-of-war sunk and white flags with a red ball in the centre for merchant victims. British submarines hoisted a rather uncharacteristically flamboyant Jolly Roger pirate flag, the first of which had been flown by HMS *E-9* (Lt Cdr Max Horton) in September 1914 after sinking the German battlecruiser *Hela*. On a subsequent patrol after sending the German destroyer *S-116* to the bottom, Horton hoisted a second flag on approaching the British base at Harwich. Before long there was no room to fly a separate flag for each sinking and Horton substituted one large Jolly Roger bearing the appropriate number of bars for the total number of enemy vessels he had sent to the bottom. The custom prompted an acid comment from the Admiralty when the Chief of the Russian Naval Staff asked, in 1915, if Max could take over as Senior Naval Officer at the British base in the Baltic. The Second Sea Lord wrote on the document: 'I understand that Commander Horton is something of a pirate and not at all fitted for the position of SNO . . .'

At least one other British submarine copied Horton's idea, but it was not until World War II that it caught on; and then it was the submarine Flotilla Commanders in

the Mediterranean who instigated what was to become a tradition throughout the second underwater war. It started with HMS *Osiris* sinking the Italian destroyer *Palestro* well inside the heavily guarded Adriatic which Mussolini has boasted no enemy could enter. *Osiris* was told by signal lamp on return to Alexandria that 'a special recognition signal in a sealed package marked JR to be opened by Commanding Officer only is being sent to you in my motor boat. It will meet you at the boom. *Osiris* is not to come alongside until this identity signal is showing.'

The captain of *Osiris* (Lt Cdr Harvey) broke open the package, hauled up the Jolly Roger it contained and carried on in. Thereafter the Captain (SM) of a Flotilla presented each of his submarines with the dreaded skull and crossbones flag of the old-time Spanish Main when the boat had achieved its first success. Not all commanding officers followed the custom. Lt Ian McGeogh in *Splendid*, for example, felt it was unduly boastful and, anyway, that actual as opposed to hoped-for sinkings were not known. It was up to the submarine itself to keep the record up to date with suitable symbols sewn on by the signalman. The signalman's needlecraft was sometimes rough and ready. This was noted by the famous and respected Carmela Cassar who kept one of the finest lace shops in Malta. Carmela's lace was made in the convents of Malta and she decided in 1941 to arrange for the nuns to make beautifully embroidered

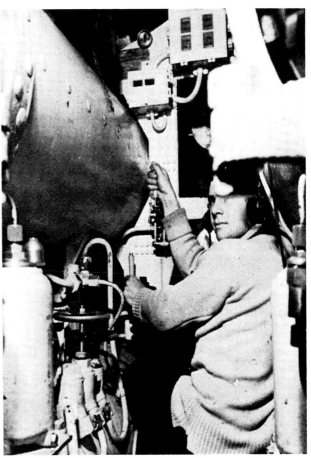

Top Left
Lookouts on the bridge of *U-552* **(Kptlt Eric Topp) known as the Red Devil boat because of its emblem. This boat was the third highest scorer in the German Fleet. Note the wire binding on the periscope to give strength and minimise vibration without periscope standards. The man on the left is using dark glasses for aircraft watch into the sun.**

Top Right
The business end of a 1940 British S-class submarine.

Bottom Right
Torpedo firing levers in the Polish *Sokol* **(ex HMS** *Urchin***).**

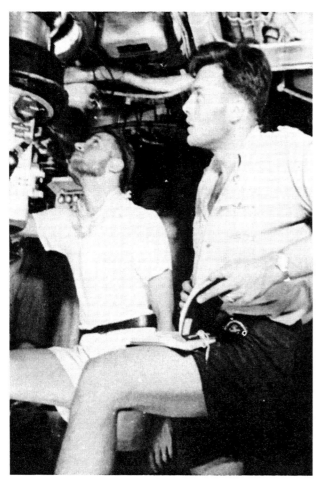

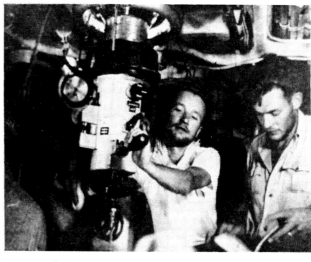

Jolly Rogers, each about 12 by 18 inches, with a realistic skull and cross bones and all the appurtenances to which a particular submarine was entitled; these were presented to the individual commanding officers operating from Malta. Jolly Rogers well illustrated the extraordinary variety of operations carried out by British submarines, and several Allied boats under British control adopted the same idea. The flags displayed a submarine's exploits in graphic detail as patrol succeeded patrol until, all too often, a boat went out and did not come back. Then Carmela's little flags, left behind in the Depot Ship or ashore, were all that remained to tell the story.

Success flags of one kind or another gave returning submarines a certain transient glamour which the German Navy amplified with bands, bunches of flowers and glamour-girls at the quayside. But submarine torpedo attacks themselves were far from glamorous. There was no audience to applaud and a long, dangerous haul back to harbour remained before hands could be shaken and medals pinned. Ultimate success depended upon arduous training, ruthless elimination of sub-standard officers and men, and long periods of wearisome waiting.

However, one kind of attack offered instant rewards for marksmanship with all the fun of the fair thrown in—gun action.

Bringing a gun into action reversed the principles of torpedo fire. American and German boats made comparatively little use of their guns. When they did, they usually stalked their prey on the surface using light conditions to best advantage. The British used guns much more and, with the stated aim of patrolling primarily submerged, perfected a technique of not surfacing until the very last moment and then opening fire immediately. The drill was exciting and several of the crew who did not usually see action were able to lend a hand even if only in the ammunition chain. It was the one time that submariners shouted; and they put their utmost into it in a way that would have gladdened the hearts (if they had any) of the leather-throated instructors on the parade ground at Whale Island, the noisy home of naval gunnery.

On sighting a suitable (unarmed) target through the periscope 'Stand-by Gun Action' was ordered and the crew raced to diving stations while the magazine hatch was wrenched off leaving a large open manhole in the centre of the passageway through which many a hastening, sleepy body dropped. It was a painful occurrence, because, usually, only one leg went down through the aperture so that the victim performed a sort of sideways splits.

The Gunlayer and Trainer inspected the target through the periscope while the captain estimated range, angle-on-the-bow and target speed in the usual way so that range and deflection could be set on the control room transmitter (if proper gunnery instruments were available) or passed directly to the sight-setter who was probably the submarine's chef in private life.

With the submarine still at periscope depth, the captain gave the executive order 'Salvoes shoot' followed by 'Man the gun tower'. In U-class submarines, which had no separate gun-tower, the gun's crew had to climb up the conning-tower ladder, and force themselves out of the hatch with the surfacing officer-of-the-watch and the lookouts before flinging themselves over the forward end of the bridge down to the waiting gun.

At 'Stand-by to surface' the layer removed both safety pins that secured the upper gun-tower hatch and reported 'Tower manned, pins out'. Meanwhile, the First Lieutenant bled HP air into the boat until three or four inches above atmospheric pressure showed on the barometer. The motors were put to Half Ahead Group Up (about $6\frac{1}{2}$ knots) for the hydroplanes to have maximum effect, and

the captain ordered 'Surface' and all the tanks were blown.[5] When, despite the hydroplanes, the boat could no longer be held down against the rapidly increasing positive buoyancy and when the depth gauge was passing the 20-foot mark, the First Lieutenant blew a whistle. The gunlayer released the last hatch clip; the planesman put the plane to hard a-rise; the hatch, still under water but very close to the surface now, flung itself open under pressure from inside and the gun's crew followed, jet-propelled, as air whistled out around them. The heavy thud of the first round going away could be heard throughout the submarine before the boat had settled herself properly on the surface.

The first round was unlikely to hit the target because it had to cope with a cold gun as well as water and anything else that had found its way into the barrel, factors which affected range unpredictably. The first round cleaned the gun: the second was the one to watch for. A range of one or two thousand yards from just abaft the target's beam was the ideal position to combine surprise with ease of aim. With a shell leaving the barrel every ten seconds or so it was not long before spotting corrections from the Gunnery Officer on the bridge succeeded in putting the target out of action or sinking it outright.

If an aircraft came in sight, the captain simply shouted 'Down below' It was an emergency order and the gun's crew, lookouts, officer-of-the-watch and, last, the captain dropped vertically down the ladder irrespective of crushed fingers or the state in which the gun had been left. It was the first lieutenant's job to get the boat under as quickly as possible, not to worry about what was going on up top; and he did not hold up the dive for any concern about whether the

The asdic dome on HMS *Sentinel*. The hydrophone and asdic set were tuned at about 10 Kc/s. Although used primarily for listening (with a very short range by modern standards) transmissions could also be made, usually for underwater morse signalling between submarines (SST).

captain would make it. With two conning tower hatches, one ten feet below the other, there was always the lower one to be pulled shut if the upper lid was still open when the sea lapped over.[6]

Torpedo attacks were often prolonged and, for most of the crew, boring and frightening by turns. Hits were unpredictable, usually unobserved and all too often followed by a depth-charge hammering. Gun actions, in contrast, offered instant results with little chance of retribution from puny unescorted targets. In this respect, as has already been suggested, submarines which used guns deserved, perhaps, some of the 'unsporting' epithets which had for so long been flung at them since the beginning of the century. But, sporting or not, gunnery was, frankly, a good game.

9 The Enemy Above

The ingenuity, effort and expense in countering the underwater threat was out of all proportion to what was spent on submarines themselves, as submariners well knew. For the Allies, the costly defeat of the U-boats was, as Churchill said, the essential prelude to all effective, aggressive operations. Anti-submarine measures taken by the Axis powers did not inhibit their own offensive capabilities to anything like the same extent; but Germany and Italy were to feel keenly the lack of adequate protection for convoys in the Mediterranean; and Japan was ultimately to collapse due to not having assembled sufficient A/S ships and aircraft to combat the American underwater onslaught on the Empire during the last two years of the war. The Japanese debacle was due primarily to the offensive spirit which entirely dominated the Imperial Navy's thinking, along Mahanian and Jutland principles, which led to destroyer groups being trained, almost exclusively, to fight a fleet action rather than to escort merchant vessels.

World War II started with the Allies, advised by Britain, enjoying sublime confidence in the effectiveness of Asdic (from the initials of the Allied Submarine Devices Investigation Committee). It was, perhaps sincerely, believed that underwater listening and echo-ranging developments had overcome the submarine menace. This totally false but comforting thought arose from unrealistic peacetime exercises, politicians taking scientific aspirations too literally, a trustful conviction in the United States that any new technology was bound to work and an incorrect appreciation of how German U-boats would go about their business in war. Intelligence reports from the Baltic had indicated that U-boats would attack submerged; but the U-boat arm under Doenitz had no such intention. Doenitz was as impressed as anybody about the supposed capabilities of Asdic and Sonar; he constantly advised his men that diving rendered a boat blind, defenceless and more liable to destruction than when on the surface although that, of course, was before Allied radar became effective. Assuming that German agents told him about exercises in the Royal Navy in the 1930s, his opinion must

have been strengthened by reports of British submarines being unable to penetrate the screens formed by escort vessels around capital ships and simulated convoys.

British submariners, or, at least, the Staff of Rear Admiral Submarines, accepted, apparently without demur, some extraordinary conclusions drawn from Fleet manoeuvres to the effect that a submarine would almost always be detected and depth-charged before reaching a firing position. No allowance was made for unwarlike safety restrictions imposed on submarines, nor for the fact that A/S forces knew, pretty well exactly, where the opposing boats would be. It is surprising that submariners took their paper defeat so tamely; but perhaps the notoriously poor promotion prospects for protesters was a taming influence. Whatever the reason for their pre-war silence, submariners began to display (outside the USN where more than a few continued to be unduly cautious) an aggressive disregard for any theoretical potential credited to the enemy above once war broke out and when they were no longer held back by peacetime rules.

Ignorance of the nature of the sea and its effect on underwater sound was a contributory factor in building over-confidence amongst anti-submariners. Sound propagation anomalies, with sound waves deflected and attenuated by temperature and salinity variations, bottom reflections and background noise, were hardly understood. They were learned about, in the main, from negative results when hunting submerged targets; and submariners tended to discover the sea's peculiarities (and put them to good use) before the hunters. Most sea areas had negative gradients where temperature decreased with depth, bending sound waves downwards by refraction without any indication for Asdic operators that this was happening. A surface vessel might well not be aware that its listening range was being severely curtailed to the point where a submarine could approach undetected by powerful active transmitters or passive, listening hydrophones which should have revealed its presence several thousand yards away.

False Asdic reflections or echoes from

'non-subs' abounded and fish-noises—icthyological gefuffles as Captain F J Walker RN, the most successful U-boat hunter of the War, called them—masked submarine screw and machinery and noises and U-boats were able to make their own gefuffles by releasing a *Pillenwerfer*. This was a small metal canister which discharged a dense, chemically generated mass of bubbles as a decoy to reflect Asdic transmissions. It was supposed to keep an attacker busy while the submarine made off; but it only fooled the most inexperienced operators. U-boat men had little faith in it. If very hard pressed it was sometimes more effective to blow main ballast tanks with the vents open or, *in extremis*, to discharge oil or fire debris through a torpedo tube in the hope that the enemy above would think another U-boat had been killed. In isothermal, well-mixed water it was difficult for a submarine trapped in a sound beam to escape and desperate measures were needed; but even in ideal A/S conditions a boat was seldom detected before it gave the game away by firing fish. Despite his fears about vulnerability submerged, Doenitz advised a U-boat captain not to think that every action by the enemy above applied to him for 'generally it did not'. He was, of course, quite right. Submariners would not have achieved much anywhere if they had paid too much attention to what the forces overhead might or might not be doing. Fortune favoured the brave: the so-called lucky ones were those who pressed on regardless. Attack was always the best means of defence. The confusion and noise following a torpedo explosion offered an excellent chance of escape while the targets were trying to avoid another attack and the escorts were milling around and trying to avoid hitting each other. At night, with all ships darkened, violent alterations of course were hazardous around a convoy even when radar was fitted; a submarine with three dimensions at its disposal was much better placed than its pursuers.

When escorting other ships A/S vessels were obliged to sweep out the waters ahead of them with active sound impulses emitted in searchlight beams which could be heard many miles away and used as homing beacons by submarines. German and Italian forces more often used sensitive passive hydrophones when looking for a submarine in a restricted area; their own speed, and hence self-noise, could then be low enough to hear sounds from unalerted and unwary submarines. Submarines therefore learned to keep very quiet. But apart from going below a density layer and presenting the smallest possible target by keeping end-on, there was little a submarine could do to avoid its hull returning a detectable echo if caught in an *active* beam. Experiments were made with sound-absorbent coating but, in most cases, the sea soon tore it off and the added drag cut speed by about 10 per cent. U-boat designers were notably successful, however, in quietening auxiliary machinery by insulating it acoustically from the hull and all captains endeavoured to suppress the unmistakable sound of propellor cavitation—caused by too rapid, inefficient rotation of the screws at shallow depths—by going sufficiently deep when increasing speed. When trying to evade or escape it was, above all, vital not to give away the boat's presence by the sort of easily recognised noise which could be made by a careless member of the crew clattering a bucket, stamping on a deckplate or opening a valve with a spanner which was not rubber-coated. When on the defensive it was also prudent to switch off all unnecessary lighting and machinery to conserve the battery: it was impossible to tell how long a hunt might last although British crews in the Mediterranean, where the going was especially rough for

Top Right
Depth charge from HMS *Verity* **set to explode at shallow setting (pre-war photograph).**

Centre Right
A depth-charge, to a submariner, felt even worse than it looked to a surface-sailor!

Bottom Right
Captain F J Walker conducting an A/S attack from the bridge of HMS *Starling.* **This brilliant officer, whose career had frankly been a failure in peacetime, commanded A/S ships and groups which accounted for 23 U-boats in the Atlantic. He was a genius by the definition of having an infinite capacity for taking pains: unlike some other A/S captains whose patience ran out before that of the U-boats they were hunting, Walker never gave up. His persistence and the tactics he invented, particularly the 'creeping attack' in which he held his target on asdics while directing a consort to 'creep' over the contact and drop depth charges, were amply rewarded.**

NAVAL MESSAGE.

Originators Instructions (Indication of Priority, Intercept Group, etc.)		Codress/Plaindress	No. of Groups
TO: C. inC. PLYMOUTH ® Ad'. C. inC. WA Aug 1969. Capt D Liz		FROM: STARLING	

HAVE SUNK U-BOAT BY DEPTH-CHARGE
AND RAM IN POSITION 44° 59' N 11° 24' W
AT 0830 AM NOW INVESTIGATING WRECKAGE
"STARLING'S" A AND B MAGAZINES FLOODED

240935Z

NAVAL MESSAGE.

Originators Instructions (Indication of Priority, Intercept Group, etc.) IMMEDIATE		Codress/Plaindress	No. of Groups
TO: C. inC. PLYMOUTH ® C. inC. W.A. ADMIRALTY		FROM: E.G.2	

SITUATION AT 1900 B ⊙ SUPPLY 'U-BOAT
"U461" SUNK BY AIRCRAFT IN POSITION
45° 33' N 10° 47' W AT 1206 SURVIVORS
IN "WOODPECKER" ⊙ SUPPLY U-BOAT "U411"
SUNK BY GUNFIRE OF SECOND SUPPORT
GROUP NEAR SAME POSITION AT 1214
SURVIVORS IN "KITE" AND "WREN" ⊙
A THIRD U-BOAT 750 TONS SUNK BY DEPTH-
CHARGE ATTACKS OF SECOND SUPPORT GROUP
IN POSITION 45° 33' N 10° 56' W AT 1543

MUCH WRECKAGE, HUMAN REMAINS AND
OIL, NO SURVIVORS ⊙

301925 B

---

submarines, found, thankfully, that Italian chasers were apt to give up at dusk.

Just as some submarines were much more efficient than others due entirely to human factors, so certain A/S units stood head and shoulders above the rest. It was a matter of application, determination and a refusal to ever give up after hours, days or even weeks of fruitless hunting.

Depth charges were the principle weapons used on all sides throughout the war. They were superseded towards the end by ahead-throwing weapons (hedgehog) but it was 'ash-cans' in large quantities (at £37 apiece in the Royal Navy) which submariners had to contend with mainly.

Being depth-charged was an experience which no submarine wished to repeat. The commanding officer of HMS *J-2* had felt in 1917 that a hammering was a good experience because it 'added to the keeness and efficiency of a boat's crew and shortened the time of a crash dive'! He may have been right (although he must have been almost unique amongst submariners in using the expression 'crash dive') but his added prediction that in the next war it would break the nerve of many submarine officers and men did not prove true. A few nerves broke[1] and there were hardly any cases of claustrophobia (which was not, despite public opinion, a disease endemic to submariners); but there were isolated incidents of boats giving up the fight or surrendering before being damaged beyond hope of recovering the situation. A few captains, too, apparently turned away from heavily defended targets; but they were a very small minority.

Top
This was *U-119*, a Type XB minelayer commanded by Kptlt von Kameke, sunk off Cape Ortegal by HMS *Starling*.

Bottom
Confusion in the Bay of Biscay! This signal from the famous U-boat killer Captain F J Walker commanding the Second Escort Group captures the excitement of 30 July 1943 when a total of six U-boats were destroyed by air and sea forces. Ironically, *U-461* was sunk by aircraft 'U' of No 461 Squadron, RAF. This U-boat was a valuable Milch Cow as was *U-462* mistakenly referred to as *U-411* by Walker. His wording of the signal makes it appear that he was responsible for the sinking but the U-boat had been mortally wounded by the aircraft before he arrived. *U-504* was the third U-boat in the signal and was acting as an escort to the other two; it was actually a large 1120-ton Type IXC commanded by a U-boat ace, F K Poske.

Out of many hundred recorded Allied and Axis submarine attacks there were only a handful of occasions when the threat of depth-charging deterred submarines from obtaining their objective entirely as their captains wished. On the other hand submariners kept their heads down during an actual going-over and were then unable to fire torpedoes (other than Gnats) with any accuracy. It was therefore tactically sound for A/S vessels to plaster the general area even if not in firm contact; but the number of charges which they carried was limited and had to last for the whole period of escort duty. Submariners counted the explosions carefully and were able to judge pretty well when stocks were running low.

The killing range of a standard depth-charge was about 30 feet and its effect increased with depth. It was a prematurely surrendered U-boat, *U-570* (Kptlt Hans Rahmlow), later taken into British service as HMS *Graph*, which in due course provided the most detailed indications of underwater explosive effects. *U-570* surfaced off Iceland in misty weather on 27 August 1941 under the nose of a patrolling Lockheed Hudson aircraft from No 269 Squadron, RAF. The Hudson (Squadron Leader Thompson) instantly straddled the target with four depth-charges which so shook the captain and crew that it was decided to surrender without a fight. Subsequent investigation showed that there was nothing in the hull damage which would have made it impossible, or even difficult, to dive the U-boat: nor would cracked battery cells have prevented escape. Supplies to the main motors, lighting and auxiliaries could have been restored very quickly and the steering and hydroplanes could have been put in hand-control; but no attempt was made to do any of these things. Although the captured crew said chlorine gas was escaping from the batteries no trace of this was found by the party sent by the Royal Navy to take the boat over. It was a case of total surprise leading to panic.

As well as subsequently patrolling usefully under the White Ensign *Graph* yielded valuable secrets, not least the results of depth-charge trials made against her when she decommissioned. These showed that a charge detonated beneath the hull was the most dangerous: one-third to one-half of its value did the same damage as a charge above the hull; and if a charge was detonated opposite to a transverse bulkhead or a large fitting attached to the pressure hull its effect was considerably magnified.[2] It was therefore correct, when avoiding counter-attack, to go as deep as possible and that is what submariners, instinctively, were doing. German

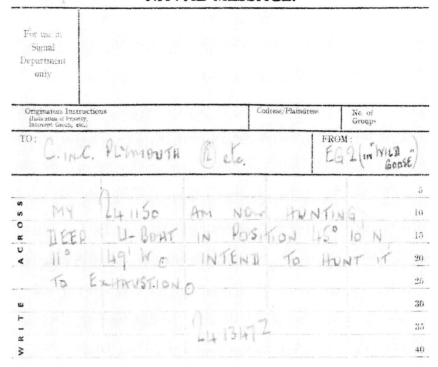

NAVAL MESSAGE.

This signal from HMS *Wild Goose* spelled the end for *U-449* (Oblt Otto).

USS *Scamp* (Lcdr J C Hollingsworth) was on the surface endeavouring to pass an enemy report on 7 April 1944 off Mindanão when a Japanese seaplane came out of the sun. Hollingsworth dived immediately but a bomb exploded close to port as the boat was passing 40 feet and forced her down to 320 feet. Despite severe internal damage, *Scamp* regained trim and remained dived until dark. External damage can be seen here. *Scamp* was to be lost eight months later, probably on a mine.

and Italian submarines were helped by being well supplied with information about standard Allied hydrostatic depth-charge settings—which were frequently too shallow. The normal diving depth of a Type VIIC U-boat was 100 metres, well below D/C settings early in the war, and it could go much deeper, although at 200 metres the internal wood-work started to crack (an unpleasant sound) as the hull compressed. The laid-down limit was 230 metres in emergency but that only left a narrow margin of 20 metres before the hull could be expected to collapse. The ultimate collapse depths predicted by de-signers on all sides were, incidentally, ac-curate (as proved by post-war trials) to within a few feet.

U-boat men were also aware of another significant advantage of going deep. This arose from the fact that an Asdic sound beam, being conical in shape, covered a narrower and more shallow volume of water as the range closed. An escort therefore lost contact with a U-boat at 200 metres at a range of about half-a-mile even in isothermal water: when running in to carry out an attack on a 'collision' course there was therefore nec-essarily a brief period during which contact was lost. This, added to the time which depth-charges took to sink to a given depth, allowed a submarine about two minutes to make a radical and undetected alteration of course and speed to place itself some 300 yards outside the lethal range of the pattern. Depth-finding Asdic sets and ahead-throwing weapons to overcome this problem for escorts were not generally available until after the critical part of the Battle of the Atlantic had been fought; at the height of the battle skilled U-boat captains who kept their nerve were able to avoid being sunk by the great majority of surface ships' attacks. How-ever, quite distant depth-charges could damage a boat's equipment to the extent that it could no longer fight. The more delicate, sophisticated fittings were the first to go. Doenitz insisted that equipment be kept

Top Left
Hauling an A/S net aboard a boom vessel.

Centre Left
Submarine surfacing after being caught in an A/S net during trials.

Bottom Left
Japanese search-receiver aerial (70–430 mc/s) for giving warning of enemy radar. The antenna was rotated by hand by an operator on the bridge equipped with headphones: audio warning only was given.

simple and easy to repair at sea with 'hand-raulic' alternatives where possible. The best commanding officers in all navies exercised breakdown procedures at every opportunity and constant training paid dividends. A lazy commanding officer who did not bother to keep his crew at the peak of efficiency during slack periods on passage or patrol may have enjoyed some superficial popularity but it was apt to be, literally, short-lived.

When below periscope depth a submarine had to rely on its hydrophones which were directional but, at best, only accurate to within one degree of bearing. Range could only be guessed. Submarine hydrophone operators had some indication when escorts were in contact from the way in which their transmissions remained constant (searching) or started to shorten (attacking). However, shouts of 'in contact' and 'attacking' were discouraged because they did little to help morale. It was usually obvious enough, from propellor noises throbbing through the hull, when depth-charges were about to rain down. The attacking ship could plainly be heard speeding up on a steady bearing and that was the moment for the submarine to start energetic evasive action. A brief but hideous pause was followed, audibly, by the faint

click of pistols striking before the successive sledge-hammer blows of explosions hit the hollow hull and overcame all rational thought. Gauge-glasses shattered, lights went out and the boat was thrown about uncontrollably by the colossal force of pressure waves at depth. If a sea-water connection fractured it did not just leak; the resulting water jet at, say 200 metres was like a bar of steel, quite strong enough to break a limb.

Amidst the damage and the darkness it was imperative to remain quiet and that made essential repairs difficult and trimming more so, for the ballast pump and high pressure blows were clearly audible to the enemy above. Any tendency to over-react, let alone panic, was bound to make the situation worse. But a well-drilled crew who were able to keep calm stood a far better chance of escape than anti-submarine forces reckoned. The prize for maintaining the will to win under depth-charge attack must have gone to an American coloured boy who, somehow, failed to appreciate the significance of Japanese 'ash-cans' exploding all around his boat: his enthusiastic cry of 'give 'em hell' came as a welcome relief. It was only equalled, perhaps, by the Coxswain of a British boat being hammered from all sides

USS *England* was only commissioned in December 1943 and was new to the business of war, but under the command of Lcdr W B Pendleton she quickly became the top scoring submarine killer in any navy. Between 19 and 26 May 1944 the *England* sank the Japanese submarines *I-16*, *Ro-106*, *Ro-104*, *Ro-116* and *Ro-108*; and on 30 May, in company with other destroyers, her hedgehog projectiles sent *Ro-105* to the bottom.

who drily reassured everybody: 'It's alright men, we've got them surrounded.' Possibly the coloured boy had just knocked back one of the little two-ounce bottles of Scotch that, with the tacit connivance of certain captains, appeared on these occasions despite the US Navy being strictly dry. As for the Coxswain, he would not have been a Coxswain if he did not have access to some private hoard of refreshment. A little Dutch courage could be very helpful on occasions.

It was aircraft, though, with their much more limited attacking ability, that submariners—especially U-boat men—came most to dread. The impact of A/S aircraft on the underwater world was enormous but they were not always as effective as submariners feared. Allied aircraft were considerably

Top
AA armament strengthened in a Type VIIC U-boat to one 37 mm and two twin 20 mm guns

Centre Left
U-79 going down, with two survivors still waiting on the stern, after being depth-charged by HMS *Hasty* **and** *Hotspur* **off Bardia on 23 December 1941.**

Bottom Left
U-977 hit by a test torpedo fired by USS *Atule* **on 13 November 1946.** *U-977* **commanded by Oblt Heinz Schaeffer, was at sea when the cease-fire was ordered. Schaeffer decided to make for the Argentine but first landed, by dinghy, 16 of the crew in Norway who wanted to return home. He used his schnorchel for most of the way and arrived on the 17 August 1945, the boat being interned on arrival.** *U-977* **was subsequently handed over to the USN for use as a torpedo target.**

more skilled in anti-submarine operations than their Axis counterparts; but out of 767 attacks delivered on U-boats between September 1939 and December 1942 only 31 were lethal, although a further 73 resulted in serious damage. The main effect of A/S air operations, from a submariner's point of view, was to make surface-running exhausting and dispiriting. Boats had constantly to be alert to dive for any aircraft, whether or not it seemed to be an immediate danger. Crews were continually dragged from their bunks by the diving klaxon in an area of high

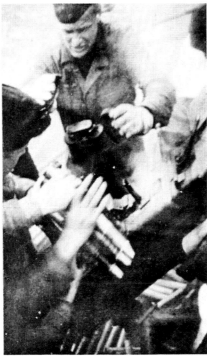

A sequence of photographs taken during an action in which *U-427* was repelling aircraft with the 37 mm in January 1945.

air activity, battery charging became a problem and mundane domestic evolutions such as sight-taking, ditching gash or blowing the heads were dangerous. Air crews returning from apparently fruitless missions probably did not realise that their presence alone was an effective deterrent to submarine operations.

Allied submariners also learned to their cost that there was no such thing as a friendly aircraft; they were frequently bombed in 'safe' zones by over-sanguine aircrews. Rear Admiral Lockwood USN was prompted to remark that he was 'not impressed with the earnest desire of the Army Air Force to co-operate with other forces.' Wise submariners dived for anything with wings and were not ashamed if, later, it turned out to be a seagull.

The nets and obstacles that had been so extensively used from 1914–1918 were seldom employed in the second underwater war except in the Baltic; but the inherited World War I concept of laying anti-submarine mines proved disturbingly effective and a number of submarines on all sides were lost because of them. If sent to a mined area, which might or might not be known by its operating authority, a submarine depended largely on luck. In good conditions a submarine sonar set fitted with a short-transmission unit was theoretically able to detect a moored mine at about 1500 yards, but negotiating a minefield with this device was not a proposition that submariners welcomed. It was better to go below the expected depth of the minefield and hope for the best. Magnetic mines on the sea bottom could not, in any event, be detected; nor was degaussing and wiping (to neutralise the permanent magnetism of the hull) a sure defence. American operators in the Pacific insisted on rigorous demagnetising procedures before a boat sailed on patrol, only to

declare (wrongly) after the war that the Japanese had no magnetic mines; but other Allied submarines suffered heavily, especially in the shallow waters around the Mediterranean. Some 26 out of 82 British submarines lost between 1939 and 1945 were reckoned to have succumbed to mine warfare (although, statistically, a small proportion of these were probably lost by accident, for the sea itself was more powerful than any devices of the enemy and accidents due to human error were not unknown).

Deliberate ramming, another tactic from World War I, sent a number of boats to the bottom. Two ramming incidents deserve mention. The first was an unrelieved moral tragedy resulting in the loss of HMS *Oswald* at midnight on 1 August 1940 off Cape Spartivento. It was a dark night and *Oswald* was on the surface charging batteries when a lookout sighted an Italian destroyer one-and-a-half miles on the starboard quarter. The officer-of-the-watch sounded the night alarm but when the captain climbed to the bridge he was unable to see because he had been decyphering a signal in the wardroom without wearing night-adaption red goggles. The destroyer, *Vivaldi*, turned to ram and increased speed but *Oswald* took no avoiding action and no effort was made to man the gun or bring the torpedo tubes to bear. The subsequent investigation[3] established beyond reasonable doubt that the captain ordered 'Abandon ship' before the submarine was struck.

When the collision came it was only a

During the period 1904 to 1939, for which international figures are fairly reliable, 181 men in sunken submarines were rescued by salvage, thirty-three by bell (USS *Squalus*): sixteen escaped and survived using breathing sets and two escaped but did not survive. During the same period over two thousand men died in submarine accidents. Whether some of them tried to escape and failed will never be known. The chances of escape in war, especially in deep water, were very slight and submariners in all navies took little comfort from the escape sets carried; the emphasis on escape throughout submarine history resulted from the pressure of public opinion and the press and not from submariners themselves who preferred to concentrate on not having an accident in the first place!

Submariners learning to use DSEA (Davis Submerged Escape Apparatus) sets in the escape tank at HMS *Dolphin*. All navies used broadly similar apparatus which supplied pure oxygen, dangers of which were only fully appreciated long after the war although K E Donald fully reported 'the affects of Oxygen under pressure on Man' in 1943. Men were taught to clear their lungs completely before breathing from the oxygen bag but, in fact, it was probably those who neglected to do so and hence breathed a lesser concentration of oxygen during their escape, who fared best. However dangerous it may have been during an actual escape, the inflated bag was invaluable for support on the surface. Note the instructions at top!

glancing blow and the depth-charges that followed were not particularly close. However, the submarine was scuttled by the captain's order. The chief ERA opened main vents when all the men were out of her. Fifty-two very unhappy members of the crew were rescued and made prisoner. The Commander-in-Chief, Levant was able to say that commendable courage and devotion to duty was displayed by many of the ship's company, notably by Lieutenants Pope and Hodson, but the affair was not one to be proud of.

The other incident, concerning HMS *Proteus* (Lt Cdr P S Francis), was much more enlivening and creditable. *Proteus*, with a number of successes already embroidered on her Jolly Roger, was patrolling on the surface during the night of 8 February 1942 when Francis thought he saw a U-boat: he immediately turned towards in order to attack, but the target turned out to be the Italian torpedo boat *Sagittario*. The two antagonists met head on, causing considerable damage to *Sagittario*'s port side which was ripped open by the submarine's forward hydroplane. But the collision started several rivets in *Proteus* who had, reluctantly, to abandon the patrol. Both sides retired gracefully from the arena.

It was astonishing how much punishment a submarine could take and still survive. When a boat did give up the fight—and that was not often—it was men, badly led, who cracked before the pressure hull. It is, of course, easy enough now to criticise the few who went under when they might have finally escaped. But when tired—and submariners were often very, very tired after days or weeks in action—or when confused by what Nelson had called the fog of war and when concerned for the lives of shipmates, prospects sometimes simply looked too bleak to carry on. Nonetheless, so long as a boat could somehow stay submerged in one piece, however battered, submariners came to learn that they always had the edge on the enemy above.

Left
The engine room hatch of a British S-boat. Note the external securing bolts which made it impossible to open from the inside; it was usual to secure hatches in this way to prevent their jumping under depth-charge attack but they were, of course, thereby rendered useless for escape.

10 The Mediterranean

With such a formidable array of Italian submarines at the starting line it was reasonable to expect the Axis powers to take the lead in the underwater Mediterranean war. They did no such thing. The Italian High Command was timorous and examined risks too closely to permit a positive strategy for the submarine force. Caution bred more caution and brought about a conviction, which spread rapidly downwards through the ranks, that risks could not be tolerated. Submariners in other navies regarded their Italian counterparts with more liking than professional respect. In many cases that attitude was justified, but certainly not in all.

Italian strategy decreed that the surface fleet should look to Italy's defence while the underwater fleet took the war to the enemy; but the submariners were scarcely cheered on in battle. When the war began 55 boats were already stationed in various areas of the Mediterranean with a vague hope of their ambushing unspecified targets. Two boats, *Finzi* and *Cappellini* were heartlessly sent through the perilous and heavily patrolled Straits of Gibraltar into the Atlantic but they, too, lacked any clear directive. Three days after the beginning of hostilities half the boats at sea returned to their bases with one problem or another and thereafter there were never more than 25 to 30 submarines on patrol. The boats that stayed out were pushing their luck: no less than ten were sunk during June 1940, the first month of the war for Italy. Losses thereafter declined to about ten boats every six months but this was only because there were less boats at sea. A schnorchel device would have done much to reduce losses: a prototype had in fact been successfully tested in the Italian submarine *H-3* in 1926 but the project had been abandoned, for no given reason. Italian submarines found themselves exposed to concerted attacks in the Mediterranean by British submarines, ships and aircraft and their slow reactions, both in human terms and diving performance, rendered them frighteningly vulnerable. The 32 boats transferred to German control at Bordeaux, primarily for Atlantic operations, from September 1940 to February 1943, with the majority arriving in France at the beginning

of this period, fared, for the most part, no better; worse, they suffered humiliating criticism from the German U-boat Staff. Nor did the half-dozen Italian boats in the Red Sea and Indian Ocean enjoy success and several crews in these areas were incapacitated (they said) by an illness caused by faulty air-conditioning. Morale in the Italian submarine service was, with notable exceptions, not good.

Against the 79 Italian boats lost on operations, the principal successes achieved were three British cruisers, one destroyer, one corvette, one minesweeper, and about half-a-million tons of merchant shipping. However, the figures quoted in various sources vary widely and many original records were destroyed.

To be fair, the German U-boats despatched to the Mediterranean in 1941 and

again in 1943 and 1944 did not find their task easy in those generally calm, clear and confined waters. Nor, for that matter, did the British boats. But U-boats were much smaller and handier than their Italian counterparts and, although Doenitz was reluctant to take any boats away from the Atlantic convoy battles, the handful that operated in these unfamiliar conditions so far removed from

HMS *Uproar* (Lt L E Herrick) arriving in Algiers from England in April 1943, having been attacked by two American Bell Airacobras en route. Although not a high-scoring submarine she had amongst her several successes sunk the small 731-ton German controlled *Andrea Garallino* off Elba with three torpedoes out of three fired and, at the incredible range of 7800 yards, torpedoed the 11,718 ton liner *Vergilio* (ex-Yugoslav *Dubrovnik*) which became a total loss as a result.

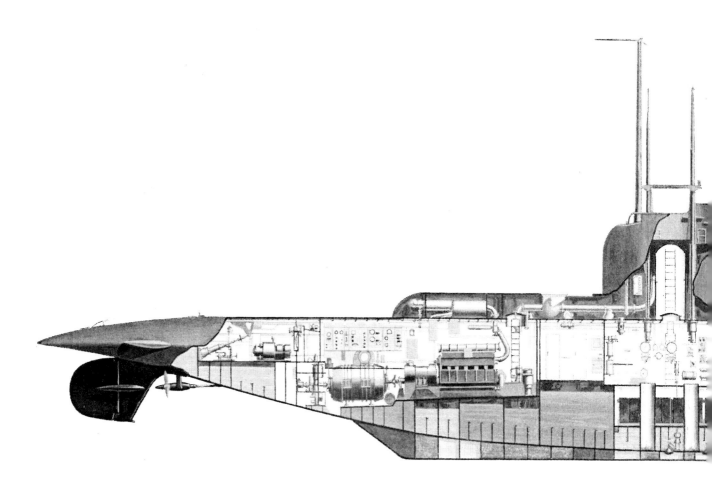

the Atlantic caused more than sufficient havoc to justify their presence. In November and December 1941 they sent the aircraft carrier *Ark Royal*, the battleship *Barham* and the cruiser *Galatea* to the bottom. In the first six months of 1942 the cruisers *Naiad* and *Hermione* were sunk by *U-565* (Kptlt Jebsen) and *U-205* (Kptlt Reschke) respectively; and the submarine depot ship *Medway*, five destroyers and 12 assorted transports and tankers were also torpedoed. The loss of HMS *Medway*, the largest and best depot ship afloat, was a severe blow to the British Flotillas. The aircraft carrier *Eagle*, escorting a convoy, went down to *U-73* (Kptlt Rosenbaum) in August 1942 and towards the end of the year U-boats opposing the Allied landings at Algiers and Oran sank six transports totalling 66,000 tons and four destroyers. In 1943 and 1944 they followed these successes, whilst attempting to dislocate Allied sea lines of communication, by sinking a fast minelayer (see also Chapter 8) and about 30 merchant vessels. These achievements went some way towards off-setting Italian failures but they did not count for nearly as much, strategically, as the destruction wrought upon Rommel's supply lines by British boats.

The Mediterranean saw submarine activity of every kind and it was here that the most advanced tactics in the underwater war were developed, practised and perfected, particularly by the British and the two Polish and three Dutch boats under British control. Submariners, especially those operating from Malta, struggled under conditions which were more testing than in any other theatre; but with typical perversity they performed even better as the difficulties became greater.

The Royal Navy's Mediterranean flotillas enjoyed outstanding leadership and no better than that of Captain 'Shrimp' Simpson[1] commanding the Tenth Flotilla in Malta and backed to the hilt by the forceful, implacable Max Horton, Vice Admiral (Submarines) from his London Submarine Headquarters at Northways.

Politics in the Mediterranean were traditionally a national pastime and it was always difficult to know who was on what side. When Italy entered the war and when the collapse of France in Europe followed ten days later, the situation was, to say the least, confused. But the Middle East was such a vital arena that one thing was clear to all: the Mediterranean sea lanes would be challenged by both sides and the victor in that dispute at sea would gain final victory. Simpson grasped the point immediately.

Shrimp was junior for the job. He was only a commander when appointed Senior Officer Submarines, Malta in August 1940 and had only recently been promoted to a Captain when his group was established as the Tenth Flotilla. At the far end of the Mediterranean submarines from the Far East had been transferred to the First Flotilla at Alexandria and were by now patrolling against the enemy ships supplying North African possessions and armies; but the old O, P and R class boats were not suitable for inshore operations and suffered heavy losses; nine out of 15 were sunk in the last half of 1940. At the end of the year some of the new U-class submarines were sent out from England destined for Alexandria but were ordered to Malta where these small, handy craft quickly showed their worth in the Tenth Flotilla. Their endurance was short but Malta was ideally situated for them. From Lazaretto harbour they sailed principally to strike at the Sicily–Tripoli–Tunisia route favoured by Axis shipping; but they were also sent to patrol off the main Italian naval bases in South Italy in the hope of attacking heavy enemy units, for at that stage the British Mediterranean surface fleet was numerically at a disadvantage.

The early Italian air attacks on Malta

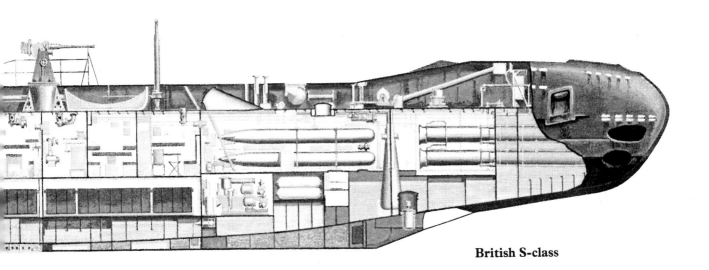

British S-class

Lt A D Piper RNR. This outstandingly successful reservist from the Merchant Navy commanded HMS *Unsparing*, operating mainly in the Mediterranean, from August 1942 to October 1944. The Submarine Service was fortunate to include a number of these very experienced seamen whose training in the Merchant Navy, especially as regards seamanship and navigation, proved invaluable. Piper, as a third hand, First Lieutenant and Commanding Officer, made no less than 39 patrols in *Ursula, Unbeaten* and *Unsparing* and survived the war.

scarcely dented the island's defences; submarines were able to return in relative peace for rest and repair at the improvised base on Manoel Island. That state of affairs was not to last. At the end of 1940 German forces entered the Mediterranean battle and the effect was soon felt. Air attacks on Malta were stepped up and soon the surface units based on Malta had to be withdrawn. The submarines remained: they were the island's only offensive force. There was now little rest for the crews between patrols. Workshops and accommodation were heavily damaged in air raids and submarines in harbour were themselves bombed making it necessary for them to spend daylight hours submerged which did nothing to assist maintenance and relaxation. However, Rommel's Afrika Corps was building up for an assault: it was imperative that the Malta submarine base kept going as usual. Although false economy before the war had prevented submarine underground pens from being built, the Maltese limestone was easy to burrow into. Shelters and makeshift workshops were rapidly excavated. In matters of maintenance and making-do the Flotilla was fortunate in having an outstanding Engineer Officer in Commander Sam MacGregor who was resourcefulness and improvisation personified. MacGregor's de-

termination to avoid all paper work was helped by a fortuitous Luftwaffe bomb on the Naval Store Officer's records. As a cloud of paper forms and flimsies floated away on an easterly breeze at the height of the bombardment in February 1941, Sam was heard to remark with satisfaction: 'I reckon that must have loosened things up a bit.' Thereafter submariners helped themselves to whatever stores they needed without formality.

The German and Italian Commands were unaccountably rigid in their routing of convoys between Italy and North Africa. They adhered to similar routes for as much as three months at a stretch. This obliging consistency favoured the submarine onslaught on Rommel's supply lines and useful guidance was also obtained from intelligence reports which did not, in the garrulous Mediterranean, depend wholly on intercepted radio traffic. Thus, submarine operators, who at various times controlled boats from Gibraltar, Algiers, Alexandria, Beirut, and Maddalena as well as Malta, were able to concentrate the very limited number of submarines available at the most favourable positions. From January 1941 until February 1943 it was usually possible to maintain four submarines, including Polish and Greek boats, on patrol. During these

77

Top Left
Commissioning ceremony for the Greek
submarine *Pipinos* at the Vickers yard, Barrow-in-
Furness. Despite arriving late in the war *Pipinos*
under the command of Lt Rallis, and later, Lt
Loundras carried out several aggressive patrols in
the Aegean Sea during one of which the German
controlled ex-Italian destoyer *Calatafimi* was
torpedoed and sunk. Although hampered by
political problems and outdated weapons the
Greek submarine service embodied the fine
fighting spirit of that country with its
determination to attack its enemies.

Top Right
U-95 survivors coming ashore after being sunk by
the Dutch submarine *O-21*, east of Gibraltar. *U-95*
had sunk over 50,000 tons of shipping.

Centre Right
The Dutch submarine HNMS *O-21* (Lt Cdr J F van
Dulm RNN) returning from patrol off Naples
encountered the *U-95* in the Gibraltar area at
night. The Dutchman was keeping a better
lookout and sank the U-boat, rescuing the
German captain, Kptlt Gert Schreiber, four
officers and seven ratings. Some of the survivors
from *U-95* are pictured, still carrying their
excellent U-boat clothing, leaving HNMS *O-21*.

Bottom Right
HNMS *O-21* arriving at Gibraltar with German
prisoners from *U-95* which she had sunk on 28
November 1941 just off Gibraltar.

Top Left

HNMS *Dolfijn* **(British U-class) at Holy Loch,
Scotland.** *Dolfijn* **under Lt Cdr H van Oestrom
Soede patrolled very successfully in the
Mediterranean where, on her first patrol, she sank
the Italian U-boat** *Malachite* **on 9 February 1943.
Two important merchant ship sinkings followed
later and the boat returned safely to England after
fifteen Mediterranean patrols on the 7 June
1944. During a working-up patrol in UK waters in
January 1945** *Dolfijn* **was fired at by a Mosquito
aircraft (in an area of total attack restriction),
causing damage to both periscopes and other
equipment which delayed her completion
programme by one month and, in effect, ended
the war for her.**

Top Right

The last of 'Mum'. The British depot ship *Medway*
sinking after being torpedoed by *U-372* **on 30 June
1942 on passage from Alexandria to Haifa. Only 30
ratings from a total complement of 1,135 officers
and men were lost: the remainder were quickly
picked up by the exceptionally heavy (but
ineffective) escort of one cruiser and seven
destroyers. The serious loss of stores, repair
facilities and torpedoes was somewhat mitigated
by 47 torpedoes, out of the 90 carried, floating
clear and being recovered.**

Centre Left

HMS *Unseen* **(Lt M L C Crawford) alongside
survivors of the 985-ton** *Rastrello* **which she sank off
Bari, 21 August 1943. Four survivors were taken
on board** *Unseen* **and food and morphine tablets
were given to the remainder on the raft.**

Bottom Left

**Caught at night on the surface, the Italian
submarine** *Uarsciek* **dived to escape the Greek
destroyer** *Queen Olga* **and the British destroyer**
Petard **but a severe depth-charging forced her to
the surface where she was engaged by gunfire.
Under tow by** *Petard* **for eleven hours the
submarine finally floundered on 15 December
1942. Despite having 25 patrols to her credit the**
Uarsciek **had sunk no enemy ships.**

Valetta, Malta, during a lull in the bombing 1942. Despite the heavy bombing and extensive damage, submarines continued operating from the Island except for the period 26 April to 20 July 1942 when no air cover was available for the minesweepers endeavouring to keep the approaches to Malta clear of mines laid by German E-boats.

critical two years more than 600 torpedoes were fired and about 100 enemy vessels were sunk by torpedoes and gunfire, varying from small schooners to liners of 20,000 tons. Warship casualties inflicted by the Tenth Flotilla alone included two cruisers, four U-boats and several destroyers. Meanwhile Malta suffered some 2,000 air-raids resulting, in just over a week from 26 March to 4 April 1942, in the loss of four submarines in harbour including the Greek *Glaukos*. Losses were correspondingly heavy at sea in 1941 and 1942; a dozen boats failed to return to Malta from patrol, half of them being sunk by mines.

On the success side of the scales, HMS *Utmost* (Lt Cdr R D Cayley) started the count in February 1941 with a ship north of Tripoli, followed by *Upholder* (Lt Cdr M D Wanklyn) who got two a week later. In March, *Upright* (Lt E D Norman) carried out a brilliantly executed night attack, on the surface, against two Italian cruisers, hitting and sinking the *Armando Diaz*, going very fast, with a salvo fired fine on the bow at short range. This particular sinking gave the Flotilla confidence and a much needed boost to morale. It also fully justified the intensive 'Perisher' training back at home!

Successes mounted during the summer and reached a peak during the Autumn of 1941. HMS *Upholder* sank the large liners *Conte Rosso* in May and *Oceania* and *Neptunia* in September. They were all southbound full of troops and their loss significantly curtailed shipborne troop movements. In five hours the last two attacks accounted for as many enemy men as the total number of Allied submariners employed during the whole Mediterranean war. *Oceania* and *Neptunia* were hit at night with *Upholder* rolling heavily on the surface and the gyro-compass out of action. Wanklyn did

not trouble, in his patrol report, to make the point that the attack was exceptionally tricky with the helmsman steering erratically by magnetic compass and the boat yawing several degrees either side of the true course; he simply remarked that he had to spread his torpedoes over the full length of both targets by anticipating the amount of swing between the order to fire and the torpedo leaving the tube. The first torpedo was aimed, as normal, at the target's bow; a violent yaw to starboard obliged him to fire the second where his fourth would normally have been aimed; and

A night air-raid on Malta. Attacks like this were almost as critical as attacks at sea on submarines themselves.

Above
Kptlt Rosenbaum (*U-73*), having just received the Knights Cross for sinking the British aircraft carrier *Eagle* on 11 August 1942. He is standing on the deck of his boat at La Spezia with the Italian Flag Officer Commanding U-boats and the Senior German U-boat Officer in the Mediterranean.

Below
U-616 (Oblt Siegfried Koitscka) returns to Toulon with victory pennants flying. *U-616* endured the longest A/S hunt in any navy — three full days — before being sunk off Oran on 14 May 1944 by eight US destroyers and a squadron of Wellington bombers. Note the extreme youth of the crew in these photographs and also the individual boat's badge (in this case a red devil brandishing pistols) worn on their forage caps.

Above
Kptlt Helmut Rosenbaum (*U-73*) with the customary floral tribute given to U-boat commanders after a successful patrol.

numbers three and four tubes were fired to fill in the gap on the swing back to port. This skilful timing covered the combined targets with accuracy and resulted in two torpedo hits, one on each ship. The attack took place on 18 September 1941 and was the culmination of a carefully planned operation involving four submarines placed across the probable line of advance of the convoy as it approached Tripoli. *Unbeaten*, *Upholder* and *Upright* were positioned ten miles apart on a line drawn 30 degrees off the expected enemy course and *Ursula* was stationed some 50 miles closer to Tripoli where it was expected she would have an opportunity to attack soon after dawn, Simpson reckoning that the convoy would aim to arrive at Tripoli at 0900. A strong air escort was expected and it was therefore planned that the other three boats should make their attack by night which is exactly what *Upholder* did, firing soon after 0400. It was an exemplary engagement.

Wanklyn had already been awarded the

Victoria Cross, one of five Mediterranean submariners who received the highest decoration, some four months earlier, following his fourteenth patrol. It was nominally given for sinking the liner *Conte Rosso* (17,879 tons) in failing light with the Asdic gear out of action and a very real risk of being rammed inadvertently by one of the numerous escorts; but submariners preferred to think of the award being made for Wanklyn's ability, during a long series of patrols, to assess chances quickly and accurately and take calculated risks when there was a proper, if very narrow, margin in his favour. He had a brilliant mathematical brain which served him perfectly, however fraught the situation was; and, above all, he had the knack of inspiring his crew into being a cut above average. His success did not, however, come easily: his first four patrols had been failures to the point that Simpson began to wonder if he could retain a commanding officer who was using up valuable torpedoes with no result. But Wanklyn studied the circumstances which had caused him to miss and meticulously set out to polish the techniques necessary to succeed. And succeed he did: in the 16 months that *Upholder* operated in the Mediterranean Wanklyn sank two U-boats and one destroyer, damaged a cruiser and another destroyer and sank or damaged 19 of Rommel's supply ships totalling 119,000 tons. (A third U-boat on *Upholder*'s Jolly Roger was subsequently disallowed.)

Upholder failed to return from her twenty-fifth patrol, falling victim to the small Italian torpedo boat *Pegaso* off Tripoli on 14 April 1942. *Pegaso* carried out an urgent attack on a smoke-float datum dropped by an escorting seaplane and then gained an unclear sonar contact. When she had depth-charged the position with no apparent result and lost contact after two hours the little A/S vessel modestly made no firm claim for having destroyed anything. But she had sunk the Royal Navy's finest submarine. It was a sadly low-key ending to *Upholder*'s career. It may well be that Wanklyn and his crew had simply done one patrol too many and were mentally and physically burned out by the strain. Full alertness was not limitless.

Returning to the attack on *Neptune* and *Oceania*, which showed submarine strategy and tactics at their best, it is worth noting that Captain S M Raw, in his covering letter on *Upholder*'s patrol report considered that the principal credit for the operation 'must be accorded to Captain S10 (Simpson) not only for his most excellent and intelligent appreciation of the enemies' probably movements—which proved to be uncannily accurate—and the subsequent dispositions, but also for the

Above
Italian submarine *Bronzo* lying in Malta Harbour after being captured off Augusta by three British minesweepers on 12 July 1943. The German influence can clearly be seen in this design based on the *Argonauta*. This boat, eventually transferred to the French Navy in 1944, became the *Narval*.

Below
HMS *Parthian* steaming into Camnavitsa Bay during her bombardment of the Axis Resin Refinery. Her gun, its muzzle visible in the foreground, is about to fire at the iron pier, which appears just to the right of *Parthian*'s jumping wire. The burning caiques were loaded with turpentine and resin.

very high state of efficiency of the submarines under his command. A better *esprit de corps* than that prevailing in the Tenth Submarine Flotilla could not be found . . .'

Neither Simpson nor his commanding officers were prone to exaggerating their successes; claims by nearly all submarines were correctly assessed. Between January 1941 and August 1944 an attack success rate of 28 per cent was achieved and a torpedo hitting rate of 53 per cent, much higher than elsewhere and almost exactly what was forecast by submariners in certain uniquely realistic Spring Exercises of 1939. With the experience of attacking fast, zigzagging, heavily escorted ships behind them, the Tenth Flotilla boats, commanded from January 1943 by Captain G C Phillips and operating towards the end of the war from a new base at Maddalena in Northern Sardinia, found coastal targets and transitting U-boats were easy game off Toulon and along the Riviera coast. The rate of hitting here rose as high as 64 per cent. It was an unequalled example of professionalism and precision.

Gunnery, however, was not always the Tenth Flotilla's strong point. When HMS *Unbending* (Lt E T Stanley) encountered a schooner full of mule and camel fodder in the Gulf of Sfax and went to gun-action stations it was the gunlayer's first war experience. At 1,000 yards he was wide of the target so

Stanley closed to 500 yards and then to 100 yards. The gunlayer missed. So the Torpedo Petty Officer (TI) was summoned to see what he could do. *Unbending* went alongside the target, the TI jumped on board with a can of shale oil and the schooner was soon blazing. It took the arrival of *Safari* (Cdr Ben Bryant), on loan from the Third Flotilla, to show what a three-inch gun in competent hands could achieve. Bryant favoured gun actions and calculated that he averaged ten tons of enemy shipping sunk for every 16-pound round fired. Guns came to be used extensively, especially in the Mediterranean backwaters where the air threat was less: and shore bombardment was a popular pastime when sea-borne targets failed to appear. Gunnery targets were usually small, of course, but sinking caiques and schooners, which often carried valuable stores and troops, was undoubtedly bad for the enemy's morale even if the steady rate of attrition did not amount to a formidable tonnage in comparison with torpedo sinkings.

At the end of his time in the Mediterranean, Simpson suffered the infuriating experience of having the ship in which he was taking passage, HMS *Welshman*, sunk under him by *U-617* but he survived to take command of the Western Approaches Escort Group from Londonderry. It was largely because of 'Shrimp' that Rommel's Chief of

Parthian is firing at the caique visible behind the smoke. Both this and the one in front of the smoke were sunk; and fire was then shifted to the railway tracks on the left, all of which were hit. The railway embankment can be seen stretching across the picture behind the houses, but the signal box, water tower and station (all of which were hit) are not visible. All the tracks were damaged and set on fire; about thirty hits were registered on, or very near, the line in the gaps between the houses before *Parthian* was forced to dive by machine-gun fire from the right of the picture. Only one dwelling was hit, the fourth from the left, whose roof appears damaged in this picture. One man of the submarine's gun crew was killed by machine-gun fire. This was *Parthian*'s third Mediterranean war patrol from 30 April to 12 May 1943.

Staff was moved to say 'we should have taken Alexandria and reached the Suez Canal if it had not been for the work of your submarines on our lines of communications.' This tribute from an enemy is fully substantiated by history but historians have seldom given Allied submarines in the Mediterranean the full credit for victory in an area where, as the Commander-in-chief Mediterranean wrote to the Admiralty on 17 September 1941, 'every submarine which could be spared was worth its weight in gold.' Even at 540 tons apiece, he may have been right.

11 Operations from the United Kingdom

German U-boats were intermittently active in UK home waters and the Norwegian Sea—witness Gunther Prien's brilliant attack on HMS *Royal Oak* in Scapa Flow on 14 October 1939 and the (largely abortive) shots at British transports and naval vessels during the German invasion of Norway in April 1940—but German preoccupation with the Atlantic left the field open, for the most part, to RN submarines and Allied boats under British control.

The seas around England were often shallow, treacherous, heavily mined and beset by violent bouts of bad weather and poor visibility. In summer months the hours of darkness in the northern areas were short, which made battery-charging hazardous. Sea-water densities changed abruptly from place to place and at different depths, especially off Norway where the density could be 1.022 at periscope depth and 1.025 a little deeper which made it necessary to reverse normal trimming procedures and flood water into the compensating tanks to get below the layer around 60 feet. A/S defences were concentrated in focal areas and the Skaggerak, in particular, was 'alive with escorts'.[1] Floating mines were a serious threat and a dozen or more might be sighted every day on patrol along the Norwegian coastline: HMS *Sturgeon*, for instance, encountered 73 on passage to and from Lerwick between 25 June and 12 July 1942.

The battle commenced tragically when, on 10 September 1939, HMS *Triton* and HMS *Oxley*, patrolling off Oprestad, encountered each other on the surface with the result that *Oxley* was sunk with only two survivors. *Oxley* was out of position and replied to *Triton*'s challenge with an ineffective signal lamp but, *de mortuis nil nisi bonum*, *Oxley*'s captain was absolved from blame.

One result of this accident was to increase the spacing between submarines on patrol, but before this could be done *Sturgeon* fired three torpedoes at *Swordfish*, happily without result. On 17 September HMS *Seahorse* managed to survive bombing by an RAF aircraft which heralded a long series of attacks on submarines in all areas by 'friendly' aircraft. Notoriously inaccurate air navigation and lack of adequate co-operation and co-ordination between submariners and airmen at Staff level was to become horrifyingly evident throughout the war.

HMS *L27* (launched in 1919 but completed many years later) got three hits on a 7000-ton merchant ship on 15 October 1940 off Cherbourg, passing through a screen of seven A/S trawlers to do so. But on the next patrol inshore the old lady hit what was probably a fixed defensive mine off Fécamp with the result shown here.

Above
HMS *Sunfish* in dry dock at Wallsend after a near miss from a 250 kg bomb in the River Tyne on 2 October 1941. She was later transferred to the Soviet Navy.

Below
A triumphant German procession. A/S trawler *UJ-128* towing HMS *Seal* into Friedrichshafen. *Seal*, a minelayer, was too large for the task allocated — the laying of a minefield in a particularly restricted part of the Kattegat. Herself falling victim to a German mine on 4 May 1940 and badly damaged, *Seal* managed to struggle off the bottom but while striving to make for neutral Sweden, and unable to scuttle herself, she was taken by German forces which could hardly have failed to find her when daylight came at 0250 on the next day.

Above and Right

The British submarine *Seal*, flying the Swastika (*above*). *Seal* was renamed *UB*. Of little use to her captors, *Seal-UB* was eventually scuttled in Keil harbour at the end of the war. One young German rating, fed up with boring trials in *UB* was drafted to *U-570* which was captured by the British on her first patrol; thus he served in a British submarine captured by the Germans, and a German submarine captured by the British.

Submarine War Orders were indicative of the British Admiralty's poor appreciation of submarine capabilities: 'the primary object ... is to report movements of German war vessels but no *favourable* opportunity of attacking them should be neglected, providing that this can be done without prejudice to the primary object ...' The old, first war Mahanian concept of bringing about a major Fleet action was firmly at work. Enemy reports were by no means easy to pass in the face of enemy air cover and the War Orders hedged instructions in a curiously unaggressive, unctuous way: 'Commanding officers must decide for themselves, according to circumstances, whether the importance of the enemy to be reported and the possibility of the submarine being detected by enemy surface ships or aircraft, justifies surfacing to pass a report, if necessary flying a kite[2] or waiting until more suitable opportunities exist.' Even on the distant China Station, where there was no air threat, British submarines were ordered 'to report not attack'. The War Orders were, therefore, not inspiring at the start; but on 20 September 1939 they were drastically amended to say that 'the object of all submarines is to attack enemy war vessels.' Commanding officers were duly thankful!

However, the Government was determined to adhere to international law and attacks on all merchant shipping were restricted just as in the German Navy. This led to a loudly-voiced uneasiness in the minds of submariners who were unsure about their aim and object, particularly after the sinking of MV *Heddernheim* on 19 March 1940 by HMS *Ursula* (Cdr G C Phillips) and the attack on MV *Edmond Hugo Stinnes* (subsequently scuttled) on 23 March by HMS *Truant* (Lt Cdr C H Hutchinson). Both attacks took place in the Kattegat and the

Top Left
HMS *Sealion* (Lt Cdr Ben Bryant — in the Sou'wester) returning from patrol in the Kattegat. Note the White Ensign laid over the bridge for identification from the air. The small box-like instrument on the side of the bridge is the port emergency navigation light.

Centre Left
Note the HMS *Sealion* cap-tallies. For security reasons the names of boats were not usually worn; 'H M Submarines' was the general rule as the war progressed.

Bottom Left
Submarines based in the UK did not have to go to the Arctic to find ice — HMS *Sealion* at Parkstone Quay, Harwich in 1939 or 1940.

safety of the crews was ensured; but it was held that the commanding officers had exceeded their orders. Nonetheless, Vice Admiral (Submarines), by now Max Horton, decided not to restrain other submarines from following these examples, as 'neutrals were unlikely to be offended so long as territorial waters were respected'. The correctness of this view was borne out by a report from the Military Attaché at Copenhagen which stated that the sinking of these ships had a 'splendid effect upon the Danes'. On 4 April, with the Norwegian invasion imminent, commanding officers were ordered to give priority to transports over warships. This important signal was the forerunner of the Polish submarine *Orzel*'s sinking of the transport *Rio de Janeiro* east of Kristiansund on 8 April and the Cabinet decision approving the first of several 'free for all areas' whereby all German merchantmen would be treated as transports and sunk without warning.[3] Thereafter, restrictions were lifted along a pattern similar to that of the German Navy but, if anything, preceding it. Doenitz pointed out that, by April 1940, British submarines were permitted to attack all German ships by day and ships of any kind without warning by night, even if sailing with full lights, in the 'free for all' areas in the Kattegat and Skaggerak. He also argued that Allied merchant ships making the signal 'SSS' together with their position on sighting

a U-boat, could only have resulted from general instructions issued by the British Admiralty contrary to the provisions of the 1936 London Submarine Agreement. His suspicion was entirely confirmed by the 'Defence of Merchant Shipping Handbook 1938' which enjoined merchant vessels to send enemy reports and never 'tamely surrender to a submarine' but to 'open fire if fitted with defensive armament.' The claim by Doenitz that the German Naval High Command reacted only with extreme caution, and step by step, to British measures constituting a breach of Agreement was not without foundation.

Operations around the United Kingdom and northwards into the Norwegian Sea were so scattered that no clear pattern emerged which can tidily be summarised. An international mixture of submarines were employed including French, Dutch, Polish and Norwegian boats as well as British. The French submarines were not up to Allied standards of mechanical efficiency and their crews were not contented, which was hardly surprising in view of the condition of France; most French boats returned to France at the end of May 1940 leaving, however, *Rubis* (CC Georges Cabanier and later CC Rousselot) who performed outstandingly as a minelayer throughout the war. Her early operations had clearly shown her usefulness and the British Admiralty were insistent that she remained

behind to continue minelaying operations (minelayers being short in the Royal Navy) when the other French submarines were recalled.

When the Armistice talks between France and Germany began on 18 June, *Rubis*, at Dundee, had taken aboard a complete new outfit of mines and the British Admiralty urgently requested the French Vice Admiral Jean Odend'hal to allow the boat to sail for a last patrol on 21 June: a promise was made that when the Armistice went into effect *Rubis* would be recalled. The Armistice was signed on 25 June but *Rubis* continued in accordance with her orders, which were not revoked by the British, and laid mines in the approaches to Trondheim on 26 June. After returning to Dundee she was formally taken over (the French said 'seized') on 3 July. The appropriation went smoothly because most of the crew were on leave ashore but, in any case, Cabanier and his men decided, after a week's deliberation, to continue the fight.

Taking over the giant *Surcouf* at dawn on the
same day at Portsmouth did not go so
smoothly: some of the French crew fought
back with revolvers and four men were killed,
three of them British.

Vague accusations were subsequently to be
made about *Surcouf* carrying out some kind
of Fifth Column activity off Bermuda, but
claims that she torpedoed Allied vessels were
not upheld by the records. She was, however,
politically unpopular and eyebrows were
raised on all sides when she reinforced,
with her 8-inch guns, Admiral Muselier's
annexation of the Saint Pierre and Miquelon
Islands on 24 December 1941, an event
which stirred up considerable controversy in
the American hemisphere and imperilled the
US State Department's agreement with
Vichy. *Surcouf* had the knack of being at the
centre of political trouble. Her unhappy
career was terminated when she was rammed
on 19 February 1942 by the American
merchant ship *Thompson Lykes* seven days

after leaving Bermuda for the Pacific where
she was due to reinforce French forces after
the declaration of war on Japan. Despite
rumours to the contrary, there is no reason to
believe that this ramming was anything but
accidental; but 159 men went down in her,
the greatest number ever to be lost in any one
submarine until USS *Thresher* was accidentally lost 21 years later.

The total of 12 Dutch submarines (including three transferred from the Royal Navy)
enjoyed exceptionally high morale but achieved no sinkings, in contrast to the marked
success of Dutch boats operating in the Far
East. The three Norwegian boats operating
from the UK sank eight vessels between them
including *U-974*; they benefitted from an
intimate knowledge of Norwegian waters
and, despite the small size of the Norwegian
Navy and the comparatively limited training
available, their crews were notably efficient.

In August 1942, the planners of Operation
Torch, the Joint North African landings,
wanted more submarines in the western
Mediterranean. Six *Gato*-class boats were
therefore sent with USS *Beaver*, an old
depot ship, to form Subron 50 operating
primarily from the Gareloch in Scotland;

these submarines would hopefully release some smaller British boats for use in the Mediterranean. They achieved no success during 27 patrols and none of their four claimed sinkings, which included a U-boat, was substantiated. Nonetheless, Anglo-American co-operation took a turn for the better and the Royal Navy grasped the opportunity of studying American men, methods and material at first hand. Furthermore, operations in European waters enabled the USN to overcome a number of teething troubles and useful experience was gained. Subron 50 remained on the eastern side of the Atlantic until, in June 1943, Admiral H R Stark USN, commanding the American naval forces in Europe, stated that these boats were required in the Pacific. They left during June and July carrying out uneventful patrols in mid-Atlantic on the way back.

On their departure Flag Officer Submarines stated, with necessary politeness but evident sincerity, that Subron 50 had been invaluable to the submarine campaign during the winter and spring of 1942 to 1943: 'without them it would not have been possible to have staged operations on anything like the scale we have. It is pure bad luck that they have not achieved more successes, especially so in the case of USS *Shad* who carried out one of the most outstanding attacks that have ever come to my notice.' The latter remark was prompted by *Shad* (Lcdr MacGregor) detecting, by radar, an inward-bound blockade runner escorted by three destroyers off Bilbao on 1 April 1943 at a range of about six miles. MacGregor handled his submarine expertly and fired three torpedoes at 0342. When the torpedoes exploded everything on the radar screen was blotted out; it was conjectured that the

Top Left
HMS *Sturgeon* **('a virgin sturgeon needs no urging' according to the ribald ditty) at Blyth. Under three captains,** *Sturgeon* **certainly needed no urging to sink 24,000 tons of shipping, operating from the UK.**

Centre Left
Lt. M R Wingfield at *Sturgeon's* **periscope. The boat was evidently shallow, hence the crouch, but the picture may have been posed because the fore-planes should certainly have been to dive — which they are not!**

Bottom Left
The Norwegian submarine *Ula* **(ex-HMS** *Varne***), seen post-war, which had a successful war and sank** *U-974* **on 19 April 1944 off Stavanger. Like other Norwegian boats she gained much from an intimate knowledge of the difficult home waters.**

blockade runner and at least two of the escorting destroyers had been sunk—hence Flag Officer Submarines' congratulations. But analysis showed that the target, *Pietro Orseolo*, was only damaged by a torpedo in number one hold which threw most of her cargo of rubber into the sea (and may have caused radar blanketing) while one of the escorts, *Z-23* was struck by a torpedo which failed to explode. It was, despite the relatively disappointing results, 'a masterly attack and deserved better success.'[4]

Torpedo successes by submarines based on the United Kingdom amounted to 89 enemy ships destroyed, including the cruiser *Karlsruhe* and eight U-boats with a further 15 vessels damaged including the battle-cruiser *Gneisenau*, the pocket battleship *Lutzow*, which was put out of action for 12 months, and the cruisers *Leipzig*, *Nuremburg* and *Prinz Eugen*. Magnetic torpedo exploders, detonating the warheads beneath the targets, would have achieved greater damage and more sinkings. These figures do not include the heavy damage done by X-craft whose charges detonated under the ships attacked (see Chapter 16).

Minelaying was an important function and the fighting French *Rubis* easily led the field with 683 mines laid in a record-breaking 28 patrols which resulted in the sinking of 14 supply ships (totalling 21,410 tons), seven A/S ships and minesweepers and damage to one supply ship and a U-boat.

The specialised British minelayers were also kept busy although they were not confined to minelaying operations. *Narwhal*'s fields claimed 12 victims, *Rorqual*'s one and *Seal*'s four. After *Seal* (Lt Cdr R P Lonsdale) had completed a lay at 0945 on 4 May 1940 in a very dangerous position inside the Kattegat (which Max Horton had approved against the advice of his Staff, although this statement is based upon verbal evidence only) she started to retire westwards, with German E-boats threatening from the North East, between two unsuspected lines of German mines laid, respectively, at a depth of 15 and 30 metres. By 1000 the E-boats had not been shaken off so *Seal* went to 70 feet and stopped all auxiliary machinery. Half an hour later, nine miles east of Skagen lighthouse, there was a heavy explosion forcing *Seal* to bottom in 22 fathoms. The mining compartment, part of the crew space, the auxiliary machinery space and the motor room were flooded and the submarine lay on the bottom at an angle of 18 degrees bow up. *Seal* had picked up and towed one of the German mines earlier in the day and this had finally detonated. At 2300 Londsale endeavoured to pump the boat off

Lt R P Raikes, commanding HMS *Tuna* in 1942, looking grim — perhaps as the result of arduous and probably unwelcome misemployment on convoy escort duties following successful patrols in *Seawolf* earlier.

the bottom to escape under cover of darkness; but it was not until 0100 on the next morning that she broke surface when she proved completely uncontrollable. It was decided to try to make for Swedish territorial waters, stern first if necessary, which was the only way in which the submarine appeared manageable. But daylight came early and at 0250 *Seal* was sighted by German aircraft and attacked. Fire was returned until the Lewis gun jammed and no further retaliation was possible. A German seaplane then landed near *Seal*, held up the crew with its guns and took the captain prisoner. The officers remaining on board were loathe to sink the boat with the crew, including two badly wounded men, still on board and, anyway, by the time a German trawler *UJ-128* arrived *Seal* appeared to be sinking gradually by the stern of her own accord. She was towed to Friedrikshavn still sinking gradually—but not fast enough. Fortunately the damage caused by the mine and the destruction of secret apparatus by the crew prevented the German Navy from reconditioning the boat.

The *Seal* (*UB*—not numbered for there was only one U-Boat, British) was laid up in June 1941 but not before Doenitz had sarcastically asked the German Torpedo Department why they could not copy *Seal*'s British torpedoes which had *working* detonators.

When the crew were freed from their prisoner-of-war camp at the end of the war, Lonsdale was court-martialled but honourably acquitted. The Admiral (Submarines) of the time wrote to the Admiralty: '. . . it must be remembered that the officers and men must have been suffering from the mental after-effects of their prolonged dive without the modern assistance of oxygen and

CO_2 absorbent which may well have clouded their judgement. In actual fact the task of sinking the submarine, with all pressure gone in the telemotor (hydraulic) system would have offered some difficulty to men in an exhausted condition.'

The least popular occupation for submariners in these waters, and one for which they had absolutely no training in peace or war, was escorting convoys. The reason for employing submarines in this role, mainly between Britain and Russia, was to provide protection against German surface raiders. The French had advocated submarines for escort duty from the beginning of the war and it may have been politically expedient, even if tactically imprudent, to use British submarines for the same purpose. Submariners heartily disliked the idea, although Lieut R P Raikes (HMS *Seawolf*) did his best to justify two periods of Russian convoy duty in May and June 1942. *Seawolf*'s presence, said Raikes, materially assisted the Merchant Navy's morale, and that was borne out by the boat's enthusiastic reception at Murmansk when she passed along the line of merchant ships on her way up harbour to Polyarnoe. It cannot, however, have been much compensation for being so wastefully employed when submarines were in such short supply.

12 The Atlantic

The U-boats which fought the Battle of the Atlantic have usually been regarded, outside Germany, as an anonymous menace reduced to cold statistics, an impersonal war-machine which, set into motion, advanced and then, finally, retired. It was not like that at all. U-boats were manned by individuals. Each boat had its own distinctive character and its own individual problems, often even harder to overcome than those faced by submariners in other navies.

A few figures to set the scene are inescapable. During the 51 months of the 1914–1918 war Germany had built 365 U-boats, lost 178 and sank 4,837 Allied merchant vessels totalling over 11 million tons. In the second underwater war, covering 68 months, 2,775 Allied merchant ships, amounting to 14,573,000 tons, were sent to the bottom for the appallingly high number of 784 U-boats lost from all causes. The great majority of these losses, on both sides, were incurred in the Atlantic.

Doenitz held, quite contrary to American, British and Japanese thinking, that submarine operations against naval vessels promised little hope of success. Even on the surface, he said, a U-boat had no margin of speed to haul ahead for an attack and enemy aircraft were expected to forestall such action anyway. The low underwater speed of a U-boat would not permit it to attack fast warships except when it was directly in their path and 'that happens very seldom.' Nor did Doenitz believe that U-boat operations in support of German surface forces would be a profitable proposition. Hence, from the start, U-boat captains devoted almost their entire attention to the destruction of Allied merchant shipping and formulated their individual standing orders and domestic arrangements accordingly.

In September 1939, the first wave of U-boats was ordered to wage war against merchant shipping 'in accordance with the revised issue of the Prize Regulations until such time as danger areas are declared.' The regulations were those of the London Protocol (1936) whereby merchant ships (other than those on military service, resisting inspection or under escort) could be sunk only after being stopped and searched and

after steps had been taken to ensure the safety of their crews. This would clearly be impossible in many cases, particularly near an enemy coast.

Nonetheless, Doenitz stuck by the rules although he pointed out that the British Admiralty were breaking them by instructions (issued in 1938) to Merchant Vessels to the effect that they were not to submit tamely and should signal reports of U-boats sighted.

Unfortunately, on 4 September, the day after war was declared, Oblt F J Lemp in *U-30* torpedoed the liner *Athenia* in the belief that she was an auxiliary cruiser. A thorough enquiry was held and Lemp was exonerated (and told to improve his ship recognition). The mistake was almost certainly genuine but it caused the Fuehrer—who was trying to avoid any extensions of the war—to order that no liners whatever were to be attacked, whether sailing independently or in convoy. The incident did not help Doenitz in his struggle with the politicians for more freedom of action; but he succeeded, step by step, in getting the U-boat restrictions lifted; and there was some justification in his claim, already noted in Chapter 11, that he only did so successively in response to breaches of the Agreement by the British Admiralty. However, from the outset tankers were considered separately. They were of such importance to Britain's war effort that U-boats were permitted to attack neutral tankers (other than American, Russian, Japanese, Spanish and Italian ships) but were to 'remain unobserved and use electric (trackless) torpedoes in order that the illusion of an internal explosion may be created.'

With certain restrictions, which were fairly easy to observe, U-boats in most vital areas were, by May 1940, no longer significantly hindered by the provisions of the London Protocol and were able to concentrate uninhibitedly on the destruction of Atlantic shipping. They flung themselves into the task with grim enthusiasm.

The German radio interception, codebreaking and intelligence services provided a great deal of information but there was still the problem of location. On the face of it, a large number of ships ploughing smokily

along at eight or ten knots would seem easy to discover but that was not true in practise. Doenitz remarked in his War Diary for December 1940 that the first contact was a matter of chance. Unfortunately for the Allies chance chose to favour the U-boats.

Doenitz never succeeded in getting adequate air reconnaissance from Reichsmarschall Goering who disliked the Navy and was jealous of his own powers, but, amongst other measures, U-boat men devised a sort of do-it-yourself autogyro, a rotary winged kite which, in the South Atlantic outside Allied air cover, could be used for reconnaissance. It was primitive but more effective than the alternative of a collapsible mast. It consisted simply of a metal tube frame mounting a pilot's seat, a conventional autogyro head rotor and a foot-operated rudder. The whole kite could be dismantled and stowed very quickly in the Type IX boats which carried them. The machine was launched at the end of a cable with a slight backward tilt when an air speed of 25 kms per hour had been attained: the minimum airspeed to maintain it in flight was about 17 kms per hour. Up to 165 metres of cable could be veered to give the autogyro a height of about 100 metres above sea level and enabling the pilot to search over a distance of 60 to 70 miles. Reports were made down a telephone to the submarine bridge. It was found that ordinary German seamen could easily learn to handle these kites, which could be recovered safely: one U-boat launched its machine no less than 80 times without mishap. However, the pilot was in danger if he reported an enemy warship necessitating a rapid dive by his parent submarine: he was then supposed to jettison the rotor and descend by parachute into the sea where, according to a laconic report circulated in the Royal Navy, 'he drowned in the normal way'.

Autogyros apart, initial detection usually depended on binoculars or a periscope sighting. Even with advanced underwater sonic equipment such as *Balkon* and *Nibelung* the human eye was always the most reliable sensor by day or night. An unlit ship was no more than the faintest shadow against a dark horizon; the trick was not to look directly at it

94

but a little above. Not everybody had good night vision; the few that did were prized members of the crew and were apt to be hauled up to the bridge as lookouts whatever their proper jobs were.

Although the principle of concentration was all important, U-boats making up a wolf-pack did not act as a team, as commonly supposed, and they were never intended to. Boats were drawn, usually, from a patrol line strung across likely convoy routes through the Atlantic and directed onto a convoy by signals from U-boat Headquarters (BdU) situated for most of the battle at Kerneval near Lorient. They did not communicate between themselves (other than, exceptionally, by signal lamp) and only signalled their intentions and convoy positions by short two or four-letter HF radio signals to shore to minimise the chances of being pinpointed by Allied D/F stations. Co-ordinated attacks were launched in 1940. The first spectacular success came when, over a two day period, 20 out of 34 ships in Convoy SC 7 were sunk, most of them during the dark and rainy 'Night of the Long Knives' off the Rockall Bank, on the night of 18/19 October. Kptlt Otto Kretschmer's War Diary for *U-99* told of his part in the action:

18 October

0200 On receipt of urgent radio message "To *U-100*, *U-28*, *U-123*, *U-101*, *U-99* and *U-46*. Be in position in patrol line from naval grid square 2745 to naval grid square 0125 AM by 0800," I proceed to my position at maximum speed, although I cannot arrive until 1100. I therefore report by short signal to FO U-boats: "Owing to position, cannot comply with dispositional order. My position is naval grid square 41 AM." [Some 100 miles southwest of the new patrol line position.]

0903 Sight a U-boat conning-tower, bearing 060. Shortly afterwards a medium boat appears on the horizon, proceeding in a north westerly direction. It must be *U-46*, the boat on the left flank of the patrol line.

1128 In position. Proceed up and down across the patrol line. Medium U-boat in sight, bearing north. It must be *U-101*, which is proceeding up and down along the patrol line.

Radio message received at 1208: "... To FO U-boats from *U-38*: Convoy in 1539 AM at 0200 [some 100 miles northwest of the patrol line] course 110, no contact ..." That means that the convoy will pass the patrol line to the north. At 1530 the patrol line is cancelled by radio from FO U-boats: "... *U-100*, *U-123*, *U-101*, *U-46*: Operate on *U-38*'s report. Convoy probably in 2580 at 1400." [Some 30 miles north of the north end of the patrol line.] Flag Officer U-boats cannot suppose *U-99* to be in the patrol line. I proceed in an east-north-easterly direction.

1745 Wind south-east, force 3; sea 3; moderate cloud. *U-101*, which is two or three miles north, signals by light: "Enemy sighted to port."

1749 A warship is sighted, bearing 030, steering east. Soon afterwards, smoke to left of her. Finally the convoy. While hauling ahead to attack, we sight a steamship to the southeast, apparently on a westerly course.

1928 Submerge for attack. [These were early days. It was much more usual to remain on the surface.]

1950 Surface, as the ship is making off slowly to the east. Haul further ahead: at 2000 pass within a few hundred metres of a U-boat on the surface, apparently *U-101* again.

Kk **Werner Hartenstein** (*U-156*) who torpedoed the *Laconia* on 12 September 1942 in the South Atlantic. A humane man, he was determined to save the huge number of people on board his victim which included women and children, Poles and 1800 Italian POWs, as well as British troops. Doenitz ordered other U-boats to assist and requested help from French ships at Dakar but during rescue operations an American Liberator, ignoring a makeshift Red Cross flag and all that was obviously going on, dropped bombs. The incident prompted Doenitz to forbid, by signal, all such rescue operations in the future because they were clearly too hazardous. His signal was to be used in evidence against him at Nuremberg. A very skilful captain with a high score, Hartenstein was to go down with his boat off Barbados when depth-charged, this time accurately, by a US aircraft from VP-53 on 8 March 1943.

Right
U-26, a Type 1A U-boat which scored several successes in the early months of the war before falling victim to HMS *Gladiolus* and aircraft of No 10 Squadron, RAAF on 3 July 1940 South-West of Bishop Rock.

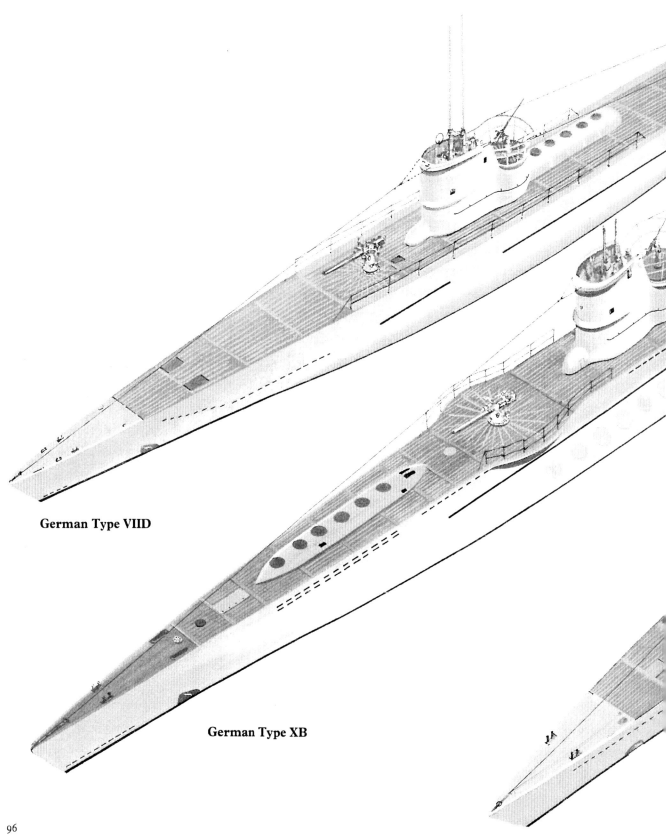

German Type VIID

German Type XB

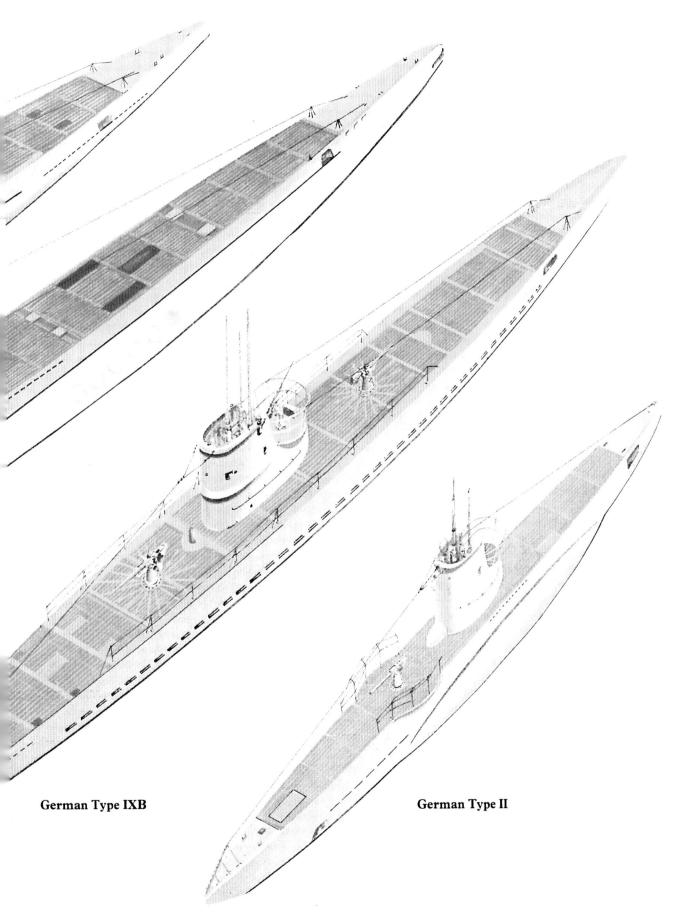

German Type IXB

German Type II

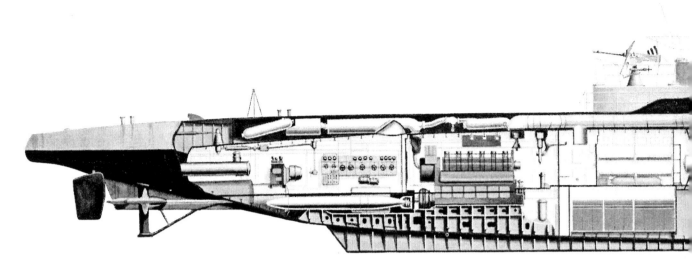

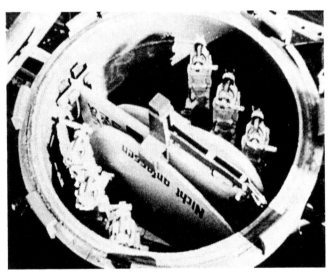

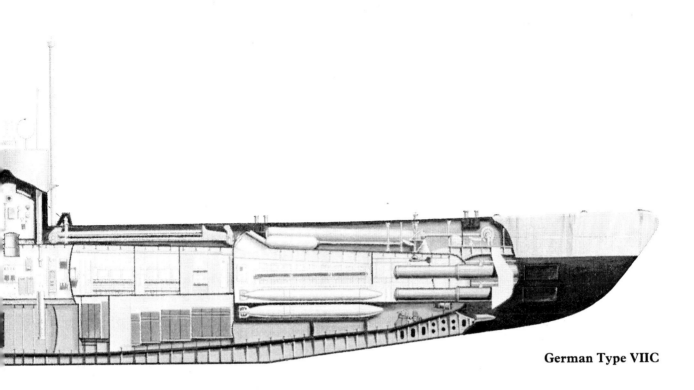

German Type VIIC

Assembling and launching a Focke-Achgelis
Fa 330 rotary-winged kite—the '*U-Bootsauge*' (U-
boat's eye)—in the South Atlantic. Assembly from
the pressure-tight storage tubes could take four
men as little as three minutes. The 180 lb kite was
placed on a platform abaft the conning tower and
the 12 ft blades were spun by hand until the
U-boat's own speed ahead kept them rotating.
The field of vision was, of course, greatly extended
by this device but there is no firm evidence of it
contributing greatly to sinkings.

2024 Another U-boat has torpedoed the ship. Shortly afterwards exchange recognition signals with *U-123*. Convoy again in sight. I am ahead of it, so allow my boat to drop back, avoiding the leading destroyer. The destroyers are constantly firing starshells. From outside, I attack the right flank of the first formation.

2202 Weather: visibility moderate, bright moonlight. Fire bow torpedo by director. Miss.

2206 Fire stern torpedo by director. At 700 metres, hit forward of amidships. Vessel of some 6,500 tons sinks within 20 seconds. I now proceed head on into the convoy. All ships are zig-zagging independently.

2230 Fire bow torpedo by director. Miss because of error in calculation of gyro-angle. I therefore decide to fire the rest of the torpedoes without the director, especially as the installation has still not been accepted and adjusted by the Torpedo Testing Department. Boat is soon sighted by a ship which fires a white star and turns towards us at full speed, continuing even after we alter course. I have to make off with engines all out. Eventually the ship turns off, fires one of her guns and again takes her place in the convoy. I now attack the right flank of the last formation but one.

2330 Fire bow torpedo at a large freighter. As the ship turns towards us, the torpedo passes ahead of her and hits an even larger ship after a run of 1,740 metres. This ship of some 7,000 tons is hit abreast the foremast, and the bow quickly sinks below the surface, and two holds are apparently flooded.

2355 Fire a bow torpedo at a large freighter of some 6,000 tons, at a range of 750 metres. Hit abreast foremast. Immediately after the torpedo explosion, there is another explosion with a high column of flame from the bow to the bridge. The smoke rises some 200 metres. Bow apparently shattered. Ship continues to burn with a green flame.

19 October

0015 Three destroyers approach the ship and search the area in line abreast. I make off at full speed to the southwest and again make contact with the convoy. Torpedoes from the other boats are constantly heard exploding. The destroyers do not know how to help and occupy themselves by constantly firing star-shells, which are of little effect in the bright moonlight. I now start to attack the convoy from astern.

0138 Fire bow torpedoes at large heavily-laden freighter of about 6,000 tons, range 945 metres. Hit abreast foremast. The explosion sinks the ship.

0155 Fire bow torpedo at the next large vessel of some 7,000 tons. Range 975 metres. Hit abreast foremast. Ship sinks within 40 seconds.

0240 Miss through aiming error, with torpedo fired at one of the largest vessels of the convoy, a ship of the *Glenapp*-class, 9,500 tons.

0255 Again miss the same target from a range of about 800 metres. No explanation, as the fire control data were absolutely correct. Presume it to be a gyro failure, as we hear an explosion on the other side of the convoy some seven minutes later.

0302 Third attempt at the same target from a range of 720 metres. Hit forward of the bridge. Bow sinks rapidly level with the water.

0356 Fire at and miss a rather small, unladen ship, which had lost contact with the convoy. We had fired just as the steamer turned towards us.

0358 Turn off and fire a stern torpedo from a range of 690 metres. Hit aft of amidships. Ship drops astern, somewhat lower in the water. As torpedoes have been expended, I wait to see if she will sink further before I settle her by gunfire.

0504 Ship is sunk by another vessel by gunfire. I suppose it to be a British destroyer, but it later transpires that it was *U-123*. Some of her shells land very close, so that I have to leave the area quickly. The ship was *Clintonia*, 3,106 tons.

0530 I commence return passage to Lorient . . .

Further devastating wolf-pack attacks quickly followed. The extraordinarily efficient organisation at BdU, run by only a handful of watchkeepers, enabled Doenitz and his brilliant Staff to wield units at sea almost as though they themselves were sharing the crowded, sea-swept bridges of the boats as they raced through the Atlantic gales ahead of the convoys to be in position for attack when darkness fell. U-boat captains knew that their signals back to Doenitz—essential for a pack to gather—forewarned the enemy of his fate; but they also knew that there was very little a lumbering convoy could do except make drastic alterations of course which seldom took it wholly out of reach. It was more important to achieve concentration than surprise. Each captain aimed, quite independently, to penetrate the protective screen, diving only if immediately threatened and then only for 20 minutes or so, and make for the heart of the convoy. Once inside, between the convoy lines, a boat was fairly secure because, as Oblt Otto Westfalen (*U-968*) explained, even if the boat was glimpsed and the escorts were alerted, the convoy had to stay together and were too close to make independent course alterations without risk of collision. Nor was it then possible for escorts or merchant ships to use guns with safety. A U-boat captain was therefore able to select one target after another and fire deliberate salvoes of one, two or (rarely) three torpedoes at each. If convoy ships were at their usual spacing, one thousand yards in line abreast and five hundred yards in line astern, it was usually best to maintain the same course as the convoy and angle torpedoes right or left when the bridge-director sights came on. In these conditions the First Lieutenant looked through the sights and directed fire-control while the Captain acted as General Manager and took his boat into the right positions for successive attacks. It was almost impossible to miss such large, steady targets at a few hundred metres.

Allied submariners, on the relatively few occasions when they acted in groups, invariably sought to establish each other's positions by radio or underwater signalling for safety but Doenitz considered this unnecessary. In fact (probably unknown to BdU) two out of 17 U-boat collisions were directly due to pack tactics. The worst, which sank two boats, occurred in pitch darkness during the early morning of 4 May 1943 off Cape Ortegal. May was, anyway, a disastrous month with 41 U-boats lost; but there was a certain uniquely hideous nightmare quality about the disaster which overtook *U-439* (Olbt H von Tippelskirch) and *U-659* (Kptlt W Sporn).

The two boats were hotly pursuing a pair of adjacent south-bound convoys. By about 0130 they had unknowingly come very close to one another while steering to head off their targets. Meanwhile, another U-boat had

Above
Atlantic convoy seen from HMS *Thunderbolt* **in the Atlantic acting as an escort in early 1941. A recognition grenade is prudently loaded and ready to fire. Convoy duties were understandably unpopular: a submarine was not suited for the task, could achieve little in the event of attack by German surface units (which they were supposed to guard against) and was itself in danger of being rammed or mistaken by Allied units for a U-boat.**

Bottom Right
Oblt V Varendorf, who had been Gunther Prien's Second Watch Officer in *U-47* **during the spectacular Scapa Flow attack, thanking the Bandmaster who provided the customary martial music for a send-off in July 1942. It was to be the last patrol for Varendorf, now commanding** *U-213* **which was lost with all hands after depth-charging off the Azores a few days later on 3 July.**

launched its attack. The First Lieutenant of *U-439*, reported to be by nature lazy and easy-going, became so interested in the resulting display of starshell that he neglected to look out on the port bow (which was his sector). Then, not knowing it was exactly the wrong moment, the captain ordered a slight alteration of course to port. There was not merely a glancing collision: *U-439*, making 7 knots, squarely struck *U-659*, travelling at full speed, in the control room. Water poured in. A few minutes later a huge wave swept over *U-659* and sent her to the bottom.

U-439 went full astern after the impact but her torpedo space was flooded and an attempt to compensate the bow-down angle by flooding the after tanks only settled the boat deeper in the water. In the end, a wave down her conning tower sent her down in the same way as her sister. She may have drifted helplessly just below the surface because, two hours later, HMS *Coverley* struck a submerged object, probably the doomed U-boat. If so, she put out of their misery any men who may still have been alive.

Even if the incident had happened three years earlier and been reported to Doenitz, it is most unlikely that he would have imposed safety restrictions on the pack tactics which he so rightly believed were essential to success. Certain risks had to be accepted.

U-boats did, of course, take any opportunity of torpedoing capital ships that offered themselves as targets and, occasionally, deliberate operations were mounted against them; but Doenitz refused to be deflected from his main aim. He also strenuously resisted untrue propaganda put out by Goebbels whose purpose was better suited by

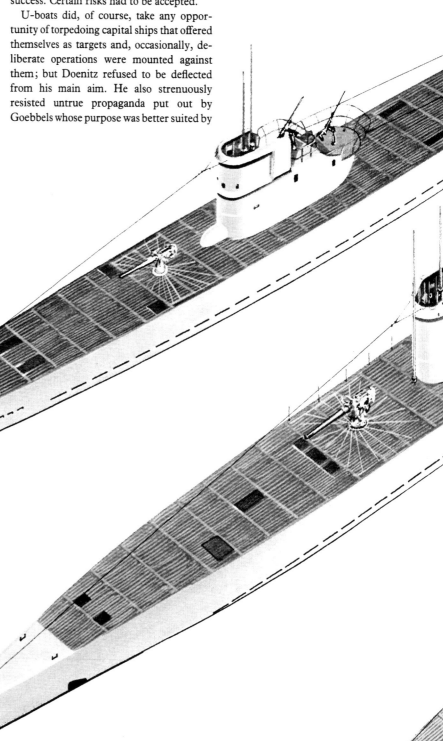

German Type IXC

German Type IXD2

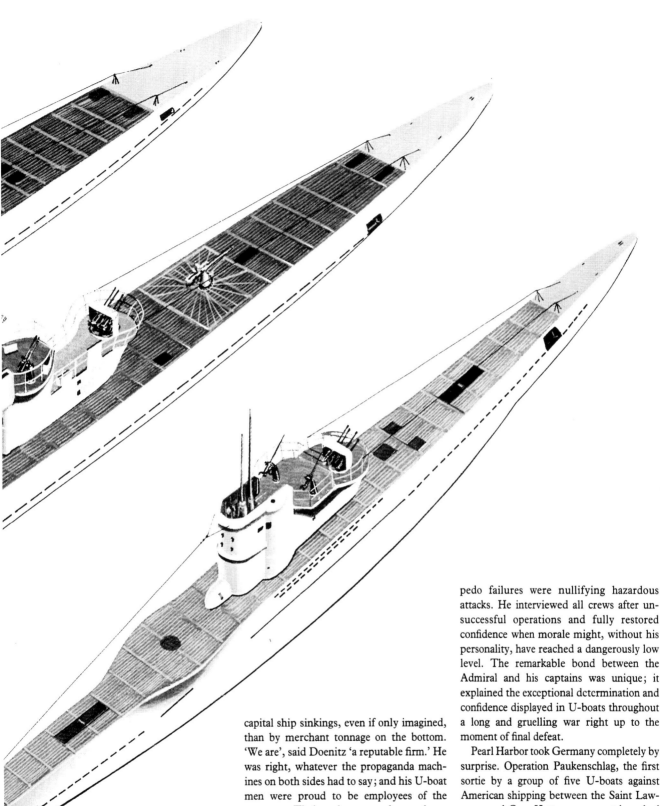

German Type VIIC

capital ship sinkings, even if only imagined, than by merchant tonnage on the bottom. 'We are', said Doenitz 'a reputable firm.' He was right, whatever the propaganda machines on both sides had to say; and his U-boat men were proud to be employees of the company. Their orders were clear and unambiguous (except when the politicians interfered); their direction from shore was skilled and purposeful; and yet their captains retained freedom of action.

The loyalty of U-boat captains to Doenitz was understandably absolute. It became strikingly obvious in early 1940 when tor-

pedo failures were nullifying hazardous attacks. He interviewed all crews after unsuccessful operations and fully restored confidence when morale might, without his personality, have reached a dangerously low level. The remarkable bond between the Admiral and his captains was unique; it explained the exceptional determination and confidence displayed in U-boats throughout a long and gruelling war right up to the moment of final defeat.

Pearl Harbor took Germany completely by surprise. Operation Paukenschlag, the first sortie by a group of five U-boats against American shipping between the Saint Lawrence and Cape Hatteras, was not launched until five weeks after Germany and America were at war. The object was to sink vessels over 10,000 tons. Despite the delayed start and the small number of attackers, the 'Roll on the Kettledrums' was highly profitable. The traffic was so dense that it was impossible to sieze all opportunities. Targets were often

The Battle of the Atlantic is being lost!

The reasons why:

1. German U-boats, German bombers and the German fleet sink and seriously damage between them every month a total of 700 000 to 1 million tons of British and allied shipping.

2. All attempts at finding a satisfactory means of defence against the German U-boats or the German bombers have failed disastrously.

3. Even President Roosevelt has openly stated that for every five ships sunk by Germany, Britain and America between them can only build two new ones. All attempts to launch a larger shipbuilding programme in America have failed.

4. Britain is no longer in a position to secure her avenues of supply. The population of Britain has to do with about half the ration that the population of Germany gets. Britain, herself, can only support 40% of her population from her own resources in spite of the attempts made to increase the amount of land under cultivation. If the war is continued until 1942, 60% of the population of Britain will starve!

All this means that starvation in Britain is not to be staved off. At the most it can be postponed, but whether starvation comes this year or at the beginning of next doesn't make a ha'porth of difference. Britain must starve because she is being cut off from her supplies.

Britain's losing the Battle of the Atlantic means

Britain's losing the war!

Bottom Left

Kptlt Topp drafting a sinking signal to BdU in his cabin in *U-552* with the Fuehrer's portrait in the background.

Bottom Right

SS *Beacon Grange* (10,160 tons) hit by three torpedoes abreast No 2 hatch, the engine-room and No 4 hatch at about 1430 on 27 April 1941. When a U-boat broke surface, moments later, 500 yards on the starboard beam, the Master was able to see a red devil painted on the conning tower – Kplt Erich Topp's *U-552*. When the stricken ship's crew had pulled clear in lifeboats (*Beacon Grange* had been proceeding independently) Topp fired a fourth fish but still, apparently, had to finish off his victim with gunfire that evening.

lit and held straight courses against the brightly illuminated background of the shore where there was no blackout. The only problem for the U-boats was an insufficiency of fuel and torpedoes. Trimming tanks, washing-water tanks and even drinking-water tanks were used for extra fuel and every compartment was filled with spares, stores and provisions. In the early weeks of these long-ranging patrols there was no seating accommodation for the crew in the bow or stern compartments and there was no room anywhere to stand upright. Messes and bunks were stacked with cases, leaving only a narrow gangway between them. But the crews made no complaint. The enormous successes achieved off the eastern American coastline and, later, in other distant areas off South America, the West Indies, West Africa and in the Indian Ocean were adequate compensation for discomfort.

Allied submariners could look forward to a triumphal return to base when the fuel or torpedoes were expended. The U-boat men were not always so lucky. Kk Eitel-Friedrich Kentrat, for example, commanding *U-196*, was at sea continuously for seven months from 13 March to 28 October 1943, taking in fresh supplies and torpedoes at sea. Even if torpedoes were expended and could not be replenished a boat was liable to be kept out to act as a weather station; and as for fuel running out, one captain who reported that he had not many litres left was told by Doenitz to carry on regardless: 'Attack and sink. I never abandon a U-boat.'

Long patrols were made possible by a number of supply ships which waited at secret rendezvous (several were sunk when their rendezvous was compromised) and by 'Milch-Cows'—specially adapted Type IX and Type X U-boats. These replenishment boats could resupply up to a dozen U-boats with spare fuel and torpedoes. Transfers on the surface, in anything other than flat calm, demanded good seamanship and when there was a possibility of attack from the air they were hazardous. The first refuelling operations were started on 22 April 1942 by *U-459* about 500 miles off Bermuda but it was not until 12 June 1943 that the first Milch-Cow fell victim to aircraft (from USS *Bogue*): from this time, greatly assisted by code-breaking, Allied air attacks on Milch-Cows became very damaging to the U-boat campaign. The cumbersome grocers suffered heavily and so did a number of shoppers making for the market place. The concentration of U-boats around a replenishment submarine would, of course, have been a rich target for A/S units; but it was important not to indicate that the position of

a Milch-Cow was known until the time was ripe to strike. The Allies grew cunning and feints were made by American forces in the hope that a Milch-Cow would think itself safe and gather a valuable herd around it; but a herd was never actually discovered when A/S forces came to attack.

U-boat losses had amounted to 152 in all areas from September 1939 to the end of 1942 and, during the same period, 3,862 merchant vessels had been sunk—a profitable exchange rate. But in the following year the tide turned. Long-range maritime-patrol aircraft with centimetric radar, carrier-based aircraft, overwhelmingly powerful A/S escorts fitted with HF/DF, improved A/S tactics and weapons forced U-boats to patrol and attack, for the most part, submerged: from that time the Battle of the Atlantic was lost. The month of May 1943 saw the beginning of the end of the U-boat arm. The fatal date could, however, have been advanced considerably if Fleet Admiral Ernest J King USN (C-in-C Atlantic) had agreed to an earlier proposal for basing a couple of US Navy Consolidated Liberator squadrons on Newfoundland to close the mid-Atlantic gap and, equally, if more British air effort had been directed towards maritime operations instead of being concentrated on bombing Germany and German-Occupied territories which, in the long term, was a much less effective occupation.

The U-boats struggled on with successive improvements to radar-warning devices, AA armament and schnorchels but they never succeeded in regaining the initiative. During the full year of 1943, 237 U-boats went to the bottom in exchange for only 597 merchant ships. They continued thereafter to achieve isolated sinkings in all areas but there was no longer any hope of bringing the British war effort to a halt by breaking the supply chain from America. Towards the end, in 1944, Kptlt Siegfried Koitschka, a most experienced commanding officer, reluctantly arrived at the conclusion, shared by others, that none of the standard wartime U-boats had any chance of success in action and little chance of survival. None of the planned new generation of Type XXI U-boats was ready in time to affect events.

As it was, the U-boat arm was fighting a continually losing battle during the last two years of the war. A final, desperate effort was made to stem the flood of invasion forces between 6 June and the end of August 1944; but, of the schnorchel boats taking part in 45 sorties, 30 were destroyed. However, against these heavy losses, a number of escorts and landing craft as well as 12 very valuable supply ships were sunk. The latter totalled

56,845 tons—a paltry amount, it seemed, to what had gone before. But a close look at what a dozen supply vessels could carry (assuming they were all loaded with military cargoes) shows the sort of Allied losses entailed (their actual cargoes are not known; the figures given have been extrapolated from a US Army Air Force manual of the time):

> 105 tanks
> 36 6-inch howitzers
> 400 25-pounder guns
> 180 40 mm guns
> 110 armoured patrol vehicles
> 225 Bren guns
> 25,000 tons of munitions
> 2,700 rifles
> 1,1750 tons of tank spare-parts
> 4,500 drums of petrol
> 10,000 tons of rations

About 9,000 aircraft sorties would have been needed to destroy that quantity of stores on land: the comparative economy of submarine warfare is clear. Although Allied merchant ships in the Atlantic were certainly not all loaded with munitions, the figures, in relation to the Atlantic losses, indicate how close the U-boat campaign came to winning the war for Germany. No wonder that Churchill said it was the only thing that really frightened him.

On 4 May 1945, Grand Admiral Doenitz, signalling his boats to cease hostilities, issued the following Order of the Day:

'My U-boat men, six years of U-boat warfare lies behind us. You have fought like lions. A crushing superiority has compressed us into a very narrow area. The continuation of the struggle is impossible from the bases which remain. Unbroken in your warlike courage, you are laying down your arms after a heroic fight which knows no equal. In reverent memory we think of our comrades who have died. Comrades, maintain in the future your U-boat spirit with which you have fought most bravely and unflinchingly during the long years ...'

Nearly 30,000 U-boat men went down with their boats, ten times the number of submariners lost both in the Royal Navy, and in the United States Navy. Whatever prejudices and memories remain, it would surely be difficult for submariners on any side to refute the spirit of that final message.

13 Indian Ocean

German underwater operations in the Indian Ocean arose from an exceptionally high number of 30 new U-boats being made ready for operational duties in each successive month of July, August and September 1942. Doenitz was always reluctant to undertake any operations which detracted from his main objective in the Atlantic but he was ready to make thrusts further afield if these would contribute significantly to the tonnage war on merchant shipping bound for British ports. Hence, when an accumulation of Allied shipping was reported in the Cape Town area and when Type IXC boats and replenishment facilities by submarine tankers became available to make possible the 6,000-mile transit, he despatched the Polar Bear Group (Type IXCs) followed by three long-range Type IXD2 boats. Between them, in October alone, they sank three large and irreplaceable British troopships and 27 cargo vessels, many of which were loaded with important military stores.

Doenitz was well pleased. His boats had done more damage than the disguised German surface raiders, their predecessors in piracy in these waters, at far less cost to the Navy's resources. The three Type IXD2 boats further extended their operations into the Indian Ocean itself and sank a further 20 ships off Lourenço Marques before the year was out. Besides their immediate consequences, widely separated lunges of this sort had the far reaching effect of forcing the Allies to disperse their already inadequate anti-submarine resources as the British Admiralty ruefully recognised.[1]

When the Battle of the Atlantic started to go against Germany in the spring of 1943, Doenitz agreed to send more Type IXC and IXD2 boats to the Indian Ocean where the German Naval Attaché in Tokyo, Admiral Wenneker, had been trying to organise co-ordination between the German and Japanese war efforts. When Doenitz was satisfied that the new Japanese base at Penang could provide suitable fuel and lubricants as well as European food (something he insisted upon) he guardedly accepted the Japanese plans for co-operation and at the end of June 1943 started to sail long-range U-boats to Penang, intercepting targets of opportunity en route.

Submarine tankers were essential for the long transit but by now, their security having been breached by code-breaking, they had become vulnerable priority targets. The tanker *U-462*, which was to have proceeded in company to refuel Group *Monsun* comprising nine Type IXC and two Type IXD boats, failed in two attempts to break through the Biscay Blockade; *U-487* was ordered to take her place and be ready to refuel the Group by 14 July in a position 700 miles south of the Azores. But *U-487* had replenished eight Type VIIC U-boats since 6 July and was 120 tons of fuel short of the requirement to provide each boat in Group *Monsun* with 40 tons. *U-160*, an outward bound Type IXC, was therefore directed to transfer the bulk of her fuel to the tanker leaving only enough to return to base. However, *U-487* succumbed to attacks by aircraft from USS *Core* on 13 July and *U-160* was sunk by aircraft from USS *Santee* the next day. Meanwhile, two of the transiting U-boats had also been sunk by aircraft while proceeding independently through the Bay of Biscay. The replenishment was eventually carried out by *U-155* and *U-516* 600 miles west of the Cape Verde Islands; but of the 11 boats of Group *Monsun* only five remained to continue their passage through the South Atlantic to the Indian Ocean. In June and July 1943 Allied carrier-borne aircraft accounted for two more U-tankers and six operational boats in the Azores area while seven operational boats, who in consequence had to be used as tankers, could no longer be employed in the distant areas for which they were destined. Furthermore, six Type VII boats destined for the Atlantic areas were unable to refuel and had to be diverted to the vicinity of Freetown contrary to the original intention. One way and another, Group *Monsun*'s passage to Penang proved expensive.

The remnants of Group *Monsun* refuelled from the surface tanker *Brake* on 11 September and commenced operations in the northern part of the Indian Ocean; but the strain of the long voyage had evidently taken its toll and opportunities of attack were not seized with great vigour. Moreover, although it was not realised at the time, the hot climate caused the batteries of electric torpedoes to

deteriorate with the result that the torpedoes ran slow. Reinforcements for Group *Monsun*, all Type IXD boats commanded by highly decorated and experienced officers who had distinguished themselves in the North Atlantic or the Mediterranean, also suffered severely on passage. By the end of the war no less than 22 of these boats sent to the Indian Ocean had been lost, 16 being sunk by aircraft. The majority were sunk long before rounding the Cape of Good Hope. The Indian Ocean offered splendid opportunities for independent U-cruiser interceptions but the comparatively clumsy Type IX boats were obliged to traverse the same exceedingly dangerous seas of the Bay of Biscay and Eastern Atlantic as the much handier Type VII's: the fact, therefore, that the big boats were quite well suited to long-range and tropical operations was not (apart from their torpedoes) very relevant.

U-177 (Kk R Gysae) made two particularly noteworthy patrols in the South Altantic and Indian Ocean between November 1942 and October 1943. *U-177* was a happy boat and Gysae was an outstanding captain and sank over 88,000 tons of shipping during two cruises. These lasted four-and-a-half months and six months respectively under very trying conditions, but morale stayed high and Gysae never resorted to punishment. Temperatures inside the boat were commonly 35 to 45 degrees Centigrade rising to 80 degrees in the Engine room. Gysae was not only a skilful tactician; he was an excellent psychologist. With very limited facilities, he took care to provide plenty of entertainment: when no targets were in sight, competitions of every kind were held. There were painting, chess and card competitions and a singing contest was held over the loudspeaker system. Appropriate privileges were awarded as prizes; for example, the captain might keep a winner's watch. Gysae's personality, as much as his submarine expertise, kept the boat safe on passage and successful on patrol. But he did make one mistake. On 28 November 1942 he sighted a steamship and, through the periscope, took her for an Armed Merchant Cruiser. She went down to three torpedoes fired from dived. When he surfaced and closed the few lifeboats and rafts

found floating, he found to his horror that his victim had been the *Nova Scotia* carrying some 500 Italian prisoners-of-war and internees from Abyssinia to South Africa. Gysae did what he could to redeem the error, signalling for the Portuguese authorities to send assistance; but he felt so ashamed, although he really had no need to be so, that before returning to Bordeaux he made every member of the crew give a written promise never to mention the incident. When he closed the survivors of his next victim, the Greek *Saronikos*, he did his utmost to make sure of their safety and gave them bandages and other medical supplies.

When Gysae left *U-177* he was relieved by a man with a totally different idea of discipline who handed out frequent punishments. *U-177*'s third cruise would probably, according to survivors from the crew, have ended in mutiny had not the U-boat been destroyed after she had been at sea for five weeks. The new captain's disciplinary measures included daily emergency gun-drills and these were so frequent that they eventually dulled the alertness of the crew. On 6 February 1944 a US aircraft from Ascenscion was allowed, in good visibility, to get within a mile of the U-boat before being spotted. It was too late. Accurately bombed, *U-177* sank in a few moments, taking with her two thirds of the crew.

Top Right
HNMS *K.XVIII* at Soerabaja before the war (1934). Submarines contributed significantly to the defence of the Dutch East Indies.

Centre Right
HNMS *O-20*, one of two submarines based on the design for two minelayers built for Poland. The mines were stored in vertical shafts amidships in the saddle tanks with two mines in each shaft. The experimental schnorchel mast can be seen in the retracted position at the after end of the bridge superstructure. *O-20* was sunk by Japanese destroyers in the Gulf of Siam on 19 December 1941. By Christmas, little more than two weeks after commencing hostilities with Japan, only three out of seven Dutch boats under British Control in the Far East remained in service. Their determination in the face of impossible odds resulted in two being lost in minefields, and one (*O-20*) being sunk by A/S vessels; *K-XIII* was at the same time put out of action by a battery explosion.

Bottom Right
HNMS *O-23*. This Netherlands submarine made seven patrols off Penang, Sabang and in the Andamans area between July 1942 and August 1943 before returning to the UK for refit. She sank two large Japanese passenger-cargo ships on her first patrol. The large hatch abaft the bridge covers a hydraulically raised 20 mm AA gun.

The guns crew of HMS *Statesman* standing down after setting fire to three small coasters in the Malacca Straits, 1944. The scarcity of worthwhile torpedo targets necessitated the use of the gun and British submarines, 'like foxes in a hen coop', shot up and sank anything that floated, operating in water as shallow as 20 feet and as close to the target as 25 yards! In nine patrols *Statesman* (Lt R G P Bulkeley) destroyed or damaged 49 vessels totalling 10,000 tons, mainly with her 3-inch gun at the small cost of 1200 rounds. Japanese seaborne supplies in the waters of Burma, Siam, Malaya, and Sumatra were badly disrupted by British submarines.

Wounded men on board HMS *Petard* after a gun-battle with the Japanese submarine *I-27* which sank the troopship *Khedive Ismail* (with a loss of over 1200 lives) one of five troopships whose escort from Kilindini to Columbo included HMS *Paladin* and *Petard*. In the action on 12 February 1944, *I-27* was eventually sunk by a torpedo (the seventh fired) from HMS *Petard* but not before the submarine's gun had inflicted casualties during a running battle lasting one hour.

Kptlt Eck commanding *U-852* did not have the same attitude towards survivors as Gysae. On 13 March 1944 en route to the Indian Ocean he sank the Greek ship *Peleus* (4,695 tons) off the west coast of Africa. Fearful that the presence of wreckage and survivors would betray his position to Allied air patrols, he opened fire on the floating remains but in fact failed to kill all the crew, three of whom were rescued. They reported what he had done. It was the only known case in World War II of a U-boat captain deliberately setting out to kill survivors. Other U-boats had endeavoured to complete a sinking by opening fire on ships that refused to go down after being hit by torpedoes; but Eck went an important step further than that. He and those of his officers who shared the responsibility were condemned to death by a British court-martial and shot on 30 November 1945. Doenitz himself by no means approved Eck's action but remarked that 'a U-boat captain was responsible for the safety of his boat . . . in an area where at least four boats had recently been bombed.' Submariners may have felt bound to compare Eck's fate with undeniable, unpunished, Japanese submarine atrocities and the blandly ignored shooting of Japanese survivors in the water by Lcdr 'Much' Morton in USS *Wahoo* (see Chapter 14).

The Japanese attached great importance to their strategic underwater offensive against Allied sea communications in the Indian Ocean and, hence, to the establishment of Penang as a base for the Eleventh Submarine

Flotilla in February 1942 and as a Headquarters for the Eighth Submarine Squadron from April 1943. At the end of that month, *I-10*, *I-16*, *I-18*, *I-20* and *I-30* sailed to carry out a reconnaissance of important points on the African coast. Rear Admiral Ishizaki controlled the operation from *I-10* following the Japanese decision to use command submarines for the direction of certain operations, a concept which had been rejected by Doenitz before the war. *I-10*'s aircraft reported a *Queen Elizabeth* class battleship, one cruiser and other ships at anchor in Diego Suarez on 30 May and at midnight *I-16* and *I-20* launched midget submarines ten miles from the harbour entrance. The midgets failed to return but one large tanker, the

Top and Centre Right
The end of *I-27* seen from HMS *Petard* off the Maldive Islands. *I-27* was one of the Japanese submarines which had launched midgets seven miles east of Sydney Harbour in May 1942. From September to December 1943 this boat operated in the Arabian Sea and on 4 February 1944 sailed from Penang to intercept shipping in the Western Indian Ocean.

Top Left
HMS *Shakespeare* (Lt D Swanston) was hit by gunfire from a merchant ship which was being attacked in the Andaman area on 3 January 1945. The Engine Room and Control Room were partially flooded, making diving impossible, and the steering was damaged. One main engine and both motors were put out of action. Throughout the day, *Shakespeare* fought off 25 air attacks, shooting down one aircraft but suffering fifteen casualties (two killed). The 3-inch gun's crew are here enjoying a well-deserved smoke between attacks. *Shakespeare* eventually reached Trincomalee under tow assisted by two destroyers sent out to meet her.

Top Right
Medical supplies from HMS *Stygian* being ferried by canoe to the crippled *Shakespeare*.

Centre Left
Lt Cdr E P Young, the outstandingly successful RNVR captain of HMS *Storm* whose story is told in what is probably the best personal account of a submarine's exploits ever written in his book *One of Our Submarines*.

Bottom Left
Torpedo tracks viewed through the periscope. It can be seen that HMS *Trenchant's* full salvo fired at the Japanese cruiser *Ashigara* would indeed have looked like 'an arterial road'.

British Loyalty, was sunk and the battleship *Ramillies*[2] was hit by one torpedo which made it necessary for her to disembark oil and ammunition and go to Durban for extensive repairs. These First Division submarines enjoyed considerable success and sank some 20 merchant vessels totalling 120,000 tons during a month of operating unscathed by anti-submarine vessels or aircraft.

Japanese boats, mainly those from Penang, continued to amass impressive totals of tonnage sunk during the remainder of 1942; and they planned heavier attacks for 1943. The latter, however, did not materialise in full because Pacific victories by the US Navy drew Japanese submarines out of the Indian Ocean to Pacific waters where they proved no match for the rapidly increasing skill of American A/S forces. The boats left in the Indian Ocean also felt the weight of improved Allied defences and started to suffer heavily. Penang-based Japanese submarines lost 19 of their number between February 1943 and June 1945.

British submarines operated from Depot Ships lying at Trincomalee. At one time or another there were eight T-boats, eight S-boats, *Porpoise* and *Severn* patrolling from this base. The operating areas were mainly in the Malacca Straits, off Java and the South China Sea. Worthwhile targets were not plentiful; the deployment of such a substantial submarine force in south-east Asia resulted from a political desire to show, quite late in the war, that the Royal Navy was undertaking its fair share of work in the Far East while the United States Navy was so clearly dominating the Pacific. By 1944 there were not, anyway, many other areas where British boats could usefully be employed and they did not have the range to operate further afield in the Pacific.

Top Right
HMS *Tally Ho* **returning to Trincomalee after sinking the Japanese cruiser** *Kuma* **on 11 January 1944 with two hits from a seven-torpedo salvo at 1900 yards on a 95 degree track angle on 11 January 1944.**

Bottom Right
HMS *Tally Ho* **(Lt Cdr L W A Bennington) sank** *U It-23* **(ex-***Giuliani***) with a three-torpedo salvo on a 120 degree track angle at 3500 yards in a brilliant snap attack in the Malacca Straits at 0525 on 15 February 1944. Going on to pick up secret agents on 17–19 February she was unsuccessful in doing so because no contact could be made with them; and Bennington, in a mood of frustration which was scarcely justified (he had sunk the cruiser** *Kuma* **only a month before) fired five torpedoes at the unescorted 510-ton** *Daigen Maru* **and hit with one. On 24 February he encountered a Japanese torpedo boat at night, too close to take avoiding action by diving. The enemy's attempt at ramming ripped open the port main ballast tanks as shown here; but** *Tally Ho* **made it safely back to base with a heavy list.**

Patrols in these inshore and often very shallow waters were testing and frequently fraught with undue interest. But, surprisingly, the lack of air-conditioning in the relatively small submarines, which were grossly overcrowded when carrying landing parties,[3] did not detract from efficiency although prickly heat and heat-exhaustion were a continual problem.

Japanese A/S activity was sparse, sporadic and inefficient. Submarine chasers were apt to work singly and submarine commanding officers quickly realised that the poorly protected little vessels were vulnerable to gunfire. HMS *Tally Ho* (Cdr L W A Bennington), rather than submit to a hammering in shallow water where she could not even go below periscope depth, surfaced and demolished Chaser *No 2* with five four-inch rounds out of 19 fired on 6 October 1944 in the southern part of the Malacca Strait. The geographical restrictions under which boats operated in these waters were well illustrated by an earlier torpedo attack by *Tally Ho* against a coaster which failed due to the torpedo hitting native fishing stakes set up parallel with the beach. *Tally Ho* had a particularly successful war in the area and her victims included the ex-Italian *UIT 23* and the Japanese cruiser *Kuma*. All of Bennington's six torpedo salvoes sank their targets and nine hits were registered for 33 torpedoes fired. Nor did any of his 14 gunnery targets escape entirely although one merchant ship made off damaged and another ran aground: a total of only 204 four-inch shells were expended on these targets. *Tally Ho* had one narrow escape, however, when an enemy torpedo boat was encountered at night too close to avoid by diving. Drastic avoiding action on the surface prevented direct ramming but a glancing collision ripped open the port main ballast tanks. This did not prevent the submarine from diving to shake off her pursuer but the return passage was made on the surface, in bad weather, with a heavy list to port.

Cdr A R Hezlet in *Trenchant* made what may rank, for a submarine tactical purist, as the most brilliant attack of the war on 8 June 1945 when, off the Sumatran coast, he sank the heavy cruiser *Ashigara* bound for Singapore and carrying a large number of Japanese troops from Batavia. The target's masts were sighted through the periscope at 1148 at a range of about six miles and it was soon clear that Hezlet could not improve his firing position to better than 4,000 yards off track. At this long range it was essential to optimise target estimations and Hezlet made his calculations with cold precision during the 21 minutes which elapsed before the DA came on. He fired a full bow salvo of eight torpedoes aimed individually from a quarter of a length ahead to a quarter of a length astern. To avoid breaking surface in the flat calm sea on firing, speed was increased to five knots and the foremost trim tank and Q tank were temporarily flooded at the critical moment. The correct depth was thereby held within four feet. Complete control was regained within three minutes when a quick look through the periscope revealed the torpedo tracks stretching towards the target 'like an arterial road'. Because of the shoreline to port the target could only alter to starboard, towards *Trenchant*, which was the worst possible avoiding action with torpedoes approaching from just abaft her starboard beam. At 1212 five torpedoes hit, over a period of seconds, along the length of the ship while Hezlet's ship's company queued up to watch through the search periscope, a luxury which attracted retaliatory fire from the cruiser's AA battery. Meanwhile Hezlet was turning fast to bring the stern tubes to bear. He fired two more torpedoes at 1244 using the DA for a reduced speed of five knots. While these last two torpedoes were running *Ashigara* altered further round to starboard, probably in an attempt to beach on a nearby shoal, and the torpedoes missed astern. They were not, in any case, necessary: the cruiser capsized under the effect of the initial salvo while a destroyer patrolling in the vicinity dropped three 'face-saving' patterns of depth charges at least three miles from *Trenchant*. Hezlet remarked modestly in his patrol report on 'the ease with which the cruiser was sunk' but it was an exceptionally expert piece of work.[4]

Dutch submarines also achieved notable successes running from Ceylon in, for them, familiar waters. They included the sinking of *U-168* which went down to *Zwaardvisch* (ex-HMS *Talent*) commanded by Lt Cdr Hans Goossens. There were not enough opportunities for the Dutch to show their paces properly with such a paucity of targets; but it was very clear that their submariners were very professional and proficient.

Three British and four Dutch submarines were lost on operations in the Far East for two cruisers, two destroyers, five U-boats, 13 minor naval vessels, 47 sizeable merchant ships and numerous junks and other small vessels. These figures include seven ships known to have been sunk as a result of 30 mine-laying operations (640 mines) and the cargo vessel *Sumatra Maru* (4,859 tons), which was sunk in Puket Harbour by Chariots launched from HMS *Trenchant*. All these sinkings were positively confirmed and amounted to about 130,000 tons, a figure which, by the end of the war, virtually exhausted target opportunities.

14 The Pacific

By the time that Japan and America went to war in December 1941, the niceties of submarine attack restrictions were sensibly forgotten. It would have been absurd to have observed them in what was undeniably a total war. The United States declared the whole Pacific to be an operational area—which meant unrestricted warfare. This declaration did not, however, lead to an immediate wholesale onslaught on merchant shipping or even to a long-term war of attrition (although that, for the USN, was to develop); on the contrary, both sides concentrated their attention, initially, on naval vessels and neither formulated a clear-cut strategic policy to cover the vast expanse of the Pacific Ocean.

The Japanese submariners were confused. The Imperial Navy had spent the pre-war years endeavouring to assimilate and adopt whatever lessons were to be learned from the European powers, notably Britain and Germany, as well as from the United States Navy who had long been seen as the inevitable enemy. Since these powers were by no means sure themselves about their underwater objectives the Japanese were presented with a welter of conflicting evidence. This led to changeable and insecure doctrines which, in turn, made it difficult for their large and increasingly varied submarine force to adopt a coherent strategy although individual units developed rational submarine tactics. It remained to be seen whether these tactics would succeed within the framework of the Japanese naval plans as a whole.

In December 1941 the organisation of the Japanese Submarine Fleet consisted of squadrons comprising between two and four divisions of two or three units each. Most squadrons had an old light cruiser of the *Kuma* or *Nagara* class as a flagship (an old idea derived from the disastrous British K-class plans in World War I) and each submarine division had its own submarine flagship to co-ordinate operations. Pre-war exercises showed that the standard of the force was high and morale was certainly excellent, the force being composed entirely of volunteers. However, the concept of direct command being exercised by these submersible flagships was not proven in realistic manoeuvres.

The huge Japanese submarines *I-400*, *I-401*, and *I-41* alongside the tender USS *Proteus* in Tokyo Bay. This picture clearly shows the open hangar door on *I-400* and the catapult launching ramp for her floatplanes on the forward deck.

Japanese *I-400*—class hangar door showing the
anti-sonar paint extensively used on Japanese
submarines. The highly secret formula for this
was, by weight: 21% rubber, 6% kasein mixture,
30% silica sand powder, 11% lock fibre powder,
10% Paris white, 2% iron black. The coating
decreased speed by up to one knot and was not
used on the faster boats. It adhered better than
the seemingly ineffective German equivalent and
was applied in three or four coats, 3 mm thick.

On 18 November 1941 *I-24* slipped her
moorings at Kune and, carrying a midget
submarine, headed out into the Pacific.
Within a few days the rest of the Sixth
Submarine Fleet set out towards their assigned patrol stations to await the dawn of
Sunday, 8 December. By the time that
Admiral Nagumo's carrier strike force had
reached its launching point some 275 miles
due north of Pearl Harbor, 27 submarines
were in position around Oahu. Five of the
newly constructed *I-16* class submarines
carried midget submarines which, it was
hoped, would be able to penetrate the harbour defences and be able to inflict further
damage upon the American warships at
anchor. Although Admiral Yamamoto doub-
ted whether the midgets would make any
impact on the American defences, believing
that they could never return and were in any
event unnecessary, he let them go ahead.
Yamamoto's doubts were justified. However,
Imperial HQ was confident that the larger
submarines could carry out their principal
task of preventing reinforcements reaching
Pearl Harbor. More was expected from
submarine warfare than the immediate strike.

As things worked out, only one submarine
succeeded in making an attack: all of the five
midgets which were launched and one large
submarine were lost without sinking a single
American ship. The Japanese boats were
packed into a dense patrol zone more than 60
miles from the harbour entrance where they
were wasted; but, even if they had been free

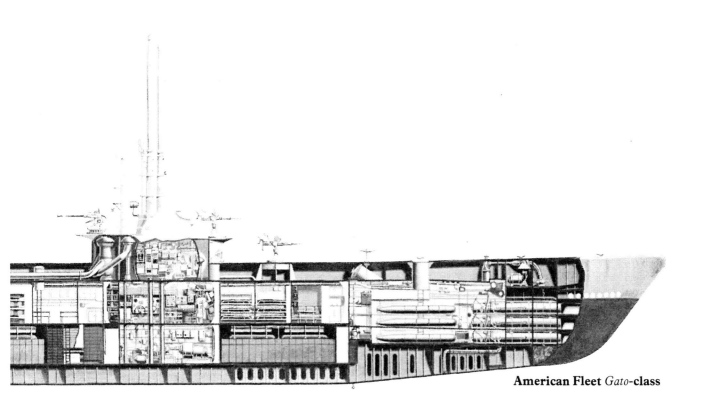

American Fleet *Gato*-**class**

to move, the hornet's nest of American destroyers which had been stirred up would have interposed a formidable barrier between them and their targets. When it was clear that the underwater part of the Pearl Harbor operation had failed the Japanese ruefully revised their ideas and gave belated thought to attacking supply ships; but advanced bases were needed for that—and there were none.

So far as their dispositions allowed, the Japanese submarines were well handled on reconnaissance and raiding operations for which they were well-suited. Submarine *I-156*, for example, on patrol off Malaya, was responsible for making the crucial enemy report which sealed the fate of HMS *Prince of Wales* and HMS *Repulse*; and several of the large boats which carried seaplanes carried out a valuable reconnaissance of Allied bases. Other boats conducted spectacular night bombardments on Johnston Island, Palmyra, the Hawaiian Islands and Midway; *I-17* even attacked shore installations near Santa Barbara on 24 February 1942, while *I-25* was ordered to despatch her seaplane to start a forest fire in Oregon with incendiary bombs in August. None of these operations affected the course of the war but they helped to make American citizens realise that the Imperial Navy was 'for real', a counter-productive result so far as Japan was concerned.

On patrol duties the Japanese performance was patchy. On 10 December, two days after Pearl Harbor, five submarines were detached to patrol off the western seaboard of the United States. On the way *I-6* was responsible for the first major Japanese submarine success of the war when she succeeded in putting the aircraft carrier *Saratoga* out of action for three months. By mid-December there were nine submarines off the west coast of America but by the end of the month they were forced to return to Japan for replenishment. They had achieved very little but their presence had forced the United States Navy to adopt a comprehensive convoy system with extensive A/S patrols in the Pacific at a time when every available escort was needed in the Atlantic.

On 1 March 1942 Naval Directive No 60 called for 'the utmost efforts [to secure] the destruction of enemy lines of communication throughout the Pacific and Indian Oceans.' All vessels were to be sunk on sight with the exception of those flying Axis, Soviet or Swiss(!) flags.

The directive was duly and successfully implemented in the Indian Ocean from April 1942; but Admiral Yamamoto in the Pacific was still intent on bringing the United States Fleet to battle and, preparing for the Coral Sea and Midway offensives, he kept a tight rein on the Sixth Fleet submarines to back up these operations.

At Midway both the Japanese and United States Navies employed large numbers of submarines in almost identical roles. The Japanese disposed 16 boats in two patrol lines north and south of French Frigate Shoals and the Americans disposed 19 submarines near or around Midway itself. In each case the aim was to intercept the enemy's advancing carriers and in each case the submarines failed to inflict any damage on enemy forces at any crucial stage of the action. The Japanese patrol line was late in getting into position and, having missed the American Task Force at the start, was unable to catch up with them before Admiral Nagumo's carriers were already sunk by US carrier aircraft. Meanwhile, American submarines, despite being geographically in position to meet the Japanese forces, found themselves unable to bring their torpedoes to bear on the fast warships speeding by while being constantly harassed by Japanese destroyers. Some face was saved on both sides by *I-168* sinking the already crippled carrier *Yorktown* and the destroyer *Hamman* and the claim of Lcdr W Brockman, commanding USS *Nautilus*, that he had finished off the carrier *Soryu*, already severely damaged by bombing. Postwar analysis determined that Brockman actually fired at *Kaga*: of the four torpedoes fired, one failed to leave the tube, two missed and the fourth struck amidships but failed to explode. *Kaga* was already sinking and the air-vessel which was thrown loose by the last torpedo served as a welcome life preserver for several of *Kaga*'s crew.

Their catastrophic naval defeat at Midway halted Japanese plans for further expansion. Imperial HQ rescinded Directive No 60 and on 22 June 1942 substituted Directive No 107 which again called for unrestricted

Top Left
The conning tower of *I-153*. This boat, completed
in 1926, had some remarkably modern features
but normal diving depth was limited to 80 metres
(195 ft) and, with the rest of its class, was
relegated to a training role in 1942.

Top Right
The Control Room of an old (1923) Japanese
Ro-57-class training submarine showing a marked
similarity, except for the periscope, to the British
L-class on which the design was based.

Centre Right
The crew's mess table in *I-169*. The Japanese Navy
made every effort to ensure that submarines were
provided with good food but it was not easy
amidst wartime privations.

Bottom Right
Tube space in *I-153*. Note the absence of the tube
space bulkhead separating the tubes from the
torpedo stowage compartment common to all
British boats. Several early Japanese boats owed
their layout to British L-class design but *I-153* and
her sisters were based on the German *U-125*
(World War I) and U-boats did not have this
compartmentation which was instituted in the
Royal Navy to minimise risk of serious flooding
following a collision: it was expected that, *in
extremis*, a submarine would endeavour to ram
rather than be rammed in a peacetime collision
situation, hence the provision of a bulkhead
forward.

Top Left
Sonar operator in *I-169*. Japanese sonar gear was not up to the standard of USN equivalents but *I-169* was equipped with quite reliable Type 93 hydrophones and Type 91 echo-ranging equipment. Data was adequate for evasion but not for accurate blind attack.

Top Right
Hydroplane operators in *I-169*. This large fleet boat (1785/2440 tons) was to be lost at Truk on 4 April 1944 due to flooding after an air raid.

Centre Left
Main ballast LP blowing manifold in *I-153*. In submarines of all navies high pressure air from bottles was only used to blow sufficient water out of selected main ballast tanks to achieve the minimum positive buoyancy for surfacing. The remaining water was blown out by a low-pressure system using either the exhaust gases from the diesels, as in German U-boats, or a large rotary eccentric air-pump known as the blower in British and related designs.

Bottom Left
Tubes crew in a Japanese training submarine (possibly *Ro 27*). The Petty Officer on the left of this posed photograph is probably working the forward hydroplane hand emergency control.

submarine attacks on Allied commerce but deleted the central Pacific as an area of operations and disposed all submarines around Australasia and in the Indian Ocean. If all Japanese boats had indeed been transferred to the Indian Ocean they might have had a most serious effect on the Allied war effort in the west. It is conceivable that they could have prevented the Suez Canal being used as a supply route to Egypt with incalculable consequences on the outcome of the war in North Africa.

As it was, the split force achieved little; but in the Pacific, during the long and bitter struggle for Guadalcanal, Japanese submarines fought savagely, particularly in the narrow waters at the eastern end of the passage between the Solomon Islands which became known as 'Torpedo Junction'. Here, I-boats disposed of the US carrier *Wasp*, the cruiser *Juneau* and two destroyers and inflicted further heavy damage on the luckless *Saratoga* and the battleships *North Carolina* and *South Dakota*. At the same time they succeeded in sinking or damaging several merchant ships and smaller warships and obliged the Americans to make a number of supply runs with their large fleet submarines.

After the defeat of the combined Japanese Fleet during a three-day battle from 12 to 15 November 1942 and the steady deterioration of the Japanese position on Guadalcanal itself, the positions of the two submarine forces were reversed. Now, because of the alarming losses of surface ships on the nightly 'Tokyo Express' run to the beleagured island, the Japanese resorted to submarines as blockade-runners. The decision was not popular with Japanese submariners but the plight of the Japanese soldiers was so dreadful they felt obliged to do their utmost in the new unwelcome role. They did their best, but by the end of 1943 no less than 14 submarines had been lost on transport duties in the Solomons area. The evacuation of Guadalcanal by the Japanese was optimistically seen, by those who still clung to the original concept, as the beginning of the expected Third Phase (see Chapter 2) when the hopefully weakened United States Fleet would be brought to battle in Japanese controlled waters. Even if really believed, it bore the markings of a defeatist policy but the Japanese did not view it as such. On 25 March 1943 Directive No 209 laid down still more fresh instructions for the future conduct of submarine operations. It included a reversion to traditional Japanese submarine doctrine and ordered that 'in the event of an attack by the main strength of the enemy fleet the submarine force will maintain contact with it and endeavour to reduce the enemy's strength.'

The diminishing submarine force was not capable of fulfilling the directive. By the beginning of 1944 it was fully occupied in transport duties and desperate, ineffectual attempts to halt the steady American advance across the Pacific. Supply and transport duties came to be seen as all-important. A programme was launched to build a permanent force of transport submarines consisting of very simply constructed boats, without offensive armament, which could be used exclusively for what submariners themselves regarded as a thankless, fruitless task. Two new classes for the purpose were initiated by the Japanese Army who by now had great influence over submarine operations.

By the middle of 1944 great advances in American anti-submarine equipment, developed from experience in the Atlantic, made Japanese submarine attacks even more hazardous. Few boats were fitted with effective radar and submarine sonar was rudimentary. Throughout 1944 and the first half of 1945, ill-equipped to fight an increasingly efficient enemy, fewer and fewer submarines returned from each attempt to pierce the American A/S screens. By the time of the Okinawa landings in April 1945 the combined fleet was able to deploy only four operational attack submarines. *Kaitens*, human torpedoes converted from standard Type 93 weapons with an effective range of about ten miles, offered one means whereby large submarines could attack targets without themselves coming within reach of American sonar equipment. They achieved scant success and only USS *Underhill* is known to have been destroyed by a *Kaiten* (see Chapter 17).

However, *I-58* succeeded in sinking the heavy cruiser *Indianapolis* on 29 July 1945 and she also damaged a destroyer while *I-53* torpedoed a large transport. When the *Indianapolis* went down shortly before midnight on 29 July, some 800 out of the 1199 men on board got into the water or clambered into life-rafts; but the American authorities failed, almost unbelievably, to note that the cruiser did not arrive on time. Distress lights fired from the life-rafts and seen by an American aircraft were disregarded; and an intercepted contact report from *I-58* to Headquarters was dismissed as Japanese boasting. When they were eventually sighted by a naval aircraft 84 hours after the torpedo had struck home the number of survivors had dwindled dramatically; only 316 were rescued alive. It was not always wise to discount Japanese claims which were necessarily modest but generally accurate.

Amidst the disintegration of their force and the ominous threat posed by Germany's surrender, the Japanese submariners planned a dramatic raid on the Panama Canal using *Seiran* aircraft to be launched from the gigantic 4,550-ton *I-400* class submarines which had been laid down early in 1943. Two of these were ready for service by the beginning of 1945 and each carried three of the *Seiran* single-engined aeroplanes capable of dropping either torpedoes or bombs. The aim was to block the Panama Canal and hold back the tidal wave of Allied forces now pouring into the Pacific. Captain Ariizumi, commanding the First Submarine Flotilla with its underwater aircraft carriers, was confident of success and the pilots were thoroughly well trained. The suicidal nature of the mission was accepted but by the middle of June a crippling attack against Allied Forces, already within striking distance of the homeland, was more urgent than this further-reaching strategic mission. Order No 95 therefore directed the First Submarine Flotilla to expend their *Seiran*'s in a suicide attack against US Navy aircraft carriers at Ulitha Atoll. If the invasion of Japan could somehow be delayed there would be more time to prepare defences.

This attack, Operation Hikari, called for prior reconnaissance so *I-13* and *I-14* went ahead of the flagship *I-401* and its sister ship *I-400* intending to launch reconnaissance aircraft on 16 August. *I-13* was sunk by US carrier aircraft en route but *I-14* succeeded in reaching a point off Truk and its aircraft duly reported that the United States Fleet was still at anchor. However, on 15 August the Emperor announced Japan's surrender which, for some reason, only resulted in Naval Headquarters postponing the attack until 25 August although this last order was countermanded on the following day when all submarines were called back. Captain Ariizumi was instructed to destroy all offensive weapons and important documents. In the last order to fire torpedoes in the Imperial Japanese Navy, one torpedo circled and actively pursued *I-400*, passing dangerously close although it was set to safe. The *Seiran* aircraft themselves were either catapulted pilotless or punctured and dropped overboard. On 31 August, just before *I-401* entered Tokio Bay, Captain Arriizumi placed a service pistol to his head and shot himself. In a last letter he expressed remorse for subjecting the men under his command to the shameful situation of surrender which Imperial Navy men and ships had never before experienced.

Japanese submariners had, for nearly four years, suffered from misemployment. When,

Top Left
Torpedoed Japanese destroyer photographed through the periscope of USS *Wahoo*.

Top Right
Lt J P Biena USNR, Engineer Officer of USS *Silversides* receives the Navy and Marine Corps Medal from VADM Charles Lockwood on 21 March 1943 for his work in keeping the submarine going when she suffered a spate of problems on her fourth war patrol. Reservists performed outstandingly well, both in the USN and RN.

Centre and Bottom Right
Unusual photograph taken at Brisbane, Australia of damage sustained by USS *Growler* during her action with the Japanese supply ship *Hayasaki* (900 tons) off the Bismark Archipelago on the night of 7 February 1943 (see text). The effect of the Japanese machine-gun fire which seriously wounded *Growler's* Captain, Lcdr Howard Gilmore, and killed two others on the bridge, can clearly be seen, as can the damage to the bow which resulted from *Growler* unintentionally ramming her adversary. It was on this bridge that Gilmore gave the most famous and selfless order in US submarine history—'Take her down'.

all too seldom, their submarines had operated singly in broad patrol areas they had done what submariners expected of them; but even if they had been better directed they could not, against the might of the United States, have brought victory to Japan or even seriously delayed the outcome of the war.

The United States Navy in the Pacific also had problems at the beginning of the war; but it was to overcome them magnificently. The period from December 1941 until the end of 1942 saw the US submarine force hampered and dogged by torpedo defects and by command weaknesses at sea and on shore. Submariners elsewhere could only admire the way in which fresh, younger commanding officers and overdue dynamic leadership from above revitalised the force from the beginning of 1943 and led it to final victory.

During 1942 American submarines sank 180 Japanese ships for a total of 72,500 tons: this was unfairly compared with the 1,160 Allied ships totalling 6 million tons destroyed by U-boats during the same 12 months. Without question, more reliable torpedoes and more skilled, agressive commanding officers could have achieved much more than they did; but it was poor training, leading to over-caution and unskilled direction from force commanders, as well as unreliable torpedoes, that were to blame. If commanding officers were wrongly selected, wrongly employed and poorly equipped that was not their fault. There were blatant cases where submarine captains did not carry out their orders properly but, in the main, the fault lay fairly and squarely on the shoulders of senior officers ashore. Time and again throughout the underwater war good leadership and skilful direction were seen to count for much more than material; poor leadership and lack of loyalty downwards affected submarine operations to a greater extent than in any other kind of ship. Although moderate in terms of tonnage, the 1942 sinkings were creditable in the circumstances; and targets in the Pacific were nothing like so plentiful, where the submarines were sent, as those which U-boats were offered on a plate in the Atlantic.

The continuous angling applied to torpedoes in the tubes was much envied, especially by the British; but it was all too easy to fire from the hip without accurately determining the target's course, speed and range. Periscope ranging must have been haphazard for reasons discussed earlier in Chapter 8. Unavoidable radar vagaries were not taken into account when radar bearings were used and it is doubtful whether the sets were calibrated for range as carefully as they should have been. Reports from sonar were apt to be believed implicitly: and sonar

inaccuracies, both with regard to bearing and turn-count, were not allowed for. The impressive quality of the equipment in American boats was such that a US submariner might well not question the answers it supplied; but its very excellence militated against surety of success. Over-credulity was almost certainly responsible for many failures when other problems of command and weaponry had eventually been solved. Fortunately, during the successful campaign against Japanese merchant shipping during the latter part of the war most targets were simple to attack and inadequately escorted so that approaches did not necessarily call for the same degree of skill and precision as that required in, for example, the Mediterranean. If comparisons have to be made, these rather unflattering generalisations are unavoidable; but they in no way detract either from the gallantry so frequently displayed throughout the United States submarine force nor from the conclusive and decisive result which it ultimately achieved.

The first commanding officer to complain about faulty torpedo performance was Lcdr Tyrell Jacobs of *Sargo*, himself a torpedo expert. The first fish fired by *Sargo* exploded prematurely, so Jacobs disconnected the magnetic feature on his remaining torpedoes and altered their depth-setting to hit with contact exploders. During six successive attacks he fired a further 14 torpedoes readjusted in this way and still none exploded. Jacobs reasonably concluded that Mark XIV torpedoes either ran deep or that the contact as well as the magnetic exploders were faulty, or both. He was rewarded by ComSubAsiatic (Captain John Wilkes) with a severe reprimand and a refusal, reportedly due to a shortage of torpedoes, to allow a test firing through a fishnet. However, a representative from the Bureau of Ordnance was flown out to investigate. The expert busied himself in ensuring that *Sargo*'s crew were following the correct drills and maintenance procedures. In so doing he turned a gyro back to front. That scarcely gave submariners confidence in the Bureau of Ordnance; but somehow the Bureau managed to blame the crew of *Sargo* for all the failures.

This habit of blaming the boats was to continue in varying degrees until Rear Admiral Charles Lockwood arrived to command the Asiatic Fleet submarines in June 1942. Besides relieving one quarter of his commanding officers immediately and berating some of those remaining for lack of aggressiveness, Lockwood soon applied himself to the torpedo problem. It was Lcdr Dan Daspit in *Tinosa* who decided Lockwood to make some thorough tests. Daspit was an

exceptionally skilled attacker. When homed by Ultra radio intelligence onto a 19,000 ton floating whale factory on 24 July, his target estimations were, by any standards, good. He fired no less than 15 torpedoes in conditions that were nearly perfect, despite a Japanese destroyer which tried to interfere. Eleven fish failed to explode although hits were clearly observed. The subsequent trials arranged by Lockwood proved that when a warhead hit at an ideal 90-degree angle the exploder mechanism was invariably crushed before it struck the detonating cap. At a smaller angle of 45-degrees, which could only result from a less favourable firing position, the failure rate was about 50 per cent. That was still alarmingly bad but Lockwood had no alternative, while modifications were urgently being carried out, than to tell his commanding officers to shoot on fine track angles, a tactic which all their training had taught them to avoid. It took no less than 21 months of war to end the sorry saga and provide American submariners with reasonably reliable weapons.

Not all the American boats were modern. The S-boats sent to the Alaskan area to oppose the Japanese landings on Kiska and Attu found it hard enough to survive, let alone defend the islands. The weather was atrocious and the charts were unreliable. Navigation was difficult and *S-27* (Lcdr H L Jukes) ran aground on Amchitka Island on 19 June 1942. *S-27* was abandoned and the crew, sheltering on the deserted island, were not found for six days. During the next few weeks seven fleet boats were sent to the area and one was lost. Despite a generally poor showing by most boats, *Growler* (Lcdr Howard Gilmore) gained distinction by attacking three destroyers anchored off Kiska; two were damaged and one sunk. During this spirited action Gilmore showed initiative not common amongst CO's at that time. It was perhaps significant that he was an ex-enlisted man and had won his way to the Naval Academy by competitive examinations. After a distinguished but short career he died on *Growler*'s bridge during a surface action against the *Hayasaki*, a 900-ton provision ship, on the night of 7 February 1943. *Hayasaki* sighted *Growler* a mile away and turned to ram. *Growler* was slow to detect the course alteration (inevitably, if the control party was depending on radar) and when Gilmore realised what was happening his use of full rudder only resulted in the submarine hitting the target amidships at 17 knots. The Japanese ship opened fired on *Growler*'s bridge killing or wounding the exposed personnel. Gilmore, wounded, ordered the bridge to be cleared and then, unable to climb down the hatch himself, gave his last order—

'Take her down'. His Executive Officer, Arnold S Schade, reluctantly obeyed. Gilmore, posthumously, became the first submariner to be awarded the Medal of Honor.

Despite more energetic and loyal support from shore, the Asiatic Fleet submarines were still not directed to focal points and bottle-necks where, as in the Luzon Strait, traffic crossed and was often heavy. In any case, by early 1943 interest was focused on the island-hopping campaign in the central Pacific and submarines which had been operating from Australia were transferred back to Pearl Harbor to participate. One of these was *Wahoo* (Lcdr 'Mush' Morton) who, in his first patrol, transformed a formerly discontented crew into an effective fighting unit. He took chances and pressed home attacks relentlessly, making in all six patrols in which he sank 19 ships totalling 55,000 tons (but claiming 17 for 100,500 tons) Morton told his crew before sailing from Brisbane for the first patrol that *Wahoo* was expendable. It was this sort of talk in a Kentucky accent that had earned him the nickname 'Mushmouth' and it was natural to wonder whether his performance would match his words: generally it did although, like other submarine captains, he was apt to put his tonnage figures on the high side. He was fortunate in having a brilliant Executive Officer in Lieutenant Dick O'Kane who was himself to win fame and the Medal of Honor later in command of *Tang*, although he also caught the habit of overestimating sinkings which, in his case, turned out to be 41 per cent of what he claimed. Morton gave O'Kane the periscope during attacks and concerned himself with getting *Wahoo* into the right position. This arrangement re-

Top Right
British and Australian prisoners of war rescued by USS *Sealion* on 15 September 1944. They had been aboard Japanese transports, en route from Singapore to Japan, when their ships were sunk in attacks by US submarines *Sealion*, *Growler* and *Pampanito*, in position 18–24N, 114–30E.

Centre Right
HMS *Rainbow* off Vladivostock in December 1939 with the temperature inside the boat 17 degrees below freezing. It was a mistake to think of the Pacific as being a sea of sun throughout its vast expanse!

Bottom Right
Final victory and homecoming. Mail call for USS *Gurnard* on return to Hunters Point Shipyard, San Francisco, after an oustandingly successful war, on 15 September 1945. The crew, typical of US submarines, were obviously fit and clean—a tribute to the excellent living conditions on board.

sembled the practise usual in German U-boats making surface attacks. In *Wahoo* it worked for submerged approaches; but it is doubtful whether it would have succeeded with lesser men than O'Kane. One unpleasant incident is recorded in Clay Blair's *Silent Victory* although other histories gloss it over.[1] On the convoy route between Wewak and Palua, Morton found himself in the path of a four-ship convoy. He hit one freighter, damaged a second and stopped a large troop transport dead in the water. A second torpedo fired at the latter failed to detonate but a third resulted in a massive explosion and Morton watched large numbers of Japanese soldiers—he said thousands—jumping over the side. Unable to pursue the other targets submerged with the battery low, *Wahoo* surfaced in the midst of 'a sea of Japanese'. Morton is then said to have ordered the guns to be manned and turned on the survivors. His patrol report (apparently) described their killing during a nightmare hour of carnage Some of the survivors returned the fire with ineffective pistol shots; Morton may have felt that this justified an action which most submariners would find repugnant.

No comment seems to have been made on this incident by Morton's superiors who endorsed *Wahoo*'s patrol report in glowing terms.[2] The appalling treatment meted out by the Japanese to submariners taken prisoner, exceeding anything experienced in European theatres of war, may have been held to offset a murderous act but it was still, at the very least, distasteful. If there was lack of comment by senior officers, one way or the other, they were scarcely gifted with moral courage.

Wahoo, with O'Kane no longer on board and evidently missed by Morton, was lost in October 1943 on her way out of the Sea of Japan where Lockwood had started to send his boats into the busy shipping lanes. Meanwhile, submarines were being sent hither and thither to follow Ultra intelligence reports. These enabled force commanders to predict Japanese naval movements with reasonable certainty; but a natural desire to home submarines onto glamorous warship targets blinded the Admirals for a long time to the strategic advantage of concentrating submarines against the merchant shipping on which Japan was wholly dependent for survival. On a wall-chart, Ultra findings and interceptions looked good but in practice navigational discrepancies, common both to hunters and hunted, quite often resulted in a top secret rendezvous being missed. Warships steamed at high speed and a submarine could easily find itself separated by a tantalising score of miles from a target which swept past and offered no second opportunity for attack. The total dedication of Commander J P Cromwell, commanding Division 43 and riding in *Sculpin* with a detailed knowledge of Ultra abilities, resulted in his refusing to leave the sinking boat with the rest of the crew after a devastating series of attacks by the singularly capable destroyer *Yamagumo* on 19 November 1943. Cromwell knew only too well that code-breaking secrets might be forced out of him if the Japanese took him prisoner. He elected to ride the boat down to the finish and richly deserved his posthumous Medal of Honor. Half of the surviving crew, who had been put about the carrier *Chuyo*, were killed when the carrier was torpedoed in the middle of a typhoon by *Sailfish* (Lcdr Bob Ward). It was bitter irony because *Sculpin* had found and stood by *Sailfish*, then *Squalus* but renamed, when she had sunk accidentally off Portsmouth, New Hampshire on 23 May 1939.

October 1943 saw the first attempt at wolf-pack tactics. Captain 'Swede' Momsen, commanding Squadron 2 selected *Cero* (Lcdr Dave White) as his flagship taking *Shad* and *Grayback* with him to the East China Sea near Okinawa. The idea was not for the three boats to attack a convoy simultaneously, because of the danger of hitting each other (a risk which Doenitz had discounted in the Atlantic where there was no case of torpedoes hitting another U-boat although there were collisions). Instead they were to co-ordinate their approaches for maximum effect. However, rather than finding themselves stationed as planned, on either flank and astern of a convoy, the three boats scattered while chasing contacts and at best the pack could be described as a joint search unit rather than a joint attack unit. With all the Ultra information available it might have been better to control attacks from shore like Doenitz. It would have avoided unsatisfactory communications between the boats on TBS (Talk Between Ships) radio although it would, on the other hand, have risked boats being located by D/F and code-breaking which the USN, because of their own ability, were sensitive about. Teething problems were surmounted in due course and wolf-packs were to achieve notable successes after a few months of trial and error; but it is hard, in retrospect, to believe that formal co-ordination between submarines at sea was any real improvement over what would have been accomplished by totally independent but concentrated operations, even at the risk of mutual interference and enemy radio interception, against designated convoys.

Ultra intelligence reports continued to dominate the positioning of submarines whether in packs or operating singly; and they still pointed primarily to naval rather than merchant targets until 1944. Then, in the third year of the Pacific war, US policy changed radically and Japanese shipping began to be devastated by submarine attacks. Although the Japanese building programme managed to keep up with the tanker losses during 1944, one half of its other merchant vessels went to the bottom virtually without replacement during the year. From September to December oil imports were cut by more than two-thirds and reserve stocks were at a dangerously low level. 1944 also saw the loss of one Japanese battleship, seven aircraft carriers, two heavy cruisers, seven light cruisers, about 30 destroyers and seven submarines with another carrier and four heavy cruisers severely damaged. All these fell victim to what had now become an extremely agressive and effective submarine force, well led and amply supplied both with Mark XIV steam and Mark XVIII electric torpedoes. It had taken a long time to learn the lessons leading to success but now the General Instructions for Seventh Fleet boats typified the new approach:

'The primary mission of submarines is to torpedo and destroy enemy men-of-war and shipping. As the war progresses, the attrition of his ships and shipping is causing the enemy to employ anything that floats to transport important cargoes.

'Press home all attacks. Long-range shots offer too little chance of hitting and too much chance for the target to maneuver to avoid. ... Pursue relentlessly ... do not let cripples escape or leave them to sink—make sure they do sink ...'

The mission and the method were now both clear. A new generation of commanding officers took their submarines into action with daring and skill. John Paul Jones and Nelson would have approved their efforts to engage the enemy more closely! Criticism has been implied by figures showing that, on average, it took ten torpedoes to sink a ship: that was high in comparison with other navies; but the fact is that large salvoes were fully justified while torpedoes were plentiful. The important thing was that enemy ships *were* sunk. If the warheads had been larger or if magnetic pistols had detonated them beneath their targets, the sinkings would have been much higher; as it was a large number of Japanese vessels escaped with only moderate damage.

The total tonnage claimed by American submarines in the Pacific amounted to 10,657,800 tons which was reduced by post-war analysis to 5,325,208 tons. The discrepancy record was held by Commander Roy M Davenport (*Haddock, Trepang*) whose wartime assessments were 17 ships for 151,900 tons brought down to 8 ships for 29,662 tons by JANAC.

These exaggerated claims, exceeding actuality in total by almost 100 per cent, call for some explanation. They were common in the USN but, except in a few cases, they were not likely to have been made wilfully or knowingly. Of course, optimism and wishful thinking played their part; but there must have been other factors at work for American submariners, as individuals, were not prone like the Russians to deliberate falsification for political reasons even if lack of success was seen to doom promotion prospects. The real culprits were almost certainly the fire-control angling system and the torpedoes themselves, as suggested in Chapter 8, together with the inevitable tendency of sonar operators to register each and every explosion as being on the target's bearing when it was, in fact, extremely difficult to determine the bearing of any short burst of noise, however loud. Torpedoes hitting the bottom, colliding, exploding in a wake, exploding prematurely or for no particular reason all gave rise to high hopes of success when nothing actually happened to the enemy.

For comparison, a thorough review of German claims and a random check of British successes has been made. It suggests that the majority matched contemporary assessments quite well although even the most cautiously compiled reports occasionally proved, after the war, to have been over optimistic. It was, though, fairly easy for German and British successes to be checked at the time: merchant vessels torpedoed by U-boats in the Atlantic almost invariably announced the fact on the distress frequency; and excellent intelligence sources gave Simpson, and others, in the Mediterranean the information which they needed to compile an accurate list of British sinkings. Furthermore, both the German and Royal Navy were well practised in analysing attacks critically, mathematically and in detail. This was not true of the United States Navy which, frankly, preferred to hope for the best.

The loss of 19 American boats in 1944 was small in relation to their achievements which ensured, as early as December 1944, that the war against Japan was won. By that time the merchant shipping left to the Empire was plying its trade almost wholly in the confined waters of the Sea of Japan and the Yellow Sea, keeping close to the coast where the American submarines, neither designed for nor practised in operations inshore, would, the Japanese hoped, be unable to reach them. But, singly and in packs, the US submarines probed deep into Japanese home waters. The Inland Sea had not been exploited since October 1943 and, besides heavy air and surface A/S cover, it was known to be guarded by new minefields. However, sensitive, short-pulse FM active sonar was now available and was capable of detecting moored mines at, submariners were assured, a suitably safe distance. Six boats were sent in April and May 1945, to locate and plot the minefields with this gear. That they succeeded in doing so, apparently producing comprehensive charts, is remarkable: following experience elsewhere with mine-detection gear and knowing how imprecise navigation could be even within sight of the land, it is difficult to believe that their plots were trustworthy. No submariner cared for this kind of work which was hazardous in the extreme and promised no rewards. Lcdr W J Germershausen in *Spadefish* was admired for confining himself to the remark that 'mine hunting was dull and unrewarding . . .'. *Spadefish* had incidentally, another unrewarding experience when, on the night of 13 June, Germershausen sank an 11,000 ton Russian ship in error. Earlier in the war this would have rated a court-martial in which three other Russian-sinking captains would have joined him; but in 1945 loyalty downwards was abundant; neither Lockwood nor Nimitz prosecuted.

As the war at sea gradually petered out during the first few months of 1945 targets became scarce. With the minefields (supposedly) known, nine FM-equipped boats, 'the Hellcats', were fitted with clearing wires, to prevent mine cables from being caught by bow or stern planes, and were sent ('Damn the torpedoes') into the Sea of Japan. The Hellcats aimed to pass beneath any uncharted fields and managed to do so safely although on two occasions wires were heard scraping down the sides of *Skate* and *Tinosa*. For some reason the Japanese did not lay deep fields. At depths below 120 feet boats were relatively safe from the buoyant mines and the Japanese only laid ground magnetic mines in enemy waters. Getting out again, with the Japanese fully alerted by the havoc of the Hellcats, promised to be difficult. It was decided to make an exit through the La Perouse Strait at night on the surface. Lockwood sent *Trutta* (Lcdr F P Hoskins) to divert the enemy by shelling an island in the Tsushima Strait to the south in 'a purposely conspicuous manner' and this served its purpose. Some hours later on 24 June eight submarines assembled in darkness just inside the La Perouse Strait and then, in line ahead at 18 knots, made for the open sea encountering fog but no obstructions on the way. A second wave repeated the operation in July and August and mopped up what was left. On 14 August 1945 *Torsk* (Lcdr B Lewellen) sank coastal defence vessels *13* and *47*. They were the last Japanese ships to be sunk and *Torsk* fired the last torpedoes anywhere in World War II.

The 'Third Phase' of the war at sea, during which the Japanese High Command had planned to annihilate an exhausted American Fleet approaching the mainland of Japan, was entirely reversed by the United States Submarine Force who fought their way to the homeland quite unexhausted and at remarkably little cost in either men or materials. Submarines were long denied public recognition of their major share in victory, in part because of inter-service rivalries but also because their operations had depended so heavily on Top Secret Ultra radio intelligence that they were little known outside a relatively small circle of submariners. However prejudiced a historian may be in favour of the other services, it would be difficult now to deny that submarines, quite apart from sinking a significant proportion of the Japanese Navy, brought the island nation of Japan to a standstill by virtually destroying the merchant marine upon which its livelihood and war-making potential depended. All this was achieved for the loss of 49 Pacific submarines. Notwithstanding mines laid by aircraft, which took a heavy toll around Japan during Operation Starvation from March to August 1945, it is arguable that it was the submarine force which finally won the war and that the two atom bombs dropped on Hiroshima and Nagasaki were superfluous.[3]

15 Soviet Submarines

When Germany invaded Russia on 22 June 1941, 35 boats were at sea or ready, by Soviet standards, for operations in the Baltic; a further 50 boats, approximately, were re-fitting or obsolete, and it may be that as many as 65 boats, in all, were theoretically available in the Baltic. However, the principal base at Libau had to be evacuated three days after the start of hostilities. The boats which could not move were scuttled and the others retired to Riga and then, when that was threatened, moved to Reval where they were joined by boats of the Second Flotilla when these were forced to leave their base at Hango in the Gulf of Finland. They were only able to remain at Reval until August when they had to withdraw still further to Leningrad and Kronstadt—and both these ports were under siege. The rapid succession of moves must have been disastrous for maintenance, logistics and operational control to say nothing of facilities for submariners themselves. Nor were matters made easier by mines, which the Germans laid from every available craft in the Baltic, and by the energetic activities of German air and sea A/S forces in an area which it was extremely important for Hitler's Navy to control—not least for U-boat training and trials.

Shch-307 enjoyed the only notable *confirmed* success in the first year of the Baltic war when she torpedoed *U-144* on 9 August although three merchant ships were to be sunk by torpedoes or submarine-laid mines before ice conditions from December prevented any further submarine operations. The Soviet submarine effort in the Baltic had, in fact, so little effect that the Germans reopened normal shipping routes on 12 July after three weeks of no underwater action being apparent and soon afterwards decided that escorts were unnecessary. With little on the credit side, no less than 27 Soviet submarines were lost in the Baltic or destroyed in harbour before the end of 1941.

In the Spring of 1942, when the ice had cleared, the Red Banner Fleet prepared its submarines for a breakout through the Finnish-German minefields and A/S patrols into the open Baltic. The boats were thickly painted, presumably in a vague hope that this would give some protection against magnetic mines and sound detection apparatus, and wooden frames around hydroplanes and other projections were fitted to supplement the standard jumping wires for brushing aside mine-mooring wires. Commanding officers were directed to try and avoid mine-fields altogether by keeping to shallow water and, when that was not possible, to pass beneath suspected minefields at as great a depth as possible. When the noise of a mooring wire was heard scraping along the hull, they were to 'stop motors until the sound ceased, indicating that the wire had slipped past.' Soviet submariners left no record of their reaction to this bland instruction!

Despite the mines, between 12 and 19 June, eight submarines traversed the first barrier in the vicinity of Lavansaari Island losing only *M-95* on the way. They then roamed the eastern Baltic sinking a dozen fair-sized merchant ships, *S-7* and *Shch-317* accounting for four ships each. The Soviet government had not declared a zone of blockade and three neutral Swedish ships, torpedoed without warning, were amongst the victims. Despite Soviet commanding officers being ordered not to attack Swedish vessels, 17 attacks were made on them and a total of five Swedish ships were sunk in 1942. The Swedish government thereupon introduced a convoy system and did not hesitate to use depth-charges if they suspected the presence of a submarine (the habit has continued in recent years). Over-statement of Soviet submarine successes, against declared enemies of course, became habitual from this time as the difficulties of making successful attacks mounted and underwater explosions of one kind and another became more frequent. *Shch-317*, for example, with Captain Second Rank V A Jegorov commanding the Submarine Division on board, claimed five ships for 46,000 tons when the actual figure was four ships for 8,000 tons. Ship identification was not a strong point. *Shch-320* claimed the important submarine tender *Mosel* while actually firing at (and missing) the smallish merchant ship *Gudrun*. It was the practice to go deep after firing and assume that any subsequent bangs signified a sinking—an assumption not unknown in

other navies but much more common in the Red Fleet than elsewhere.

Two further Baltic sorties, in August and September 1942, resulted in claims of 14 merchant vessels for 100,000 tons sunk when five ships for 10,000 tons actually went down in exchange for two submarines lost and another severely damaged by mines.

Eighteen boats were sent out between 18 September and early November 1942 but by then the minefields had been reinforced and the defences alerted. Four *Shch*-class were mined on passage and *Shch-305, 306* and *S-7* were sunk by Finnish submarines. The Soviet group claimed 18 ships for 150,000 tons but post-war German findings fixed the total at six ships for 12,000 tons with a further four ships damaged. However, three more ships (12,000 tons) were destroyed by mines which were probably laid by *L-3*. Curiously enough the Soviet Official History for this period gave exaggerated credit to individual boats and cited some entirely imaginary happenings[1] but, if anything, under-estimated the total damage caused. Soviet statistics could not, it seems, be agreed internally, let alone be made credible externally.

Vice Admiral Friedrich Ruge (German Navy) mildly remarked that it was a slight exaggeration, therefore, for Admiral Isakov (Soviet Navy) to write that 'Soviet submarines put terror into the heart of the enemy'. However, the Soviet submarines were indeed potentially dangerous and had to be guarded against throughout the Baltic war at a cost which was unwelcome when German forces were badly needed elsewhere to counteract the operations of British and Allied submarines off Norway and in the North Sea. Traffic outside the Gulf of Finland was vital and, during 1942 when 400,000 soldiers had to be transported through the Baltic, it was no longer possible to ignore the underwater threat.

As soon as ice conditions permitted, the German Navy, assisted by the Finns, laid further minefields in the Gulf of Finland and in April completely shut off the Gulf with a double submarine net at the western end. This barrier proved impenetrable. Soviet boats were entirely prevented from operating in the Baltic until Finland and the Soviet Union effected a truce on 4 September 1944 when the Finns were obliged to clear a way through the defences close to the Finnish coastline.

Navigating with the aid of Finnish naval officers, *Shch-310*, *Shch-318* and *Shch-407* made their way out into the Baltic a fortnight after the truce was arranged, soon followed by 12 more boats. Armed with mines and torpedoes they succeeded in destroying a score of ships including a minesweeper and *U-479* which struck one of the mines laid by *Lembit* on 12 December.[2] Fortunately for Germany, the 1944 Soviet submarine offensive was too late to interfere with the numerous transports evacuating Reval from 18 to 23 September; but in the following year the Germans were to be faced with near catastrophe as withdrawal and rescue operations intensified.

Twenty operational submarines remained to the Baltic Fleet at the beginning of 1945. They now had ice-free bases and were able to mount more patrols throughout the winter months; and they started to press home their attacks with more vigour. On 30 January 1945, *S-13* (Captain Third Rank A E Marensko) torpedoed and sank the 25,000 ton liner *Wilhelm Gustloff* off the Bay of Danzig. Marensko was more expert than his colleagues and hit his target with three torpedoes. The liner was urgently ferrying 6,000 fugitives, including U-boat men, from Pillau and it had no escort because none was available, nor was the ship zig-zagging: speed was the essence. On 10 February Marensko torpedoed another large liner, the *General Stuben* of 14,700 tons which, in this case, was escorted. On 16 April *L-3* sank yet another transport carrying 6,000 men. Between January and May 1945, Soviet submarines torpedoed 13 transports altogether totalling 63,000 tons and three more ships totalling 4,000 tons. Four warships were sunk by submarine-laid mines and Soviet submarines maintained a continual threat against supply ships going to Courland and troop-transports leaving Libau. There was sometimes direct

Top Right
Shch-303 (Captain Third Rank I V Travkin) made two bold claims of sinkings in the Baltic but no post-war evidence can be found of the attacks she reported which included a troop-transport.

Bottom Right
Ships of all classes were used in the Baltic in 1945 to rescue many Germans from Russian captivity but they were vulnerable targets even to the rather inept Soviet submarine commanding officers.

co-operation between submarines and reconnaissance aircraft; and quite effective tactical sub-air co-operation, of a type not attempted by Doenitz, was also employed in some areas. It is impossible to assess its value but the concept was good and it may have worked better than contemporary American sub-air procedures in the Pacific; in any event, Soviet secretiveness prevented the other Allies from knowing much about it.

The Soviet Black Sea Fleet was well supplied, from the beginning, with more than 47 submarines of all sizes, and they were mostly new. Throughout 1941 ten boats were at sea and they contributed, with other forces, to the loss of 29,000 tons of Romanian, Bulgarian and German shipping; but their share of sinkings in relation to the naval air arm is not known. As in the Baltic, commanding officers paid no attention to neutral flags and a number of small Turkish vessels were destroyed. Although gunnery was much favoured, torpedoes were fired at every opportunity, even against shallow-draught targets which, very occasionally, were hit, presumably by setting torpedoes to run on the surface. Torpedo depth-keeping and firing mechanisms do not seem to have been better than in any other navy; in all areas there were reports of torpedoes passing under ships (not only shallow draught) and detonating without hitting a target. The Soviet fish seemed particularly prone to explode in a wake and at the end of their run; but these phenomena were rather more easy to observe in the Black Sea than elsewhere and the proportion of malfunctions may not, in fact, have been unduly high. In general torpedo failures in the Soviet Fleet bore a marked resemblance to those in the German and United States Navies but, in contrast, defects were not corrected before the end of the war. During 1943 the Soviet Admiral in

Top Left
D-4 in the Black Sea, date not known but possibly before the war.

Centre Left
A Black Sea 'baby' sailing for patrol.

Bottom Left
Shch-205 **(Captain Lieutenant P D Sukhomlinov) returning to its base at Poti in the Black Sea. A Soviet account simply states that** *Shch-205* **gunned and destroyed a transport on 18 May 1942: the German version is that this was the Turkish MV** *Duatepe* **(250 tons), inside territorial waters, which had to be run aground after 70 rounds had been fired by the submarine's gun. The same boat sank a 400-ton Turkish ship a few days later with the 45 mm gun.**

the Black Sea said that the Soviet submarine arm had made considerable progress in its training and that 139 operations had been undertaken. Post-war analysis shows that 2.7 per cent of the total enemy tonnage escorted through the Black Sea in 1943 was lost due to submarine attacks.

The Soviet Official History admitted that by 1944 only 16 of the 29 submarines still available in the Black Sea were able to operate due to inadequate repair facilities. Some quite successful sorties were made along the Caucasus coast but they failed to interrupt the German convoys. Their activities gradually diminished and finally terminated when Romania and Bulgaria capitulated at the end of August and the beginning of September 1944 respectively. During the course of the Black Sea underwater war the Soviets lost about 20 boats, 40 per cent of the total operational number operating. Six small Type II German U-boats, which had been sent overland and via the Danube, operated at one time or another in the Black Sea and these were joined by six Italian Type CB midget submarines which arrived by rail in April 1942. *Shch-207* and *Shch-208* may have been destroyed by the midgets and *Shch-214* was certainly sunk by *CB-2* (Sdv A Russo). The Axis boats destroyed 33,630 tons of Soviet shipping but, to balance the picture in comparison with the Russians, it should be noted that German false claims amounted to about 41,600 tons more than the real total. These claims, not subject in the Black Sea to the usual rigorous examination by Doenitz, were even wider of the mark than Soviet boasts. However, the Romanian boat *Delfinul* (CC Costachescu), with its sole attack on 6 November 1941, earned a high place in the long international roll of records for exaggeration throughout the war: Costachescu reckoned his target, the Soviet merchant ship *Uralles*, to be 12,000 tons when in fact she displaced a mere 1,975 tons. He must have fired all his fish at point-blank range, presumably believing his target was some three times more distant than it really was.

Although the Baltic and Black Sea submarine operations were important during the German advance and subsequent retreat, it was the Northern Fleet that was most crucial to the defence of the Motherland. Despite the large number of submarines in readiness on paper in the northern bases, and an even larger number available in the Far East which could presumably have been transferred westwards when weather conditions allowed, only 16 Arctic boats were able to start operations on 22 June 1941. Three took up defensive positions around the Rybachiy

Peninsula, two off the Kola Inlet and four were sent to attack shipping between Petsamo and the North Cape. They contented themselves initially with observing shipping movements and it was not until the middle of July that any attacks were reported. The submarine command organisation ashore was not well organised and the Stalin purges of 1937 and 1938, aimed at individualists, had cut a wide swathe through the ranks of those experienced senior officers who should now have been operating the submarine fleet.

The Commander-in-Chief Northern Fleet, Admiral A G Golovko, took a personal interest in submarine activities but his memoirs show that he, like the staff officers and submarine captains under him, was very inexperienced. His memoirs, besides suggesting a pettishly parochial outlook, an extraordinary unawareness of global strategy and an inflexible belief that the Soviet Union's allies were treacherous, displayed a remarkable ignorance of the way in which his submariners went about their business. Some of his accounts, in which he showed the utmost loyalty to his subordinates, were touchingly naive but they do give some idea of the difficulties under which commanding officers and crews were operating. The British Senior Officer (Captain, later Rear-Admiral, R H L Bevan), became quite friendly with the C-in-C who remarked that the 60-year-old British officer (he was actually 50) was an expert on agriculture who could discuss it 'until the cows came home.' Perhaps Bevan politely steered conversation in that direction knowing that the Russian Admiral had himself been educated at the Timiryazev Argricultural Academy: he wrote home that the C-in-C was a young man of '45 or even less'; Golovko was in fact 35 so honours were even.

The Soviet system of command and con-

Shch-class 'Pike' submarine putting to sea. More than 100 boats of this class were commissioned from 1933 onwards, the last being completed in 1948. Most displaced 590/705 tons and were 192 ft long. Twenty-six were lost by mines or enemy action and another five by accident including *Shch-402* destroyed in error by Soviet aircraft in the Barents Sea on 21 September 1944.

trol was rigid in the extreme. Commissars had been reinstated during the Great Purge of 1937 and on 16 July 1941 a commissar was appointed to almost every naval unit including submarines. There they remained until 10 October 1942 when 'individual freedom of action and personal responsibility were restored' (for commanding officers)[3] but, although the title disappeared, extremely influential party members remained and unmistakable commissars were plainly evident in boats being taken over from the British in 1944. Commissars wore uniforms and were officially under the orders of their commanding officers; but they retained the power to make reports directly through Party channels both officially and unofficially.

The constant presence of commissars and Party officials in submarines, with the widest possible powers to praise or condemn, must have made it impossible for commanding officers to act quickly or resolutely in fast changing situations when every action could be argued on the spot or criticised later. The only thing to do was to obey their dauntingly detailed operation orders strictly and literally; any deviation was dangerous and initiative was stifled. Submariners anywhere else would have found such close and frequently inexpert supervision intolerable. Furthermore, it was customary for Divisional Commanders (themselves inexperienced) to accompany their submarines to sea and tell captains, step by step, how to do their job. This was well illustrated in Golovko's account of an approach by the small *M-172* (Captain Lieutenant I Fisanovich) on the roadstead of Liinakhamari Harbour through a narrow, heavily protected fjord. 'The steadiness and patience of Kalyshkin (the Flotilla Commander) who knew,' said Golovko, 'as nobody else, how to choose the right moment for attack, had a most beneficial influence on Fisanovich ... First of all he suggested postponing the entry of *M-172* into the enemy harbour for 24 hours ... to study the position ... on the second day Kalyshkin again advised delaying the entry. This was simply a test of patience for the captain to school him for independent operations later on.' Fisanovich duly heeded all this advice, successfully passing through the fjord, and fired a salvo at a merchant ship lying alongside a pier. *M-172* then retired to sea and attacked the hospital ship *Alexander van Humboldt*. Both attacks were greeted with wild acclaim; but the truth was that the first salvo hit the pier, without damaging the target, and the second missed altogether. Perhaps genuinely unaware of these disappointing results, Golovko was moved to make the artless comment that 'such was the outcome of the first combat sortie of Captain Fisanovich, achieved under the supervision of the Flotilla Commander.'

There were other difficulties. Torpedoes froze in their tubes on the surface in winter; submarines had to dive at intervals throughout the night, while endeavouring to charge their batteries, in order to clear ice from the casing and the conning tower hatch; guns froze up; lubricating oil solidified; main vents stuck shut; periscope top windows cracked; lookouts could barely hold binoculars (which, anyway, froze over); periscopes were intolerably stiff to turn; and canvas mats (liable to jam the hatch) had to be laid on the bridge deck to prevent watchkeepers from slipping. Visibility clamped down suddenly and the sea alternated from glassy calm, sometimes with a heavy swell which made depth-keeping tricky and quickly ran the batteries down, to high waves during violent storms which blew up quickly and without warning. And in harbour external maintenance routines could not be carried out.

For one reason and another, the achievements of submarines in the Northern Fleet were understandably modest. It is possible that nothing at all had really been sunk in this area by the time that HMS *Tigris* and HMS *Trident* started operating from Murmansk in the second half of August 1941. Within a few days the two British boats despatched four German ships for 16,000 tons which made the Russians feel uncomfortable and led them to augment their own supposed sucesses still further. Even Bevan, on the spot, believed the claims they put forward; and it may be that the Soviet Staff succeeded in convincing themselves that their boats were wreaking havoc with the German communication lines.

The captains of the 'baby' M-class boats consistently showed dash and offensive spirit, according to Bevan, in contrast to the Staff who displayed 'lack of offensive, excessive caution, concentration on minor details and a lack of commonsense, practical sense and foresight ...'. Unfortunately, spirit alone at sea did not make up for lack of training which resulted in single torpedoes or very loose salvoes being fired, apparently more in hope than in anger. Bad recognition did not help either: *M-172* fired two torpedoes at a tanker reckoned to be carrying 8,000 tons of fuel: one torpedo hit, but only because it was running so shallow; the victim was the *Vesco* of only 331 tons. The British Staff had high hopes for *D-3* who was supposed to be using British salvo-firing methods and Bevan was delighted when *D-3* claimed four successes between 26 September and 11 October (although he cautiously noted that the last was 'very doubtful'). *D-3* actually hit nothing belonging to the enemy but there is reason for inferring, from missing correspondence and signals (which the British—presumably in the interests of good relations—destroyed in entirety) that *D-3* mistook Allied ships for Germans. The difficulty in assessing Soviet sinkings can be gathered from the exploits of *K-3* (Captain Lt V Utkin) who claimed a 6,000-ton eastbound vessel with one hit from a four-torpedo salvo and the subsequent sinking by gunfire of an armed trawler and an MTB. German records showed that he missed entirely with his torpedoes but had more luck with his guns. *K-3* was armed with two 100 mm guns but the small A/S vessel *UJ-1708* had only one 88 mm and two 20 mm guns while the other escorts in this engagement had nothing larger than 20 mm weapons. At 3,000 metres—long range for submarine gunnery—a fortuitous hit aft caused depth-charges on *UJ-1708* to detonate and the boat sank. The other two boats, outgunned, retreated behind a smoke-screen. Although the odds were in her favour, *K-3* certainly fought a spirited gun-action, something that Soviet submariners were quite good at, but the Commander-in-Chief found this of little interest and only recorded in his memoirs the fictitious 6,000-ton torpedo sinking.

Soviet boats made radio signals freely and the German monitoring service was easily able to establish what submarines were at sea. However, the Germans did not have sufficient A/S craft to counter the threat, which anyway proved small, and radio intelligence therefore had little significance.

By the beginning of 1942 the Soviets had about 30 operational submarines in the northern theatre including six large K-class and

Senior Political Officer E V Gusarov reading out political information in *D-3*.

12 small M-class boats. Their successes continued to be minimal but were sometimes rewarded by undeniable persistence: *M-173* got into position for an attack no less than five times on one occasion and at last sank *MV Blankenzee* (3,240 tons). The Soviet boats were not afraid of gun duels but these became increasingly hazardous: German reinforcements on the surface and in the air sank *K-23*, with the Divisional Commander, Captain Second Rank M I Gadziev on board, on 12 May, but the Russians continued to trust guns more than torpedoes, probably for the excellent reason that they had little or no idea of how to calculate a DA. This was particularly evident during an attack by *K-21* (Captain Lt N A Lunin—a Hero of the Soviet Union) on the German battleship *Tirpitz* during the disastrous passage of convoy PQ 17 to Murmansk. Lunin claimed a disabling hit on *Tirpitz* and an accompanying destroyer but the Germans did not even notice that an attack had taken place. No amount of evidence has since convinced the Soviet Union that this attempt failed to secure what would have been a most significant strategic victory.

During the winter of 1942–3 five Russian submarines undertook the long trail from Vladivostok to Murmansk via the Pacific and Atlantic. Three of these boats, all S-class, arrived at Rosyth in early January 1943 and were given a minor refit which included the fitting of Asdics. *S-55* and *S-56* were able to sail for the Kola Inlet on 1 March with new batteries: but *S-54* had to be given a thorough overhaul in Portsmouth Dockyard where the crew were instructed in the use and maintenance of their new Asdic sets together with what knowledge could be imparted about radar in the time available. Dockyard relations were not happy with any of the boats but that was not due to the crews. The attendant, watchful commissars were to blame; the Soviet submariners could have learned so much more without them.

During 1943 the Soviets had as many as 20 submarines at sea in the Arctic area. The M-class 'babies' patrolled for between three and six days on station while the larger boats stayed out for somewhat longer but rarely for more than two weeks. Their achievements were unimportant because they aimed, primarily, for any small German naval vessel that happened to come within easy reach and sought no larger targets. German minefields were now protecting their shipping routes and were a significant deterrent to operations against transports and cargo vessels. Mines probably claimed five submarines in September and October 1943 and, while the number of submarine sorties steadily diminished, a

handful of relatively invulnerable MTB's took over most of the operations against convoys.

Shch-421 (Captain Third Rank F A Vadyaev) struck a mine while surfacing in the mine-strewn waters. All propulsion was put out of action; but Vadyaev, prompted by the ubiquitous Flotilla Commander, Captain Kolyshkin, raised both periscopes and hoisted diesel-engine covers between them as a sail in the hope that wind and tide would carry the heavily damaged boat out to sea and away from the enemy occupied Norwegian coastline. The improvised rig worked well for some three hours with a favourable wind and tide giving the submarine a speed of about four knots. The wind then changed leaving *Shch-421* still in sight from the shore. Reluctantly, the boat was made ready for scuttling and, in accordance with Russian naval tradition, she was cleaned throughout and the brightwork was polished as if for an admiral's inspection. When all was done, an open Party meeting was held. Those sailors

M-172 (**Captain Lieutenant Fisanovich**), **one of the 205/256 ton M-class 'baby' submarines in Northern Waters. More than 200 boats of this class were commissioned between 1934 and the end of the war. They could quite easily be dismantled and shipped by rail and/or barge to the Pacific and Black Sea. Twenty-three were probably lost due to enemy action, four were lost by accident (including one sunk off the Caucasuses Coast in March 1943 by Soviet surface craft) and a number were destroyed or dismantled to avoid capture by the Germans in the Baltic. There must have been very little room for the omni-present Division Commander and commissar.**

HMS *Sunfish* and HMS *Ursula* being handed over to the Soviet Navy where these boats were renamed *V-1* and *V-4* (often wrongly called *B-1* and *B-4* in Western histories due to confusion with the Russian alphabet). Only three of the eleven British ratings lent to *Sunfish* were willing to accompany her to Russia and these men were lost with the entire Soviet ship's company when the boat, on its way North, was bombed in error by an RAF aircraft.

who were not already Party members were accepted into the All-Union Communist Party of Bolsheviks. Soon after this prudent precaution had been taken the rescue boat *K-22* (whose navigation had apparently been erratic) at last succeeded in finding *Shch-421*. After several fruitless attempts to take the stricken submarine in tow with enemy reconnaissance aircraft gathering ominously overhead, the crew were taken off and the boat went down. The Flotilla Commander and the captain left last and in that order. Vadyaev went on to command *Shch-422*, replacing the former captain Malyshev who had been court-martialled for cowardice despite acknowledged displays of courage earlier. The only reference to the latter's court-martial[4] throws a particularly sinister light on the role of commissars in submarines. Malyshev was said to have returned from patrol, on several occasions, with unexpended torpedoes. Senior Political Instructor Dubik reported that there had been ample opportunity to fire them and that the commanding officer 'bore the stamp of excessive, inexplicable caution'. When a new commissar, Senior Political Instructor Tabenkin, relieved Dubik and went on patrol he soon signalled the base asking for recall in view of the captain's palpable cowardice. It

seems that the boat's gyro became unserviceable and that the captain, who had been the Division's Navigating Officer, personally tried to repair it. His efforts put the gyro completely out of action. At the subsequent court-martial Malyshev admitted to having caused the damage deliberately 'because he was afraid to carry on with his patrol.' It was said that Malyshev and other prisoners were killed when the building in which they were being held was hit during an enemy air raid. This small fragment of Soviet submarine history makes abundantly clear the reason for commanding officers firing torpedoes extravagantly at small (but reportedly large) targets.

Another example of a commissar's standing was evident after a battery explosion arising from incorrect battery-ventilation procedures in *Shch-402* (Captain Lt N (Stolbov). The captain, commissar and most of the officers were killed. Naturally, the Secretary of the submarine's Party organisation, Warrant Officer Yegorov, took charge. The first thing to do, of course, was to appoint a new commissar and Yegorov lost no time in telling the crew that he was taking over himself. Having settled that, he got down to the less important question of who should be the captain. In his new capacity as Commissar it was obviously up to Warrant Officer Yegorov to make the choice and his suggestion that Engineer Captain Lt Bolshakov should move into the vacant post went unopposed. There was never any doubt about priorities; the all-powerful Party invariably came first.

Another Engineering Officer, Karatayev, also saved the day for *M-172* whose captain, Lysenko, had been a sound peacetime commanding officer who handled his submarine 'without any glaring errors' but found the

strain of war too much for him. One day, returning from patrol, Lysenko mistook a friendly aircraft for an enemy and hastily dived in shallow water close to the coast whereupon the boat hit a submerged rock and stuck there. According to his Division Commander, he immediately panicked and screamed, 'It's a magnet! The Germans have special magnets to attract our submarines. We're trapped!' However, the Engineer Officer, with 'skill and presence of mind', sorted the situation out and made sure the submarine surfaced and reached base safely. Not all engineers were so dependable. When *Shch-402* sprang leaks in her external fuel tanks after an air attack, her captain, believing he had plenty of fuel left in the internal tanks, blew everything out of the externals to prevent the possibility of oil slicks giving away the boat's position. Unfortunately, he was wrong. The Engineer Officer had forgotten to fill the internals. A K-class boat had to put to sea and transfer 15 tons of fuel and lubricants. Neither boat was damaged during what was unquestionably a magnificent feat of seamanship; but the Division Commander coldly (and understandably) recorded that 'we have no right to create difficulties ourselves in order to overcome them heroically later.' There was a strong thread of improvisation and dogged perserverance running through Soviet submarine operations during the war and it seems that the engineering specialists, like those in other navies, were generally the most dependable and steadiest men behind these admirable attributes. The Soviet practice of keeping a man in one boat (or ship) for a large part of his naval career—sometimes for many years—probably helped to stiffen many a backbone when a newcomer captain was weak.

One of the submarines which had been given Asdics in Rosyth during her break in the 7,000 mile voyage from the Pacific to Kola put its new equipment to immediate use. *S-56* (Captain Lt G I Shchedrin) carried out an Asdic (bearings-only) attack on 4 March 1944 without using the periscope. One hit, blind, was claimed on a 6,000-ton merchant ship although it was not explained how the target was identified! German records show no sinkings on that day but it appeared that Shchedrin handled his boat confidently and competently; and, ultimately, he had more real success than most of his comrades. He became a Hero of the Soviet Union and *S-56* was made an Order of the Red Banner Guards submarine flying the coveted Guards Flag. As in all good Soviet boats accredited Party men were the aristocrats of the crew; but when Shchedrin passed the word, during a lengthy counter-attack by

German A/S units, that non-Party men could take a rest 'while the Communists hold on', the reports from all compartments were said to have been: 'We have no non-Party men. We shall all stand on watch till the end.' The boats from the Pacific seem, incidentally, to have been more efficient than the rest. It may be that training facilities at Vladivostok, well away from Head Office, were less restricted than in the Northern Fleet and, besides, the winters were rather less severe and somewhat shorter.

Four veteran British submarines, *Sunfish*, *Unbroken*, *Unison* and *Ursula*, were handed over, after refitting, to the Soviet Navy on loan in July 1944. They sailed for Polyarnoe at the end of the month. A number of British ratings were appointed to help the Russians acquaint themselves with the British boats. Eleven Royal Navy submariners were lent to *Sunfish* who, it must be said, was not in mint condition after a 250 kg bomb had exploded close alongside (although her condition was certainly not the cause of her subsequent loss).

One British submariner, a Leading Stoker, left a record of his impressions which, shared by all the British sailors sent to *Sunfish*, resulted in no more than three remaining on board for her voyage north despite threats of severe disciplinary action from the politically minded Admiralty. The Leading Stoker and his companions were distinctly unhappy. There was an immense gulf between Soviet officers and ratings—greater than in any other submarine service including German U-boats with Prussian aristocrats, 'vons', in their wardrooms. The proclaimed Marxist equality for all did not seem to apply to submariners; officers were noticeably more equal than the ship's company! Yet the officers were not outstandingly competent. Professionalism was lacking and there was a distinct reluctance to ask questions and learn how to use foreign equipment efficiently and safely. When filling tanks, for instance, valves and vents were apt to be opened and shut by trial and error whatever advice was offered.

It may be that the Leading Stoker's outlook was unduly darkened by the Russians refusing to accept the rum ration provided for them by the Admiralty as for all British boats. Rum was not strong enough for some of the Soviet sailors who did their best to give it more body by topping up their tots with metal polish (thereby getting through several weeks' issue of cleaning gear in a few days) and vodka had to be hurriedly obtained instead, much to the disgust of the British submariners. However, it was a much more disturbing event which finally decided them that they had absolutely no wish to stay with

Rear Admiral Kharlamov with members of the Soviet mission looking around HMS *Tigris* in mid-1941. *Tigris* was to operate with *Trident* from Polyarnoe from August 1941 until the late autumn when they were relieved by *Sealion* and *Seawolf*. Besides political expediency and a clear need to demonstrate how submarines should be operated, the stated purpose of these boats in the Arctic was to intercept German supply lines running up the coast of Norway and around the North Cape.

the Soviet Navy.

It occurred while *V-15* (ex-*Sunfish*) was still refitting at Rosyth. The British Leading Stoker and his Russian opposite number were hooking a chain purchase on to a cylinder head, preparatory to lifting it, when the commissar, in full uniform, stalked into the Engine Room. He pounced on the pair, making it clear by extravagant gestures that in the Soviet Navy cylinder heads were always lifted by hand. For some reason, perhaps because he thought the message was not getting across, he became furious and knocked the British man to the deck. The Russian Stoker put up his arm to ward off a similar blow and, in so doing, knocked off the commissar's cap which fell into the oily bilges. He was promptly arrested and the boat was quickly made ready for sea. When outside territorial waters, the unfortunate man was brought up onto the casing, shot and disposed of over the side.

Submarine *V-1* sailed for the North in good mechanical order. She was allocated a safety lane and stayed within it, albeit over to one side. But she was taken for a U-boat and sunk with all hands by an RAF aircraft on 27 July 1944. The Board of Enquiry had no doubt that RAF navigation was at fault. The tragedy did nothing to help Anglo-Soviet relations.

From the end of 1944 until the war finally finished, it seems that the submarines of the Northern Fleet were scarcely employed at all; but in November *V-2* (ex-*Unbroken* with a distinguished career behind her) claimed notable successes in the Barents Sea under Captain Third Rank Y Iosselini. However, the 'unescorted tanker of 3–4,000 tons' which went down to *V-2*'s torpedoes was actually the small Norwegian coaster *Stortind* of 168 tons; the rather large disparity in size

explains why Iosselini had to fire three salvoes before obtaining a hit! His other claims, which included a 10,000-ton transport, were not substantiated by post-war analysis. Admiral Kolyshkin, some 20 years after the war, noted, the 'scrupulosity' of Soviet submarine captains in assessing the results of their attacks but went on to acknowledge that 'the subjective element would inevitably creep in'. This was seen to be true not only in the Soviet submarine service: it happened everywhere to a greater or lesser extent; but Soviet exaggerations were quite unequalled in other navies and almost certainly arose from a mixture of politics and fear—the fear of what failure would cost an individual submariner when he returned to base.

The other Allies were forced to conclude with regret that Soviet submarines in all areas contributed very little to winning the Great Patriotic War. The crews were smart, keen and did their best with old-fashioned equipment, unformed tactics, inadequate maintenance, poor training facilities and a super-abundance of political control; but the sum of their achievements was not impressive.

16 The Monstrous Midgets

Secrecy was not the only reason that so little was heard about human torpedoes and midget submarines. Only a handful of men in any navy understood them and they were not conversation pieces. The mini-monsters embodied in one dimunitive hull everything about submarines that was most disliked and feared by surface sailors. Most midgets were intended for destroying targets in harbour, alongside a jetty or at anchor: it may have been thought this unsporting habit plumbed the depths of submarine depravity. In British terms, midget operations were definitely 'not cricket'! Nonetheless, the British Navy scored heavily with these craft and the Admiralty was unstinting in recommending decorations for the crews who manned them.

Midget submariners, K-Men, charioteers and the like tended to treat naval customs,

rank and courtesies with cheerful disregard. The message flashed from HMS *X-24* to the battleship *Duke of York*—'what a big bastard you are'—did little to foster big and little ship relationships. Nor were the extra-curricular activities of German K-men any more endearing to authority: training at Venice in 1943, they played endless pranks which were not calculated to improve Public Relations with the inhabitants of that watery city. Publicity, though, was the last thing that midget submariners sought anywhere. They were perfectly happy to grow up as a race apart.

When Italy entered the war on the side of Nazi Germany, the Royal Navy still dominated the Mediterranean just as it had done for the better part of two centuries. It was now left to Italian *Maiale*—pigs—to put the situation right for Mussolini.

Two Italian engineer officers, Lieutenants Tesei and Toschi, invented a type of human torpedo in the middle of 1935 and put their plans to the commander of the naval base at La Spezia on 22 October of that year. At a subsequent demonstration Admiral Falangola was much impressed by the tiny submersible which could make three knots for about five hours and, hopefully, dive to 30 or even 40 metres. The operators wore water-

tight rubber suits and oxygen masks for breathing underwater, not knowing that oxygen would soon have proved fatal at the craft's maximum depth. During early trials, Tesei had to abandon one of the vehicles and it sank. His first words to the men who fished him out were 'that pig got away again!' The name stuck.

The first attempts in 1940 by the MAS (*Motoscafi Sommergibile*) against Alexandria were frustrated. It was probably due to the excellent British intelligence service that the parent submarines *Iride* and *Gondar* were sunk before the pigs, lashed to their decks, could be launched. Early attacks against Malta and Gibraltar also failed, but valuable lessons were learned which led to future victories.

At 0200 on 20 September 1941 six frogmen, wearing improved Pirelli breathing apparatus, climbed out on to the deck of the submarine *Sciré* lying off Algeçiras, straddled the three pigs which she carried and set off for Gibraltar harbour. The three craft pressed forward slowly with the operators' heads and shoulders above the water. British patrol craft, dropping random charges into the Bay, were easily evaded. Lieutenant Visintini's approach was typical. When just short of the anchorage, he carefully calculated his position and pushed the control lever forward, taking his mount down to 10 metres. The expected anti-submarine net loomed up ahead but its meshes were so large that the small craft was able to slip through. When safely on the other side, another look above the surface revealed a fat merchant ship silhouetted against the night sky less than 200 metres distant. Edging closer Visintini planed the pig gently downwards until its nose scraped the ship's plates. Feeling his way, he clamped one end of the securing wire to one bilge-keel and then drove the pig right under the hull and up again to attach the other end. With the 300 kg explosive charge held by the wire, he had only to turn a knob and the delayed action fuse was set.

All three crews attached charges to different targets in the same way and then scuttled their craft in deep water before swimming ashore to a Spanish house, the Villa Carmela, that had recently been pre-

The delectable Conchita on the beach below the Villa Carmela, bought with funds from the Italian government in June 1942 by the Italian 'Gamma' volunteer Antonio Ramognino for himself and his very pretty Spanish wife in Spain overlooking the Bay of Algeçiras and in plain sight of Gibraltar Harbour. The Villa was clandestinely used by a fighting unit of 11 'Gamma' men.

pared for them. From start to finish it was a model operation.

The pig-men themselves had no way of knowing immediately what they had achieved. But the Italian propaganda machine could not resist telling the world as soon as intelligence sources revealed the extent of the damage:

'Attack craft of the [Italian] Royal Navy have succeeded in penetrating the Roads and the Grand Harbour of Gibraltar where they sank a 10,000-ton tanker and a 6,000-ton merchant ship loaded with munitions. A 12,000-ton merchant ship loaded with war material was hurled against the rocky coast by the force of the explosions and can be regarded as lost.'[1]

The British correctly interpreted the implications: security measures of all kinds were immediately strengthened. Meanwhile, German and Japanese naval experts were much interested and soon started a series of visits to La Spezia, the MAS headquarters, where the secret weapon—no longer quite so secret—was on show.

It was now decided to mount a second expedition against Alexandria. Every effort was made to preserve security and mislead Allied intelligence. On 5 December 1941, the same parent submarine *Sciré* left La Spezia for the island of Leros where rumours were circulated to the effect that she was damaged and in need of repair. On 14 December, three pig-crews arrived secretly by flying-boat and on the following evening *Sciré* slipped out of harbour and set course for Alexandria where German reconnaissance had reported that the British 30,000-ton battleships *Valiant* and *Queen Elizabeth* were moored. On 17 December CC de la Penne, the leader of the mission, received the order to attack.

Sciré risked a known submarine minefield and surfaced at 2047 on 20 December to launch the pigs no more than one kilometre from the fairway which was heavily patrolled by anti-submarine vessels. There would be ten hours of darkness to complete the operation. Passing fully submerged through the patrolled approaches the three craft were delighted, on breaking surface, to see two warships steaming into harbour. The anti-submarine net must therefore have been lowered: there would be no need to use compressed air cutters. De la Penne was able to lead his team, deep, through the harbour entrance in the wake of these ships without hindrance: he selected *Valiant* as his own target.

At 2215, as previously agreed, the three crews made contact with each other on the surface well inside the harbour and then set off for their respective targets whose torpedo

nets proved no obstacle. Bianci, de la Penne's Number Two, was having trouble with his breathing apparatus and, during the final stage of the attack, was swept off his seat. He swam to a buoy and managed to remain unseen while de la Penne carried on by himself. The 300 kg charge could not be attached to the hull by one man alone so de la Penne dropped it on the sea-bed a few feet beneath the giant keel. He then sank the pig and, unwilling to leave his companion, joined him on the buoy, allowing the British to take them both prisoner.

They were interrogated on board without giving anything away and were sent ashore under arrest. However, at about 0900, when Admiral Cunningham in HMS *Queen Elizabeth* heard of their capture he ordered them to be returned to HMS *Valiant* and placed below the water line. The boats of all ships were called away to drop scare-charges and the ship's companies were turned out to rig

Keeping up appearances! Admiral Cunningham C-in-C Mediterranean, directed that the ceremony of Colours, with Guard and Band and himself attending, would be carried out as usual on board his Flagship, HMS *Queen Elizabeth* **following the devastating attack by Italian human torpedoes. The hope was that the world would think the battleship was undamaged and the Royal Navy was still supreme.**

British 'chariot' on the surface.

Winston Churchill, Britain's Prime Minister, took careful note of the spectacular Italian success. In a memorandum to the Chiefs of Staff dated 18 January 1942 he wrote:

'Please report what is being done to emulate the exploits of the Italians in Alexandria Harbour and similar methods of this kind . . . At the beginning of the War Colonel Jefferis had a number of bright ideas on the subject which received very little encouragement . . . One would have thought we should have been in the lead . . .'

The Navy was, in fact, already engaged in producing self-contained midget submarines (X-craft). The production of human torpedoes, based on an Italian machine salvaged at Gibraltar, was now started in parallel. The British Chariot was, like the Italian *Maiale*, basically a slowed-down torpedo driven by batteries, with a detachable warhead. Number One of the two-man crew who straddled the machine steered and controlled it submerged; Number Two assisted him in negotiating anti-submarine nets and in fixing a time-fused charge to a target.

The task of providing a breathing system for the riders was given to the newly formed Admiralty Experimental Diving Unit where many of the divers, says a report, 'were taken to the point of unconsciousness and convulsions . . .' Diving with a closed-circuit, oxygen apparatus and with a built-in carbon dioxide absorbent unit to avoid tell-tale bubbles, was not an enjoyable occupation. Pure oxygen was dangerous below 30 feet (although that was not fully appreciated then) and if sea-water reached the absorbent it effervesced, forcing a corrosive 'cocktail' down into the diver's lungs. Cold water, too, made life unpleasant for the Charioteers. Although British crews scored successes in Norway their major triumphs were in the warmer waters of the Mediterranean and Pacific where the climate was a good deal kinder to the poorly protected operators in their frogman suits.

By way of return for the damage that the pigs had done earlier, British chariots sank three Italian cruisers and damaged other vessels at Palermo and La Spezia in 1943 and 1944. The last attack, on the *Bolzani* (which the Germans had taken over when Italy abandoned the Axis and joined the Allies), was a joint British-Italian effort.

Charioteers in the Royal Navy were not accredited to the Submarine branch. Indeed, the submarine arm was by no means anxious to promote chariot operations: 'the diversion of submarines for chariot carrying and recovery duties gravely interrupted normal

chain bottom-lines for dragging along the bottoms of all warships in harbour. The bottom-lines revealed nothing (understandably in the case of *Valiant*) and it is surprising that the British ships did not attempt to shift position in the light of a probability of ground mines: this action would certainly have saved *Valiant*. Admiral Cunningham noted sardonically that, as time went on, 'the prisoners became very restive'. Eventually de la Penne sent a polite message to Captain Morgan (commanding *Valiant*) to the effect that his ship was due to blow up in five minutes. The subsequent explosion was punctual and devastating. Four minutes later the Admiral, on the quarterdeck of the other major target *Queen Elizabeth*, felt rather than heard a dull thud and was tossed about five feet into the air by the savage whip of the great ship as the charge secured to the bilge detonated. There had already been a heavy explosion under the tanker *Sagona* which also severely shook the destroyer *Jervis*.

Investigation revealed a hole 40 feet square under the foremost boiler room of *Queen Elizabeth*. All steam was lost for 24 hours and submarines had to be secured on each side of the stricken battleship to provide power. *Valiant*'s damage extended over 80 feet, including the keel.

Six brave men had put two battleships, one destroyer and a valuable tanker out of action and radically changed the balance of power in the Mediterranean within the space of a few minutes.[2] None of the operators was lost although they spent the remainder of the war in prisoner-of-war camps. Once crew swam ashore and nearly avoided capture altogether despite some difficulty in changing an English £5 note in Egypt; but they were finally arrested on 23 December by a policeman in Rosetta.

When the war, for Italy, was finally over in March 1945, the Italian Crown Prince awarded de la Penne his country's highest decoration, the Medaglio d'Oro: it was pinned to his breast by none other than Vice Admiral Sir Charles Morgan, the man whose ship he had disabled more then three years earlier.

British 'chariot' (Mark I) being floated from a submarine.

'Chariot' attack by Lt Greenland RNVR and Leading Signalman Ferrier on the Italian cruiser *Ulpio Traiano* in Palermo harbour on 3 January 1943 (from the painting by D A Rapkins).

HMS *Trooper* alongside HMS *Titania* in Lock Cairnbawn with chariots out of their containers for inspection. Three T-class submarines were fitted with containers and chariots with the intention of attacking the Italian battleships at Taranto. The three, *Trooper, Thunderbolt* and *P-311* sailed in November 1942 direct for Malta, passing Gibraltar at night to avoid watching Axis spies who were very active in the area. The Italian battleships changed their base to Naples and alternative targets were chosen at Maddalena, Cagliari and Palermo but the loss of *P-311* in the area, probably from mines, resulted in Palermo only being attacked. Five chariots were launched from *Trooper* and *Thunderbolt* on 2 January 1943 but only two penetrated the harbour; the other three broke down. The liner *Viminale* (8,500 tons) was badly damaged and the new cruiser *Ulpio Traiano* sunk but three limpet mines were removed from the hulls of three destroyers before they could explode. *Thunderbolt* carried out a later operation against Tripoli harbour with partial success but chariot operations not only caused the loss of *P-311* but diverted submarines from their more valuable task of operating against the Axis supply line to North Africa.

This collection of *Koryu* midgets assembled at Kure gives some idea of the importance which the Japanese Imperial Navy attached to midget submarines. The two torpedo tubes were muzzle-loaded by large supply submarines or other vessels. These craft had immense potential although it was never developed. Great thought was given to the design, which was far in advance of other navies', with particular emphasis on control surfaces to counteract the rotating effect of the single propeller's torque at the exceptionally high speed of 15 knots submerged which could be maintained for one hour. A crew of five were well supplied with equipment which included a hydraulic system and a raisable radio mast. The welded construction was only fair but it is extraordinary that the Western Powers discounted this excellent design because, with a range of 1,380 miles on the surface, it could have been—and could still be, if brought up to date—a very powerful weapon. It is more than likely that the Soviet Navy gained full details of this important but inexpensive weapon.

patrol activities at a time when there were many valuable targets at sea on the Axis supply routes to North Africa.' Submariners also felt that, directly or indirectly, two T-class submarines had been lost on chariot operations due to their being obliged to surface and launch them dangerously close to the enemy coastline.

Japan, meanwhile, had very little luck in waging dwarfish underwater warfare. The Japanese midgets and human torpedoes—*Kairyus*, *Koryus* and *Kaitens*—were manufactured in great quantities and made numerous gallant attempts to prove their worth; but they were not effective. The reason was tragically plain: they were suicide weapons which Italian and British craft emphatically were not. It was not technically difficult to fly an explosive aircraft into a ship during a straightforward *Kamikaze* attack requiring minimal flying skill and no thought beyond the honour of dying for the Emperor; but it was quite another matter to control a human torpedo or midget submarine over a long period in the unpredictable, rapidly changing tactical situations common to any type of underwater operation. It must, above all, have been extremely difficult to concentrate on accurate navigation when certain death lay not far ahead.

The Japanese expected the US Navy to attack their harbours with midgets or human torpedoes and ingenious underwater defence ports were built into old ships scuttled for the purpose: Tokyo itself had three of them. But,

despite having originated the idea some 170 years earlier, American submarine authorities did not pursue it: they had no need to and it would not have been in character. This was, perhaps, best evidenced by the US Navy's insistence that boats were manned by subma*ri*ners and not subma*ri*ners—the latter pronunciation (as used in the Royal Navy) suggested, it was felt, that they were substandard mariners.

British X-craft, the first of which was laid down in September 1941, were built originally with one clear purpose—to destroy the German battleship *Tirpitz* ('The Beast' as Churchill called her) lying holed up in a Norwegian Fjord where no other kind of vessel could reach her.

X-craft were quite different to Chariots. They were perfect submarines in miniature, about 60 feet long with an average hull diameter of six feet. Although towed by full-sized submarines to the target area, they were thereafter entirely independent and capable of operating for several days on their own. Endurance was only limited by crew fatigue.

X-craft proved to be exceptionally powerful weapons of war but so little was known about them that they deserve some explanation.

A midget was divided into four compartments. The battery was right forward. Then came the diving lock known as the Wet and Dry Compartment which also contained the WC, a cramped, hand-pumped, hazardous and very public inconvenience; it could not, by any stretch of imagination, be called a comfort station. The Control Room amidships was the largest section of the craft; and a diesel engine filled the tapering stern.

From main-vent hand-levers to the electric switchboard everything was ingeniously scaled down. Taking command of a midget for the first time was rather like being given a new toy train for Christmas. A battery of small cells fed the motor which gave a maximum speed submerged of nearly six knots. The designers placed a bunk right forward on top of the battery whose cells fizzed merrily on charge. Even if the bunk's occupant managed to avoid trailing a sleepy hand across the terminals below him, he was sure to wake up with lungs full of battery gas and a splitting headache. Anyone off watch usually preferred to sleep on a foreshortened couch in the control room or coiled around the periscope. There were two crews—one of three men for the exhausting period under tow and the other of four for the actual operation.

The passage crew had an unenviable job. Their craft was submerged for most of the tow during which they had to make sure that everything was on top line for the operational team who would have, naturally, most of the excitement and rewards.

The Operational Crew were, of course, exposed to most of the dangers but the passage crew were not without a few of these themselves. If the heavy tow-rope parted, for example, its weight could take the craft straight to the bottom. On tow the craft oscillated gently up or down through a hundred feet or more; it was unwise to try towing submerged in shallow water! At two hourly intervals the towing submarine called the passage crew by telephone—if the telephone worked. Its cable was wrapped inside the tow rope; a few contortions of the latter when leaving harbour were enough to ensure that communications would be non-existent for the remainder of the tow. Life thereafter became a series of surprises. Every six hours, the midget was brought up to 'guff through', changing the stale air by raising its induction mast and running the engine for ten minutes—or longer if the battery and air bottles had to be re-charged. In rough water this was a miserable, unwelcome interlude despite the fresh air.

For much of the time the passage crew worked hard. In northern waters this at least helped to keep away the cold—a damp, grey almost tangible variety that no kind of clothing could keep out. There was, needless to say, no galley. A carpenter's glue-pot in the control room served as a double boiler and for a day or so some attempt was made to cook meals. The first four tins which came to hand were emptied into the glue-pot, heated and stirred into an unidentifiable potmess. It was not an attractive meal but its memory remained until the next 'guff through'; the odour of potmess pervaded the craft and condensation trickled drearily down the inside of the pressure hull. It was difficult to be truly thankful for food in these circum-

Top Right
A Japanese two or three-man *Kairyu* **midget. This version carried two 21-inch torpedoes externally and a suicidal warhead in the bow if required. The torpedoes were angled astern at 35 degrees by bevelled wedges on the torpedoes themselves which fitted into tapered slots built onto the hull. Displacing 20 tons, this** *Kairyu* **had a maximum diving depth of 330 feet (100 metres). The second periscope in the three-man version was raised by hand and it seems likely that the original purpose of the type seen here was for training with a 'teacher' embarked.**

Bottom Right
A *Biber* **(Beaver) on the surface with the conning tower open.**

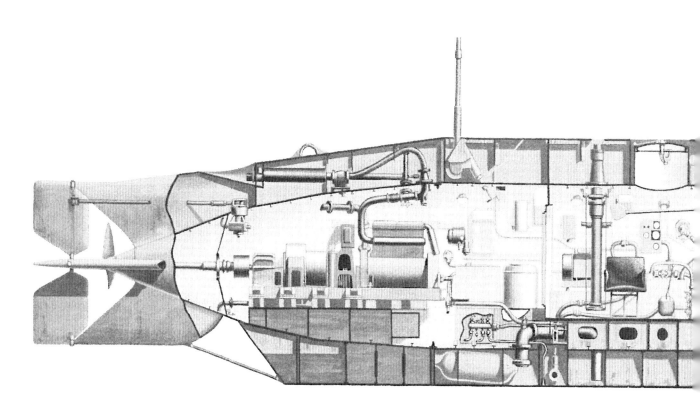

stances but one Engine Room Artificer, whose gratitude could only be admired, knelt to say an aggressive grace before and after each meal. Appetites dwindled rapidly after the first day. Cooked food, biscuits, oranges, apples, coffee, tea and fruit-juice were rejected one by one—usually in that order.

There was a more popular way of going from one port to another in the UK. The complete craft was small enough to be loaded onto a railway truck. Rail was the quickest means of transport from one shore base to another and far more tolerable than a tow although it gave rise to some unlikely situations. The crew travelled with their craft and soon found that railwaymen were a congenial crowd, quite willing to accede to midget sumariners' eccentric whims and wishes. Trains were known to stop for the crew to shoot pheasant or refresh themselves at favourite hostelries en route. It was not always easy to persuade the railway police, when returning from one of these sorties to a marshalling yard in the middle of England, that a few innocent sailors were simply rejoining their submarine on a railway siding.

Unfortunately there were no friendly railway lines to Norway or Singapore where the most important operations took place.

In hostile waters, when the passage crew had paddled back in a rubber dinghy to the towing submarine, the operational crew slipped the tow and settled themselves into the positions they would occupy for the next two days or more. Under cover of darkness the captains stayed on the casing while making best speed on the 42 hp Gardener engine which properly belonged to a London bus. By first light it was hoped to be within about ten miles of the objective so that the craft could submerge for the remainder of the approach. At this point the induction mast was lowered; all gash ditched; the position fixed as accurately as possible; and the gyro compass checked against the sun. The captain then lowered himself through the hatch and pressed the diving klaxon.

Diving depth was nearly as good as that of a larger submarine despite the craft having glass viewing ports above and at either side of the command position. External shutters could be drawn across these scuttles, from inside the craft, in the event of depth-charging. The controls were hydraulic and practically everything could be worked from the First Lieutenant's position at the after end of the control room. Course and depth had to be held precisely (within a degree and a few inches respectively) and the captain, when manoeuvring under a target, often required the craft to go astern or to stop suddenly and rise or descend vertically for a few feet. The trim was tender; a plate of potmess and cup of coffee passed from aft to forward could cause a bow-down angle.

Navigation looked crude; but it had to be extremely accurate. There was no space for an adequate chart-table and the chart had to be folded. It was soon sodden with condensation and the compass-rose was invariably on the wrong fold.

When approaching an anti-submarine net the diver had to struggle into his suit. It was a tiring performance in the cramped space forward of the periscope and he was helped by the captain and the helmsman. He then retired to squat, in solitary state, on the heads in the Wet and Dry compartment. When the time came, he pumped water into the lock from an internal tank to avoid upsetting the delicate trim. The water flood-

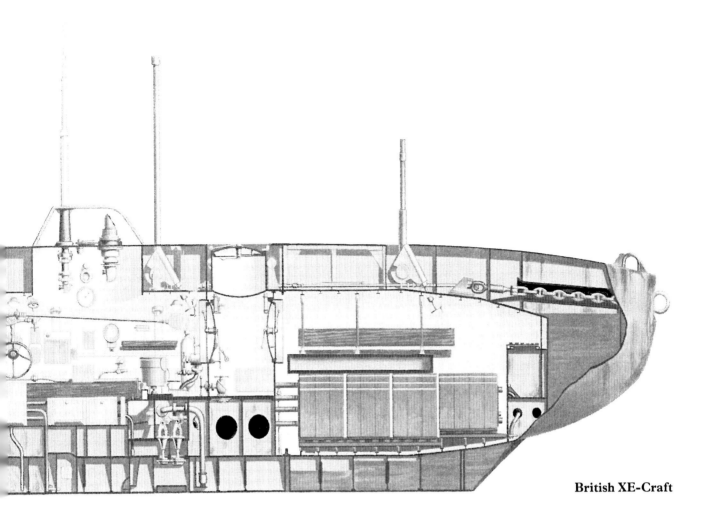

British XE-Craft

ed slowly up and over his person until it reached the top of the compartment when, water being incompressible, the pump savagely exerted its energy on each and every compressible portion of the diver's body and flattened his breathing bag. This phenomenon, experienced in solitude and utter darkness, was known, without affection, as The Squeeze. He then had to equalise pressure inside and out, open the upper hatch and haul himself up on to the casing.

A/S nets were made of thick wire-mesh interlacing steel rings suspended from telltale buoys which gave away their position to midgets trying to get through. The time of entering a net was planned, ideally, so that the craft would oppose the tide. This enabled the captain to manoeuvre into and through the net at about 25 feet with the least possible disturbance while still maintaining full control of the craft. If the tide changed the craft was liable to be swept broadside, and perhaps inextricably, into the barrier. For cutting wires the diver used an hydraulic gun which fired a toughened steel blade against an anvil in a hook which made the tool look something like an outsize tree-pruner. It was all too easy,

especially in numbingly cold water, to amputate a finger without even noticing its loss. He started by climbing down the net as far as the X-craft's keel and, from that level, cut a slit upwards in each successive strand so that the craft gradually pushed its way through while he flattened himself on the casing before crawling back into the lock.

It was best to go deep—below the keel depth of the target—when about 600 yards away. As soon as the Captain, craning his neck to see out of the upper glass scuttle, glimpsed the target shadow like a huge black cloud overhead, he ordered the motor to be put astern so as to stop directly underneath. With no movement ahead or astern the craft was then pumped very slowly up until it rested, like a fly on the ceiling, with the three special antennae which were raised for that purpose against the enemy's hull. Alternatively it hovered or rested on the bottom while releasing its weapons.

There were two types of weapon. Two large side-cargoes strapped on either side contained either a quantity of limpet mines (sometimes stowed in the casing) for attaching individually to the target or two tons each

of high explosive with a variable time fuze: these huge delayed action mines were laid directly beneath the enemy without needing the services of a diver and without necessarily coming up against the hull.

After an attack the captain did not linger. The risk of detection increased with time and it was uncomfortable to be around when limpets or side-cargoes detonated. Then there was the long journey out to the rendezvous point; an exchange of recognition signals; and finally the welcome reappearance of the passage crew.

German heavy ships based on Norway seldom ventured out into the Atlantic; but the possibility of their doing so and the carnage they could then cause amongst Russian convoys forced valuable battleships of the British fleet to remain on guard in Scapa Flow. By 1943 they were much needed elsewhere, particularly in the Far East. The greatest threat which tied them down—*Tirpitz*—had to be eliminated. September 1943 found her securely berthed in Kaa Fjord.

Six midgets set out from Scotland for the lair. They were towed by standard sub-

marines and stayed submerged for most of the long passage. One craft simply disappeared; on surfacing one night the towing submarine found the tow-rope hanging loose with nothing on the end. Another was forced to jettison its explosive charges, one of which exploded correctly after the maximum time delay but still severely damaged the retreating midget. A third reached the outer fjord but was suffering mechanical problems. Its Australian captain, Lieutenant Ken Hudspeth, reluctantly turned back so as not to put the entire operation at risk: it was morally a gallant and selfless decision. *X-5* (Lieutenant H Henty-Creer) apparently reached the inner fjord but was probably sunk by gunfire before reaching her objective.

X-6 (Lieutenant Donald Cameron) and *X-7* (Lieutenant Godfrey Place) were the only two craft to reach the target. By the early morning of 22 September both were approaching the inner defences—an anti-submarine net at the entrance to the fjord and a triple line of anti-torpedo nets closely surrounding the battleship.

At about 0400 *X-7* passed through the gate in the A/S boom but was forced deep where, blind, she tangled for an hour with an unoccupied anti-torpedo net, putting her trim pump and gyro out of action. At 0600 she was on her way again, precariously trimmed at periscope depth. Meanwhile Cameron in *X-6* was having trouble with his periscope which had flooded and was virtually useless. Determined to gain his objective at any cost he surfaced to pass through the A/S boom-gate, conning through the short net-cutting (or 'night') periscope, diving again when safely past. Both craft fouled the A/T nets but after 'wriggling and blowing' and 'some extraordinarily lucky chance' they groped their way into the lair:

Top Left
German *Seehund* **craft at Keil. These two-man midgets were conventionally propelled with a surface range of 120 miles at 8 knots and a submerged range of 20 miles at 3 knots. Two torpedoes were carried externally on either side of the keel. Approximately 250 boats were built between September 1944 and April 1945 and a few were equipped with a primitive schnorchel. German midget constructors learned useful information from wreckage recovered after the British X-craft attack on** *Tirpitz* **in 1943.**

Centre Left
A German *Biber* **stranded after the Normandy invasion.**

Bottom Left
German *Seehunds* **lying in harbour.**

the compasses in both had by now gone off the board due to sundry collisions, groundings and steep angles.

X-7 hit *Tirpitz* at full speed at 20 feet below B turret. Place let the craft slide gently down below the keel where he went astern for an estimated 150 to 200 feet and let go the port charge approximately under X turret. Cameron in *X-6* was snared in one more obstruction which forced the craft up to the surface again close on the battleship's port bow where he was greeted with a brisk fire from hand grenades and small arms—he was much too close for the big guns to bear. Realising that escape was impossible, he destroyed the most secret equipment, went astern until *X-6* was scraping the giant hull abreast B turret, released his charges and scuttled the craft. As he started to sink, a power boat from the battleship came alongside to take off the crew but were too late to stop the craft following her charges to the bottom.

Tirpitz had a Ship's Company of 2,500, displaced 42,000-tons, mounted eight 15-inch guns along with 96 smaller weapons and was sheathed in armour 15-inches thick. At breakfast-time on 22 September 1943 HMS *X-6* and HMS *X-7*, each with four men inside their fragile, half-inch pressure hulls, slipped four two-ton delayed action mines beneath the pride of the German Navy at her moorings. 'The Beast' never put to sea again.

But X-craft did. Not content with sinking ordinary ships they quickly added a floating dock to the mounting score and then turned their attention to affairs in the Far East. On 26 July 1945 *XE-1* and XE-3 set out under tow for Operation STRUGGLE to attack Japanese cruisers berthed off Singapore with priority being given to the 10,000-ton *Takao*.

Before setting off the crews were addressed by Admiral Fife USN whose flag HMS *Bonaventure*, their depot ship, happened to be flying. 'Jimmy' Fife, the senior American submariner in the Pacific, was a great supporter of the British 14th Submarine Flotilla (*XE-1—XE-6*) commanded by Captain W R Fell RN. British reserve was somewhat shaken when he barked, at the end of his address: 'You're the little guys with a lotta guts. Good luck!'

Neither *XE-3*'s diver, Leading Seaman 'Mick' Magennis, nor his captain, Lieutenant 'Titch' Fraser, realised just how much luck they would need when they paddled across from the towing submarine *Stygian* with the other two operational crew-members to take over from the passage crew some 40 miles short of Singapore in the early morning of 30 July. They slipped the tow and went on alone at 2300 that night. Fraser

found the Singapore harbour net boom open and passed through in dangerously clear, shallow water without being seen despite the proximity of a Japanese Boom Defence Vessel. At one stage *XE-3* inadvertently bottomed on a mine but luck held and it failed to explode.

Their real difficulties started when Fraser tried to position his craft beneath the cruiser. There was too little space beneath the target—even for such a small submarine as *XE-3*—and the tide was falling. There was no room to open the hatch fully for the diver, let alone to raise upright the folding antennae which were supposed to ensure a clear three feet beneath the top of a craft and the bottom of a target.

No X-craft diver's job was easy; but Magennis in *XE-3* had the toughest task of any. He found the awkwardly sloped hull covered in weed and heavily encrusted with barnacles. These had to be scraped off with a knife and although the six limpet mines which he extracted from the port side-cargo container were slightly buoyant it was hard work attaching their magnetic pads. It took him half-an-hour to do so; and by the time he wriggled his way back into the craft he was near to collapse. A slow leak from his oxygen set did not help and he was barely able to shut the hatch behind him.

Fraser turned the release wheel inside the craft and the starboard side-cargo fell away onto the sea-bed under the cruiser. He then turned the other handwheel and assumed that the port container had also freed itself. *XE-3* now found herself tightly wedged between the hard sea-bottom and the menacing hull above. Sub-Lieutenant Smith, the New Zealander First Lieutenant, worked the motor full ahead and astern, flooding and blowing tanks for 50 minutes. Eventually his increasingly desperate struggles extricated the craft from its precarious position alongside a huge quantity of time-fused high explosive. Fortunately, the Japanese did not hear the commotion or notice *XE-3* break surface momentarily when it finally pulled free; but Fraser's problems were by no means over. For some reason the empty port limpet carrier had failed to jettison and it was making the craft impossible to control. Magennis, despite his exhausted condition, immediately volunteered to go out and clear it. After seven minutes work with a large spanner he persuaded the side-cargo to drop clear and *XE-3* was able to head back over the obstacle-course of harbour defences for the pre-arranged rendezvous with *Stygian*. Fraser's crew had been in action continuously for 52 hours. Operation STRUGGLE was well named!

Takao was damaged beyond repair and the threat of her eight-inch guns to Allied troops planning to advance along the Singapore causeway was annulled. Magennis and Fraser, like Cameron and Place, were awarded the Victoria Cross.

X-craft were extraordinarily versatile. Amongst other diverse sorties they severed the underwater telephone cables linking Japanese-occupied Hong Kong, Singapore and Saigon. This obliged the enemy to revert to radio communications which could be intercepted and deciphered by Ultra units. It was an exceedingly valuable operation.

In the West, X-craft were given an even more unlikely task. Two were selected to act as beach markers for guiding amphibious DD tanks to British-Canadian landing areas at dawn on D-Day.

Invasion planners knew that if the X-craft failed a vital part of the invasion forces might never land on the narrow strips of beach that shelved gently enough for the cumbersome amphibians to crawl ashore: and if they were discovered the whole invasion might be jeopardised. The boats chosen were *X-20* (Lieutenant Ken Hudspeth who had been forced to turn back from the *Tirpitz* attack) and *X-23* (Lieutenant George Honour who had exceptionally long command experience).

On the night of Friday, 2 June 1944, the pair put out from HMS *Dolphin*, the submarine base at Gosport. They were escorted by a tug and trawler past the Isle of Wight where, parting company, they dived. Their subsequent experiences were similar: *X-23*'s are followed here. Except for a one-hour battery-refresher during hours of darkness, Honour and his crew motored southerly, submerged, at an average speed of three knots to a point off what was to be SWORD Beach close to the mouth of the River Orne at Ouistreham. They arrived at dawn on Sunday, 4 June.

The crew, besides Honour, consisted of the normal First Lieutenant and ERA but two COPP (Combined Operations Pilotage Party) specialists in beach-landings were also embarked: one of these was a qualified navigating officer. When the position had been precisely fixed by bearings, Honour let go a small anchor and bottomed.

X-23 came stealthily to the surface at 2300 to listen for a pre-arranged radio signal from Niton on the Isle of Wight and to 'guff through', changing the air. The beach by night looked dangerously close. Honour reflected on the code name for their part in these activities—Operation Gambit. He had checked gambit in the dictionary: as he darkly suspected it referred to a move in a game of chess where 'a pawn is sacrificed for position'. Whoever named X-craft operations had a sardonic sense of humour.

The expected radio message duly arrived while the craft lurched and plunged to its anchor in an increasingly heavy sea that swept over the casing. The coded signal told Honour that Operation OVERLORD would be delayed. It did not say for how long; but the weather made the reason obvious. There was nothing for it but to dive back down to the bottom, play a few rounds of singularly vicious liar-dice and go to sleep. This pause in the proceedings came as a relief to one of the COPP party who had suffered agonies of sea-sickness on the surface.

On Monday night *X-23* came up again to learn that the landing was now due on the following day. At 0530 on Tuesday, 6 June Honour surfaced finally. The sea had moderated and he was able to prepare his craft for the job in hand. A mast, 18 feet high with a green light shaded to landward, was hoisted to signify that *X-23* was in her correct position; a radio homing device was also triggered and an underwater sonic beacon switched on. A red and white international flag H ('I have a pilot on board') proudly announced HMS *X-23*'s qualifications; and Honour prudently added, in case anybody should mistake the craft for a German U-boat, a huge White Ensign of a size normally issued only to battleships.

The incoming fleet appeared from the north exactly on time. It was an impressive sight. Invasion craft clustered trustingly around *X-23* and poured their canvas-clad DD tanks into the water. Honour watched with awe and sincerely hoped that the enthusiastic amateur sailors in khaki understood the Rule of the Road at sea. The tanks, as if on a parade ground, sluggishly formed up in line abreast and chugged their way towards the beach. Two of them sank on the way but their crews (rather pessimistically) had been provided with submarine DSEA (submerged escape) sets and no lives were lost. Honour and Hudspeth watched for a while from their respective vantage points at either end of the beach before being taken in tow by the trawlers assigned to them and changing over with the passage crews. When they eventually got back to the base at Gosport they were indignant to find nobody willing to believe that two midget submarines had spearheaded the invasion and been first off the beaches.

Meanwhile, there was frenetic midget submarine activity on the German side.

By the Autumn of 1943 the German Navy was in a poor state. The Atlantic tide had turned against the U-boats in the spring and was now running strongly in favour of the Allies. An invasion of Europe was clearly imminent; but neither the regular U-boat arm nor the German surface fleet was in any shape to meet the threat. In desperation, Doenitz turned to human torpedoes and midget submarines as one means of defence during the forthcoming crisis. The German Naval Command had, up until now, rejected this kind of underwater warfare; but the damage inflicted by the Italian 'pigs' and British X-craft, especially the outstandingly successful *Tirpitz* operation, heavily influenced the decision to create a new naval commando unit, to be called the Kleinkampf-mittel-Verband (small battle-weapon force or 'K-force'). It was composed of explosive motor-boats, frogmen, human torpedoes and small submersibles inspired by British fragments dredged up from Kaa Fjord. All were produced amidst an air of urgency that amounted almost to panic.

The K-force was hastily conceived, inadequately equipped and poorly trained; and its assorted craft were flung into the fray long before they were ready for combat. But if the K-men achieved little of real significance it was not for want of trying. They had, essentially, the same independent, superficially irresponsible character as Italian and British charioteers and midget submariners. Indeed, in seeking to become a select Nelsonic 'band of brothers', a stated aim of their commander Vice Admiral Heye, they went further towards non-conformity than their opposite numbers by discarding all badges of rank.

Human torpedoes were cheap, easy to produce and, by adapting existing Type G7e torpedoes, the *Negers* or Niggers, as they came to be called, needed no precious raw materials. On 10 March 1944 Doenitz, in Berlin, sent for Lieutenant Hanno Krieg, a promising young U-boat commander whose boat had been put out of action in Pola harbour by enemy bombing. As usual, Doenitz came straight to the point. A single prototype one-man torpedo awaited trials at Eckenforde; all trials must immediately be completed and ten complete weapons made ready within four days. They were then to be transported to Italy, fully prepared for action, within a fortnight. Further Allied landings at Anzio behind the German lines in Northern Italy were expected hourly and it was here that the Niggers, launched from the German occupied coastline to the south, were to be baptised. The Admiral had one more thing to say as Krieg turned towards the door: 'I can spare no U-boat men . . .'.

Looking back on that remarkable interview it is difficult to believe that Doenitz, with his unequalled experience of underwater warfare, really believed that the K-force could be anything more than a diversion. But desperate measures were called for. None of the General Staff any longer believed that the Allies could be altogether stopped; but any conceivable means of hindering their advance was worth putting to the test.

A Nigger was basically two modified type G7e electric torpedoes. One, a range-reduced weapon to save weight, was slung below the other converted to a carrier. The pilot sat, sheltered by a perspex dome, in a small cockpit which replaced the warhead in the carrier fish. He had a start-stop lever, a column for horizontal and vertical rudders (although none of the models was able, in practise, to submerge completely) breathing apparatus, a compass and a handle for firing the weapon-torpedo which started automatically when released from the two-clamp cradle which connected it to the carrier. Drinking water and concentrated food tablets were also stowed in the cockpit. The aiming device consisted of a graduated scale marked on the canopy and a spike striking up from the body to serve as a foresight. The weapon was, in every sense, cheap and nasty. The carrier's endurance (there and back) was 12 hours at four knots (six knots after the torpedo had been fired).

In theory, especially to shore-based tacticians, the Niggers seemed attractive. They were quick to produce (the all important factor), capable of inflicting appreciable damage and there was a real chance of the pilots coming back. The first snag arose when it was discovered that they were very difficult to launch from the shore: 500 (admittedly reluctant) troops only managed to push 17 out of 30 Niggers into the sea for initial and wholly unsuccessful operation in Italy. When one eventually settled in the water a pilot was much too low down to see properly and any oil on the surface smeared the canopy and made him blind. Potential targets were thus almost impossible to evaluate; and aim-off was more a matter of luck than good judgement. For the same reason it was difficult to take avoiding action and, being unable to dive fully, a pilot had no defence if sighted. As one pilot gloomily remarked, an enemy motor boat had only to 'come alongside, remove the canopy with boat hooks and strike the pilot. The torpedo would then fill with water and sink!'

In a vain endeavour to distract the omnipresent opposition milling around the invasion landing areas a number of canopies were painted to simulate the head and shoulders of a pilot: these dummies were floated off on the tide but did not decoy the

Top
A German *Neger* **being winched out for trials.**

Centre
A German *Molch* **awash in harbour showing how easily such craft could operate in tight spaces.**

Bottom
A German *Biber* **being taken alongside a launch.**

opposition sufficiently to alleviate heavy losses amongst the real K-men.

Some 200 Niggers were constructed and a large number endeavoured to harass the mass of Allied ships and landing craft off Normandy. But they were little more than a nuisance to the enemy. They claimed three or four small vessels sunk but the Polish cruiser *Dragon* (built in 1917) and HMS *Isis* (a destroyer) were their only significant successes.

A quite different one-man submersible, christened *Biber* (Beaver), was developed in parallel with the Niggers. The Beaver was petrol-driven and had several features of a full size U-boat including a periscope and a rudimentary schnorchel. Each craft carried two torpedoes. A small top-secret flotilla arrived in trucks towards the end of August 1944 at Fécamp on the Channel coast. The Beavers were by no means ready for action: their first expedition had to serve as their only trials and training period. Nevertheless they managed to send one landing craft and a liberty ship to the bottom despite the additional handicap of unfavourable weather. Between December 1944 and February 1945 a larger group made 110 sorties from Rotterdam; these were all without result but a number of Beavers were sunk, mainly by accident.

An accidental explosion in Rotterdam harbour, probably due to a Beaver's torpedo running wild when being prepared, finally put paid to the activities of this flotilla. It was the end of German midget operations.

In summary, the Japanese midgets failed largely because suicide tactics militated against the high degree of professional skill demanded in all types of submarine, large or small; and the German K-force had scant successs because there was too little time to practise and plan sufficiently.

In contrast, the Italian *Maiale*, British Chariots and X-craft, all thoroughly well prepared, practised and equipped, achieved major strategic victories of greater importance than most normal submarines. The adopted motto of *X-6*, one of the two X-craft which put the massive *Tirpitz* out of action, was '*Piscis minimus maximorum adpetens*' or, loosely, 'the smallest fish with the biggest appetite'. It stood for all those midgets that left such a memorable mark on the underwater war.

17 Special Operations

Submarines were called upon to undertake a number of tasks outside their normal attack role. Some were exciting but few were rewarding and most were hazardous.

Cargo-carrying submarines were first conceived during World War I when the 2,000-ton *Deutschland*, built with private funds, made a round trip from Bremen to Baltimore in 1916. The venture (a commercial success) was widely noted: during World War II the concept was broadened extensively.

The Japanese made much use of submarines to supply their captured island garrisons and their widespread employment, or misemployment, in this way was such that it overshadowed numerous runs of the same kind undertaken by American boats. USS *Seawolf* led the way by delivering 37 tons of .50 calibre ammunition to Corregidor at the end of January 1942 and bringing off 25 Army and Navy pilots, a quantity of submarine spare parts and 16 torpedoes. She was followed in February by *Trout* who delivered 3,500 rounds of 3-inch anti-aircraft ammunition and brought back to Pearl Harbour two tons of gold bars and 18 tons of silver pesos. Submarines contined to deliver ammunition and supplies and evacuate personnel from beleagured garrisons until January 1945 when *Nautilus* made the last run that was needed. Altogether about 1,400 tons of stores and ammunition were conveyed by American boats as well as secret agents and raiding parties. The USN was not, however, so hard pressed as the Imperial Navy's submariners whose landing points were more often under heavy fire. So that Japanese submarines could stay submerged, rice was packed into external drums which rose to the surface when released; and at Guadalcanal, in January 1943, miniature submersible freighters were used. They were propelled by two torpedoes at 3 knots, piloted by one man and could carry two tons of supplies for about two miles. These contraptions, which worked surprisingly well, could be released from a submarine submerged. A dracone was also devised capable of carrying 50 tons of cargo for towing submerged. A vast amount of effort and ingenuity went in to Japanese supply operations—but they scarcely constituted real submarining.

The United States Navy, on the other hand, managed to combine special operations with offensive patrols. Amongst the hundred or more United States submarines employed at various times on special missions it is worth following the career of USS *Nautilus*. This giant 2,700-ton vessel, armed with ten torpedo tubes and two big 6-inch guns, was called upon to do things which submariners did not, as a rule, expect when the war started. With her broad flat casing, *Nautilus* took a long time to dive and was very slow to turn: she was not the ideal boat to send into restricted waters but that is where she was largely employed.

Following what was thought to be a successful torpedo attack in the Battle of Midway (see Chapter 14) her first wartime captain, Lcdr W H Brockman, was propositioned by Rear Admiral English in June 1942 with the startling idea of surfacing to bombard Emperor Hirohito's summer residence close to the entrance of Tokyo Bay. Amidst shoals and rocks and a multitude of Japanese anti-submarine vessels it would have been more than risky: Brockman accepted the idea in the Admiral's office but wisely changed his mind on patrol, contenting himself with three torpedo attacks, one of which sank the destroyer *Yamakaze* and resulted in heavy depth-charging. When *Nautilus* returned the Admiral was disappointed but, with an excellent periscope photograph of *Yamakaze* going down by the stern (which was published as *Life*'s picture of the week), Brockman was awarded another Navy Cross, his second in five weeks.

On 8 August, with depth-charge damage made good, *Nautilus* sailed from Pearl Harbor in company with *Argonaut* (Lcdr J R Pierce). The two boats carried a group of marines from the Second Raider Battalion led by Colonel Evans F Carlson who had with him Major James Roosevelt, son of the President. In all there were 13 officers and 198 men in the group and their orders were to carry out a raid on Makin Island which Admiral Nimitz hoped would divert Japanese forces from Guadalcanal. Carlson's raid was successful, thanks to *Argonaut* and *Nautilus*, but only just! The two boats arrived off Makin Island safely and at 0300 on

17 August the marines disembarked in rubber boats. Several boats were swamped on launching which made their outboard engines impossible to start. The survivors towed the remainder as best they could; but the landing plan went by the board and Japanese snipers provided a warm reception. Communication between the landing party and the submarine was only sporadic but Brockman gathered that the raiders wanted fire-support. *Nautilus* immediately brought her two large guns into action and fired 24 rounds into an area where Japanese reserves were thought to be. She was then invited to direct her fire, blind, into a harbour seven miles distant. By great good luck a barrage of 65 shells hit a 3,500-ton transport and destroyed a small patrol yacht. The submarine gunners must have been as surprised as the Japanese victims.

During the forenoon the two submarines remained on the surface for as long as they could but had to dive several times for aircraft; and in the afternoon they were forced to remain submerged continuously until dusk when they surfaced to recover the raiders. Fifty-three marines were on board by 2130 but, with many still missing, *Nautilus* closed to within half-a-mile of the barrier reef at daybreak on the following morning to recover the remainder. While waiting for them, Brockman was forced to dive in the very shallow water where *Nautilus* was seen by an aircraft and attacked, fortunately without effect. That evening, the two boats again surfaced and, guided by a signal light from Carlson, cautiously edged once more towards the beach. By midnight, all but 30 marines were accounted for. With several wounded on board, the wardroom became a crowded, unsterile operating theatre. The air-conditioning was totally inadequate for the number of men carried and, with sea-sickness and exhaustion adding to the marines' misery, the conditions below were horrible. The Makin Island episode was widely acclaimed and went down in history as the greatest commando raid of the Pacific war; but the submariners were rather neglected in the general junketing that followed.

In January 1943 *Nautilus* set off again, this time to evacuate a flock of Catholic missionaries, including 17 women and three children, from Bouganville. En route Brockman sank a small freighter, damaged two other ships and missed an attacking destroyer.

In May, 109 Army Scouts were embarked at Dutch Harbour and transported, submerged for most of each day, through the foggy, submarine-infested Alaskan waters to Attu in advance of the main invasion. The soldiers were distinctly unhappy and many were seasick. Oxygen was released into the boat periodically but by the end of each day there was not enough in the atmosphere to light a cigarette. The Scouts finally went ashore fearing the enemy less than a prolonged stay on board the submarine while *Nautilus* went on to reconnoitre the Aleutians.

Between 16 September and 16 October 1943 *Nautilus* conducted the first proper submarine beach-reconnaissance using periscope photography. The Executive Officer,

Top
HMS *Porpoise* **store-running to Malta.**

Bottom
HMS *Severn***, one of two submarines employed to supply and reinforce the garrison at Leros, experimenting with a landing craft on the after casing.**

Lcdr R B Lynch was a camera enthusiast. The mission required accurate photography of three areas in the Gilbert Islands where amphibious forces planned to make landings. A bracket for holding a camera was attached to the search periscope and the lower sound room was converted to a dark room for processing film because films had to be developed immediately to see whether any shots had to be retaken. Three cameras were provided: an Eastman Medallist, a National Graflex Series II and an Eastman 35 which was specially designed for periscope photography. None of them were good enough. Although the periscope tube was made of steel it vibrated sufficiently to blur the photographs unless high shutter-speeds were used. Unfortunately, light-losses through the periscope amounted to 65 per cent and that demanded *low* shutter speeds. It was fortuitous that Lynch had his own Primarflex camera on board. This had a single-lens reflex view-finder and a focal-plane shutter which stopped the action better than a between-lens shutter. Primarflex units were made in Germany; but advertisements in trade journals produced the ten that were needed. The press seized on the story, proclaiming that a Nazi camera contributed to the downfall of Japan; but, 'Ozzie' Lynch must have thought that was a slight over-statement.

In November, *Nautilus* stood by off Tarawa to rescue any naval aircrews who might come down in the sea during the massive fleet operation directed at capturing the island. At sunset on 19 November, the eve of the amphibious landings, the captain (now Cdr W D Irvin) went close inshore to report surf-conditions before turning south towards the neighbouring island of Apamama where eight officers and 70 men of the Marine Amphibious Reconnaisance Company were to be landed. Irvin was rounding a reef in pitch darkness when, at 2154, radar reported a 25-knot ship approaching. It was the destroyer USS *Ringgold* who took the submarine for a Japanese patrol-boat and opened fire. Irvin immediately fired the correct green recognition grenade and dived but *Nautilus* was hit on the way down by the first shell. Fortunately it was a dud. The diving drill was less than perfect and the conning tower and main induction trunking took in water. Another shell, this time of the exploding variety, ruptured the port main motor cooling system and started leaks in the bilges. The marines did not enjoy the experience and nor, come to that, did Irvin's crew; with control eventually regained, the 'friendly' destroyer was evaded and the marines were duly landed.

Back on normal patrol in March 1944, *Nautilus* damaged two ships in a convoy and, a few days later, obtained four hits with four torpedoes which damaged another ship and sank the *Amerika Maru* which, unhappily, was taking seventeen hundred civilians, including women and children, back to Japan from Saipan. In June, with Cdr G Sharp as captain, *Nautilus* landed one man and 98 tons of cargo at Mindañao in the Phillipines. A fortnight later she landed four men and supplies and evacuated 17 people including five women and one German prisoner from Balatong Point. In July she put two more lots of men and supplies ashore in the same area and took off special cargo. In September, after landing 65 tons of cargo, 20 drums of gasoline and two drums of oil for guerillas on the south east coast of Cebu *Nautilus* ran aground on a shoal at about 2200. Radar ranges had enabled Sharp to remain 600 yards off shore during the unloading operation but there was no way, in the darkness, of determining lateral drift. Not one to waste stores, Sharp lightened the boat by sending another 40 tons of cargo ashore, but had reluctantly to blow 5,900 gallons of oil fuel overboard and jettison 190 rounds of 6-inch ammunition. The boat finally came off under full astern power at 0336 with sunrise only three hours away. Vigorous efforts were made to readjust the trim but in his haste the Engineer flooded about 40 tons too much water into the compensating tanks. When daylight came, *Nautilus* dived in what was for her a record-breaking 75 seconds. And she went on down. Every trick in the submarine trade was used and control was regained after a few long, fraught minutes. On the next occasion when she dived, five days later after yet another supply and evacuation mission, the Engineer Officer was more cautious with the trim: *Nautilus* took seven minutes and 31 seconds to reach periscope depth.

During October she carried out three more similar operations and was then sent to destroy *Darter* (Cdr D H McClintock). McClintock, despite assurances from his Navigator that he was 19 miles from the nearest land, had run aground five days earlier at the southern end of the Palawan Passage and could not get off the reef. The crew were safely transferred to *Dace* but all efforts to blow up *Darter* with demolition charges, torpedoes and shells, aided by what was, unfortunately, a hopelessly inaccurate bombing attack by a Japanese aircraft, failed. Nor did 55 creditable 6-inch hits out of 88 rounds fired by *Nautilus* succeed; but *Darter* was by now so badly holed that she could not have been salvaged by the Japanese. She remained on the Bombay Shoal as a monu-

ment to bad submarine navigation for many years afterwards.

Under her third commanding officer, Lcdr W Michael, *Nautilus* made two more cargo deliveries in January 1945 before being deservedly retired. Her special missions had not been glamorous or sensational or newsworthy; but they all involved dangers which submariners, in the normal run of things, did not contemplate.

In Germany, as the war ground on, a need was seen for underwater blockade-runners to bring in vital raw materials from overseas. One solution, already explored in Japan, was for submarines to tow submersible barges; and a prototype of 90-tons displacement was successfully towed by *U-1163*, a Type VIIC, in October 1943. Trials on the surface and submerged were successful but the towing boat had to make at least 4.1 knots underwater because at anything less the barge lost the dynamic force necessary to hold it below the surface. If barges of this type could be made safer by fittings that would allow them to be slipped or sunk from the towing U-boat the Naval Staff seriously considered organising a service between Europe and East Asia. Surface vessels were to cover the stretch from East Asia to the South Atlantic and outward or homeward bound operational U-boats were to negotiate the final leg from the South Atlantic to Europe. But further trials proved that it was still impossible to reduce the minimum towing speed; U-boats had insufficient battery capacity to maintain four knots for any length of time and it was already dangerous enough in 1944 for a U-boat to transit at its normal speed without towing anything, so the idea was abandoned.

On 8 February 1943, at his first conference with Hitler as Commander-in-Chief of the Navy, Doenitz had suggested using the few serviceable Italian U-boats for cargo-carrying to and from the Far East. The Italian naval command eventually sanctioned the use of ten Atlantic boats, operating from Bordeaux, but losses en route, politics and engine troubles prevented these bringing a single ton of cargo to Europe. In parallel with this enormous amount of misplaced effort, it was planned that the operational boats deploying to the Indian Ocean would carry cargo in place of ballast. The principle shipments to Japan were mercury and lead and the most needed imports were tin and wolfram ores. Boats returning home also had to find cargo space for rubber, molybdenum, opium and quinine; with careful stowage it was possible for Type IXC and IXD boats to carry 110 to 130 tons of cargo in the keel and outside the hull and 20 to 30 tons inside the boat.

The fore-ends of HMS *Seraph*, frequently overcrowded, and on one occasion carrying the corpse of the 'Man Who Never Was', during special operations.

Surface blockade-running ceased all together in January 1944 and the shipment of raw materials to Germany became a prime and urgent responsibility for U-boats returning from Penang; but even if every available boat was loaded to capacity, only a fraction of the required shipments could be carried. In January 1944 calculations showed that rubber, tin and wolfram requirements would be met if 1,000 tons of cargo were brought in by the end of 1944 and the same amount each month thereafter. Heavy losses made this impossible. Of 14 planned U-boat supply voyages, only the Japanese submarine *Kiefer*, and *U-178* and *U-188* reached Bordeaux from East Asia.

The British without detracting too much from the main aim, employed submarines to supply Malta under siege. The largest boats were the obvious choice for transport duties and *Clyde*, *Olympus*, *Rorqual* and *Parthian* were notably successful in running the Mediterranean blockade to Malta from June 1941 to October 1942. With her mine-casing doors removed *Rorqual* was able to carry, on one trip from Alexandria, 24 personnel, 147 bags of mail, two tons of medical stores, 62 tons of aviation spirit and 45 tons of kerosene; she returned with 17 personnel, 146 cases of 4-inch ammunition, 10 tons of miscellaneous stores and 130 bags of mail. The rats with which *Rorqual* was notoriously ridden did not, oddly enough, participate in

these voyages; they joined the boat in Haifa later in the war!

Without the submarine 'Magic Carpet' Malta would not have been able to stay in business as a base. Between June 1941 and the end of the year 16 stores trips were made averaging one every 12 days. In July alone, 126 passengers, 84 thousand gallons of petrol, 84 gallons of kerosene, 12 tons of mail and 30 tons of general stores were safely brought in. Not listed in official reports, but equally important, were several cases of gin and, on one occasion, 100 gramophone records for the Governor.

Store carrying was not so simple as it sounded. Boats were crammed from deck to deckhead. Emergency operations, such as putting the after hydroplanes in hand, were slowed down and trimming was a problem. When cans of petrol were carried externally, depth had to be limited to 65 feet and that only for periods not exceeding five minutes. Full buoyancy had to be maintained on the surface to avoid the external cargo being damaged by the sea; and wooden packing boxes in the casing absorbed so much water that *Cachalot*'s First Lieutenant had to pump out one thousand gallons from internal tanks to compensate. In *Rorqual*, carrying aviation spirit in external oil fuel tanks which vented fumes in the normal way through the expansion system, the smell of petrol on the bridge was so strong that pyrotechnic recognition signals had to be forbidden. Judging from the experiences of submariners generally, though, these signals, which were primarily intended to prevent attacks by Allied aircraft, conferred no guarantee of safety from 'friendly' forces and were not much missed!

Various techniques were evolved in the USN for rescuing downed aviators: one involved a pilot hanging on to the perisocope for a lengthy tow until it was safe for the submarine to surface. Amongst numerous aviators on all sides rescued by submariners those plucked out of the water by USS *Skate* off Wake Island in October 1943 resulted in a memorably grateful message from the carrier *Lexington*: 'Anything on *Lexington* is yours for the asking. If it is too big to carry away we will cut it up in small parts.' Lifeguard operations were not always so well rewarded.

HMS *Seraph* (Lt N L A Jewell) was a standard S-class submarine but her special operations were anything but normal. In mid-1942 *Seraph* found herself at Gibraltar where she started training for special operations with a team of Royal Marine commandos. During the early Autumn she reconnoitred, with other submarines from the Eighth Flotilla, beaches and landing places for the Allied invasion of North Africa but *Seraph* had two more important tasks to carry out before the landings could take place.

The first was to land General Mark Clark in North Africa. On 19 October General Clark, Brigadier-General Lemnitzer and three other United States officers were embarked at Gibraltar and subsequently sent ashore, in folbots paddled by bootnecks (one of several terms used within the Royal Navy for Royal Marines), on the North African coast about 50 miles west of Algiers. Making contact with senior French Army officers, they successfully arranged for French cooperation when the time came for the Allied landings to take place. They were safely brought back by *Seraph* to Gibraltar on 25 October. Jewell was painfully conscious of the need to ensure General Clark's goodwill and comfort; the forthcoming landings, to say nothing of lasting Anglo-American relations, might well be jeopardised if the United States officers were not properly looked after. He accordingly gave them the Wardroom and transferred his own officers to the Leading Seamen's Mess forward. In a commendable effort to be hospitable, *Seraph*'s Engineer Officer, Mr Sutton, even offered to teach the guests traditional submarine games like cribbage and 'uckers' (a vicious form of Ludo) but they politely declined to be distracted from non-stop rubbers of bridge, a game that submariners considered rather lofty.

The lasting impression made on *Seraph*'s crew was of the Americans' imperturbable air of calm. While on board they placed themselves entirely in the hands of the crew and paid no attention to the submarine's dangers or

Top Left and Right
Major H G Hasler RM starting to trim down a Sleeping Beauty. This one-man electrically propelled submersible canoe was designed especially for operations from submarines and 15 were carried in the torpedo stowage compartment. This type was officially known as an MSC—Motor Submersible Canoe.

Centre Left
Japanese *HA.101*-class boats (1944–45). These small 429-ton boats were built solely as transport submarines with no tubes and the forward compartment devoted to cargo and crew space. Each could carry 60 tons of provisions, 38 tons of fuel and ten 18-inch torpedoes for *Koryu* midgets. Mass production methods enabled some of these boats to be completed in the very short time of five months. With a single shaft, they were slow (10 knots surfaced, 4 knots dived) but could dive in 37 seconds; quick diving was essential when supplying beleauguered garrisons. The conning towers were coated with anti-radar non-reflective material but it is doubtful if this gave any real protection against increasingly efficient US Navy radar sets.

Cockle Mk I being manhandled down the torpedo loading hatch of an S-class submarine. This was the type of craft used by the 'Cockleshell Heroes'.

difficulties. They did not even comment on the efforts of the Chef who, as one of the British officers remarked, was the only cook he knew capable of mutilating porridge. If Clark's mission succeeded, thousands of troops crossing the Atlantic to take Casablanca would be unopposed; if it failed, French troops and the British-American force might slaughter each other on the beaches. Neither Clark nor his colleagues gave any hint of concern for the tremendous responsibility that rested on their shoulders during this bizarre, uncomfortable and hazardous operation. Besides their reputation for unflappability, the Americans left one other lasting legacy—an extraordinary and unique compound of the American and English languages which was to become internationally known as Seraphese.

No sooner had the first party returned than *Seraph* embarked upon a second operation which required even greater diplomacy. During General Clark's mission, the French General Mast was able to guarantee the loyalty of only the Algerian garrison he directly commanded. The French forces at Oran and Casablanca were pro-Vichy and Mast told Mark Clark that only one man could enlist their loyalty to the Allied cause—General Henri Honoré Giraud. Giraud had escaped from captivity in Germany and was now in Vichy France where Petain and Laval were planning to give him back to the Germans in exchange for certain concessions. The General meanwhile indicated to the Allies that he was willing to be smuggled from France to North Africa provided he was given a command in keeping with his rank and dignity. Dignity was the key word. Operation 'Kingpin' (the code name for Giraud) was therefore mounted to rescue the proud general but there was a difficulty: he flatly refused to deal with the British. A submarine was the only conceivable means of extracting the General and only His Britannic Majesty's *Seraph* was available; there was no American boat within three thousand miles. After some wrangling and heart-searching the Royal Navy agreed to appoint Captain Jerauld Wright USN to the command of *Seraph* for the operation to avoid all possibility of offending Giraud's tender susceptibilities. The change of command ceremony, conducted by Captain G B H Fawkes RN, commanding British submarines at Gibraltar, was impressive: 'You are hereby commissioned to take command of His Majesty's Submarine *Seraph*. You will at all times command her in the best interests of your Sovereign and conduct your operations to the benefit of the British Commonwealth and Empire.' Fawkes then handed Wright an impressive looking scroll to seal the appointment. Unwrapped, it was found to contain an exceptionally revealing picture of a Varga girl in an advanced state of undress. USS *Seraph*, with her new captain on the bridge (as a polite onlooker) sailed to the accompaniment of a gramophone record blaring out from HMS *Maidstone*, the depot ship. It was Vera Lynn, Sweetheart of the Forces, singing *Yours, till the end of Life's Story*.

Jewell took pains to practise behaviour that would look like a junior officers, while the ship's Company and the three commandos who were embarked cultivated what they fondly believed was an authentic American accent. The passage, to a beach 20 miles east of Toulon, was uneventful except for the unusual appearance of steak on the menu. After some delay and a brief glimpse of a German E-boat while *Seraph* was on the surface a few hundred yards off shore, soon after midnight on 6 November the bridge lookout sighted an old, white fishing boat. General Giraud, in civilian clothes and wearing a grey Fedora hat, was sitting in the stern with gloved hands folded over a walking stick; his son, Chief of Staff and Naval Aide were huddled together looking rather less dignified. Giraud made a leap for *Seraph*, missed the casing and nearly got crushed between the submarine and the boat. After a few anxious moments he was dragged up safely by the reception committee headed by the 'Commanding Officer', Captain Wright USN. An alarming cocktail was mixed from a strange variety of bottles in the wardroom wine-cupboard to restore equilibrium all round; and abundant Seraphese seemed to reassure the General who was said to speak no English whatsoever. *Seraph*'s officers thereupon talked uninhibitedly, in plain submariners' English, about the success of the deception not knowing that Wright had already broken the truth to Giraud in private, presumably because he thought *Seraph*'s crew would not be able to keep up the act. It was disconcerting to discover, at breakfast that morning, that the General not only knew all about it but was capable of conversing fluently in English (as opposed to Seraphese). Giraud gave no sign of discomposure or annoyance, but he let it be known that he had no intention of making a political broadcast to rally the French on the lines strongly suggested by General Eisenhower. Although Giraud was in due course to lead the French Division in North Africa (he had expected to be made Allied Commander-in-Chief) the real purpose of his rescue was therefore not achieved. As Churchill remarked about him, no one was more deceived than he about the influence he had with the French governors, generals and indeed the officer Corps in North Africa.[1]

In March 1943 Jewell was told to report to the Central Intelligence Headquarters in St James Street, London where he met, amongst others, an Air Intelligence Officer splendidly named Squadron Leader Archibald Cholmondley. From him and Lt Cdr Ewan Montague of Naval Intelligence he learned of the macabre mission which *Seraph* was now called upon to undertake. The aim was to deceive the Axis into thinking that a major invasion, for which the Allies were obviously preparing, was aimed at Sardinia when it fact it was intended to land on Sicilian Beaches. The deception was to be achieved by conveying a corpse in the uniform of a Royal Marine officer to the coast of Spain where it would be dropped close inshore carrying convincing papers pointing to an assault on the wrong island. Central Intelligence reckoned rightly on the Spanish authorities finding the body and passing the papers straight to the Germans. The ghoulish code-name Operation Mincemeat was assigned to the mission; secrecy was imposed and very few men knew about it.

On 18 April a long metal canister was brought on board *Seraph*, who was lying alongside HMS *Forth* in Holy Loch. Its true contents, a corpse packed in dry ice, were known only to Jewell himself. The other four officers and 50 ratings were told that the canister was a secret weather-reporting device to be floated experimentally off the coast of Spain. It was marked 'Handle with care—Optical instruments—for special F O S shipment'. The spot selected for floating ashore 'Major Martin', the fictitious but realistic character invented to carry the papers, was 1,600 yards off the mouth of the Huelva River. *Seraph* reached this point, after ten days of cautious transit, on the 29 April. At 0430 the next morning the submarine surfaced in pitch darkness with the ebb tide on the turn. The officers were ordered on to the casing and all ratings sent below. Jewell then revealed the gruesome nature of the casket and the officers, with commendable composure, set to work unlocking the bolts with a spanner conveniently provided with the canister.

After ten minutes work the blanketed body was revealed. There had been more decomposition than expected; but it still matched the condition of a body which had supposedly been floating half-immersed in the sea for several days. When the 'Major's' uniform, badges and the all-important despatch case had been checked, Jewell said the few prayers he could remember from the burial service for the man whose true identity was never made known. With secrecy paramount, he included the following words from Psalm 39: 'I will keep my mouth as it were with a bridle while the ungodly is in my sight. I held my tongue and spake nothing: I kept silence, yea, even from good words; but it was pain and grief to me.' His officers took the hint.

'Major Martin' slid gently and unostentatiously into the water to do his posthumous duty. He performed it admirably. On 9 May, news of the documents reached the German High Command. An appreciation of them, dated 14 May, was given very limited and personal distribution which included Admiral Doenitz. The carefully selected readers were assured that: 'The genuineness of the captured documents is above suspicion [although] the suggestion that they have intentionally fallen into our hands . . . is being followed up . . .'. Whether followed up or not Doenitz, after a visit to Mussolini, noted that 'the Fuehrer does not agree with the Duce that the most likely invasion point is Sicily . . . the planned attack will be directed mainly against Sardinia and the Peloponnesus.' As a result, the Axis defensive forces were dispersed and the Allied invasion of Italy through Sicily suffered relatively small losses.

Appropriately, *Seraph* acted as a navigation beacon for the invading American Western Task Force coming in to land at Cent Beach when Operation Husky, the invasion of Sicily, was launched on 10 July. It was the task of *Seraph* and six other British boats carrying Beach Reconnaissance Parties to mark release positions for the respective landing craft convoys and to lay navigational markers to assist Landing Craft Flotillas in finding their beaches. Everything went without a hitch. 'But of course', the crew of *Seraph* might have said.

HMS *Seraph* had a reasonable claim to the first prize for Special Operations anywhere. It was the custom for British naval officers to use references to the Bible and the English Hymnal for signalling thinly veiled insulting messages on the assumption (not always correct) that every wardroom carried appropriate religious publications in the bookcase. It was thus only necessary to signal the number of an appropriate verse to convey a barbed shaft with due delicacy. A suitable message for *Seraph*, remembering the glittering galaxies of brass she was apt to embark, was quickly found in Hymn Number 30, Verse 5. Using the Hymn Book decryption system this became, in plain language, 'Thus spake the Seraph; and forthwith appeared a shining throng . . .'

Top
HMS *Seraph* **(Lt N L A Jewell, second from left) returns to Fort Blockhouse on Christmas Day 1943 after a unique series of special operations. Ferdinand the Bull painted on the bridge signified instructions not to be belligerent while engaged on special duties; but this did not prevent Jewell making 12 torpedo and gun attacks.**

Bottom
U-532 **(Fk O Junker) arrived back too late from Japan with 100 tons of tin, 60 tons of rubber, eight tons of wolfram and five tons of molybdenum—which had all been vitally needed for the sagging economy of the Reich. Still at sea when Doenitz signed the surrender document, Junker was obliged to take his valuable cargo to Loch Eribol and thence to Liverpool where this photograph was taken.**

18 An All-Round Look

No submariner would be so unwise as to look astern without sweeping the periscope quickly all round to see what might be coming up on either side and ahead. Regrettably, it is not within the scope of this book to review the present or predict the future and certainly not to pontify; but it may be thought that certain points which have arisen during a look from below at the last underwater war raise some questions. And those questions may suggest at least some of their own answers if World War II experience is related to the present day—making, of course, due allowance for modern technology. Nobody could seriously think we will ever fight the same war again: all battles are different; and submarine battles have often deviated from the general pattern. Even when the underwater scenario was firmly established (which it is not today) practically every tactical turn of events was, to some degree, unexpected and the unusual was usual. Extreme flexibility and rapid decision-making were essential for survival and success; and they were attributes almost as necessary to submarine operators on shore as to commanding officers at sea. Inflexible control of submarines may suit certain peacetime operations and they are obviously essential for nuclear deterrence; but experience from 1939 to 1945 showed that

commanding officers needed the greatest possible freedom of action and the loosest rein in war. Soviet submarines in particular, which today seem so formidable in peace, lacked that freedom and failed in war. The need for independence emerged clearly, and not only in the Red Fleet. There are other conclusions which may be drawn: they can be summarised quite briefly.

Men and morale were much more important than machinery and material. Comfort, though, had absolutely nothing to do with efficiency; on the other hand, over-dependence on instruments and gadgets detracted from it. Paradoxically, the more a submariner was stressed and the more challenging the conditions under which he worked, the more effectively he fought. There was a limit, and there is reason to think that some of the crews who were lost, especially in the Mediterranean, were pushed beyond it; but the general rule held good whether it was consciously recognised or not.

Of course, men needed reasonably good material to fight with; but simplicity, in every way, was superior to sophistication in action and stood up to a 'hammering' much better. Above all, it was most evident that the qualities required for success and safe return in war conflicted—sometimes dramatically—

Above

Some of the surrendered U-boats lying at Lisahally, the focal point from where they were sent to their ultimate destinations (which included Russia). The number of boats shown here, only a proportion of the total, gives some idea of the continuing strength of the U-boat Fleet even after its appalling losses.

U-boats, including three Type XXI's, surrendering at Bergen in Norway, May 1945.

Top Left and Right
Bow and stern views of a Type XXI U-boat in dock (post-surrender photographs). This excellent submarine did not emerge in time to affect the course of the war and it is now known that its sonar and weapon system would not have enabled fully submerged attacks to have been carried out as effectively as hoped. However, Kptlt Adalbert Schnee, en route to Bergen to surrender after the cease-fire order, made a dummy attack on a heavily escorted British cruiser, closing to within 500 m of the 'target'. In Schnee's capable hands it was easy to slip in and out of the screen but it would have taken time to train a whole new generation of U-boat commanders to captain the new 'Electro' fleet. It must be emphasised that this incident did nothing whatever to prove the Type XXI weapon system.

Left
Stern and motor room section of a Type XXI U-boat in mass production (post-surrender photograph).

with what peacetime considerations of safety, convenience and political showmanship demanded. The multi-purpose boats, built for a long life in peace and capable, supposedly, of tackling a wide variety of tasks were not so good as the boats designed with the one clear aim of war, and a single-minded total war at that. It was still perfectly possible to bring forward new designs and tactics to keep pace with war as it developed; but there were strong indications that new technology was best kept in check until fully proven. It is true that Germany, exceptionally well equipped for underwater war at the 1942 Atlantic level, waited *too* long to mass-produce the revolutionary, fast, schnorchel-fitted Type XXI electro-boats, which did not, therefore, figure in the story of the war; but the delay was due partly to a distracting and unmerited fascination with Dr Walter's steam-turbine propulsion and partly to procrastination at the highest levels which led to wrongly assigned priorities.

It has been said that if the Type XXI had been ready a few months earlier the balance between submarines and A/S forces would have shifted back in favour of the U-boats; but that is probably wrong. Certainly, the surface and underwater fleets had see-sawed, one-up, one-down and back again, throughout submarine history and it was fortunate for the Allies that they were able to stop the see-saw in 1943 before Doenitz could pile more weight onto his end of it. But it would have been quite impossible to mount a fresh and effective campaign with the technologi-

Top Left
Bridge and conning tower of a scuttled Type XXI U-boat. To keep British confidence Doenitz did not signal the code word for scuttling all boats: *Regenbogen* (*Rainbow*); **but no less than 221 boats were taken to sea after the cease-fire and sunk by their crews in the North Sea and Baltic. However, 156 boats surrendered in strict accordance with the terms of the cease-fire agreement.**

Centre Left
Periscope photograph of a Soviet *Whisky*-**class submarine. This class gained a lot from the German Type XXI but not so much as has widely been assumed. These Soviet boats, in peace, have not been handled so well or so daringly as their theoretical capability allows. It would be interesting to see how one would perform in the hands of a World War II German U-boat Commander.**

Bottom Left
A representative collection of US and British submarines alongside at Fort Blockhouse in 1960. Most of these boats were converted World War II veterans streamlined to make them faster but, above all, quieter. Only HMS *Trenchant* (**far left**), **with an outstanding wartime record, appears much as she was.**

cally advanced Type XXIs as soon as the boats were physically ready for sea. It would have needed many months of training and exercises with first class facilities—entirely lacking by 1944—to make the new boats capable of realising even a part of their great potential. That became abundantly clear when broadly similar designs ('Guppies' and the like) were brought into the United States, British and Soviet navies after the war. In short, men always had to be the masters of material and there was no quick way to mastery.

Submariners were incapable of fulfilling their functions when held back by politicians. The underwater war meant total war if it was to have any meaning at all. It was no use politicians pussy-footing and trying to impose restrictions, especially when it must have been obvious that those restrictions were bound to go by the board eventually. Peace-time politics, inter-service jealousies and the widespread, withdrawn 'private navy' attitude adopted by submariners themselves, led to some disastrous situations when the boats went into battle. Crews, especially in the United States Navy, were too often given training that would by no means equip them for war. Unrealistic exercises resulted in dangerously false conclusions and, in some cases, bred the wrong type of commanding officer. It was not always so, but there were a fair number of good peacetime captains who were not the best for war.

Not nearly enough time, effort and money were spent on weapon-system tests and evaluations in peace. False economy, and trials which were heavily biased by interested parties, brought the United States and

Top Right
Whisky **(twin-cylinder Cruise-Missile Carrier) and** *Tango* **class. In maintaining a huge submarine fleet the Soviet Navy has clearly learned one of the outstanding lessons of World War II—submarines oblige an enemy to mount a disproportionate A/S effort, so great that he has little left with which to carry out, or even threaten, offensive operations in peace or war.**

Centre Right
The Soviet answer to American Polaris—a *Yankee* **class. The design has obvious similarities to USS** *George Washington* **and her successors but the Soviet Union continually lags about ten years behind the USN in terms of real capabilities.**

Bottom Right
Soviet nuclear attack (torpedo) submarine. Although fast and deep-diving, the huge Soviet submarine force's capability, seen as such an important threat by NATO, has never been demonstrated in actual war.

```
              MOST IMMEDIATE
Have U heard the news OG ?????
No what is it
The complete capitulation of Germany
My a; TTS marvellous
When did U hear it
It came over the wireless at 20 mins to nine they broke into
the programme   there are to be more details at nin clock
isnt it marvellous
Everything except Norway and they wont be long now
Gosh I can hardly believe it can U
Seems too good to be true
I know I feel all queer somehow
Wish I had been at home for it
Yes same are still so long as its    over TTS the main thing
Now I must tell the news to SDO
TKS   a lot OG and all the very best
Same to you OG    AR for now  AR


T/P P/L R 2045
Typed by Blake
```

German Navies near to catastrophe and cost vastly more in strategic terms than could possibly have been spent on properly proving their weapons while time allowed. It is probably true to say that no weapon in any navy behaved in war exactly as had been expected in peace.

With hindsight, it is not difficult to spot these errors and omissions. Perhaps, when the war came to an end, they were fully appreciated. Perhaps steps were taken to ensure they would not occur again. Perhaps.

The mistakes were serious but there is no need to dwell on them. Despite their handicaps and an increasingly tough opposition, submarines, with the exception of the unfortunate Soviet boats, arguably dominated the war at sea from below; and they had a very marked affect on land battles. The war was

Top

A happy chat between two teleprinter operators—the Wren at Flag Officer Submarines HQ at Northways and her 'oppo' at Rosyth on 8 May 1945.

Bottom

Loading a modern, wire-guided, homing Mark 24 torpedo into a nuclear submarine. Torpedoes are now so immensely expensive and sophisticated that practice firings are severely limited. It was, however, very clearly demonstrated during the early part of World War II that the saving achieved by limiting exercises and test firings was a disastrous form of false economy.

over before the most advanced designs came into service but in most respects their potential was subsequently analysed and developed, culminating in the nuclear monsters at sea today. But some basic capabilities appear to have been given rather less attention amidst the powerful upsurge of nuclear propulsion. For example, the effect of massed attacks by much cheaper diesel-electric boats has been, if not entirely forgotten, somewhat neglected, not least because of peacetime safety rules. Preference in new construction has been given to far fewer and much larger submarines designed to deliver their attacks at long range; but there were indications during the war that a sufficient number of small, quite basic submersibles could swamp even the strongest defences and make devastating onslaughts, albeit at great risk to themselves, from close range given simple, reliable torpedoes. At the bottom end of the size-scale, midget submarines no longer have a place in western navies and practically no defence has been retained against them. It may be worth recording that small as well as large navies on the Allied side were able to produce very fine crews for smaller submarines, X-craft and chariots. Their achievements were outstanding and extremely economical. In fact, economy of effort, a most significant principle of war today, was a marked feature of *all* wartime submarine operations notwithstanding the losses on all sides.

The gains in the underwater war were huge but the losses were indeed heavy. For the men who went down with their boats, the Admiralty's message following the sinking of HMS *Upholder* on 14 April 1942 may serve as a memorial for all, in whatever navy they served:

'The ship and her company are gone, but the example and the inspiration remain.'

Polaris A3 missile at launch. There are submariners today who prefer to think of maintaining the nuclear deterrent as something entirely by itself and not really submarining. In fact, any submarine, not by any means necessarily nuclear propelled or nuclear armed, can be a very effective deterrent to war and, during a war, a very effective deterrent to enemy operations.

Footnotes

Chapter 1

[1] Rightful parenthood for warlike submersibles belongs to the Irish-American J P Holland (1841–1914).

[2] Public Records Office, London.

[3] Letter dated 26 September 1787 to Thomas Jefferson in Paris. Jefferson had written to Washington more than a year earlier enquiring about Bushnell's invention.

[4] *Niles Register* 7 August 1813.

[5] Public Records Office, London.

[6] *The Birth and Development of the American Submarine* by Frank Cable (1924) pages 132–133.

[7] A letter from Admiral J A Fisher dated 20 April 1904 concluded (with typical capitals) ... 'I don't think it is EVEN FAINTLY realised—THE IMMENSE IMPENDING REVOLUTION WHICH SUBMARINES WILL EFFECT AS WEAPONS OF WAR. ...'

[8] *Naval Policy Between the Wars*, Stephen Roskill.

Chapter 2

[1] *Jane's Fighting Ships 1941* (Finland).

[2] Surviving U-boat captains insisted that all men were volunteers but British and American listeners believed that the Germans volunteered on the 'you, you and you' principle! When a man joined the U-boat arm, he stayed in it for the rest of his career.

[3] Captain (S) One's report following the loss of *Narwhal* in December 1940.

[4] *The Submarine and Sea Power* by Vice Admiral Sir Arthur Hezlet.

Chapter 4

[1] Otto Kretschmer (*U-99*) received the Knights Cross from Admiral Raeder at Lorient while wearing British battledress and German forage cap.

[2] Interrogation of survivors from *U-135* sunk in July 1943.

[3] Interrogation of survivors from *U-606* sunk in February 1943.

[4] The sudden release of pressure and hence drop in temperature produced a dense mist inside the submarine as the dew-point was reached.

[5] Not nearly so good as in the German and US navies.

Chapter 6

[1] The first H/F D/F set compact enough to be fitted in an escort vessel underwent successful sea trials in the US coastguard cutter *Culver* in July 1941.

Chapter 7

[1] Admiral Doenitz' Memoirs.

[2] *Silent Victory* by Clay Blair page 391.

[3] CB 04050/39(9), monthly anti-submarine reports.

[4] Doenitz Memoirs page 99 and British monthly anti-submarine reports.

[5] Doenitz to HQ Naval Command Secret Command Document M261/41.

[6] Memorandum No 83/1/42 signed by Grand Admiral Raeder 9.2.42.

[7] Summary of interrogation.

[8] Naval Staff History (Submarines) Vol II page 90.

[9] Naval Staff History (Submarines) Vol I page 215.

[10] Captain (S/M) 2—Monthly General Letter 4 September 1945.

[11] Commander Ben Bryant in HMS *Sealion* would not have agreed; he felt that the pressure hull was fairly well protected by the sea, but this view was not shared by others.

Chapter 8

[1] The book of that name by Rear Admiral Ben Bryant was subsequently retitled *Submarine Command*.

[2] Captain R M Bevan, RN, SBNO Murmansk, noted in 1941 that (from a K-boat with six bow tubes) three torpedoes were fired almost simultaneously followed after a short delay by a second salvo. He also remarked that, initially, the Russians had no attack instruments although they kept records in an Attack Book! It seems that the attack records were suitably worded to keep the political controllers happy.

[3] Lt Cdr Tsoukalas, Royal Hellenic Navy perfected a particularly invaluable spreading and spacing calculator which became known as the Greek Slide Rule.

[4] German naval records assembled by Fkpt Gunther Hessler, latterly SOO to Flag Officer commanding U-boats and Doenitz' son-in-law.

[5] The only way to blow all tanks, including those fitted with Kingston valves instead of free-flood holes, was to blow HP to LP, HP air being passed in to the LP blowing line normally used only to achieve complete buoyancy after surfacing.

[6] The heroic action of Cdr Howard Gilmore USN, who elected to remain, wounded, on *Growler*'s bridge, and ordered 'Take her down' to save his submarine, followed *Growler*'s collision with a Japanese gunboat after an unsuccessful surface torpedo attack: it was not the result of a typical gun-action 'down below' situation.

Chapter 9

[1] In HMS *Urge* a seaman paced the control-room reciting the Lord's Prayer and in HMS *Upholder* another tried to climb out through the conning tower at 200 feet.

[2] Quoted from Secret Trials Report on HMS *Graph*.

[3] Investigation into the loss of HMS *Oswald*: report from Captain (S) One to C-in-C Levant 7 April 1943.

Chapter 10

[1] It was (then) Lt Cdr G W G Simpson who had reported so fully to British Intelligence on the German-Finnish activities before the war (Chapter 2).

Chapter 11

[1] HMS *Tetrarch* patrol report April 1940.

[2] Kites carrying aerials to increase HF radio range were a standard issue to many British boats. Even during peacetime trials they were notoriously unreliable.

[3] Naval Staff History (Submarines) Vol I.

[4] Naval Staff History (Submarines) Vol I.

Chapter 13

[1] Roskill Vol II, page 270.

[2] 130 years earlier another HMS *Ramillies* was supposed to have been attacked by a much more primitive midget submersible; see Chapter 1.

[3] HMS *Thule* had 93 men on board during one operation, more than a 50 per cent addition to her complement.

[4] HMS *Trenchant*'s patrol report for her sixth patrol.

Chapter 14

[1] As in Roscoe's *US Submarine Operations in World War II* and Grider's *War Fish*.

[2] *Silent Victory* by Clay Blair, pages 384–386.

[3] This proposition is objectively supported by the fact that the USSR did not declare war on Japan until a few days before the atom bombs were dropped; this strongly suggests that Stalin, if not the other Allied leaders, was clearly convinced that victory was imminent.

Chapter 15

[1] *Shch-303* (Captain Third Rank J W Travkin) was said to have sunk a transport carring 1500 troops and *D-2* another carrying 3,000 troops. No names were specified, however, and no such events could be identified by post-war analysis

[2] Nineteen U-boats were operating in or near the Gulf of Finland from June to December 1944. Six were lost, five on mines not necessarily laid by Soviet forces.

[3] According to the *Great Soviet Encyclopedia* 2nd edition 1951.

[4] *Submarines in Arctic Waters*, Rear Admiral I Kolyshkin.

[5] Often listed as *B-1* owing to misunderstanding of the Russian alphabet.

Chapter 16

[1] Italian Admiralty Communique No 476.

[2] HMS *Ark Royal* had been torpedoed by *U-81* on 13 November and HMS *Barham* had gone down to *U-331* 12 days later. The only capital ships remaining were *Valiant* and *Queen Elizabeth* against five Italian battleships.

Chapter 17

[1] *The Second World War* Vol IV, Winston Churchill.

Index